Ethics in Early China

For
Chad Hansen
— colleague, teacher, friend

Ethics in Early China
An Anthology

Edited by

Chris Fraser, Dan Robins, and Timothy O'Leary

香港大學出版社
HONG KONG UNIVERSITY PRESS

This publication was generously supported by a subvention from
the Department of Philosophy, University of Hong Kong.

Hong Kong University Press
14/F Hing Wai Centre
7 Tin Wan Praya Road
Aberdeen
Hong Kong
www.hkupress.org

© Hong Kong University Press 2011

ISBN 978-988-8028-93-1

All rights reserved. No portion of this publication may be reproduced or
transmitted in any form or by any means, electronic or mechanical,
including photocopy, recording, or any information storage or
retrieval system, without permission in writing from the publisher.

British Library Cataloguing-in-Publication Data
A catalogue record for this book is available
from the British Library.

10 9 8 7 6 5 4 3 2 1

Printed and bound by Kings Time Printing Press Ltd., Hong Kong, China

Contents

Foreword: The Professor's *Dé* 德, or the Many-Sided Chad Hansen   vii
   Donald J. Munro

Preface   xi

Contributors   xiii

Introduction   1

Part One: New Readings
1. Were the Early Confucians Virtuous?   17
   Roger T. Ames and Henry Rosemont, Jr.

2. Mencius as Consequentialist   41
   Manyul Im

3. No Need for Hemlock: Mencius's Defense of Tradition   65
   Franklin Perkins

4. Mohism and Motivation   83
   Chris Fraser

5. "It Goes beyond Skill"   105
   Dan Robins

6. The Sounds of *Zhèngmíng*: Setting Names Straight in Early Chinese Texts 125
Jane Geaney

7. Embodied Virtue, Self-Cultivation, and Ethics 143
Lisa Raphals

Part Two: New Departures

8. Moral Tradition Respect 161
Philip J. Ivanhoe

9. Piecemeal Progress: Moral Traditions, Modern Confucianism, and Comparative Philosophy 175
Stephen C. Angle

10. *Agon* and *Hé*: Contest and Harmony 197
David B. Wong

11. Confucianism and Moral Intuition 217
William A. Haines

12. Chapter 38 of the *Dàodéjīng* as an Imaginary Genealogy of Morals 233
Jiwei Ci

13. Poetic Language: Zhuāngzǐ and Dù Fǔ's Confucian Ideals 245
Lee H. Yearley

14. *Dào* as a Naturalistic Focus 267
Chad Hansen

Afterword 297
Chad Hansen

Index 303

Foreword:
The Professor's *Dé* 德,
or
the Many-Sided Chad Hansen

Donald J. Munro

Chad Hansen was a graduate student at Michigan and I was a junior faculty member when I first started making judgments about some of our analytic philosophers. They made useful and intriguing contributions to philosophy. They made me especially aware of the importance of precise argument, consistency, clarity of meaning of the terms we employ, and many issues about language. At the same time, their definition of philosophy was narrow, unlike anything I had studied among the Platonists in the early period or among the American pragmatists in the modern United States. Chad and I shared an approval of those in the James, Peirce, and Dewey tradition. The analytic colleagues were quick to dismiss a colleague's words as "not doing philosophy." Disinterest in the findings of other fields relevant to some enduring philosophical questions was one of their traits. They also seemed not to care about the social or cultural context in which people formulated positions. Chad wrote a wonderful Ph.D. dissertation, which drew him gradually into the analytic approach. However, he has remained something of a classical pragmatist (to which, add some Rawls). Among the people who influenced him were Stich and Sklar at Michigan, plus, later on, Chomsky, Montague, and Quine elsewhere. There was much positive about this dissertation-writing phase, as Hansen had begun exploring the logical side of meaning. But, my goodness, unlike some of his teachers, how he has manifested charity in listening to the views of others, how he has embedded his knowledge of other fields into his own philosophical work, and what a deep understanding he has for the cultural variations among Chinese and Western philosophers! One would hardly recognize him among some of those who long ago helped train the many-sided Professor Hansen.

He is quick to identify the strengths in parts of positions with which he otherwise disagrees, and this is not all charity. The authors of several of the chapters in this collection will recall his balanced and favorable comments on parts of them after they were delivered as papers at the conference in Hansen's honor at the University of Hong Kong in May 2008. In my own case, I am a non-traditional utilitarian. Hansen is nothing of the kind. I once talked to him about my views as a "two-realm utilitarian." One of these realms is all humans (the subject of public morality), where worth is derived from the law. The other is close relatives, neighbors, and communities with which a person bonds (private morality), where worth for these individuals comes from the degree of my emotional commitment to them. Traditional utilitarians would say that each human is of equal worth, to be counted as one unit in measuring "the greatest happiness." On the contrary, I would treat the targets of private morality as having greater worth than the others. The analytic Hansen would not approve, and say that the rules of public morality should include each person taking care of those closest to him or her, an efficient single-tier way to achieve utilitarian general happiness. But another side of Hansen was perfectly willing to go beyond rule utilitarianism. He admitted the emotional change that colored his commitment to his own children when they appeared on the scene, and set them off from other people. In my view, this was an acknowledgement of differential worth. In brief, being concerned with a workable ethics, I care about motivation. I am more motivated to act from an emotional (private) bond than I am from an abstract rule.

In contrast to my utilitarianism, Hansen has an ethical perspective that derives from his "structural systems" view of what our minds construct. "Systems" implies that we identify interconnected parts. By examining these systems, we can understand *how* we perceive and *what* we value. I think that Hansen likes the concept of *dào* in classical Chinese Daoism partly because it describes an exemplary structural system. It is natural when it works smoothly; in change, there will be "an easy flow." These are values to be prized. As Chris Fraser has noted, Hansen likes the value of toleration, also inspired by Zhuāngzǐ's *Dào*. But Hansen would remind us that, for imperfect humans, who are not ideal observers, there are priorities among values. Not all are the same.

I have heard Hansen poke fun when some philosophers get overwhelmed by one of the social sciences, such as evolutionary psychology, or by the fMRI-centered cognitive sciences. In some cases, he reasonably targeted them. I have been a target of such poking by some critics, and not always "in fun." In any case, from his earliest years as a graduate student, Hansen himself showed how the humanities can benefit from knowledge of an outside field, namely, the law. His focus was on its relevance to ethics and political philosophy. Unfortunately, some degree of separation of philosophy from social fields, such as the law, has been true of China and of the West. Kāng Yǒuwéi 康有為 believed in breaking down the status barriers of the nine realms (九界), such as nation, class, race, gender, family, and occupation. But Kāng's tool in overcoming the barriers was restricted to only using education to transform minds. He ignored formulating and applying laws as a companion tool. And, I would add, Kāng ignored the need for stipulated punishments for breach of specific laws. I believe the law is crucial to any philosophical treatment of social change.

Acutely sensitive to cultural factors in the varying building blocks of Western and Chinese philosophy, Hansen has been one of the most convincing scholars to point to the role of Indo-European dualisms in Europe and North America. Their roots in Orphic rituals and subsequent religions that absorbed neo-Platonism, the dualists assume and begin with beliefs in these distinctions: mind-body, reason-emotion, experience-reality, and permanence-change. In the pre-Qin period, Chinese philosophers did not think in these dual terms. As Hansen has noted, some change occurred later, when certain Chinese Buddhists denied the difference between mind and body, indicating that they had some idea of the dualistic claim. But the non-dualistic approach remained strong up to the modern period.

No wonder Chad Hansen has been such an influential scholar and teacher. When his many-sided breadth of perspective is added to his analytic command of the role of language in thinking, he has been and will remain an exemplary model for students and for teachers. This is Hansen's *dé* 德.

Preface

This anthology was conceived and published in honor of Chad Hansen, chair professor emeritus of Chinese philosophy at the University of Hong Kong. The volume grew out of a conference held in Hansen's honor on the occasion of his retirement from the University of Hong Kong in 2008, at which earlier versions of nine of the fourteen essays included here were presented.

Since the 1970s, Hansen has ranked among the world's foremost philosophical interpreters of classical Chinese thought. His original, provocative insights into the conceptual structure, driving issues, and substantive doctrines of early Chinese philosophical discourse have had a far-reaching impact on international scholarship, both through the many features of his theories that have been adopted by younger scholars and through the thoughtful critical responses his work has inspired. This volume aims to honor Hansen and his career by presenting a collection of original contributions to early Chinese ethics, a field that has been among his main interests for nearly four decades. The volume is not a *festschrift* in the usual sense of a collection of essays discussing the honoree's work, typically accompanied by replies. Only two or three of the essays included here focus directly on Hansen's views. Instead, we have assembled a collection of previously unpublished papers pertaining to early Chinese ethics that in various ways — sometimes directly, sometimes obliquely — take their departure from, engage with, or bear on themes in Hansen's writings.

The editors wish to express their gratitude to the Department of Philosophy, the School of Humanities, and the Faculty of Arts of the University of Hong Kong for financial support of the conference from which the volume evolved and for a grant to facilitate publication. We thank Michael Duckworth and Hong

Kong University Press for their enthusiastic support of the project. We are deeply grateful to our authors for contributing their work and to two anonymous referees for HKU Press for their many helpful comments on the volume. We also thank Donald Munro for writing a memorable Foreword and Chad Hansen for a fitting Afterword. Above all, we thank Chad for his inspiration, guidance, and friendship over the years.

Contributors

Roger T. Ames is professor of philosophy at the University of Hawai'i at Manoa and editor of *Philosophy East and West*. He has authored many interpretative studies of Chinese philosophy and culture, including *Thinking through Confucius* (SUNY, 1987), *Anticipating China: Thinking through the Narratives of Chinese and Western Culture* (SUNY, 1995), and *Thinking from the Han: Self, Truth, and Transcendence in Chinese and Western Culture* (SUNY, 1997) (all with D. L. Hall). His publications also include translations of Chinese classics, such as *Sun-tzu: The Art of Warfare* (Ballantine, 1993), *A Philosophical Translation of the* Daodejing: *Making This Life Significant* (with D. L. Hall) (Ballantine, 2001), the *Confucian Analects* (Ballantine, 1998), and the *Classic of Family Reverence: A Philosophical Translation of the* Xiaojing (University of Hawai'i Press, 2009) (the latter two with H. Rosemont). He has most recently been engaged in attempting to define Confucian role ethics (with H. Rosemont) and writing articles promoting a conversation between American pragmatism and Confucianism.

Stephen C. Angle received his B.A. in East Asian studies from Yale University and his Ph.D. in philosophy from the University of Michigan. Since 1994 he has taught at Wesleyan University, where he is now professor of philosophy. Angle is the author of *Human Rights and Chinese Thought: A Cross-Cultural Inquiry* (Cambridge, 2002), *Sagehood: The Contemporary Significance of Neo-Confucian Philosophy* (Oxford, 2009), and numerous scholarly articles on Chinese ethical and political thought and on topics in comparative philosophy.

Jiwei Ci is professor of philosophy at the University of Hong Kong and the author of *Dialectic of the Chinese Revolution: From Utopianism to Hedonism* (Stanford, 1994) and *The Two Faces of Justice* (Harvard, 2006).

Chris Fraser is associate professor in the Department of Philosophy at the University of Hong Kong. He is the author of *The Philosophy of Mozi: The First Consequentialists* (Columbia, forthcoming) and numerous scholarly articles on classical Chinese philosophy of language, ontology, epistemology, ethics, and psychology.

Jane Geaney, associate professor of religious studies at the University of Richmond, is the author of *On the Epistemology of the Senses in Chinese Thought* (University of Hawai'i Press, 2002). Her recent essays include "Grounding 'Language' in the Senses: What the Eyes and Ears Reveal about *Ming* 名 (Names) in Early Chinese Texts," *Philosophy East and West* 60 (2010).

William Haines holds a Ph.D. in philosophy from Harvard. His publications include "Consequentialism" (*Internet Encyclopedia of Philosophy*), "Aristotle on the Unity of the Just" (*Méthexis*, 2006), "The Purloined Philosopher: Youzi on Learning by Virtue" (*Philosophy East and West* 58:4), and "Hedonism and the Variety of Goodness" (*Utilitas* 22:2).

Chad Hansen is emeritus professor in the Department of Philosophy at the University of Hong Kong. He is the author of *Language and Logic in Ancient China* (Michigan, 1983), *A Daoist Theory of Chinese Thought* (Oxford, 1992), and numerous scholarly articles on early Chinese philosophy.

Manyul Im is associate professor in the Philosophy Department at Fairfield University. He holds a B.A. in philosophy from the University of California at Berkeley and a Ph.D. in philosophy from the University of Michigan. His philosophical specialization is early Chinese philosophy, but his interests cover a broad spectrum of Asian philosophy as well as ancient Greek thought and the history of Western philosophy and ethical theory. He is the author of journal articles in *Philosophy East and West*, *Journal of Chinese Philosophy*, *Asian Philosophy*, and *Tao: A Journal of Comparative Philosophy*.

Philip J. Ivanhoe (Ph.D., Stanford University) specializes in the history of East Asian philosophy and religion and its potential for contemporary ethics. Professor Ivanhoe has written, edited, or co-edited more than a dozen books and published more than thirty articles and numerous dictionary and encyclopedia entries on Chinese and Western religious and ethical thought. Among his publications are *Confucian Moral Self Cultivation* (Hackett, 2000), *The Daodejing of Laozi* (Hackett, 2003), *Working Virtue: Virtue Ethics and Contemporary Moral Problems* (with Rebecca Walker) (Oxford, 2007), *Readings in the Lu-Wang School of Neo-Confucianism* (Hackett, 2009), and *On Ethics and History: Essays and Letters of Zhang Xuecheng* (Stanford, 2009).

Franklin Perkins is associate professor of philosophy and chair of the Chinese Studies Committee at DePaul University in Chicago. He is the author of *Leibniz and China: A Commerce of Light* (Cambridge, 2004) and *Leibniz: A Guide for the Perplexed* (Continuum, 2007), and he has published articles on Chinese and comparative philosophy in journals such as *The Journal of Chinese Philosophy* and *International Philosophical Quarterly*. He spent a year at Peking University with a Fulbright Research Grant and has conducted research at the Leibniz Archives in Hannover, Germany, with a grant from the DAAD.

Lisa Raphals (Ph.D., Chicago 1989) is professor of comparative literature at the University of California at Riverside. She studies the cultures of early China and classical Greece, and has research and teaching interests in comparative philosophy, religion, history of science, and gender. She is the author of numerous journal articles and three books: *Knowing Words: Wisdom and Cunning in the Classical Traditions of China and Greece* (Cornell, 1992), *Sharing the Light: Representations of Women and Virtue in Early China* (SUNY, 1998) and *What Country*, a book of poems and translations (North and South, 1993).

Dan Robins is assistant professor at Richard Stockton College of New Jersey. He is the author of scholarly articles in *Philosophy East and West*, *Journal of Chinese Philosophy*, *Dao: A Journal of Comparative Philosophy*, *Early China*, and the *Stanford Encyclopedia of Philosophy*.

Henry Rosemont, Jr. is the George B. & Willma Reeves Distinguished Professor of the Liberal Arts Emeritus at St. Mary's College of Maryland and visiting professor of religious studies at Brown University. With Roger Ames, he has translated *The Analects of Confucius* and *The Chinese Classic of Family Reverence*. Among his other recent books are *Is There a Universal Grammar of Religion?* (with Huston Smith) (Open Court, 2008), and *Rationality and Religious Experience* (Open Court, 2001).

David Wong (Ph.D., Princeton, 1977) is the Susan Fox Beischer & George D. Beischer Professor of Philosophy at Duke University. His works include *Moral Relativity* (California, 1984), *Natural Moralities* (Oxford, 2006), and numerous scholarly articles on Chinese and comparative philosophy. He is co-editor with Kwong-loi Shun of an anthology of comparative essays on Confucianism and Western philosophy, *Confucian Ethics: A Comparative Study of Self, Autonomy and Community* (Cambridge, 2004).

Lee H. Yearley is the Walter Y. Evans-Wentz Professor in the Department of Religious Studies at Stanford University. His major interests are in comparative religious ethics and poetics, especially in China and the West. He has, for instance, written a book-length study on notions of virtue in Mengzi and Aquinas (to appear in a Chinese translation this year) as well as articles on Western poets like Dante and Chinese poets like Dù Fǔ.

Introduction

Early Chinese ethics has attracted increasing attention in recent years, both within and outside the academy.[1] Western moral philosophers have begun to devote more attention to ethical traditions other than their own, and the virtue ethics movement has sparked interest in Confucianism and Daoism. In China, both academics and the general public have been self-consciously looking to their own early ethical tradition for resources on which to draw in shaping China's twenty-first-century ethical and political culture.

Despite this growing interest, however, many features of early Chinese ethics remain unclear or controversial, and many aspects of its significance for contemporary moral philosophy remain unexplored. Moreover, as Roger T. Ames and Henry Rosemont, Jr. emphasize in their contribution to this volume, interpretations of early Chinese ethics have often been molded by Western concepts and assumptions, sometimes altering distinctive concepts from the Chinese tradition to fit the familiar categories of Western ethical theory.[2] There are indeed important similarities between many Chinese concepts and the Western concepts to which they are compared. Yet the philosophical interest of Chinese concepts and theories may lie as much in how they diverge from Western analogues as in how they resemble them, and mapping these divergences requires care and sensitivity.

Consider, for instance, the concepts of *rén* 仁 (roughly, moral goodness, goodwill, beneficence) and *dé* 德 (roughly, power, charisma, virtuosity, virtue), two candidates for Chinese counterparts to a notion of virtue. *Rén* is central to the ethics of the Confucian *Analects*, which depicts it as among the distinctive traits of the *jūnzǐ* 君子 (gentleman), for Confucians, the morally exemplary person. The *Mencius* contends that to deny or fail to fulfill one's capacity for *rén* is in effect to deny one's humanity. *Dé* is the feature of individual agents that provides the basis for moral conduct and is a distinctive characteristic of the morally exemplary sovereign. The Confucian emphasis on such concepts has understandably prompted comparisons with the role of the virtues in Aristotelian ethics (see, for example, Sim 2007 and Yu 2007), and some writers have labeled Confucianism a form of virtue ethics (for example, Van Norden 2007). Without question, there are intriguing parallels between aspects of Confucian and Aristotelian ethics, or virtue ethics more broadly. Yet, as several of our contributors argue, there are also important differences — differences deep and significant enough to call into question whether "virtue ethics" is an apt label for Confucianism. The precise nature of early Chinese ethical concepts such as *rén* and *dé* and their similarities to and differences from familiar conceptions of virtue clearly call for further exploration.

Analogous questions can be raised about many other aspects of early Chinese ethics; here we will mention just three. Consequentialist reasoning has a prominent role in the ethics of both the *Mòzǐ* 墨子 and the *Xúnzǐ* 荀子. Yet the Mohist and Xunzian ethical theories seem distinct from familiar Western forms of consequentialism, such as Mill's utilitarianism, partly because the basic goods they posit are distinct — both theories emphasize collective goods, not individual happiness — and partly because these Chinese theories are structured not in terms of acts or rules but distinctive Chinese concepts such as *fǎ* 法 (models) in Mohism and *lǐ* 禮 (ceremonial propriety) in Xúnzǐ. The theoretical roles of *fǎ* and *lǐ* overlap in some respects with those of moral rules or principles, but they are importantly distinct, since they refer to exemplary types or patterns of activity, rather than general, abstract imperatives.

Arguably, the central theoretical concept in early Chinese ethics is that of *dào* 道 (way, path, course, channel). The focus on *dào* distinguishes early Chinese ethics from ethical discourses centered on acts, rules, or character, suggesting again an interest in patterns of activity rather than particular actions or general moral principles. It also hints at a conception of moral perception and action as forms of competence and of morality as akin to a harmonious response to natural structures or patterns. Yet the nature of *dào* and its implications for ethical theory and practice remain underexamined.

A complementary set of issues concerns early Chinese conceptions of action, motivation, and practical reasoning. Ethical theories couched in principles are typically paired with a conception of action as guided by reasoning from principles. Principles serve as reasons that justify actions, their role in practical reasoning usually being spelled out roughly along the lines of Aristotle's practical syllogism. Just as early Chinese ethical theories are not structured around general principles, early Chinese conceptions of action and practical reasoning are not structured around a conception of reason or a syllogism-like form of argument. Instead, they focus on models, analogies, discrimination of similar from dissimilar kinds of things, and the performance of repeated, norm-governed patterns of conduct such as rituals and skills. On these points, as with the preceding, a deeper understanding is needed of the concepts and theories at work in early Chinese ethics and their theoretical and practical implications. Such an understanding could provide a basis for new areas of engagement between early Chinese thought and contemporary ethical discourse.

Issues such as those we have been considering motivate the guiding themes of both parts of this anthology. The theme of Part One is "new readings" of early sources; the essays in this part seek to deepen our understanding of important concepts, issues, and views in pre-Qín ethical texts. The theme of Part Two is "new departures"; two of these essays explore methodological issues bearing on the relevance of early Chinese ethics to contemporary ethical discourse, while the others undertake original projects relating early Chinese ethics to broader ethical topics.

As explained in the Preface, the volume celebrates the work of Chad Hansen, professor emeritus of Chinese philosophy at the University of Hong Kong, by presenting a collection of new contributions to a field that ranks among his main interests. Most of the fourteen essays that follow do not focus specifically on Hansen's work, but each touches on issues that have played a prominent role in his publications. In the remainder of this Introduction, we will sketch the central themes of each essay and indicate briefly how they relate to Hansen's oeuvre.

A perennial issue facing interpreters of the Confucian *Analects* is to explain the interplay between two of the text's core ethical concepts, *rén* 仁 (moral goodness, goodwill), Confucius's central term of approbation for the morally admirable person, and *lǐ* 禮 (ceremonial propriety), a body of concrete guidelines for action in various contexts. In his influential 1992 study, Hansen proposed an interpretation of *rén* as a form of intuitive moral competence in playing social roles, which he suggested were structured by the norms of conduct embodied in *lǐ* (1992, 62, 68). In the first essay in Part One, "Were the Early Confucians Virtuous?", Roger T. Ames and Henry Rosemont, Jr. present their own distinctive, role-centered account of Confucian ethics. Arguing against recent interpretations of Confucianism as a variety of virtue ethics, they contend that it is better understood as a role ethics, coupled with a relational conception of persons as constituted by the social roles they live. On their reading of Confucianism, lived social roles — especially family roles — serve as normative standards, and the family feeling associated with these roles is the starting point for moral competence. People become good by living their social roles well, beginning with the family and extending outward to the community. Ames and Rosemont contend that the Confucian conception of the person — and *a fortiori* the morally excellent person — is fundamentally different from the conceptions that ground either Aristotelian or various contemporary forms of virtue ethics. They find a deep contrast between a notion of virtues as character traits of a discrete, excellent individual, independent of his or her relations with others, and a Confucian conception of family-based relational virtuosity, which can be characterized only through reference to relationships with others. Indeed, taking a position that converges partly with Hansen's, they argue that *rén* is not aptly characterized as a virtue, in the sense of a specific, fixed character trait. Rather, it is a generic virtuosity in interacting with others appropriately in particular roles and situations according to *lǐ*, a communal grammar ultimately derived from family relations.

Manyul Im's "Mencius as Consequentialist" also takes issue with interpretations of Confucianism as a form of virtue ethics, in this case focusing on Mencius. Rather than a virtue ethicist, Im argues that Mencius is best interpreted as an implicit consequentialist, who systematically evaluates the responses and actions of the *jūnzǐ*, or gentleman, according to whether they produce better or worse consequences than alternatives. Im does not claim that Mencius presents an explicitly consequentialist normative theory, but that when making normative arguments, the justifications he offers are systematically consequentialist in structure. A gentleman should act from benevolence and propriety, for instance, because doing so yields good consequences. Moreover, Mencius's brand of consequentialism is distinctive, Im explains, in including among the goods to be promoted certain intrinsic moral values, such as benevolence and filial piety. A potential objection to this line of interpretation is that Mencius apparently regards Mòzǐ, an explicit advocate of consequentialism, as his arch-opponent. But Im contends that Mencius's arguments in fact never reject consequentialism as a justification for motivation or conduct; they reject only the Mohist doctrine of impartial concern and the general strategy of acting so as to produce greater benefit, rather than from other motives. In reading Mencius as consequentialist, Im is to some extent developing Hansen's earlier observations (1992, 178) about Mencius's consequentialist tendencies, and in particular Hansen's suggestion that, in Mencius's view, consequentialism is "self-effacing," in the sense that guiding action directly by appeal to consequentialist criteria might actually produce suboptimal consequences (1992, 170). At the same time, however, Im suggests that his account of Mencius's normative views indicates that Hansen's criticism (1992, 179–83) of them is too quick.

In "No Need for Hemlock: Mencius's Defense of Tradition," Franklin Perkins also responds to Hansen's critique of Mencius, arguing that Mencius's attempt to defend Confucianism by evading, rather than rebutting, the challenge of the Mohists' normative arguments is more defensible than it might seem. Perkins follows Hansen (1992, 172) in distinguishing between a "strong" interpretation of Mencius's appeal to people's nature (*xìng* 性), on which we have an innate tendency to conform to specifically Confucian moral norms and practices, and a "weak" interpretation, on which our innate tendencies merely lead us to acquire some form of morality, though not necessarily a Confucian one. The strong position could in principle justify Confucian morality but is implausible; the weak position is plausible but, according to Hansen, would not justify Confucianism over the Mohist alternative. Against Hansen, Perkins argues that the weak interpretation both better explains Mencius's position and introduces considerations that undermine the Mohist challenge to traditional Confucian practices. On the weak position, Mencius can contend that we are unable to settle on any reasonably simple criterion of the good — such as the one the Mohists propose — and that our ability to determine what practices will actually have the best consequences is quite limited. More likely than not, the traditions that generations of our ancestors gradually refined and passed down to us are fairly effective in meeting human needs and thus are justified on the Mohists' own consequentialist grounds. Such a Mencian defense of traditional Confucianism cannot claim to yield knowledge that Confucian practices are justified, Perkins observes. But it can claim that there is even less reason to think a Mohist alternative would be more justified.

One of Hansen's important contributions has been to clarify the various respects in which Mohist thought shaped the theoretical framework of early Chinese philosophical discourse. Central to his interpretive proposals was the insight that the Mohists employ a conception of ethics and action structured around concepts such as *dào* (way), *zhī* 知 (know-how), and *biàn* 辯 (discrimination), rather than rules or principles, reasoning, and desire (1992, 138–43). In "Mohism and Motivation," Chris Fraser employs this insight to develop a detailed account of Mohist moral psychology aimed at rebutting the widespread view that Mohism lacks a plausible understanding of human motivation. He contends that the *Mòzǐ* presents a rich, nuanced picture of a variety of sources of moral and prudential motivation that the Mohists can reasonably view as sufficient to guide people to practice core tenets of their ethics. Fraser suggests that the Mohist account is distinctive in focusing on neither beliefs nor desires as motivating states but on *shì-fēi* 是非 (right/wrong, this/not-this) attitudes. The result is an intriguing approach to motivation and action that is neither Humean nor Kantian in structure. Fraser's discussion prompts an obvious question: If the Mohists indeed have a plausible approach to motivation, why is their ethics commonly thought to face severe motivational obstacles? Impediments to practicing the Mohists' *dào*, he suggests, stem not from the inadequacy of their understanding of motivation but from weaknesses in their normative arguments.

For most of the twentieth century, the dominant view of philosophical Daoism was that its use of the term "*dco*" (way) constituted a radical break with the term's meaning in other early Chinese schools of thought. For some scholars, this supposed divergence constituted an interpretive puzzle: as Benjamin Schwartz put it in an important 1985 study, how could "a term which seems to refer in Confucianism mainly to social and natural *order* come to refer to a mystic reality?" (1985, 194, original italics). A cornerstone of Hansen's interpretation of Daoism has been his rejection of any such radical discontinuity between the use of "*dào*" in Daoist texts and in Confucian or Mohist texts. He has argued that the concept of *dào* in Daoist thought can intelligibly be construed only as an extension or development of its normal role in the broader discourse and that Daoist reflection on the metaphysics of *dào* is in effect reflection on the metaphysical status of normativity.[3] Dan Robins's essay, "It Goes beyond Skill," develops these ideas of Hansen while seeking to answer a version of Schwartz's question. Robins identifies two basic uses of the term "*dào*" in early texts: most often, it refers to a norm-governed way of doing something, but in certain passages in Daoist texts it unmistakably refers to something that exists prior to and generates the cosmos. Robins explores the significance of the two uses at length and then attempts to explain how they relate: What might it mean for a way of acting to exist prior to and give rise to the cosmos? He proposes that a crucial aspect of following a normative *dào* or following the *dào* presented by a particular context is exercising the capacity to "go beyond skill"; that is, to adapt to particular circumstances in a way that transcends any specific pattern of action one has previously mastered. Such spontaneously appropriate action, he proposes, constitutes *dào* of the same general sort as the cosmogonic *dào* by which things arise. As to *dào* considered as a thing that exists prior to and generates everything else, Robins suggests that this notion is a reification of *dào* into a thing that determines the course of the cosmogonic *dào*. The resulting use of "*dào*" shifts the term's meaning from its use to refer to a way of acting, but this shift is an intelligible one, involving no radical break from previous usage.

A prominent thesis of Hansen's first book, *Language and Logic in Ancient China* (1983a), was that, by contrast with most Western thinkers, early Chinese philosophers emphasized the action-guiding functions of language over the descriptive or fact-reporting functions: the use of language in commands and instructions captured their attention at least as much as, and probably more than, its use in descriptions and reports. This view of language helps to explain the distinctive role in classical Chinese ethical and political thought of the doctrine of "correcting names" (*zhèngmíng* 正名). For language to fill its action-guiding role efficiently and effectively, all members of a political community must use the "names" for things — especially those implicated in job titles and duties — according to unified norms, such that their use of names accords with norms of conduct and their conduct accords with the proper use of names. In "The Sounds of *Zhèngmíng*: Setting Names Straight in Early Chinese Texts," Jane Geaney presents a novel interpretation of the concept of *zhèngmíng* grounded in early Chinese ideas about the effects on listeners of speech, music, and sound in general. Geaney argues that, in early Chinese culture, discursive speech, like music, was regarded as possessing a transformative power because of its capacity to travel on air or wind and penetrate the body through the auditory and olfactory organs. Against the background of such beliefs, correcting or "straightening out" the use of discursive sounds would have been regarded as a potent means of prompting responses from listeners. Spoken instructions that penetrate the body through air would have been seen as a gentle yet inexorable force, much like the wind itself. Geaney suggests that, as a political doctrine, *zhèngmíng* can be understood as an integral part of the ideal of ruling, not through active coercion but through harmonious "influences of air" — songs, winds, and *dé* 德 (virtue, charisma) — that penetrate human subjects through hearing and smelling.

A core element of Hansen's account of early Chinese philosophical psychology is his view that ancient Chinese thinkers saw action as guided spontaneously by trained intuition, understood as "a dispositional faculty realized in our actual physical structures," whose output is "the appropriate performance . . . in the circumstances" (1992, 74). This "dispositional faculty" is akin to a "skill structure" within the agent, which Hansen suggests can be regarded as the agent's *dé* (virtue, virtuosity) (1992, 300). On this psychological model, then, the development of knowledge or virtue for early Chinese thinkers involves psychophysical cultivation similar to training in physical skills. Hansen's model dovetails well with Lisa Raphals's findings in her contribution, "Embodied Virtue, Self-Cultivation, and Ethics." Raphals draws on a wide range of ancient Chinese ethical, ritual, and medical texts — some newly excavated — to articulate early Chinese conceptions of physically cultivated and realized virtue. She considers both Chinese athletic performances, which she argues were based on notions of virtue and self-cultivation, and the broader "embodied virtue" traditions of which such conceptions of athletics were a part. As she explains, these traditions reflect a culture of physical self-cultivation whose concepts and practices structured much of early Chinese medical theory, ethics, and metaphysics. At its core were the ideas that mind and body form a continuum and that physical cultivation can transform a person's *qì* 氣 —

the dynamic, elemental stuff of which all things are formed — and thus the person's character. Raphals's chapter is explicitly comparative, examining the relation between athletics or physical cultivation and ethics in both the ancient Greek and Chinese contexts. She argues that, despite the differences between Greek and Chinese epistemology and metaphysics, particularly Greek mind-body dualism, the role of physical cultivation practices in the two traditions is similar in many respects. Indeed, she suggests that comparison with the Chinese case might prompt us to reconsider the conventional view that Greek thought embraces a profound mind-body dualism, since a mainstream expectation in both China and Greece was that moral virtue would be manifested through the body.

We turn now to Part Two of the volume. Whereas Part One focuses on new interpretations of early Chinese ethical thought, the chapters in Part Two, "New Departures," concern the development and application of ideas from the early Chinese tradition.

Hansen has long been interested in the questions of whether and how the study of diverse ethical traditions can be relevant to one's own moral thinking. One of his major claims has been that its relevance is limited in two fundamental ways. First, only moral traditions that qualify for "normative respect" warrant serious consideration. Second, learning about such traditions need not justify wholesale moral relativism or skepticism. It may do no more than "mildly destabilize" our confidence in our own reflective equilibrium, thus prompting openness to moral reform, either by drawing insights from other traditions or by synthesizing their insights with those of our own (Hansen 2004, 79–81). Beyond justifying respect for another tradition, and perhaps mild skepticism toward aspects of our own, Hansen argues, the *normative* relevance of comparative ethics is exhausted, and "normal, first-order moral discourse must take over" (82).

Two of the essays in Part Two address Hansen's views on these and related points. In "Moral Tradition Respect," Philip J. Ivanhoe examines Hansen's conception of normative respect for another moral tradition and his view of how such respect sheds light on what comparative ethics can contribute to contemporary moral theory. Ivanhoe discusses three possible construals of Hansen's conception of "moral tradition respect," concluding that it is a normative, ethical attitude stemming from a conditional, all-things-considered judgment about the moral value of a given tradition of moral inquiry, such as that the tradition in question is at least somewhat successful in getting things right (and, indirectly, that it might be of value in helping us better understand what is good or right). He then raises several questions about the role in comparative ethics of such a conception of respect for other moral traditions. Such respect may indeed sometimes play the roles that Hansen identifies,

Ivanhoe argues, but often it does not. For instance, whereas Hansen suggests that respect for other traditions tends to mildly undermine our own moral beliefs, Ivanhoe points out that the precedence may also go the other way: people may first lose confidence in their home tradition and only later, perhaps as a result, come to respect an alternative one. Or, one might learn from ideas or ideals in another tradition that build on aspects of one's own tradition without thereby undermining one's original ethical beliefs. Ivanhoe surmises that, like Alasdair MacIntyre, Hansen implicitly sees comparative ethics as directed at a grand moral synthesis of traditions and ultimately a single, unified moral order. In response, he questions whether there is any reason to expect such an outcome and whether it is even desirable. An equally or more valuable contribution of comparative ethics might instead be to help us understand the variety of defensible, appealing, yet distinct forms of ethical life.

In "Piecemeal Progress: Moral Traditions, Modern Confucianism, and Comparative Philosophy," Stephen C. Angle argues for an approach to cross-tradition inquiry that contrasts with Hansen's in emphasizing both holistic and piecemeal perspectives and in assigning a more active role to comparative philosophy. Angle concurs with Hansen's suggestion that something akin to "moral tradition respect" — with its potentially destabilizing effect on our reflective equilibrium — is needed for an alternative moral discourse to qualify as relevant today. In answer to Hansen's doubts, he argues that contemporary Confucianism is sufficiently rich, reflective, and open to cross-tradition engagement to merit such respect. Comparing Hansen's methodological reflections on comparative philosophy with those of Alasdair MacIntyre and Thomas Metzger, however, Angle finds in all three a questionable focus on wholesale comparisons between entire traditions or discourses rather than between individual ideas or theories within such discourses. While acknowledging the importance of holistic approaches — especially in determining the meaning of the terms employed in a discourse — Angle argues that an overemphasis on holism misrepresents the nature of cross-tradition philosophical learning and tends to prevent us from recognizing differences within a single discourse, similarities between distinct discourses, and changes within a discourse. In his view, philosophical development in response to stimulus from a distinct tradition typically occurs through a process of provisionally "disaggregating" selected concepts or values from some of their native discursive entailments, thus allowing philosophers to explore their significance in novel, comparative contexts. Rather than issuing from wholesale comparative evaluations of entire discourses, such development proceeds on a piecemeal, bottom-up basis, an insight Angle credits to Hansen. Unlike Hansen, however, Angle holds that comparative inquiry has an important role to play in facilitating such piecemeal progress. Once the holistic project of justifying moral tradition respect is completed, much room remains for comparative work from a piecemeal or "disaggregated" perspective. Arguably, each of the remaining essays in this part, including Hansen's, undertakes such work.

For Hansen, a constructive outcome of comparative ethics is that it may jostle our confidence in our own ethical views, prompting us to discover insights our home tradition has missed or to synthesize insights from the conflux of traditions. Angle urges us to seek such insights through a balance between holistic interpretation and "disaggregated" exploration of the significance for one tradition of ideas from another. In "*Agon* and *Hé*: Contest and Harmony," David B. Wong engages in precisely the sort of balanced comparative study Angle proposes, reaching conclusions that integrate ideas from the classical Greek and Chinese traditions in just the way Hansen envisions. Wong marshals a variety of Western and Chinese sources to examine the role in each tradition of two values that might initially appear incompatible: *agon*, or contest, a central value of ancient Greek culture, and *hé* 和, or harmony, a central value of ancient Chinese culture. He contends that, though the Greek and Chinese moral traditions differ in the prominence they give to these values, in fact contest and harmony coexist in both traditions. Despite the obvious tension between them, the two also mutually implicate each other. On the one hand, harmony is involved in *agon*, insofar as part of the point of contest is to join the interests of the competitors in striving for excellence that in some way contributes to the common good. On the other, as Wong reconstructs it, the concept of harmony in early Confucian texts entails reconciliation of different parties' potentially competing interests. Moreover, Wong argues, given that morality functions to facilitate social cooperation, contest and harmony must be balanced appropriately in order to integrate individuals' self-regarding and competitive motivations with shared ends of the group. Both the Chinese and Western traditions, he suggests, can learn from how the two values are related in the other — without our assuming that either has the uniquely right answer about how to resolve conflicts between them. Wong's work itself exemplifies the value of learning from other traditions, as his approach explicitly draws on ideas from the *Zhuāngzǐ* 莊子 concerning the benefits of acquiring insights from distinct perspectives and the plurality of ways to satisfy basic needs.

Hansen has suggested that one role of ritual, or *lǐ* 禮, in classical Confucianism is to provide models by which agents learn concrete patterns of social interaction, thus acquiring complex dispositions that transform and shape their character (1992, 71–74). This interpretation is intertwined with a distinctive view of early Chinese folk psychology. Confucius assumes neither an inner, private, subjective conception of the mind, nor a belief-desire model of action, Hansen argues. Instead, his implicit psychology concerns a range of human inclinations, capacities, and dispositions, along with the skill-like social practices, such as rituals, in which these are exercised and cultivated (1992, 75–78). Training in rituals and other practices, Hansen suggests, leads us to develop the intuitive abilities needed to perform such practices with virtuosity (73–74). In "Confucianism and Moral Intuition," William A. Haines develops a related line of inquiry concerning ritual and intuition. Haines proposes that early Confucianism may be deeply instructive in helping us to understand the mechanisms underlying intuitive knowledge, both in morality and more generally. Drawing on Charles Peirce's theory of signs, he presents a novel account of how Confucian ritual practices function to improve one's sensibility about the world, specifically concerning moral relations and proper conduct. He argues that ritual functions as a system of signs that allow practitioners to obtain knowledge through nonverbal, projective processes, rather than, for instance, deliberate verbal reasoning. Haines explains how early Confucian self-cultivation practices can be viewed as a body of procedures for extending the range of one's affective sensibility, especially in morally relevant ways. For early Confucians, he suggests, the resulting cultivation of sensibility was an important means of disseminating and acquiring moral knowledge. He offers intriguing suggestions on the role of ritual and intuition in promoting the virtues and in guiding action even within a non-Confucian normative framework, such as utilitarianism.

A central emphasis of Hansen's interpretation of the Daoist classic *Dàodéjīng* 道德經 is that the text presents a philosophical critique of positive, explicit conceptions of the *dào* — that is, of social, conventional forms of prescriptive discourse aimed at guiding conduct (1992, 203). Jiwei Ci's contribution, "Chapter 38 of the *Dàodéjīng* as an Imaginary Genealogy of Morals," examines one of the key textual sources for this critique of conventional morality, treating it as an exercise in conceptual genealogy that locates the grounds for the Daoist view in a set of observations about moral psychology. Ci identifies two key claims from this chapter. One is that moral states fall into a hierarchical spectrum — from the natural, non-moral orderliness of directly following the *dào* 道 to the spontaneous moral goodness of *rén* 仁 down to the artificial, cultivated propriety of *lǐ* 禮 — along which the lower states are characterized by their lacking the distinctive features of the states above them. The other is that the role of moral consciousness — a conscious concern with virtue —is essentially remedial, as it arises in response to a perceived lack of some moral quality. From these two theses, Ci develops two provocative conclusions: any attempt to promote moral qualities or virtues by relying on motivational resources belonging to a higher morality is practically self-contradictory, and the cultivation of any moral state must draw on motivational resources both different from and lower than those associated with it. He argues that these points have the intriguing consequence that the process of developing moral virtues will always be one in which people must draw on motives other than, and lower than, those associated with the virtues themselves, while also to some extent misunderstanding their own motives. He concludes with a series of reflections on the consequences of these points for traditional Chinese approaches to morality and politics.

The early Chinese text that has had the greatest influence on Hansen's work is the *Zhuāngzǐ*. In considering the ethical implications of Zhuangist thought, Hansen has focused mainly on the text's justification for tolerance toward others' *dào*, its open-mindedness toward novel directions in which we might modify our own *dào*, and the personal fulfillment that results from a life of virtuoso performance of skilled, world-guided activities.[4] In "Poetic Language: Zhuāngzǐ and Dù Fǔ's Confucian Ideals," Lee H. Yearley undertakes a novel approach to exploring the potential conflicts that may arise from pursuing this latter type of Zhuangist fulfillment. Through his reading of a famous poem by the Táng 唐 poet Dù Fǔ 杜甫, Yearley examines the implicit tensions between personal spiritual aims, such as the Zhuangist life of "free and easy wandering," and other ethical concerns that define the human situation, such as one's responsibility to family, service to the larger community, and participation in other projects (in Dù's case, the arts). Yearley suggests that Dù adeptly employs poetic language to articulate these enduring tensions, which in his view Zhuāngzǐ resolves in less convincing ways. Yearley finds that, because of how he affirms basic ethical and spiritual concerns while acknowledging the tensions between them, Dù Fǔ's poem expresses a considerably darker, yet more convincing, picture of the world's possibilities than Zhuāngzǐ does.

In recent work (2003b), Hansen has explored ways in which the Chinese concept of *dào* and its associated metaphysics might shed light on ethical naturalism, the view that ethical normativity is in some sense a feature of the natural world. In our final essay, "*Dào* as a Naturalistic Focus," he continues this line of inquiry. Applying Shelly Kagan's (1992) conceptual apparatus for taxonomizing ethical theories,[5] Hansen argues that a *dào* can be regarded as a distinct kind of evaluative focal point that presents an alternative to more familiar foci, such as actions, rules, motives, or character traits. *Dào*s may possess an inherent normativity, he suggests, although the character of this normativity is that of an invitation or a recommendation, not an obligation or imperative. Hansen proposes that adopting *dào* as a normative focal point helps to dispel the "queerness" that John Mackie (1977) famously associated with ethical naturalism, since, unlike moral rules or principles, *dào*s — in the form of ways, paths, or courses — can quite plausibly be considered part of the natural world. He sketches an account of how normative *dào*s might emerge from purely natural ones, such as a path of light, a riverbed, or the evolved patterns of behavior that contribute to an organism's or a community of organisms' survival. To be sure, such natural normativity stops short of distinctively *moral* normativity. But, Hansen contends, for creatures such as humans, the advent of language can prompt the invention of social practices or *dào*s in which participants challenge each other to justify their conduct, in what Wilfrid Sellars (1956) called the "game of giving and asking for reasons." The norms of such justificatory *dào*s may evolve such that appeals to the mere social acceptance of a practice are considered inadequate reasons. Such norms would have evolutionary value, because they facilitate reforming and adapting cooperative practices, and they could easily inspire a conception of what is good *simpliciter*, rather than by the norms of any particular practice. Hansen suggests that morality expresses an ideal implicit in the *dào* of language itself: it is in effect an extension of a *dào* of giving and asking for reasons — a second-order *dào* of how we use various natural *dào*. This intriguing proposal about how a core concept of Chinese thought may be relevant to contemporary metaethics is a fitting capstone to the other essays and a testament to the depth and lasting value of Hansen's philosophical contributions.

Notes

1. For the purposes of this volume, early Chinese ethics comprises the ethical thought of the classical, pre-Qín 先秦, or Warring States era, running from the fifth century BCE to 221 BCE, when the Qín Dynasty completed its conquest of the other warring states.
2. See chapter 1 "Were the Early Confucians Virtuous?". Ames and Rosemont cite an unpublished conference paper by Kwong-loi Shun commenting on the persistent asymmetry in discourse on Chinese thought, in which Western concepts are applied to interpret Chinese concepts and doctrines but not vice versa.
3. On the relation between "*dào*" in Daoism and in the wider discourse, see Hansen (1983b, 24; 1992, 207). On Daoism as examining the grounds of normativity, see Hansen (2003b) and his essay in this volume.
4. See Hansen (1992, 284, 297, 302; 2003a, 145, 150–51).
5. Kagan distinguishes ethical theories according to three types of features: the *factors* the theories identify as determining moral status, the *focal points* of normative evaluation, and the *foundational* accounts that explain the significance of the factors identified.

References

Hansen, C. 1983a. *Language and logic in ancient China.* Ann Arbor: University of Michigan Press.

———. 1983b. A *tao* of *tao* in Chuang-tzu. In *Experimental essays on Chuang-tzu*, ed. V. Mair. 24–55. Honolulu: University of Hawai'i Press.

———. 1992. *A Daoist theory of Chinese thought*. New York: Oxford University Press.

———. 2003a. Guru or skeptic? Relativistic skepticism in the *Zhuangzi*. In *Hiding the world in the world: Uneven discourses on the* Zhuangzi, ed. S. Cook. 128–62. Buffalo: SUNY Press.

———. 2003b. The metaphysics of *dao*. In *Comparative approaches to Chinese philosophy*, ed. B. Mou. 205–24. Aldershot: Ashgate.

———. 2004. The normative impact of comparative ethics: Human rights. In *Confucian ethics*, ed. K. Shun and D. Wong. 72–99. Cambridge: Cambridge University Press.

Kagan, S. 1992. A structure of normative ethics. *Philosophical perspectives* 6: 223–42.

Mackie, J. 1977. *Ethics: Inventing right and wrong.* Middlesex: Penguin.

Schwartz, B. 1985. *The world of thought in ancient China.* Cambridge, MA: Harvard University Press.

Sellars, W. 1956. Empiricism and the philosophy of mind. In *Minnesota studies in the philosophy of science, volume I*, ed. H. Feigl and M. Scriven. 253–329. Minneapolis: University of Minnesota Press.

Sim, M. 2007. *Remastering morals with Aristotle and Confucius.* Cambridge: Cambridge University Press.

Van Norden, B. 2007. *Virtue ethics and consequentialism in early Chinese philosophy.* New York: Cambridge University Press.

Yu, J. 2007. *The ethics of Confucius and Aristotle: Mirrors of virtue.* New York: Routledge.

Part One
New Readings

1

Were the Early Confucians Virtuous?

Roger T. Ames and Henry Rosemont, Jr.

We respond negatively to the question entitling our essay. While the vocabulary of virtue ethics for describing the early Confucian vision of the moral life (*dào* 道) is superior to those linked to Kantian or utilitarian principle-based ethical theories, that vocabulary, too, forces the Master and his followers more into the mold of Western philosophical discourse than they ought to be placed, in our opinion, and hence makes it difficult to see the Confucian vision as a genuine *alternative* to those with which we are most familiar.

Instead, we will claim that (1) early (pre-Buddhist) Confucianism is best described as a *role ethics*; (2) this role ethics is *sui generis* in both philosophy and religion, East and West; (3) it embodies first, a specific vision of human beings as relational persons constituted by the roles they live rather than as individual selves; and (4) it embodies as well a specific vision of the moral life that takes family feeling as the entry point for developing a consummate moral competence *and* a religious sensibility grounded in *this* world.

Giving a detailed account of role ethics is beyond the scope of the present essay, except as part of our overall argument against efforts to link the early Confucians to Aristotle or to Kant, Bentham, and Mill — or their contemporary champions — by showing the far more central place of roles, especially family roles, in Confucianism, and simultaneously our argument *for* the importance of incorporating the concept of roles and family values into any view of morals or ethics that can claim the allegiance of reflective and sensitive citizens of the twenty-first century across ethnic, national, and religious boundaries.

Aristotle first. Many competent comparative philosophers have weighed in on the question of whether or not classical Confucianism is a form of virtue ethics, a seeming preponderance of them affirming this claim. Some of them are not altogether Aristotelian in their commitments to virtue ethics — Ivanhoe,

Yearley, and others — but many others make the comparisons seriously. Two recent studies (Sim 2007, Yu 2007), for example, are committed entirely to a comparison of Aristotle and the canonical Confucian texts on ethics and to reinforcing the majority position. All of these philosophers and others have raised the bar considerably in our attempt to formulate a dissenting position.[1]

The philosophical reasons for our dissent are proffered below. But we want first to note our unhappiness more generally with narrative and methodological approaches in these comparisons that are presumed to be philosophically neutral when in fact they are not. Consider, for example, another essay by Yu. With an admirable command of both the Aristotelian and early Chinese texts, Yu argues that Aristotle's *politick zoon* bears a close resemblance throughout to the relational self of Confucius and Mencius. But unfortunately, once the comparisons have been made, it turns out that something ". . . *is lacking* in Confucian ethics" (2005, 295); "what Aristotle regards as primary happiness *is missing* in Confucius" (296); "Confucius . . . appears *to ignore* the theoretical . . ." (297) (our italics). If Aristotle and Confucius are saying pretty much the same thing, but the former is saying it more adequately and thus better, then why bother reading the latter? We do not mean to be unfair to Yu. Similar statements abound in writings in comparative philosophy juxtaposing Confucius not just with Aristotle, but with most other Western philosophers as well. In virtually all these comparisons, something always seems to be missing in Confucianism. But we never seem to see converse statements such as "The concept of the sage *is lacking* in Aristotelian ethics," or "the centrality of ritual for human flourishing *is missing* in Aristotle," or "Kant, Mill and others . . . appear *to ignore* the importance of the exemplary person (*jūnzǐ* 君子)," and so on. Why not?

We want to resist the unfortunate asymmetry that continues in the work of comparative philosophy, bolstering as it does the unannounced but persistent premise that Chinese philosophy's encounter with Western philosophy has been its defining moment, such a definition being more flattering to the West than to the Middle Kingdom.[2] In this particular instance, we want to resist tailoring what we take to be a distinctively Confucian role ethics into a familiar category of Western ethical theory. We shall follow contemporary scholars of Chinese philosophy back to the classical Aristotelian model of virtue ethics and try to articulate the ways in which we believe the Confucian vision of human flourishing and the moral life are importantly different from Aristotle's *eudemonia*.

We shall argue for an alternative Confucian basis of normativity by establishing a contrast between an Aristotelian notion of "virtue (*arête*)" as acquired character traits and a much less abstract Confucian conception of family-based relational virtuosity. For Confucius, family feeling is clearly the entry point for developing moral competence,[3] and as such, we shall insist that Confucian normativity is defined by living one's family roles to maximum effect. A person becomes good by living her life as a good daughter to her father and mother, and then by extending these developed moral sensibilities to the larger community. On our reading, lived family roles — mothering, brothering, granddaughtering — are themselves normative standards that, informed as they are by existential embodiment, are much clearer and more concrete than putative moral principles.

It is important to note that, while the general terms denoting familial and other roles might be said to be abstract, they are just barely so, unlike the key terms in Western ethics, beginning with *individual* — the locus of moral analysis in Western ethical theorizing. What is known about a person when we are told she is an "individual," as contrasted with "mother"? There are levels of abstraction, seen clearly if we think of laws. There is the bare concept of *law*, below which we will find *criminal law*. And below that, laws *against stealing another's property*; lower down the abstraction scale we have *burglary*, *robbery*, and related laws, and down again we can find *pickpocketing*, *identity theft*, and so on.

Equally important, role terms are much less abstract than terms for the virtues on the basis of the differences in instantiation. If we see someone doing something seemingly risky, how will we tell without detailed examination whether that person is an exemplar of courage or foolhardiness, or was simply unthinking in his action? Or that we misperceived the situation? But our mother is a concrete and immediate instantiation of *mother* at all times (even when she is acting in a less than praiseworthy fashion), about which we cannot be in doubt, because who we are, in significant measure, is because of who she is. Similarly with our sister, our grandma, and our Aunt Jenny. It is through knowing these people as they define *our* lives and determine in large measure the course *our* lives will take, that we come to know and internalize the roles that model the activities of the people who live in our society, many of which we already occupy ourselves, or soon will. We thus begin with the very concrete, with the particular, that is to say, and then extrapolate to a more abstract level when we need to — but not to the highly abstract — the universal principle, unless we are philosophers besotted with pure rationality. Mothers may occasionally lay down the law, but to see the two as equally abstract is to misunderstand the nature of both mothers and laws.

Here, then, is another significant difference between Aristotle (and most other virtue ethicists) and the early Confucians: the virtues characteristic of the excellent individual inhere in him, and can be described, analyzed, and evaluated, without specifying any role or relationship to or with others, which Confucians would never do, and they can be thought to do so only by presupposing that they have more or less the same notion of human beings as individuals as Aristotle does.

Another difference we must call attention to is Aristotle's reliance upon reason in determining moral conduct, as opposed to the centrality of the imagination in the Confucian texts. In so doing, we argue that the Aristotelian and Confucian views on the moral life are grounded in fundamentally different conceptions of what it means to become a person, a factor that will be important in distinguishing Confucian role ethics from the more contemporary nuanced versions of virtue ethics that we associate with the sentimentalist virtue ethics of Slote (2007), the care ethics of Noddings (2003), and the particularist ethics of Dancy (2006). It is not merely Aristotelian virtue ethics that we believe different from classical Confucianism but contemporary variations of virtue ethics as well, keeping as they do the foundational role of the *individual* and of *rationality* (for which terms there are no close lexical equivalents in classical Chinese). We would contend that the language of moral psychology familiar in virtue ethics past and present has little relevance for a Confucian tradition that makes no appeal to the notion of *psyche* as a mode of defining and individuating persons or to *logos/ratio* as their essence. In this Confucian view of the moral life, we are not individuals in the discrete sense but rather are transactional persons living — not "playing" — a multiplicity of roles that constitute who we are and that allow us to pursue a unique distinctiveness and virtuosity in our conduct, which combines our intellect and our emotions. We are, in other words, the sum of the roles we live in consonance with our fellows, cognitively and affectively.[4]

Taken on their own terms, the classical Confucian texts appeal to a relatively straightforward account of our actual life experience rather than abstract moral principles, and, in so doing, they provide a justification for reinstating the intimacy of family feeling as the concrete ground of an always emergent distinctively human order. There is a fundamental difference between the goal of Western ethical theories that are directed at enabling people to think and to talk about ethics more coherently, and that of the Confucians who not only want to provide a vocabulary for thinking through ethical issues but simultaneously seek to inspire people to become better persons. We refer to this Confucian vision as a *role ethics*, and we intend to advance it as a *vision* of human flourishing rather than as an alternative moral *theory*; it is a vision that seeks to integrate the social, political, economic, aesthetic, moral, and religious dimensions of our lives.

In the opening chapter of the *Classic of Family Reverence*, Confucius proclaims that family reverence (*xiào* 孝) is the "root of excellence (*dé* 德)" (Rosemont and Ames 2009). Of course, in our conduct we should love, respect, and honor our parents (and our ancestors), but how are these activities tied to developing qualities such as temperance, courage, and wisdom (to name only the three cardinal virtues first analyzed and discussed at length by Socrates in Plato's *Republic* and then later by Aristotle)?[5] In this text, the familiar Confucian vocabulary — "consummate person or conduct (*rén* 仁)," "appropriateness (*yì* 義)," "ritual propriety (*lǐ* 禮)," and "wisdom (*zhì* 智)" — is muted by a sustained focus upon family reverence (*xiào*) and has relevance at the outset only within the context of the flourishing family. Simply put, when family reverence is functioning effectively within the home, all is well within the community, the polity, and indeed, the cosmos. Although it is not certain that the *Classic of Family Reverence* records the actual words of Confucius, based upon the received corpus, the centrality of the notion of family reverence in classical Confucianism cannot be disputed.

To make this point, we might turn to the most frequently referenced of Confucian "excellences," *rén* 仁, which we render "consummate or authoritative conduct." Nothing is more defining of humanity for Confucius than the genuine concern of one human being for another, a feeling that typically has its origins within the life of the family. But significantly, *rén* does not precede practical employment; it is not a principle or standard that has some existence beyond the day-to-day, family-grounded lives of the people who realize it in their role relationships. *Rén* is admittedly more general than, say, obedience, but it too can only be fostered in the deepening of role relations as one takes on the responsibilities and obligations of family, and then by extension, of communal living. *Rén* is thus a shared human flourishing. It is the achievement of the quality of relationships that, like the lines in fine calligraphy or sublime landscape painting, collaborate to maximum aesthetic effect.

When the quality of these human interactions is pursued broadly within the social and political forum, consummate conduct becomes exemplary for those in the community who would defer to it. Consummate conduct (*rén*) is thus perceived as a necessary condition for becoming exemplary as a person (*jūnzǐ* 君子) in the execution of one's lived roles.[6] Becoming exemplary as a person, like becoming consummate, is thus irreducibly collaborative, dependent as it is upon a correlation with effective models rather than compliance with abstract principles:

> The Master remarked about Zǐjiàn 子賤, "He is truly an exemplary person (*jūnzǐ*). If the state of Lǔ 魯 had not other exemplary persons, where could he have gotten this from?" (5.3)[7]

Nowhere is such collaboration more obvious than in the playing of music. Four excellent musicians perform each in a distinctive way, yet what they produce as a string quartet is altogether distinct from the contribution of any one of the four artists, while each gives to the others, and to the whole, significance and beauty — and often, in the case of religious music, a sense of the sacred.[8] The centrality of music in the Confucian tradition as providing a felicitous vocabulary for consummate human conduct should not go unnoticed.

Given that Confucianism is fundamentally an aestheticism, it is not surprising to find that it uses language such as the "beautiful (*měi* 美)" and the "unseemly, unrefined, crude, coarse (*è* 惡)" to denote modes of conduct (*Analects* 20:2). But *měi* in Chinese means "beautiful" by reference to how certain relations come together within a specific context; it is not nominalized and entified to mean "beauty-in-itself." So, too, human actions can only be seen as "virtuous" by reference to how they come together within a specific context rather than by being "virtues-in-themselves." Virtue, then, is nothing more or less than a practical and productive virtuosity.

What this means is that *rén* is not a specific virtue that can be named and analytically isolated as defining of one's character, any more than what it means to behave in a consummately humane way can be stipulated and replicated without reference to specific roles and situation. *Rén* is generic as a cultivated virtuosity in role-specific dispositions that conduce to making any particular action optimally elegant and appropriate, and thus a source of significance (*yì* 義) for all concerned. Confucius gives alternative descriptions of *ren* conduct, suggesting a multivalence to the term denoting virtuosity in relations. *Rén* is not *a* "good" but an efficacious "good at, good in, good to, good for, good with" that describes a relational dexterity within the unfolding of social experience. *Rén* is "right" conduct only in so much as it is "right on" — whatever it takes to be timely in strengthening relations that is appropriate to our shared purposes. It is "correct" behavior only in so much as it is a corrective — making those adjustments in relationships needed to maximize the shared possibilities available in the circumstances. It is not primarily a retrospective "what" but a prospective "how." By requiring that the quality of (inter)action be determined and evaluated relationally — that is, in asking after what persons do with their interdependence and mutuality both in motivation and consequences — *rén* is the difference between efficacy and waste, between elegance and ugliness, between healthy relations and injurious ones.

Looking at our conventional ethical discourse from a Confucian perspective, the main problem in the way we have come to think about virtues is that we tend to "metaphysicalize" them and thus render them as one more iteration of what John Dewey has dubbed "*the* philosophical fallacy." In so doing, we take the fixed and final to come before experience (our appeal to moral principles); we mistakenly take kinds and categories as an adequate expression of what are complex, relationally defined social situations (our appeal to virtuous individuals); we think because we have abstract names we also have "things" that match up with them (our appeal to intangibles such as "courage" and "justice"). Certainly there are exceptions, important exceptions, to this generalization about the nature of Western moral philosophy past and present, but we want to establish what we consider an important difference between the Western theoretical preoccupation and the Confucian persuasion.

On our interpretation, Confucian role ethics does not begin from an attempt to abstract from concrete living to isolate, identify, and explain some causal factor in moral action, some originative principle or agency or faculty. Rather, Confucian role ethics begins by considering what is happening and ends by trying to make what is happening happen better. In Confucian role ethics, moral excellence, like a work of art, is a specific expression of virtuosity and imagination assessed as a quantum of satisfaction, and only in that sense and against that measure can it be judged in degree by applying the general terms of right or wrong, correct or incorrect. At the same time, far from entailing a strict application of some predetermined and self-sufficient moral principle or set thereof to difficult situations, *rén* accumulates as a reservoir of moral meaning that is embodied in people and that elevates and transforms the human experience, minimizing the emergence of morally problematic situations. Confucius is explicit (*Analects* 2:3) in identifying this achieved sense of belonging as the vital difference between a deference-patterned community with its self-regulating, non-coercive structure and an authoritarian society governed by the rule of law; *rén*'s function is to proactively forestall the emergence of morally deficient situations. It is a moral artistry that seeks to achieve a quality of life within the larger picture. Only occasionally and incidentally, when such inspiration fails to prevail, does a situation arise that requires the resolution of specific problems. As his ideal, Confucius looks to a community that aspires to rise above an appeal to the rule of law in its pursuit of a self-regulating sufficiency:

> The Master said, "In hearing cases, I am the same as anyone. What we must strive to do is to rid the courts of cases altogether." (12:13)

We might extrapolate from this passage that appeal to the application of moral rules or principles, like appeal to law, is in itself an admission of communal failure — too little too late. There is more justice to be found in creating a social fabric that precludes abusive situations than in punishing perpetrators of what is deemed unjust or evil actions. From a Confucian perspective, given the natural bonds of love, nurturance, loyalty, and respect between young and old, especially kin, any society that feels the need to enact laws threatening parents with incarceration as a means of dealing with child abuse is very probably in terminal decline.

Another seminal idea in the organically related vocabulary of classical Confucianism is *lǐ* 禮, or "ritual propriety," an achieved sense of appropriateness (*yì* 義) in one's roles and relations. *Lǐ* is a communal grammar ultimately derived from family relations, which begins from making robust the roles that locate us within family.[9] As a grammar, it has the potential to engender the sublime through effective coordination and placement, allowing us to take a stand and to achieve a certain status. Put simply (if, again, oddly from a Western moral perspective), one does not simply do one's communal duty, but must do it in a certain way. One must act not only with elegance and dignity, but also in a way informed by the aesthetic and religious meaning dictated by custom and tradition. Propriety in one's roles and relations does not reduce to generic, formally prescribed "rites" and "rituals," performed at stipulated times to announce status and to punctuate the seasons of one's life, however much they may have functioned in that way before Confucius rethought them. Certainly rituals played important political functions in China, but the *lǐ* of Confucius — the expression of propriety through one's roles and relations — are more, much more. They have a somatic dimension whereby body often communicates better than language the deference needed to communicate and strengthen the bonds among the participants in the various life forms. *Lǐ* have a profoundly affective aspect wherein feelings suffuse and fortify the relational activities, providing the communal fabric a tensile strength that resists rupture.

The performance of *lǐ* must be understood in light of the uniqueness of each participant and the profoundly aesthetic project of becoming a person. For Confucius, *lǐ* is a resolutely personal performance revealing one's worth to oneself and to one's community. *Lǐ* is also a public discourse through which one constitutes and reveals oneself qualitatively as a unique human being, a whole person.

Importantly, there is no respite; *lǐ* requires the utmost attention in every detail of what one does at every moment that one is doing it, from the drama of the high court to the posture one assumes in going to sleep, from the reception of different guests to the proper way to comport oneself when alone, from how one behaves in formal dining situations to appropriate extemporaneous gestures.

If these Confucian demands seem excessive, and artificial, it is in significant measure due to the decline of standards in almost all areas of interpersonal human endeavor today. Insisting on some minimum standards of dress or decorum seems to smack of elitism; verbal language that in the past would have been frowned upon even in private ("Like, ya know, I can't get into reading; get what I mean?") is now tolerated in public speech; one of the few uses of body language that continue to be "meaningful" are intentional gestures of disrespect that are an immediate source of road rage.

The continuing reauthorization of our communal roles and institutions necessary for society to function well brings with it, at the same time, an opportunity for reconstruction and consummation. Some patterns of ritualized conduct are obligatory for minor no less than major interactions among people. Indeed, as we have already suggested, we find that, for the early Confucians, there is no sharp distinction between politeness and morals. Where robust relationships are the source of appropriate conduct and felt worth, the kind of disintegrative actions that we associate with inconsiderate conduct and bad manners quite simply diminish the meaning invested in human relations, and in so doing, compromise and ultimately threaten the moral fabric of community. Confucius studies the accoutrements of ritual, not military affairs, because he believes rituals are more fundamental than law for regulating society properly.[10]

A central aim of Confucius in the *Analects*, perhaps *the* central aim, is to guide his students toward achieving the goal of becoming exemplary persons (*jūnzǐ*), requiring that they embody consummate conduct (*rén*) in all they do, and behave with propriety (that is, are *lǐ*-like) in all of their actions. Family reverence (*xiào*) permeates this instruction: "Revere the family at home and be deferential (*dì* 弟) in the community" is one admonition (1:6); "Do not act contrary to your parents' expectations" is another (2:5, 4:18); "Give your father and mother nothing to worry about except your physical well-being" is still another (2:6); "When your father and mother are alive, do not journey far, and when you do travel, be sure to have a specific destination" (4:19) is yet another.

While loyalty and obedience are necessary ingredients of family reverence, they are only part of it.[11]

> In serving your father and mother, remonstrate with them gently when they go astray. On seeing that they do not heed your instructions, remain respectful and do not act contrary. Although concerned, voice no resentment. (4:18)

This theme of "remonstrance" (*jiàn* 諫), enunciated even more forcefully in Chapter 15 of the *Classic of Family Reverence*, indicates clearly that loyalty and obedience, while necessary qualities of the *jūnzǐ*, are not sufficient; what is also needed is the desire to do at all times what is appropriate in the larger familial, moral, and spiritual context of accepted personal responsibilities.[12]

It is clear that, for Confucius, merely "going through the motions" of meeting filial responsibilities, while perhaps necessary for social harmony, will nevertheless not conduce to one's development as an exemplary person.

Something more is needed, and what that something more seems to be is a desire to do what it is right to do; we must not only perform our duties, but we must *want* to perform them. This desire to serve one's parents, then, is the substance of the following passage:

> Zǐxià 子夏 asked about family reverence (*xiào*). The Master replied: "It all lies in showing the proper countenance. As for the young contributing their energies when there is work to be done, and deferring to their elders when there is wine and food to be had — how can merely doing this be considered family reverence?" (2:8)

Here we may call attention to the Confucian terms we have been analyzing in our sketch of familial-centered role ethics, *rén*, *yì*, *xiào*, *lǐ*, *jūnzǐ*, none of which has a close counterpart in the vocabulary of Western moral theories past or present. The converse also holds. There is no close equivalent for "morals" in classical Chinese, nor for almost all of the other terms necessary for having a discussion about "morals" in English today: "freedom," "liberty," "rights," "autonomy," "dilemma," "individual," "choice," "rationality," "democracy," "supererogatory," "private," "normative," even "ought." We have argued the philosophical significance of these semantic facts elsewhere;[13] here we only note that they should not be taken as evidence of extreme philosophical naiveté on the part of Confucius or his followers.

Native speakers in every culture have vocabulary items for describing, analyzing, and evaluating human conduct, but their lexicon will be influenced strongly by a number of cultural factors, not least among them the worldview of that culture in general and the definition of what it is to be (or become) human within that worldview. Our medieval forebears used terms like "virtue," "honor," and "sin" very differently from the way these words are used today in describing and evaluating human conduct, and other terms they employed — *soke*, *sake*, *varlet*, *chivalric*, *liegeful*, and so on — we do not use at all.

Similarly, the ancient Greek account of what it is to be a person has significantly influenced what contemporary Western philosophers have presupposed, but as Yu and Sim have themselves indicated, it too is distinct from ours in many respects. A number of the basic terms employed in contemporary moral discourse absent in the Confucian lexicon are not found in ancient Greek either, and a number of key Greek words used to describe, analyze, and evaluate human conduct — *nous*, *akrasia*, *arête*, *eidos*, *logos*, *dikē*, *eudemonia*, *phronēsis*, and so on — have no precise lexical counterparts in contemporary English (or Chinese) and are difficult to translate without modifiers, circumlocutions, or a gloss.[14]

In order not to beg any important philosophical questions against the Confucians early on, we must understand how much our own moral vocabulary for describing, analyzing, and evaluating the conduct of our fellows rests on the concept of human beings as fundamentally autonomous individuals, the definition itself utilizing the vocabulary of contemporary moral discourse. This definition of the individual person permeates not only our moral thinking but the institutions of government in developed capitalist societies that now dominate the world economically and politically, and therefore requires closer examination, for it is also the default foundation of the conceptual background that Western readers are inclined to bring to Confucian philosophy. In wanting to highlight this conceptual background, we want now to contrast Confucian role ethics with the two other ethical theories that are current in Western moral philosophy today (but most of our points will apply no less to the several strains of virtue ethics).

For most of the past two-plus centuries — with a process of evolution that stretches back to antiquity — the basic conception of what it is to be a human being in Western civilization has been *individualism*.[15] That we are social creatures, strongly shaped by the others with whom we have interacted, has always been acknowledged on all sides but has not been seen as of the essence of our humanity or, at the more abstract level, of being of compelling value. Rather, what gives human beings their primary worth, their dignity, their integrity, their value, and what must command the respect of all, is their *autonomy*, or their capacity to become *autonomous* as a potential that applies to all individuals.[16]

With this basic view of human beings in place, certain other qualities must also inhere in them, or the notion of the autonomous individual would be incoherent. Individuals must be *rational* if they are autonomous; that is to say, they must be capable of going against instinct or conditioning, for creatures that can do neither are surely not autonomous. Further, human beings must enjoy *freedom*: if they were not free to rationally choose between alternative courses of action, and then act on the choice made, how could they be said to be autonomous? Finally, we must note that these qualities of individual human beings are taken as unalloyed goods in the ethical sense.

If we define human beings in this individualistic manner, it would follow that, in thinking about how we ought to deal with our fellows, we should seek as general and as abstract a viewpoint as possible. If *everyone* has the (valued) qualities associated with individualism, then their gender, age, ethnic background, religious affiliation, skin color, and so on should play no significant role in our decisions about how to interact with them, apart from concern for (ethically irrelevant) detail. Thus, on this orientation, it is incumbent upon us to seek universal values and principles; else the hope of a world at peace, devoid of group conflicts, racism, sexism, and ethnocentrism, could never be realized. And the way to do this is obviously to do all we can to ignore and transcend our own spatiotemporal and cultural locations, and on the basis of pure reason, ascertain beliefs and principles that should be compelling to all other rational persons equally, ignoring and transcending their specific backgrounds that differ from our own. Our differing heritages divide us and generate conflict; our capacity to reason unites us all, and hence offers a greater hope for a less violent human future than has been the case in the past, and at present. This emphasis on objectivity and impartiality has been a strong argument in favor of seeking universalism in ethics. Many people, and perhaps most Western philosophers, have been swayed by it, making any occasional challenges thereto seem either relativistic or authoritarian, or both.

Two such universalistic moral theories — both based on the concept of the individual we have outlined — have occupied Western philosophers since the Enlightenment: *deontological* ethics, focusing on the concept of one's duty, and *utilitarianism*, based on attending to the consequences of one's actions. Both claim universal scope, and both have been extremely influential as contributing to the conceptual grounding of the English, American, and French Revolutions. The former theory is associated with Immanuel Kant,[17] the latter with Jeremy Bentham and John Stuart Mill.[18] For Kant, logic reigns, and the focus is on compliance and consistency rather than consequences; for Bentham and Mill, the situation is more nearly — but not quite — reversed, since probabilities must weigh heavily in a moral agent's calculations about the consequences of one's actions.

Inadequate though this sketch is, it should suffice to make clear the stark contrast between the views of both Kantians and Utilitarians, on the one hand, and the early Confucians on the other, and the relevance of these differences for understanding the concept of family reverence, or *xiào*. That is, for the Confucian each situation requires the moral imagination necessary to put oneself in the place of the other (*shù* 恕) and then to invoke the conscientiousness to do one's utmost (*zhōng* 忠) to achieve what is optimally appropriate (*yì* 義) under the circumstances. Confucians do not seek the universal, but concentrate on the particular; they do not see abstract autonomous individuals, but rather concrete persons standing in a multiplicity of role relations with one another; they do not focus exclusively on either intentions or consequences (agents or their actions), but on the virtuosity and productivity of the dynamic relations themselves. In the Confucian sensibility, the appeal is to these particular persons in this particular family, defined by these specific relations. Indeed, persons are what they mean for each other.

In discussing feelings for family and community members — those to whom, in ever widening circles, one stands in a role as now benefactor, later beneficiary — we do not mean to imply there are no cognitive dimensions in an account of role ethics. Quite the contrary. But *reasonableness*, not *rationality*, is the term we want to employ in explicating Confucian role ethics. There is a seat of thinking in early Confucianism (and other schools of Chinese thought), the *xīn* 心, originally a picture of the aorta. But there is a catch: the *xīn* is also the seat of human feelings, which dooms in advance any effort to sharply distinguish the cognitive and the affective.[19]

One dimension of Confucian "family" that must not be overlooked is the role of friendship as an extension of family relations, and as a definite, often compensatory family value. In seeking out and developing our friendships we have a latitude and degree of freedom that is not characteristic of blood relatives, providing a porous border for the institution of family that allows for a more deliberate (reasonable) shaping of one's own personal relations, and hence one's own person. These voluntary relations, although surrogate, often achieve a degree of feeling and commitment that goes beyond our more formal family bonds. Where one is necessarily amicable with a brother, one can be more critical and demanding with friends (*Analects* 13:28).

Confucians must take full cognizance of, analyze, and evaluate the specific relations that obtain among members of a family in a way that is difficult for followers of Kant, Bentham, or Mill. For these latter philosophers, if all autonomous individuals are seen in the abstract as requiring equal treatment, for example, then taking the special bonds that hold between parents and children (and other special relations) into account philosophically becomes impossible. This is, in our opinion, one of the main reasons, perhaps, why a role ethics grounded in familial relations has attracted relatively little attention in the Western philosophical narrative since medieval times. A major historian of familial moral thinking in the West, Jeffrey Blustein, notes this fact but does not endeavor to explain it:

> After Hegel, philosophers did not stop talking about the normative aspects of parent-child relations altogether. What happened was that they no longer attempted to systematically apply their most dearly held moral and social values to the study of parenthood. The resolution of problems relating to the upbringing of children and to our expectations of them became a sideline, and the most profound issues affecting the lives of human beings in society were seen to lie elsewhere. (1982, 95)

In our political and legal thinking, both deontological and utilitarian ethical orientations play a major role, exerting a profound influence on legislatures and in the courts. But because both theories are rooted in the concept of a foundational individualism, developing adequate family laws and policies is difficult — another reason why the ethical studies of families has become a "sideline."

If our analyses of these positions and issues have merit, we can begin to see not only why questions of family *versus* state loyalties cannot be answered by these Western moral theories; they cannot even be asked. Indeed, *no* moral questions concerning the family can even be framed for examination because, by definition, family members are not abstract, autonomous individuals, parts of the public, but are flesh and blood, highly specific young and old, male and female, fellow human beings related to us in highly intimate ways. Thus all moral questions pertaining to family matters have been swept under the conceptual rug of a "private" realm that involves personal matters of taste and religious belief — a realm wherein moral and political philosophy do not enter.[20]

Only when we divest human beings of all qualities except their highly abstract individuality can we begin to think of developing a theory of moral principles that will hold in all instances. With respect to family, this is precisely what we cannot do if we are even to attempt to formulate the relevant moral questions about loyalties and obligations coherently. For as soon as we use the expression "my mother" in what it is not at all an abuse of language to call a "moral" situation, we are not dealing with an abstract, autonomous individual but one who carried us, brought us into this world, nurtured and comforted us, giving of herself for our benefit.

Returning now to our main narrative of the contrast between role and virtue ethical orientations, uneasiness with some of the implications of the ethics of Kant and Mill (only a few of which have we touched on above) has led some Western philosophers to undertake a re-evaluation and reinterpretation of Aristotle's virtue ethics. Instead of asking "What principles should guide my moral actions?" we should perhaps be asking "What kind of moral qualities should I endeavor to develop?" It is in the wake of these new directions in Western moral theory that many comparative philosophers have been given to characterizing Confucianism as a "virtue ethics."

Hopefully we have already shown how and why an Aristotelian virtue ethics is not the most appropriate model for understanding Confucian thought. Other, smaller but not inconsequential differences can also be noted. In the first place, Aristotle was writing largely for and about a warrior aristocracy, and the Confucians were anything but approving of warriors.[21] Confucius, in contrast, taught whoever came to him seeking to live a moral life. More importantly, Aristotle's virtue theory of ethics seems to require the postulate of universal character traits as a part of human nature,[22] and while the writings of the early Confucians certainly cohere, they are by no means in agreement on the constitution of human nature. They all presume that human beings — or in the Confucian case, perhaps "human becomings" — are open to and shaped by culturally generated patterns of behavior and taste, a position that is very different from presumed biological and metaphysical uniformities that we associate with Aristotle. That is, persons from their inchoate beginnings are to be understood as embedded in and nurtured by unique, transactional patterns of relations rather than as discrete entities defined by common traits. The notion of *lĭ* 禮 locates what we refer to as "moral" conduct within a thick and richly textured pattern of relations and consequent interactions, with instruction largely effected through emulation.[23]

Another way that Aristotelian virtue ethics differs from Confucian role ethics is that, while Aristotle does assume some *general* notion of community, the community is not in all cases *necessary* since many of the virtues may be cultivated in solitude. That is, the basic excellences he champions (as noted earlier) temperance, courage, and wisdom — *may* be cultivated in social situations, but they need not be: we can resist the temptation for third helpings of dessert when we are dining alone; test our courage by skydiving, bullfighting, or many other ways of defying death that do not require others; and of course we read, and usually reflect on things, by ourselves.[24]

Further, Aristotle's sense of the *polis* is a most *general* notion of community, the basic roles being general — male, warrior, citizen — rather than the *specific* and *constitutive* set of roles as *this* son, *this* mother, *this* neighbor, and so on, required by the Confucian ethic. As we have argued earlier, there is a world of difference between the very low level of abstraction found in the notion of *roles* and the much higher levels found in the concepts of *virtues, principles*, or *laws* — or, most importantly, *individuals*. The basic Confucian excellences can only be acquired in the process of living one's roles appropriately with the others to whom one is related, kin and non-kin alike. As a corollary, it must follow from the Confucian role orientation that we need to look at the patient no less than the agent in ascertaining the extent to which the valued habits of conduct have been properly developed and exemplified. It is not action but interaction that is the focus of the Confucian.

There are, to be sure, a number of similarities between Aristotle and Confucius in the area of what we call moral thought. We do not dwell on those similarities herein because many other comparative philosophers have done so and, more importantly, because, as we have argued throughout, we believe the differences between them are far more significant. One way to show these differences and to sum up what has been said in comparing them thus far is simply to juxtapose their writings on a similar concept. Consider laws, for example. First, from the *Nichomachean Ethics*:

> But it is difficult to get from youth up a right training for excellence if one has not been brought up under the right laws; for to live temperately and hardily is not pleasant to most people, especially when they are young. For this reason their nurture and occupation should be fixed by law; for they will not be painful when they have become customary.[25]

And continuing:

> But it is surely not enough that when they are young they should get the right nurture and attention; since they must, even when they are grown up, practice and be habituated to them, we shall need laws for this as well, and generally speaking, to cover the whole of life; for most people obey necessity rather than argument, and punishments rather than what is noble. (1984, 1180a,1–5)

From the *Analects*:

> The Master said: "Lead the people with administrative injunctions and keep them orderly with penal law, and they will avoid punishments but be without a sense of shame. Lead them with excellence and keep them orderly through observing ritual propriety and they will develop a sense of shame, and moreover, will order themselves. (2:3)

And again:

> The Master said: "If rulers are able to effect order in the state through the combination of observing ritual propriety and deferring to others, what more is needed? (4:3)

Further, virtue ethics resonates with the deontic and utilitarian models outlined above (and differs from role ethics) in that all three of them are dependent upon rational calculation to determine moral conduct. Compliance with the moral law or the application of the principle of utility is fundamentally a deliberative, rational exercise, and the less emotive content to it, the better. While Aristotle's doctrine of the mean certainly entails *practical* reason with an "uncodifiability" that is resistant to rules, his understanding of the human being is still defined by appeal to reason and indeed, the higher aspects of the human being, by appeal to *theoria*:

The actuality of God, which surpasses all of this in blessedness, must be contemplative; and of human activities, therefore, that which is most akin to this must be the most of the nature of happiness. (1984, 1178b20)

But for Confucius, one becomes distinguished as a person who behaves with family reverence just to the extent that one behaves with family reverence. One *xiào*s in order to be *xiào*, or perhaps better, one *xiào*s and is *xiào*. The Confucian excellences differ in form and content from the Aristotelian view in that, for the latter, cultivating the proper emotion and attitude, largely through study, reflection, and disciplined training, is the means for generating approbationary behavior. For the followers of the Master, the doers and the deeds are coterminous and mutually entailing. Meet your obligations consistently, attentively, appropriately — and the requisite dispositions and emotions are omnipresent in those actions. And there are exemplars of such conduct to prove the validity of the teachings when and if one's commitment to following the proper way flags. Concrete models play a greater role in guiding moral conduct than appeal to abstracted principles.

Yet another way in which Confucian role ethics differs from all theories of virtue ethics with which we are familiar is that, in the former, the ethical life is prerequisite for the spiritual, and for exemplary persons, is not distinct from it. Indeed, it is civility within the family and community that is the locus of human-centered Confucian religiousness, and it is inspired human living that is the source of spirituality. Ancestor reverence and sacrifice are important as reinforcing this more concrete and substantial human site of spiritual expression.[26]

Role ethics allows us to shave with Occam's razor a second time. Just as we might be skeptical of positing the existence of some ontological ground — God, substance, and so on as the "soul" of the totality — so too can we question whether we need to posit an individual self (nature, soul, person, character) behind the many roles we live.[27] Role ethics emphasizes the continuity of particular behavioral interactions and the personal growth entailed by them without reifying and subordinating them to longer-term, abstract dispositions. "Good with" and "good to" are more concrete than "good." Role ethics also focuses upon the aesthetic quality of our moral conduct — its intensity and appropriateness — and requires us to entertain the particular situations of our experience as they are actually felt and lived.

We would suggest that there is a tendency to make the same miscalculation in reflecting on virtues as we do in thinking about human nature. With human nature we are inclined to default to a retrospective causal or a teleological explanation of what it means to be a human *being* rather than providing a more holistic, prospective, and contextual account of what it means to *become* human — a *human becoming*, as it were. In so doing, we come to presuppose that human nature is either a ready-made potential to be actualized or some pre-existing ideal to be attained. It is believed by some scholars — Sim (2007, 13 and *passim*) being a good example — that agency and moral responsibility require the isolation of individuals from their relationships by positing such a definition of what it *is* to be human. In fact, on the contrary, such a ready-made definition of human *being* or a guiding teleological hand would on our reading compromise any robust existential notion of agency or responsibilities.

Similarly with Confucian "virtues," we are not referencing pre-existing metaphysical principles that by definition are causal and can ultimately stand as the objects of our contemplation. Nor are virtues some predetermined ideal that is to be actualized as personal character traits through the proper cultivation of human experience. Rather, "virtues," to use such language, are gerundive: "virtuing." They are an open-ended and always provisional virtuosity in our continuing patterns of relations. Such "virtues" are the activity of relating itself. And it is an activity that we are most often inclined to call "mothering" and "son-ing" and only then isolatable as abstractions such as "courage" or "justice." What we have with Confucian role ethics is a phenomenology of the concrete human experience lived within the relations of family and community as a basis for describing what it means to live life fully — morally and more than that.

Further, in ethics we usually assume that being moral has something to do with "complying with right and wrong" or "being good," as though the notions of "right and wrong" and "good" are available to us by appeal to some pre-existing standard: a pre-existing principle (causal) or some pre-existing ideal defined in the language of virtues (teleological). From the Confucian perspective, what we need instead is a phenomenology of experience as a basis for describing what it means to act in such a way as to enhance our relations. That is, we have to ask: What makes this situation comprising these particular relations better, and what makes it worse? We take the substance of morality to be nothing more or less than positive growth in the constitutive relations of any particular situation.

Within the context of cross-cultural accommodation, role ethics avoids intractable moral conflict by abjuring any appeal to universals and assuming that appropriate conduct is always a matter of continuing, collateral, or multilateral negotiation within the complexity of particular circumstances. Indeed, the collaborative nature of moral conduct requires that it be mutual and accommodating.

In sum, while Confucian role ethics surely bears more of a resemblance to Aristotle than to Kantian or utilitarian ethics, we do not believe virtue ethics, past or present, conceptually grounded in individuals, rationality, and freedom, and with little attention paid philosophically to the family, is an appropriate description of the views on the cultivated moral sensibilities of the Master and his followers. Nor do we believe that such a virtue ethics with its exaggerated emphasis on rationality as method can serve as a morality for the culturally diverse and rich world of today.

Having said this, we want to make it clear that, while we are persuaded we have much to learn from Confucian role ethics, we do not believe our current understanding of role ethics to be an ultimate and self-sufficient vision of the moral life. In fact, it is Aristotle's sustained and often unsuccessful struggle to balance and coordinate the conflicting demands of impartiality and partiality, of first philosophy and particular context, that serves as an object lesson and shows a way forward for us. At the same time, we believe that Confucian role ethics provides a basis for further reflection and expansion on how to achieve a quality of human flourishing that at once respects bottomless particularity and the indeterminacy such particularity entails, and at the same time allows for the development of a more robust sense of regulative ideals that do not require the excesses of first philosophy.

We are convinced there is much to be learned from Confucian role ethics as it was and is, and we are equally convinced that much must be done to develop it further — especially in redefining a number of roles, and hence the family — if it is to be a viable candidate as a vision of a global yet culturally specific moral life appropriate for the twenty-first century. But we believe it can indeed be such a candidate — there are parents, children, grandparents, neighbors, friends, and more in every culture — in a way that the ethics of Aristotle, Kant, or Bentham and Mill cannot.[28]

NOTES

1. A few of our criticisms of Sim (2007) have been anticipated by Ni Peimin in his close and careful critique "How far is Confucius an Aristotelian?" (unpublished manuscript). Supporting the claim that Confucianism is a virtue ethic are the papers in Ivanhoe and Walker (2006). See also Wilson (2002) and Yearley (2003), among others.
2. Shun (2008) underscores this persistent asymmetry. We are comfortable asking if Mòzǐ 墨子 is a utilitarian, but not whether or not Wittgenstein subscribes to a doctrine of "the proper use of language" (zhèngmíng 正名). See also our comments on Yu's work above.
3. We must remember, however, that "moral competence" is a Western term; as we argue below, there is no term for "morals" in classical Chinese. What *we* single out as distinctly moral and immoral behavior as opposed to legal, polite, religious, ceremonial, or other behaviors would not be parsed in anywhere near the same way within Confucian sensibilities, and it is this multiplicity of behaviors that gives rise to what we are calling "family feelings," integrated feelings of responsibility, love,

security, respect, loyalty, reverence, and more. On different categories of normative behavior, see Rosemont (1976). We follow standard usage in rendering *arête* as "virtue," but "excellence" captures the Aristotelian sense much better, we believe.
4. The extent to which the contrasting understandings of person constitute a fundamental disjunction is not lost on Sim (2007, 8, 13) or on Yu (2007, 23).
5. Aristotle maintains the centrality of the three (1984, vol. 2; 1982/1250a).
6. See, for example, *Analects* 4:5. All references to the *Analects* are based on Ames and Rosemont (1998).
7. See also 9:14, where Confucius claims that the model of an exemplary person living among barbarians would be for them transformative.
8. Rounds (1999) develops such themes in many original and incisive ways.
9. In addition to our analysis here, readers might consult Li (2007).
10. See *Analects* 15:1. Duke Líng 靈 of Wèi 衛 asked Confucius about military formations. Confucius replied, "I have heard something about the use of ritual vessels, but have never studied military matters." On the following day, he left Wèi.
11. For a psychological analysis of the relationship between loyalty and family reverence, see Hwang (1999).
12. *Analects* 2:24 and 14:22 are perhaps even clearer examples. The theme is also found in the *Mencius*, and even more in the *Xúnzǐ*, especially the chapters on the "Regulations of a king," "Human nature is unseemly," and "The way of the son." We use the term "accepted" here somewhat as Christine Korsgaard uses "autonomy." By "choosing" (her term) a "practical identity" (also her term) of being, say, a student majoring in a specific subject, she describes what in our terms would be described as accepting responsibility for all that goes with taking up a specific role. See Korsgaard (1996, 105–6), especially the discussion of her example of the math major. We are grateful to Yang Xiao for pointing out to us how apt Korsgaard's critique is for our account of role ethics (although that was certainly not her intent; Confucianism is nowhere mentioned in this or any other of her writings on ethics, and defending a Kantian orientation in her work, she would almost certainly not concur with our critique of the deontological position).
13. On the philosophical significance of the linguistic differences noted here and below, see Rosemont (1987) and the introduction to Ames and Rosemont (1998). See also note 4. Sim (2007, 6, and elsewhere), also acknowledges problems of translating moral terms cross-culturally.
14. Qian Mu, as cited in Dennerline 1988, is adamant that the Confucian concept-cluster (our expression) of Chinese terms has no counterpart in other languages.
15. Individualism has had too many philosophical and political champions to note ever since the Enlightenment began. Most of these advocates have not been overly critical of the concept — including Marx no less than apologists for capitalism — except at the margins, and to provide a needed corrective we highly recommend Macpherson (1964).
16. For a survey (and celebration) of the concept of autonomy, see Schneewind (1998).
17. The *locus classicus* is his *Critique of practical reason*, various editions.
18. Here the *locus classicus* is Mill's *Utilitarianism*, also in various editions.
19. The late Robert Solomon, beginning with his (1976), did much to overcome the Western prejudices that insisted on this invidious split.

20. The work of the late Susan Moller Okin points up this weakness in the Western philosophical tradition. She criticizes Rawls (1970) on this score but remains basically an individualist, for while she does want to retain a private realm, she wants to keep the family out of it in a separate "domestic" realm. See Okin (1989).
21. Sim (2007, 16) also sees this Aristotelian elitism as a limitation.
22. Wong (2007) explores this charge as raised by Gilbert Harman and John Doris (in separate works). He responds well to the challenge, but not in a way that would please any virtue ethicist committed to some form of foundational individualism.
23. See, for example, *Analects* 6:30.
24. Wan Junren (2004, 129) criticizes Alasdair MacIntyre and Aristotle on precisely this point. To the extent that communities matter for them, "these indispensable factors possess *only theoretical significance as part of the necessary explanatory context* for a given virtue ethic — they do not themselves *constitute the practice of virtue itself*." MacIntyre (2004a, 154) strongly denies that communities are in this way tangential for either Aristotle or himself, citing *Politics* I (1253a1–39), paraphrasing: "To be a member of a political society is to share with others a concept of the just and the unjust, the good and the bad, while to be outside political community is to be deprived of the possibility of developing the excellence specific to human beings. Only through the relationships of the household and the political community are human beings able to develop as human beings." Blum (1996), *contra* Aristotle and MacIntyre, argues for a stronger role for community in the production and practice of moral virtues than he thinks they would allow. (We thank Steve Angle for this reference.)
25. Commenting on this particular passage, Kupperman remarks, "[T]here is every reason to believe that Confucius would have been incredulous at Aristotle's suggestion that law should have an important role in the education of young children" (2004, 107). And in commenting on this and other insights of Kupperman — and others — MacIntyre notes, "But Confucianism involves not only a rejection of Western deontology and utilitarianism, but also, as Kupperman's comparison of Aristotelian and Confucian views makes clear, a rejection of the basic assumptions of most Western versions of an ethics of virtue" (2004b, 209).
26. See Ames (2003) for a characterization of this Confucian sense of religiousness. For a this-worldly analysis of *all* religious traditions, see Rosemont (2001).
27. William James, in his essay "Some metaphysical problems pragmatically considered," goes after this same problem of "substance," that is, "the phenomenal properties of things ... *ad*here, or *co*here, rather, *with each other*, and the notion of substance inaccessible to us, which we think accounts for such cohesion by supporting it, as cement might support pieces of mosaic, must be abandoned. The fact of bare cohesion itself is all that the notion of the substance signifies. Behind that fact is nothing" (2000, 42).
28. This is the subject of our current collaboration, tentatively titled *Confucian role ethics: A moral vision for the 21st century*.

References

Ames, R. 2003. *Lǐ* 禮 and the a-theistic religiousness of classical Confucianism. In *Confucian spirituality*, ed. W. Tu and M. Tucker. 165–82. New York: Crossroads Press.

Ames R., and H. Rosemont, Jr. 1998. *The Analects of Confucius: A philosophical translation*. New York: Ballantine.

Aristotle. 1984. *The collected works of Aristotle*, 2 vols., ed. J. Barnes. Princeton, NJ: Princeton University Press.

Blum, L. 1998. Community and virtue. In *How should one live? Essays on the virtues*, ed. R. Crisp. New York: Oxford University Press.

Blustein, J. 1982. *Parents and children: The ethics of the family*. New York: Oxford University Press.

Carrithers, M., S. Collins, and S. Lukes, eds. 1985. *The category of person*. Cambridge: Cambridge University Press.

Ching, J. 1978. Chinese ethics and Kant. *Philosophy East and West* 28 (2): 161–72.

Dancy, J. 2006. *Ethics without principles*. New York: Oxford University Press.

Dennerline, J. 1988. *Qian Mu and the world of seven mansions*. New Haven, CT: Yale University Press.

Hwang, K. 1999. Filial piety and loyalty: Two types of social identification in Confucianism. *Asian Journal of Social Psychology* (2): 161–83.

Ivanhoe, P. 2006. Filial piety as a virtue. In *Working virtue*, ed. P. Ivanhoe and R. Walker. 297–312. New York: Oxford University Press.

James, W. 2000. *Pragmatism and other writings*. London: Penguin Classics.

Kant, I. 1959. *Foundations of the metaphysics of morals*. Indianapolis, IN: Library of Liberal Arts, Bobbs-Merrill Co.

Korsgaard, C. 1996. *Sources of normativity*. Cambridge: Cambridge University Press.

Kupperman, J. 2004. Tradition and community in the formation of character and self. In *Confucian Ethics*, ed. K. Shun and D. Wong. 103–23. Cambridge: Cambridge University Press.

Li, C. 2007. Li as cultural grammar. *Philosophy East and West* 57 (3): 311–29.

MacIntyre, A. 2004a. Once more on Confucian and Aristotelian conceptions of the virtues: A response to Professor Wan. In *Chinese philosophy in an era of globalization*, ed. R. Wang, trans. E. Slingerland. 151–62. Albany: State University of New York Press.

———. 2004b. Questions for Confucians. In *Confucian ethics*, ed. K. Shun and D. Wong. 203–18. Cambridge: Cambridge University Press.

Macpherson, C. 1964. *The political theory of possessive individualism: Hobbes to Locke*. New York: Oxford University Press.

Noddings, N. 2003. *Caring*. 2nd ed. Berkeley: University of California Press.

Okin, S. 1989. *Justice, gender and the family*. New York: Basic Books.

Rawls, J. 1999. *Theory of justice*. Cambridge, MA: Harvard University Press.

Rosemont, H., Jr. 1976. Notes from a Confucian perspective: Which human acts are moral acts? *International Philosophical Quarterly* 16 (1): 49–61.

———. 1987. Against relativism. In *Interpreting across boundaries*, ed. G. Larson and E. Deutsch. 36–70. Princeton, NJ: Princeton University Press.

———. 2001. *Rationality and religious experience*. Chicago and LaSalle, IL: Open Court.

Rosemont, H., Jr. and R. Ames. 2009. *The Chinese classic of family reverence: A philosophical translation of the* Xiaojing. Honolulu: University of Hawai'i Press.

Rounds, D., with the Lafayette String Quartet. 1999. *The four and the one: In praise of string quartet*. Fort Bragg, CA: Lost Coast Press.

Schneewind, J. 1998. *The invention of autonomy: A history of modern moral philosophy.* Cambridge: Cambridge University Press.

Shun, K. 2008. Some methodological reflections on comparative ethics. Unpublished manuscript.

Sim, M. 2007. *Remastering morals with Aristotle and Confucius.* Cambridge: Cambridge University Press.

Slote, M. 2007. *The ethics of care and empathy.* London: Routledge.

Solomon, R. 1976. *The passions.* New York: Doubleday.

Wan, J. 2004. Contrasting Confucian virtue ethics and MacIntyre's Aristotelian virtue theory. In *Chinese philosophy in an era of globalization,* ed. R. Wang, trans. E. Slingerland. 123–49. Albany: State University of New York Press.

Wilson, S. 2002. Conformity, individuality, and the nature of virtue: A classical Confucian contribution to contemporary ethical reflection. In *Confucius and the Analects,* ed. B. Van Norden. 94–115. New York: Oxford University Press.

Wong, D. 2007. If we are not by ourselves, if we are not strangers. In *Polishing the Chinese mirror: Essays in honor of Henry Rosemont, Jr.,* ed. M. Chandler and R. Littlejohn. 331–51. LaSalle, IL: Open Court.

Yearley, L. 2003. Virtues and religious virtues in the Confucian tradition. In *Confucian spirituality,* ed. W. Tu and M. Tucker. 134–62. New York: Crossroads Press.

Yu, J. 2005. Confucius' relational self and Aristotle's political animal. *History of Philosophy Quarterly* 22 (4): 281–300.

———. 2007. *The ethics of Confucius and Aristotle: Mirrors of virtue.* New York: Routledge.

2
Mencius as Consequentialist

Manyul Im

In this chapter, I lay out the reasons for trying to understand Mencius by attributing a consequentialist moral theory to him. This is meant in part as an oblique criticism of readings on which he is construed as a "virtue ethicist." It is also meant to be something of a reply to Chad Hansen's (1992) consistently severe dismissals of Mencius as a competent thinker about ethics. However, the scope of my argument here is limited to the positive argument in favor of reading Mencius as a consequentialist.[1] I argue that, on the best systematic sense we can make of the text, Mencius judges the responses and actions of the gentleman, or *jūnzǐ* 君子, to be better or worse according to whether such responses and actions bring about better or worse consequences than other responses, lack of responses, actions, or inactions that might have been brought about. That is not to argue that Mencius himself advocates a consequentialist moral theory. Arguably, he never lays out or advocates a *theory* in any robust sense. At best the account of his sayings and conversations in the *Mencius* indicates certain patterns of concern expressed either to rulers or disciples and occasional bouts of disputation with opponents. Nonetheless, I will argue that a pattern of justification emerges from the text that is primarily consequentialist in structure. In addition, an intended bonus will emerge from my reading of Mencius. We may see from it how a consequentialist theory might look in which an important type of intrinsic moral value might be countenanced among the goods to be promoted.

The entire trajectory of this reading will seem prima facie implausible to some because of the traditional, and correct, juxtaposition of Mencius as a philosophical opponent of the Mohists' ethical position, which is standardly — and correctly — characterized as utilitarian, or more recently, as consequentialist.[2] While I take the Mohists to be consequentialists, I argue that the difference between them and Mencius lies not in Mencius being a nonconsequentialist, but in a disagreement Mencius has about two facets of the Mohists' brand of consequentialism. In essence, my argument is that Mencius is critical of the Mohists because following their teachings, as Mencius construes them, is unlikely to result in the best consequences. Mencius argues against the Mohist view that a person should act, in the usual case, *from considerations* of producing a net overall gain of benefit. Instead, Mencius argues, one ought to act from certain motives which themselves contribute to the value of the resulting behavior, value which would be lost if one always acted from the motive of producing benefit.

Characterizing the disagreement in this way, I believe, sufficiently captures the spirit and details of the textual polemic between Mencius and the Mohists. But, as I will argue, that does not commit us to attributing a nonconsequentialist ethical view to Mencius. On the contrary, it makes sense to characterize Mencius himself as a consequentialist, though one of a less straightforward type than the Mohists. After dispatching the concern that a consequentialist reading of Mencius is at odds with the proper understanding of his relationship to the Mohists, I will fill in the reading with an account of the kinds of things Mencius considers to be goods and the ways in which he thinks one can best bring them about. I then contrast this reading with a prominent consequentialist reading of Mencius, and of early Confucianism more generally, given by P. J. Ivanhoe, one that emphasizes possession of good character as the good to be promoted.

In order to make my case, however, I need to address two preliminary issues. First, we need to be clear about the ways in which an ethical view can plausibly be considered consequentialist, despite being a view far removed historically and culturally from the intellectual context in which the ethical views typically considered consequentialist developed and exist. Also, some clarification about the nature of consequentialism itself as a species of moral theory is necessary in order to construct the proper framework for highlighting Mencius's consequentialist tendencies.

Framing Ancient Ethical Views

A very general way of characterizing theories as consequentialist attributes to them views about "the good" and "the right," wherein the right is defined in terms of the good. So such theories tend to contain:
(1) A view about what things or kinds of things are intrinsically and nonmorally valuable or good; and

(2) The view that what makes something right — an act, rule, institution, etc. — depends ultimately on its resulting either directly or indirectly in the best outcome available, where the outcome is given in terms of the net nonmoral good that results from the act.

Here, I follow Frankena's characterization, though he calls such theories "teleological" in contrast to "deontological."

> A teleological theory says that the basic or ultimate criterion or standard of what is morally right, wrong, obligatory, etc., is the nonmoral value that is brought into being. The final appeal, directly or indirectly, must be to the comparative amount of good produced, or rather to the comparative balance of good over evil produced. (1963, 14)

Aside from various kinds of utilitarianism, Frankena includes ethical egoism among teleological theories. On Frankena's analysis, ethical egoism as a teleological theory is distinguished from utilitarianism only by a difference in view about *whose* nonmoral good it is right to promote. If we exclude ethical egoism from his analysis of teleological theories, I think his use of the label "teleological" corresponds to how I wish to use "consequentialist." The important feature to notice about consequentialist views is that rightness of acts, rules, or whatever is held to be dependent on the production of nonmoral good. This distinguishes such views from deontological views, in which rightness of acts is thought to be, to various degrees, independent of the production of nonmoral good.

At this point we can distinguish a common way of characterizing "utilitarian" moral theory as a species of consequentialist or teleological theory. Utilitarianism is a form of consequentialism that specifies the nonmoral good to be brought about in terms of well-being, or welfare. What well-being consists of may vary from account to account, from pleasure felt by any sentient being to preference-satisfaction of persons (see Scanlon 1993). An example of the latter is classical utilitarianism, as Rawls understands it (1971, 25). Rawls at the same time characterizes other species of teleological theory according to the way the conception of the good is specified.

> Teleological doctrines differ, pretty clearly, according to how the conception of the good is specified. If it is taken as the realization of human excellence . . . we have what may be called perfectionism. This notion is found in Aristotle and Nietzsche. If the good is defined as pleasure, we have hedonism; if as happiness, eudaimonism, and so on. (1971, 25)

Rawls's characterization of "perfectionism" contributes an important distinction between broadly teleological theories and consequentialist ones. Human excellence, as part of the conception of the good in a teleological theory, may contain goods that are not clearly nonmoral. In particular, if we take Aristotle's case, human excellence must include the virtues, which may sensibly be considered moral goods, at least broadly speaking. By contrast, consequentialist ethical theories are supposed to be concerned with the nonmoral good.

To understand better what consequentialism is — or could be — then, it is necessary to clarify the distinction between *nonmoral* good or value and the other merely suggested category up to this point, *moral* good or value.[3] The reason that this distinction is important to clarify for our purposes here is that ethical theories may attribute value not only to actions but also to traits, motives, and psychological attitudes for the further and final purpose of evaluating a *person* morally, rather than for the purpose of evaluating the value of states of affairs. Such value seems to be the kind that is typical of moral (versus nonmoral) value. But it may seem to those who are familiar with Mencius that it is exactly that kind of value with which he is often concerned.

What I will suggest is that there are at least two quite different distinctions that are glossed in the literature as the moral/nonmoral value distinction. One distinction has to do with whether or not something is good in a way *derivative* of some standard of rightness. That distinction, I will argue, is essential to the definition of consequentialism. But there is another distinction which some have used — for example, Frankena — to characterize the divide. This second distinction has to do with whether something has value in the sense of being admirable and in some irreducible sense *estimable*, as opposed to being merely desirable. I do not think this latter distinction is essential to the definition of consequentialism, though it may be of some use for describing more clearly the kinds of things a consequentialist theory can be concerned with promoting.

Right-Derived Moral Good

We can find in Rawls an analysis of the reason why any theory that is act-consequentialist cannot recognize or, at the very least, cannot concern itself in its account of right action with a certain kind of value.

> It is essential to keep in mind that in a teleological theory the good is defined independently from the right. This means two things. First, the theory accounts for our considered judgments as to which things are good (our judgments of value) as a separate class of judgments intuitively distinguishable by common sense, and then proposes the

hypothesis that the right is maximizing the good as already specified. Second, the theory enables one to judge the goodness of things without referring to what is right. (1971, 25)

Rawls's analysis has two steps. First, it identifies what is unique about consequentialism as an ethical theory by the way the relationship between what is right and what is good is structured by such a theory. This we have also seen above in Frankena's analysis of "teleological" theories. The point here, again, is that the good is normatively independent — at least by the light of common sense — from the right, according to a teleological theory. Second, Rawls's analysis identifies a class of normative judgment concerning acts or persons that is incompatible with the way a consequentialist theory must structure the relationship between judgments of value and judgments of what is right.

An example, Rawls thinks, is the judgment that the distribution of goods is itself a good. If it is counted as a good — a "higher order" good, perhaps — and hence is counted by our ethical theory as one of the goods among others that it is right to promote, Rawls argues, the theory will not be a teleological theory in the sense specified above. The reason for this is that "The problem of distribution falls under the concept of right as one intuitively understands it" (1971, 25). In other words, the value of the distribution of goods is dependent on the rightness of a fair distribution of goods. But what is distinctive about teleological, or what I call consequentialist, theories is that the goods to be promoted are thought to have their value independent of what is right. If goods were included that had value that depended on their being right to promote, then there would be a problem of circularity in the theory. For the theory of rightness in a consequentialist theory would recognize goods, some of which were dependent on its being right to promote them. Then the rightness of an act would depend on the goodness of the consequences, but the goodness of some of those consequences would depend on the rightness of the act.[4] So for reasons of circularity, one kind of value that cannot be counted by a consequentialist theory as part of the nonmoral good to be promoted is the value something has in virtue of its being right to promote that thing.[5] Now, although Rawls himself does not call this kind of value "moral good," it is worth calling this *right-derived moral good* so as not to confuse it with another kind of value also distinguishable from nonmoral good.

Esteem-Based Moral Good

We can find this other kind in Frankena's discussion of the difference between moral and nonmoral good. Frankena's treatment of the distinction is especially interesting because it reveals an ambiguity, allowing us to see how things that fall under an important construal of "moral value" actually can be of interest to a consequentialist theory. According to Frankena, what distinguishes things that are morally good from nonmorally good things is the connection that the former have to persons and elements of personality. Both in the objects that we tend to call morally good or bad and in the reasons we have for making such judgments, Frankena thinks there is an important link to personhood: "When we judge actions or persons to be morally good or bad we always do so because of the motives, intentions, dispositions, or traits of character they manifest" (1963, 62). Such judgments of moral value, Frankena calls "aretaic judgments."

Aretaic judgments of moral value, according to Frankena, are suggestive of *intrinsic* moral goodness of a sort important to identifying what he calls an "ethics of virtue."[6] Frankena thinks that judgments of moral value are especially and primarily apt when applied to people or features of people such as their motives and dispositions. He identifies moral value that is intrinsic, not derivative of what it is right to do or to promote, as a way of delineating what is distinctive about an ethics of virtue.

> What would an ethics of virtue be like? It would, of course, not take deontic judgments or principles as basic in morality, as we have been doing; instead, it would take as basic aretaic judgments like "That was a courageous deed," "His action was virtuous," or "Courage is a virtue," and it would insist that deontic judgments are either derivative from such aretaic ones or can be dispensed with entirely. Moreover, it would regard aretaic judgments about actions as secondary and as based on aretaic judgments about agents and their motives or traits. (Frankena 1963, 63)

The moral value of motives or dispositions according to this type of account is not derivative of the concept of right action. Instead, right action is derived, if at all, from the moral value of certain motives or dispositions. On such a view, what is morally good has theoretical primacy over rightness.[7] Intrinsic moral value, just like intrinsic *non*moral value, must be determined independently of other things of value and, for that reason, independently of the moral value of actions.[8]

How, then, might intrinsic moral value be determined? Though woefully short of presenting a full account, we can suggest how such an account might parallel a powerful way of accounting for *non*moral value. It is sometimes argued that judgments of intrinsic nonmoral value can be grounded in judgments of what we desire or what we would desire under certain conditions.[9] The reason is that nonmoral value seems to have an important intuitive connection to being the object of desire. A parallel way to ground judgments of intrinsic *moral* value might be to exploit a similarly intuitive connection moral value has to being the object of certain favorable attitudes other than desire: for example, moral admiration, esteem, or respect. This way of grounding moral value would be quite similar to Hume's sentiment-based argument that virtue and vice are distinguishable by certain natural kinds of reaction that we have to certain things: "An action, or sentiment, or character is virtuous or vicious; why? because its view causes a pleasure or uneasiness of a particular kind. In giving a reason, therefore, for the pleasure or uneasiness, we sufficiently explain the vice or virtue" (Hume 1740, 472). Hume also marks a difference in kinds of attitude with which he tries to distinguish the objects of moral esteem from nonmoral.

> A good composition of music and a bottle of good wine equally produce pleasure; and what is more, their goodness is determin'd merely by the pleasure. But shall we say upon that account, that the wine is harmonious, or the music of a good flavor? In like manner an inanimate object, and the character or sentiments of any person may, both of them, give satisfaction; but as the satisfaction is different, this keeps our sentiments concerning them from being confounded, and makes us ascribe virtue to the one, and not to the other. . . . 'Tis only when a character is considered in general, without reference to our particular interest, that it causes such a feeling or sentiment, as denominates it morally good or evil. (1740, 472)

Judgments of intrinsic moral value could, then, be grounded in judgments of what we admire or would admire under certain conditions. Such an account might even give a rationale for Frankena's claim that only aspects of *persons* have moral value. If that were true, it would be because only such things are objects of moral admiration or esteem. We may call this type of value, then, *esteem-based moral good*.

Important for this distinction is that the esteem, or admiration, upon which judgments of such value are based should not be reducible to further judgments about what is right, for that would not distinguish esteem-based good from right-derived good. We would have to think of esteem or admiration as, in some sense, a primitive or basic natural attitude, perhaps a species of desire, but with a psychological "shape" to it that distinguishes it from other species of desire broadly construed. So, estimability and admirability would track desirability, but under a specific rubric of it that is the basis for calling them species of *moral* desirability rather than nonmoral.

Summarizing, it may be possible to distinguish at least two kinds of moral good: (1) extrinsic, or secondary moral good, which may be derived from a prior concept of right action — or, *right-derived moral good*; and (2) intrinsic, or primary moral good that is based on esteem or admiration. Returning to the structure of consequentialism, we may question if and why things with intrinsic *moral* value cannot be part of the good, along with nonmoral goods, that are right to produce on consequentialist grounds. We have seen why right-derived moral value cannot be included. But what could be the reason for excluding things with intrinsic, *primary* moral value — *esteem-based good* — from a consequentialist theory? The answer to this question depends on an answer to the question of what role intrinsically morally good people, motives, or dispositions are to play in a theory.

Take benevolence as an example. It may be a motive that has moral value because of its admirability. It may even be admired because it moves a person to further the happiness of other people. But a consequentialist need not consider a benevolent motive good solely because of its *instrumental* value to realizing the nonmoral good of happiness. The possession of benevolent motives might also be considered an *intrinsic* moral good that is itself a good thing to be brought about. And this may be for the same sorts of reasons that a consequentialist might have for considering intrinsic *non*moral goods to be brought about, namely, because they are things with which we think the world is better off than without. The difference between benevolence and happiness that differentiates them as different kinds of good is that benevolence is the object of moral desire — esteem or admiration — while happiness is the object of a broader type of nonmoral desire.

This type of reasoning may provide the basis for including within consequentialist ethical theory certain goods that are thought of as morally valuable — more specifically, thought to be so in the esteem-based way. So dispositions or motives may be thought intrinsically valuable and among the goods which, *if brought about by an act*, contribute to a consequentialist assessment of the act as right.

Objective and Subjective Consequentialism

One last preliminary issue before discussing Mencius's ethical views is the construal of consequentialism according to what it is supposed to provide as a theory. As Bales puts it, one might think of a consequentialist ethical theory as either providing an "account of right-making characteristics" or as providing a "decision-making procedure" (1971, 261).[10] This distinction allows us to see how someone who has a consequentialist ethical view and hence is concerned with bringing about the best consequences could at the same time advocate that we act from considerations other than that of bringing about the best consequences. That will allow us to see how Mencius's criticism of the Mohists can be read as consequentialist criticisms.

To think of an ethical theory as providing an account of right-making characteristics is to suppose that it provides an account of the criterion for whether an act is right. Such an account may tell us how to go about deciding what to do in all or most situations, or in a particular one. How exactly we go about deciding what to do is itself something that can be judged right by applying the criterion of rightness identified by the account. But, so far, this tells us how to determine the right decision procedure — it is not itself the procedure used to decide how to act in some particular situation. So applying the criterion of right action can tell us what decision procedure we ought to use in deciding how to act, but the criterion of right action itself need not be included among the things we ought (according to that very criterion) to consider when deciding what to do.

Following Railton, we can call a consequentialist view *objective* if it only gives its account of right action as a criterion of the rightness of an act, and call it *subjective* if the overall good to be promoted is given in the theory as the object one should consciously take in deciding what to do; i.e., "that whenever one faces a choice of actions, one should attempt to determine which act of those available would promote the good, and should then try to act accordingly" (1984, 113).

Mencius and the Mohists

From what we read in the *Mòzǐ*, we know that consequentialist views formed a large part of the ethical and political thought of the Mohists. Mòzǐ's criticisms of Ruist, or Confucian, teachings and practices focus on the bad consequences of adopting those teachings and engaging in those practices. In particular, Mòzǐ targets the Ruist emphasis on observance of traditional ceremonies, especially funerary and mourning rituals. In the chapter "Simplicity in Funeral" (jié zàng xià 節葬下), he takes to task the expenditure of materials, time, and the sheer physical and emotional energy involved in traditional ceremonies because it is ruinous to the kingdom.

> When the sage-kings of the Three Dynasties had passed away, and the world had become ignorant of their principles, some of the gentlemen in later generations regarded elaborate and extended mourning as magnanimous, and righteous, and the duty of a filial son. . . . In my opinion, if, in adopting the doctrine and practicing the principle, elaborate funeral and extended mourning could enrich the poor, increase the few, remove danger, and regulate disorder, it would be magnanimous, righteous, and the duty of a filial son. . . . I have examined the sayings of those who uphold elaborate funeral and

> extended mourning. If they should be taken seriously in the country, it would mean: when a lord dies, there would be several inner and outer coffins. He would be buried deep. There would be many shrouds. Embroidery would be elaborate. The grave mound would be massive. So then, the death of a common man would exhaust the wealth of a family. And the death of a feudal lord would empty the state treasury.... (Mei 1973, 123–24)

Likewise, practices not necessarily advocated by the Ruists, but apparently carried on by some rulers of his day, are also targets of Mòzǐ's criticism; for example, heavy taxation and corvée, offensive warfare, the building of elaborate palaces and homes, and the performance of elaborate music and dance. To give their views rhetorical weight, the Mohists argue that the actions of historical cultural heroes, the sage kings and others, show the same concern for consequences as the Mohists themselves advocate.[11] So the appeal to consequences in assessing the acceptability of teachings and practices plays a rather prominent role not only in the debates between the Mohists and Ruists such as Mencius but also, it seems, in the Mohist scholars' more general political criticisms and even their interpretations of historical myths.

The description of the consequences with which the Mohists are particularly concerned is "the benefit to the kingdom." Benefit to the kingdom is explicated often in terms of the economic well-being, broadly speaking, of the people. Included in that is the defensibility of the kingdom from aggression. Given the prominence of consequentialist arguments within Mohist views, it is striking that, in his discussions of Mohist doctrines, *Mencius expresses no objections to justifying particular teachings or practices by consideration of the consequences of adopting them.* There are two main points Mencius argues in those discussions, both of which are compatible with consequentialist positions: (a) that the Mohists have an implausible psychological element in their teachings, and (b) that taking benefit as the goal of one's actions has bad consequences. In the case of the latter, as we will see, Mencius actually argues for the point with a consequentialist argument of his own.

Mencius's explicit discussion of Mòzǐ (i.e., actually referring to Mò by name) is restricted entirely to criticism of Mòzǐ's doctrine of "inclusive concern," *jiān ài* 兼愛 (or as more commonly translated, "universal love"). This was a key element of Mòzǐ's view that one ought not to display exclusivity or favoritism, say, toward the members of one's own family. What is important, in Mòzǐ's view, is not just that one ought to *behave* so, but that one ought to *feel* concern inclusively toward all in the kingdom, as he states in his *Jiān ài* chapter.

> But what is the way of universal love and mutual aid? [Mòzǐ] said: It is to regard the state of others as one's own, the houses of others as one's own, the persons of others as one's self. When feudal lords love one another, there will be no more war; . . . when individuals love one another there will be no more injury. When ruler and ruled love each other they will be gracious and loyal . . . . When all the people in the world love one another, then the strong will not overpower the weak, the many will not oppress the few, the wealthy will not mock the poor. . . . (Mei 1973, 82)

Mòzǐ's ethical view, then, requires concern for all — not just in one's own kingdom but for all humankind regardless of state boundaries. Mòzǐ explicitly contrasts partiality with the inclusivity (*jiān*) of the concern one ought to feel. As Mencius understands it, this means that one ought to take the very same concern one feels for members of one's own family, ruler, or state, and feel that same way inclusively toward all people. Hence, by Mencius's rendering of Mòzǐ, one ought not to have partial feelings at all toward anyone.

This was a mistaken view, as far as Mencius was concerned; he thought it assumed an implausible empirical psychology, requiring a psychologically impossible task of people. It is this point that Mencius objects to in this explicit discussion of Mòzǐ's views. In 3A:5, Mencius discusses the actions and beliefs of a follower of Mòzǐ's teachings, Yí Zhī.[12]

> [Mencius said:] I have heard that Yí Zhī is a Mohist. In the matter of funeral arrangements, Mòzǐ teaches that one ought to be sparing. . . . Nevertheless Yí Zhī buried his parents in a rich manner and so he served his parents in a way he disparages.
>
> Xú Bì reported this to Yí Zhī. Yí Zhī said: The Ruists teach that the ancients ruled like they were caring for children. What does this mean? It means that one ought to love without differences of degree. In carrying this out, the starting point is affection for family.
>
> Xú Bì reported this to Mencius. Mencius said: Does Yí Zhī sincerely believe that a man's affection for his brother's child is like his affection for a neighbor's child?

The fact that Mencius's complaint against Mòzǐ really is this — that it is futile to expect people to be able to feel concern impartially — is further supported by the Mohists' own description of their detractors: "But the gentlemen (*jūnzǐ*) of the world say: 'So far so good. It is of course very excellent when love becomes universal. But it is only a difficult and distant ideal'" (Mei 1973, 83).

In the two other places where Mòzǐ is specifically referred to by name,[13] Mencius identifies in passing the objectionable part of Mòzǐ's view by referring to Mòzǐ's principle of inclusive concern, *jiān ài* — not by referring to the motive of benefit, *lì* 利. So it is clear that Mencius was dubious about the plausibility of humans being *able* to have concern impartially. He does not seem concerned, at least explicitly, with Mòzǐ's consequentialist standards of justifying or criticizing feelings and actions that center on benefit.[14]

It might be thought that Mencius was content only to address the doctrine of inclusive concern and not worry about addressing Mòzǐ's consequentialism, because the latter is founded on the former. Hence, if Mencius can argue against the psychological underpinnings of Mòzǐ's consequentialism, he would undermine it. But there are two obstacles to this argument. First, it is clear that it is the other way around: Mòzǐ's consequentialism underwrites his view about what one ought to feel. Mòzǐ actually gives a consequentialist justification for the view that one ought to feel concern inclusively. Each of the three chapters on inclusive concern compiled in the text of the *Mòzǐ* begins with an analysis of the cause of disorder and argues that the cure for disorder is impartial concern. In the third of these *Jiān ài* chapters we find a nice summing up of the argument of Mòzǐ.

> When we come to think about the several benefits [to the world] in regard to their cause, how have they arisen? Have they arisen out of hate of others and injuring others? Of course we should say no. We should say they have arisen out of love of others and benefiting others. If we should classify one by one all those who love others and benefit others, should we find them to be partial or universal? Of course we should say they are universal. Now, since universal love is the cause of the major benefits in the world, therefore [Mòzǐ] proclaims universal love is right . . . . [We] have found out the consequences of universal love to be the major benefits of the world and the consequences of partiality to be the major calamities in the world; this is the reason why [Mòzǐ] said partiality is wrong and universality is right. (Mei 1973, 88)

So, on Mòzǐ's view, one ought to feel concern inclusively because that would result in benefit for the world, i.e., better consequences; and one ought to bring about the better consequences. Mòzǐ does not run his argument in the other direction, that one ought to bring about the better consequences because one ought to feel concern impartially. So Mencius would have to have terribly misunderstood the Mohists' position if he thought that he would undermine their consequentialism by arguing against the inclusive concern doctrine. Of course he might have been so confused. But here is where the second obstacle to this argument is relevant.

Mencius does not actually display any objections toward the view that one ought to bring about the better consequences. On the contrary, he himself takes for granted that one ought to do so. The evidence that Mencius does this is somewhat subtle, for two reasons. First, it occurs in passages that do not explicitly mention Mòzǐ or his followers but that do involve the term that is prominent in the Mohist views: *lì* 利, "profit" or "benefit." Second, there is subtlety in those passages because Mencius ostensibly argues against someone's acting for the sake of benefit. But if we look at the passages, it is clear that Mencius considers the consequences of acting for the sake of benefit to be counterproductive of the goal of attaining benefit, and *that* is the reason not to act with that motive. In 1A:1, Mencius visits King Huì of Liáng and is greeted by the king with the suggestion that Mencius has come all this way with counsels "to benefit my kingdom" (*lì wú guó* 利吾國). To this Mencius replies that Huì should not "speak of" benefit (*wáng hé bì yuē lì* 王何必曰利). Likewise, in 6B:4, Mencius corrects a fellow scholar, Sòng Kēng, who is about to try to stop the kingdoms of Qín and Chǔ from their hostilities. Sòng Kēng tells Mencius that his plan is to try to persuade the rulers of the two kingdoms that warfare between them is "not to their benefit" (*qí bù lì yě* 其不利也). Mencius responds by suggesting that his aim is fine but his plan is flawed.

> Your aim is great, but your plan is inadvisable. If you speak of benefit to the kings of Qín and Chǔ, the kings will be pleased with the thought of benefit and stop their armies.... Then this will make the ministers [of those kingdoms] to serve their lords while harboring desire for benefit; it will make sons to serve their fathers with thoughts of benefit.... Because of this, lords and ministers, fathers and sons, and elder and younger siblings will discard benevolence and propriety and cherish benefit in their interactions. In such a state, there has never been a kingdom that did not fall to ruin.

In both 1A:1 and 6B:4, then, Mencius argues that the *widespread adoption* of benefit as a goal is a detriment to the social fabric. His argument seems to rest on an empirical claim, namely, that once people start thinking in terms of benefit, they will end up acting largely for the sake of personal benefit and hence will start to disregard their duties and other moral concerns. Whatever we think of that empirical claim, it is clear that Mencius's objection to acting for the sake of benefit is that it produces bad consequences; far from producing benefit, it produces social chaos by breaking down important hierarchic relationships.

But Mencius does not stop there. In addition to objecting to acting for the sake of benefit because of its bad consequences, Mencius goes further in 6B:4 to recommend acting from benevolence and propriety because doing so brings about *good* consequences.

> Take benevolence and propriety and speak to the kings of Qín and Chǔ about them. Then the kings, taking delight in the benevolent and appropriate, will stop their armies. . . . This will cause ministers to serve their lords while cherishing benevolence and propriety, [etc.]. . . . So lords and ministers, fathers and sons, and elder and younger siblings will put aside thoughts of benefit and cherish benevolence and propriety in their interactions. In such a state, there never has been an unsuccessful sovereignty. Why must anyone speak of benefit?

Benevolence and propriety are important because they sustain the relationships that Mencius thinks important for the well-being of a kingdom. They are motives derived from valuable, natural attitudinal responses, as *Mencius* 2A:6 tells us: "The heart of compassion is the tip of benevolence; the heart of shame and disgust is the tip of propriety. . . ."[15]

Here, we should seek some clarification. If compassion is the basis of benevolence, then acting with benevolence involves responding with an emotional sensitivity, i.e., compassion, to the benefits or harms of another person. Why is this not acting from the motive of benefit? The proper contrast for Mencius between acting from benevolence and acting with the goal of benefit must lie in the difference between responding to some other particular person or group of people's needs and taking benefit *as such* as the end for which one acts. This would explain why Mencius thinks taking *lì* as one's motive would make one think of one's own benefit. For example, if one takes benefit as such as the goal, it may not matter from the point of view of the agent whether his or her own benefit is sought or that of another. Propriety, *yì* 義, bears a more straightforward contrast to the motive of benefit. Shame or disgust at the impropriety, say, of groveling for one's life is the motive for choosing one's own death, for example, in *Mencius* 6A:10.

> Life is . . . something I desire, as also is propriety; if these two are offered but I cannot have both, I will forgo life and take being proper. . . . If among the things people desire there were nothing they desired more than life, then what would prevent them from using any means whatsoever to keep their lives? . . . But in fact there are means that they will not use for the sake of life and there are things they will not do to avoid peril.

One might, for the sake of benefit, agree to some impropriety, say, giving one's approval to a ruler for attacking and annexing a neighboring state. But if one were acting instead from shame, one could not allow oneself to do so.

What we see is that, through the things Mencius says both explicitly and implicitly about Mòzǐ's views, the Mencian position relative to the Mohists' is not defined by opposition to consequentialist justification for norms of action and feeling. On the contrary, it is defined by opposition to what we might call the specifically Mohist *strategy* for producing better consequences; and the reason for Mencius's opposition is the ineffectiveness of that strategy for producing a better kingdom or a better world for all under Heaven. For on the one hand, Mencius doubts that people have the ability to feel inclusive concern. On the other hand, he thinks acting with benefit *as such* as the goal is counterproductive.

Other Indications of Mencian Consequentialism

In addition to the revealing dialectical position occupied by Mencius relative to the Mohists, there are other examples of Mencius using consequentialist justification for what one ought to do.

In 1A:7, Mencius recommends that King Xuān take compassion on his own people, because doing so would be a more effective way to attain Xuān's goal of uniting the various kingdoms under one rule than if one were to try attaining it with Xuān's military plans. Mencius's argument there and elsewhere[16] is that ruling benevolently will win the hearts not only of one's own people but also of the people in other kingdoms. Having won their hearts, the battle to unite the kingdoms under one rule would be mostly won, for one's own people would be ready to fight loyally for one, and the people of other kingdoms would defect to the side with the benevolent ruler. Mencius further argues in 2A:3 that mere pretense to benevolence will not be effective for this purpose:

> One who uses force and fakes benevolence is a hegemon. A hegemon requires a large kingdom [because he needs a large army]. One who uses the power of exercising benevolence is a true king. A true king doesn't depend on largeness [of his kingdom]. . . . Using force subjugates men, but it doesn't subjugate their hearts. Such force is not adequate. Using the power [of benevolence] to subjugate men is to delight their hearts to the core and achieve genuine submission.

Mencius's view about ruling is that a ruler ought to be benevolent, i.e., rule with compassion for his people, because benevolence is the means to uniting and bringing peace and prosperity to the kingdoms. It is not merely that being benevolent will get a ruler what he wants, but what a ruler *ought* to want is to unite and pacify the land.

By appearances Mencius seems to offer a rather diverse array of arguments for taking particular courses of action. Aside from citing the consequences, he appeals to the authority of traditional odes and the exemplary actions of the sage-kings. However, even these appeals to authority are, in fact, meant to indicate decision-making procedures that take following the authority of the ancients as a rule, but as a rule because doing so brings about good consequences. Consider 4A:1, which appeals to both kinds of authority:

> Presently there are rulers with benevolent hearts and benevolent reputations, yet the people do not receive any benefit from this nor will the rulers leave laws that will last; this because the rulers do not carry out the ways of the sage-kings. . . . The *Odes* say: "No transgressions, no forgetfulness; following the ancient laws." If one follows the laws of the sage-kings, one will not fall into error.

Finally, Mencius even seems to apply consequentialist considerations to his criticism of certain rival ethical teachings. He argues, in ways that the Mohists also do, that the consequences of people believing those teachings would be dire. This is so, he thinks, because of the behavioral implications of those teachings. He argues this in 6A:1 against the philosopher Gàozǐ's view that people can be good, but that it is not in their nature to be so. Likewise in 3B:9 he argues that the teachings of Yáng Zhū and of Mòzǐ are to be rejected because of the way people would act if they accepted such teachings. So, not only does Mencius object to rival views such as Mòzǐ's because he thinks they make implausible assumptions, but he seems also to object to them on grounds of the kinds of consequences that accepting those teachings will have on people's behavior. If that is indeed the import of his statements, Mencius would, of course, have to be appealing to consequences that are bad even on the views that he is criticizing. Otherwise he would simply be begging the question. That is, he would only be arguing against the Mohists, for example, that if people accept their teachings, the people would then act in ways that the Mohists think are right. But that would hardly count as a criticism of the Mohist view. At any rate, if Mencius is offering such criticisms of rival views, he is further displaying a consequentialist pattern of argument.

Mencian Consequentialism

The particulars of Mencian consequentialism that we can construct from the various aspects of his teachings are worth exploring, for they reveal the possibility of an ethical theory that has a complex and compelling shape.

A good path into the discussion leads through an alternative consequentialist reading of Mencius's view that is already available.[17] According to Ivanhoe (1991), both Confucius and Mencius hold views best understood if we attribute a special kind of consequentialist view to them, namely, "character consequentialism."[18] Ivanhoe argues that Mencius's concern with elements of one's character can be given a consequentialist treatment. However, there are two ways in which Ivanhoe's view might be superseded by our discussion. First, it should be pointed out that what Ivanhoe argues to be a distinctive and theoretically advantageous set of considerations in character consequentialism fails to distinguish the latter from the more familiar kind of consequentialism: act-consequentialism. Though it might be true that taking certain considerations of character seriously can make the application of act-consequentialism better (and, indeed, may be *required* according to act-consequentialism), this does not give us reason to classify the theory as a special character-centered version of consequentialism. Second, how Ivanhoe describes the kind of value, either intrinsic or instrumental, that elements of one's character have on Mencius's view could use some clarification along a different line of difference — that between having moral and nonmoral value. And as we saw earlier, there are actually two different lines of difference marked out by the moral and nonmoral goods distinction.

Ivanhoe begins to describe character consequentialism by saying that it "concentrates on the future fruits rather than the immediate results of actions . . . and it focuses its attention on the cumulative effects of actions" (1991, 55). So far, this description fails to distinguish character consequentialism from most other forms of consequentialism. A consequentialist theory sticks more closely to the *point* of consequentialism if it does not focus particularly on either immediate or the long-term results but includes both in the calculus of goods which will determine whether something is right or wrong. After all, it is good consequences *overall* that right action is supposed to produce. Ivanhoe's further description of character consequentialism clarifies things somewhat: "Since individuals carry and manifest the cumulative effects of actions, character consequentialism is primarily concerned with the formation of character" (1991, 55). So character consequentialism is to be distinguished from other forms of consequentialism by its primary concern: the formation of character.

The main reason that it might make sense for a consequentialist theory to focus on the formation of character, Ivanhoe argues, is that:

> [C]alculating the total utility of most kinds of action requires that one take into account a vast range of different and often competing factors, weight each factor with a value and assign to each a probability of occurrence. Such calculations can quickly become complex and unmanageable. . . . We have much greater control over the development of our character. It is less complex, more predictable and closer at hand than events in the world at large. (1991, 61–62)

We should note a couple of points about this. First, Ivanhoe seems concerned with what we have characterized as "subjective" consequentialist theories, i.e., ones that take the consequentialist criterion of rightness to be giving not only the criterion for something being right, but also providing the decision-making procedure for how to act. This makes it clear that act-consequentialism in its "objective" form, i.e., as a theory that only provides the criterion for an act being right, is entirely consistent with what Ivanhoe describes as the primary concern of character consequentialism: focusing on the formation of character. It might be right according to an objective act-consequentialist theory, for us to focus our actions on character formation, *if* that were in fact more effective overall for producing good consequences. To act in such a way as to cause our characters to become effective in producing good consequences would be the right thing to do on an objective act-consequentialist view. Indeed, some of Ivanhoe's discussion seems to take this point of view.

> [Confucius] realized that if one believes in and practices his Way, over the course of a lifetime, this practice will bear fruit; it will result in the formation of certain virtues and these will produce certain desirable consequences. These were the consequences that most concerned Confucius. (1991, 61)

And, according to Ivanhoe, Mencius favors the same ethical program. But then it looks like the view Ivanhoe attributes to Mencius as well as to Confucius is really an objective act-consequentialist view that takes the following to be empirical facts: (1) that formation of character is more effective in bringing about good consequences than is worrying about calculating the net results of each act, and (2) that having a character of the sort Mencius advocates is productive of the best consequences overall.

It should be noted, however, that both (1) and (2) are empirical claims that require justification through a tackling of the very same kind of complexities as one would have if one were trying to figure out what *act* would produce the best consequences overall in a particular situation. Focusing on formation of character requires one to adopt a plan of action. And showing that such a plan of action will actually produce the best consequences overall is something that requires calculation of the consequences (in all their complexity) of adopting that plan. Likewise, showing that having a particular set of character traits is productive of the best consequences overall requires calculation of the consequences of having such traits. And in either case, there must be an enormous amount of data to warrant generalizations about what types of actions or kinds of character will produce overall best consequences. So what Ivanhoe argues are the distinct advantages of character consequentialism over, say, direct act-consequentialism seem to diminish under scrutiny.

More importantly, however, we have actually seen that Mencius does not despair of making claims about what the consequences of particular acts are. In his advice to kings and to others, it is clear that Mencius judges an act to be advisable or inadvisable based on what he thinks the consequences of the act will be. So perhaps Mencius thinks it is good for people to have good characters, but that hardly makes him a character consequentialist in Ivanhoe's sense. For Mencius himself is not at all shy about assessing the direct and immediate, as well as the long-term, consequences of particular acts. Add to this the fact that Mencius seems to argue sometimes against acting with the overt goal of benefit (*lì*) in pursuing good consequences. It then makes most sense to attribute to Mencius an objective act-consequentialist view, along with a very flexible view about the proper decision-making procedures: sometimes he seems to think one ought to worry about weighing or assessing (*quán* 權) the consequences; other times he thinks one ought instead to act from other considerations, say, those of benevolence or propriety. But in either of these cases, it is because of the goods to be gained or lost as a result that Mencius advises the particular kind of decision-making procedure.

Ivanhoe identifies a certain kind of good, that of "the intrinsic value of enduring and *unique* human relationships, particularly family relationships," which is the "source and center" of Confucian moral philosophy (1991, 64). The kind of view Ivanhoe attributes specifically to Mencius "places great emphasis on the psychological good associated with certain *unique* human relationships, particularly kinship relationships" (1991, 56).[19] These ways of valuing relationships may indeed be central to Confucian ethics. Ivanhoe's further view is that character consequentialism can give such goods pride of place. Ivanhoe identifies goods such as those of kinship relationships as both intrinsically and instrumentally valuable for Mencius.

That Mencius thinks such goods are instrumentally valuable is clear from his conversations with Huì of Liáng (1A:3, 1A:5) and Xuān of Qí (1A:7). In those conversations, Mencius emphasizes the benefits to be had from proper training in filial and other proprieties. Those benefits are described in terms of such goods as relief from hard labor for the elderly. So filial piety, for example, is instrumentally valuable for bringing about certain goods. We might add that in Mencius's view there are other virtues associated with human relationships that may not be of the kinship variety, which also have this kind of instrumental value. For example, being a good ruler or subject requires being compassionate or loyal, respectively.

How, though, might the intrinsic value of such goods be explicated? Ivanhoe is not quite as clear on this point. It would perhaps help if we put Mencius's ideas in the following way. Virtues associated with various human relationships are instrumentally valuable, but they are valuable not only for bringing about non-moral goods such as comfort or economic well-being but are also valuable as constitutive parts of the human relationships that are themselves intrinsically valuable. So for example, filial piety plays a constitutive role in the *kind* of child-to-parent relationship intrinsically worth having. So filial piety has a certain intrinsic value that it brings *to* a child-parent relationship. Likewise, in the relationship of benefactor to beneficiary, Mencius points out how a certain kind of attitude can add or subtract from the value of the relationship in 6A:10:

> A bowl of rice and a portion of soup — receive them and one lives, refuse them and one dies. If they are offered along with an insult, an ordinary pedestrian will refuse them; if they are stepped in and offered, a beggar will not stoop to accept them.

It is possible, as we saw earlier, to include within a consequentialist theory certain "moral" goods, in one sense, as among the goods to be promoted. Those are intrinsic moral goods that are esteem-based, in Hume's and Frankena's sense of being objects of admiration or praise. Something we might call *Mencian* consequentialism may be construed as including such goods among the things one ought to bring about. In this way, virtues such as benevolence, propriety, or filial piety have both instrumental and intrinsic value (*pace* Cài 1987). Understanding Mencius in such a way produces an interpretation that is textually helpful for providing an organizational center for the diverse forms of justification within which he engages. And, it provides an example of how a consequentialist theory might look in which an important type of intrinsic, moral value might be countenanced among the goods to be promoted.

Notes

1. So, for example, Van Norden's (2007) formidable argument in favor of a virtue ethical reading of Mencius is not discussed here. Nor do I consider here the very challenging arguments against an earlier version of my reading provided by Wang (2005). Their arguments deserve better; hence, I will give those views fuller consideration in a future, much longer work on Mencius. Hansen's often edifying analyses of Mencius are sprinkled throughout Hansen (1992).

2. I will say more below about the possible relationships between utilitarian and more generally consequentialist patterns of ethical views.
3. I will use "good" and "value" interchangeably. I do not think anything rests on this.
4. This would not be the same problem as, say, if a consequentialist theory included in an account of the nonmoral good what people have moral preferences for — the kind of account that Harsanyi (1977) argues against. There is a surface similarity in that kind of view: if such preferences were allowed in the account of nonmoral good, then it would be right to promote what an agent prefers specified in terms that depend on what the agent considers morally right. But the problem with such a view would not be the same problem as specifying the good to be promoted in terms of what is independently considered right. Rather, in such a view, the good is specified in terms of people's preferences, whatever the source of their preferences. That is to say, what is to be promoted on that view is *the satisfaction of preferences*. And under that description, at any rate, the good is specified in morally neutral terms, in particular, in terms that do not depend on prior intuitions about what is right.
5. Again, this would reverse the consequentialist viewpoint, namely: it is right to promote a thing *because* it is a good.
6. This is especially interesting for assessing the possibility that Mencius has an ethical view that is best characterized as an ethics of virtue. One might be tempted to say such a thing if one takes virtues of character to be "central" in some way for Mencius's ethical view, as, for example, Yearley (1990) does.
7. Frankena (1963, 63) notes that Hume has such a view. We should notice that Kant also has this kind of view: the moral value of an action "does not depend on the realization of the object of the action but merely on the principle of volition by which the action is done" (Kant 1785, 13). So, it is not only "ethics of virtue" in some Aristotelian or Platonic concern with virtues that is identified by Frankena's description.
8. So, when Frankena asks later (1963, 70) what makes a motive or disposition morally good and then wonders whether motives or dispositions other than the sense of duty are also morally good, he answers those questions in a way that does not do full justice to the notion of intrinsic moral value he himself identifies here. He seems concerned with answering those questions by referring to the "morality-supporting" role of certain motives and dispositions to produce right or morally valuable *action*. That may identify one kind of moral value, but it is not intrinsic moral value.
9. See Railton (1986), for example.
10. Bales (1971). The same distinction is argued for by Railton (1984).
11. This is evident throughout the *Mòzǐ*.
12. *Mencius* translations are my own.
13. *Mencius* 3B:9 and 7A:26.
14. There are places where Mencius addresses the problems with acting in order to produce benefit or profit, *lì* 利. Those passages will be discussed shortly.
15. The formula is more or less repeated in 6A:6.
16. For example, with King Huì in 1A:5.
17. As far as I know, it is the only other such reading.
18. It should be noted at the outset that Ivanhoe's consequentialist analysis is not given with much textual evidence for the concerns he attributes to Mencius (and to

Confucius). However, I will take it that my own discussions given in the two sections above of Mencius and the Mohists and of the other indications of consequentialist views in the text are sufficient to have made the case for the broad claim that Mencius has a consequentialist ethical view.
19. For some reason Ivanhoe feels compelled to emphasize "unique" each time it is used in this context. It is not clear from his discussion why the uniqueness of these relationships is especially important.

References

Bales, R. E. 1971. Act-utilitarianism: Account of right-making characteristics or decision-making procedure? *American Philosophical Quarterly* 8 (3): 257–65.

Burnyeat, M. 1980. Aristotle on learning to be good. In *Essays on Aristotle's ethics*, ed. A. O. Rorty. 69–92. Berkeley: University of California Press.

Cài, X. 1987. 論孟子的道德決擇 (On moral choice in Mencius). 台大哲學評論 (*Taiwan University Philosophical Review*) 10: 135–74.

Eno, R. 1990. *The Confucian creation of heaven*. Albany: SU NYPress.

Frankena, W. 1963. *Ethics,* 2nd ed. Englewood Cliffs, NJ: Prentice Hall.

Hansen, C. 1992. *A Daoist theory of Chinese thought: A philosophical interpretation*. New York: Oxford University Press.

Harsanyi, J. 1977. Morality and the theory of rational behavior. *Social research* 44: 623–56. Reprinted in *Utilitarianism and beyond*, ed. A. Sen and B. Williams. 39–62. Cambridge: Cambridge University Press, 1982.

Hume, D. 1740. *A treatise of human nature*, 2nd ed., ed. L. A. Selby-Bigge. Oxford: Oxford University Press, 1978.

———. 1748. *An enquiry concerning the principles of morals*, ed. J. Schneewind. Indianapolis, IN: Hackett Publishing Company, 1983.

Ivanhoe, P. 1990. *Ethics in the Confucian tradition*. Atlanta, GA: Scholars Press.

———. 1991. Character consequentialism: An early Confucian contribution to contemporary ethical theory. *Journal of Religious Ethics* 19 (1): 55–70.

Kant, I. 1785. *Grounding for the metaphysics of morals*, trans. J. W. Ellington. Indianapolis, IN: Hackett Publishing Company, 1981.

Lau, D. 1963. *Lao tzu: Tao te ching*. New York: Penguin Books.

———. 1970. *Mencius*. New York: Penguin Books.

Mei, Y. 1973. *The ethical and political works of Motse*. Westport, CT: Hyperion Press. Reprint of 1929 edition published by A. Probsthain, London.

Railton, P. 1984. Alienation, consequentialism, and the demands of morality. *Philosophy and Public Affairs* 13 (2): 134–71. Reprinted in *Consequentialism and its critics*, ed. S. Scheffler. 93–133. Oxford: Oxford University Press, 1988.

———. 1986. Moral realism. *The Philosophical Review* 95 (2): 163–207.

———. 1988. How thinking about character and utilitarianism might lead to rethinking the character of utilitarianism. *Midwest Studies in Philosophy* 13: 398–416.

Rawls, J. 1971. *A theory of justice*. Cambridge, MA: Harvard University Press.

Ross, D. 1925. *Aristotle: The Nicomachean ethics*. New York: Oxford University Press.

Scanlon, T. 1993. Value, desire, and quality of Life. In *The Quality of life*, ed. M. C. Nussbaum and A. Sen, 185–205. WIDER Studies in Development Economics. New York: Oxford University Press.

Van Norden, B. W. 2007. *Virtue ethics and consequentialism in early Chinese philosophy.* New York: Cambridge University Press.

Wang, Y. 2005. Are early Confucians consequentialists? *Asian Philosophy* 15 (1):19–34.

Yearley, L. 1990. *Mencius and Aquinas*. Albany: SUNY Press.

3

No Need for Hemlock: Mencius's Defense of Tradition

Franklin Perkins*

Of the various labels one might use to characterize the essence of Confucianism, "traditionalist" is one of the more obvious. Certainly their opponents, from Mòzǐ to Zhuāngzǐ to Hàn Fēizi, portray Confucians as clinging to tradition, but this orientation goes back to Confucius's own self-image. Among his most famous words was this self-description: "A transmitter and not a maker [*shù ér bú zuò* 述而不作], sincere and loving the ancients, I compare myself to Old Péng" (*Lún Yǔ* 7:1). This chapter examines the problematic intersection between reliance on tradition and demands for justification, particularly the implications of this tension for the meaning of philosophy. It concentrates on the *Mencius* as an attempt to maintain the primacy of tradition while answering the demand for justification, a demand prompted by the Mohists. These issues are approached following the work of Chad Hansen, in particular by working through a dilemma Hansen sets up between two interpretations of Mencius's view of human nature: a strong position that claims that human nature determines the details of Confucian morality and ritual, and a weak position that claims only that human nature drives us to develop morality, ritual, and so on, without determining their precise forms. According to Hansen, whichever way one reads it, Mencius's account fails: the "strong" position would justify the Confucian *dào* but is extremely implausible, while the "weak" position is plausible but

---

* A version of this chapter was presented at the "Dào, Mind, and Language" conference at the University of Hong Kong. I am grateful for helpful comments from many of the participants and a response from Chad Hansen, as well as comments from anonymous reviewers for this collection. This chapter benefited from discussions with some of my colleagues, particularly Sean Kirkland and H. Peter Steeves. The basic idea of the chapter was developed through discussions at a forum sponsored by the Liberty Fund.

would not suffice as a justification (2000, 162–83). Where my account will diverge is that, while Hansen takes the strong interpretation, I will pursue the other horn of the dilemma, taking the more plausible view while admitting its failure as a direct justification. The conclusion remains close to that of Hansen, arguing that the *Mencius* is an attempt to defend tradition against philosophical critique, that is, to evade the "Mohist challenge." The chapter concludes with a brief argument that Mencius's evasion is more plausible than it seems, at least in the context of classical Chinese thought.

Tradition and the Mohist Challenge

I here use the term "traditionalist" in a specific sense, to refer to a position in which a fundamental source of justification for a claim is that it was held by certain key figures of the past, figures whose views constitute the tradition.¹ As such, a traditionalist position involves explicit appeals to authority, the authority given through one's position in the tradition. The key point is that more trust is placed in the tradition than in the judgment of the individual, which means that, in at least some cases, an individual cannot and should not demand justification of traditional claims or practices. This contrasts with a position that recognizes the value of tradition as a source of insight but still subjects it to justification in other terms. It is impossible to entirely rely on tradition. At the very least, carrying on a tradition requires some ability to interpret that tradition, to sort out conflicts within it, and even to adapt it to new circumstances. The need for *individual* judgment can be lessened by reliance on living authorities — priests or *Rú* 儒 (Classicists/Confucians) — who speak for the tradition, but one must still be able to account for this interpretative ability, even if it is available only to specialists and the highly cultivated. This aspect of carrying on a tradition is central to Hansen's account of the history of early Confucianism, which he sees as splitting over how to account for this interpretive ability, with some claiming that human beings have an innate guide for applying and interpreting the tradition and others claiming this ability must be internalized through the tradition itself, much as a master artisan develops intuitive abilities through practicing a craft (Hansen 2000, 87–93).

The real challenge for a traditionalist is not how to account for the ability to interpret the tradition, but rather: How do we justify the tradition in general? How do we claim that this tradition is better than the alternatives? These kinds of questions do not arise necessarily — Confucius may not have thought about them — but they are raised explicitly by the Mohists. We can briefly look at three points at which this challenge appears. The first is in the argument for moderation in funerals, in which Mòzǐ draws a distinction between rightness or morality, *yì* 義, and custom, *sú* 俗. Since we consider some customs wrong (such as eating one's firstborn son), we implicitly distinguish what is right from what is customary (*Mòzǐ*, 187–89). If so, then practices cannot be justified simply because they are customary or traditional. The second moment is in the "Models and Standards" chapter and focuses on authority (20–21). *Mòzǐ* begins with a series of possible authorities who might serve as models: parents, teachers, rulers. He then points out that, in each case, many are in fact not good, and thus they cannot be relied on as models. One might reply that we can rely on *some* fathers and mothers and *some* rulers, but that reveals the nature of the problem: How would we decide which ones to model? We would need some criterion that was not itself derived from listening to parents or rulers. The third point occurs in the dialogue chapters, in which one finds a mixed view of tradition, with some passages advocating it and some criticizing it. One passage brings the two sides together:

> Gōng Mèngzǐ said, "Gentlemen do not make [*zuò* 作]; they transmit [*shù* 術] and that is all." Master Mòzǐ said, "It is not so. People who are most distant from being gentlemen do not transmit the good of the ancients and do not make the good of today. Those next in not being gentlemen do not transmit the good of the ancients, but if they themselves have good then they make it, desiring the good to go out from themselves. Now transmitting and not making is no different from those who do not love to transmit but only to make. If I take something good from the ancients then I transmit it and if it is today's good then I make it. This is because I desire good to increase more." (*Mòzǐ*, 434–35 [46:17]; cf. 442 [47:4])

The passage presents a moderate position: we rely on the ancients when they have good to offer and we rely on ourselves when we have good to offer. By acknowledging that we cannot always rely on tradition, the question becomes: When do we rely on it, and when do we add to or go beyond it? Answering this question requires a point of appeal outside the tradition itself, so that individual judgment displaces tradition as the ultimate authority.[2] In each of these examples, the Mohists make the same basic point that traditions are sometimes wrong and so traditional practices or views require justification. This is the "Mohist challenge." Since this demand for justification probably marks the birth of philosophy in China, Mòzǐ's challenge can be taken as analogous to Socrates's challenges to the Athenians. In fact, Hansen goes so far as to say that Mòzǐ launched a "Socratic attack" on Confucianism, by raising the question: "Are our accepted practices correct?" (2000, 107).

Thorough traditionalists have a few possible responses to the Mohist (or Socratic) challenge. They may put the questioners in prison or have them drink hemlock (neither of which would be far from what Xúnzi might recommend).[3] Those who introduce a natural ability to navigate the tradition have more options. The same factors in human nature that allow the evaluation of competing interpretations also allow for the justification of the tradition as a whole. This position, though, runs into a different problem: If we have a natural ability to justify tradition, why do we need the tradition? The same ability that allows us to interpret, justify, and navigate the tradition itself circumvents that tradition. This analysis reflects a structural problem: a strong traditionalist position precludes any non-question-begging defense to a radical challenge. The only possible defense would appeal to something other than tradition, but in making that appeal the traditionalist has already lost, admitting something other than tradition. Thus insofar as philosophy asks the radical question of why any particular tradition is good, it is simply the enemy of the traditionalist. Hansen reaches this same conclusion regarding Mencius: "Mencius, in the end, bases his status-quo defense on the claim that one should not philosophize" (2000, 183).

Strong and Weak Sprouts

We can now consider how Mencius makes this claim for tradition and against philosophy, turning to his conception of human nature (*xìng* 性). We can begin with the key passage:

> The heart (*xīn* 心) of compassion and pain is the sprout of benevolence. The heart of shame and aversion is the sprout of rightness. The heart of declining and yielding is the sprout of ritual propriety. The heart of so and not-so is the sprout of wisdom. People have these four sprouts like they have four limbs. (*Mencius* 2A:6)

Hansen proposes two interpretations of the four sprouts or seeds (*duān* 端). The "weak" view takes the four sprouts as basic ways of reacting to the world, as natural human tendencies to feel compassion and shame, to ritualize our interactions, and to make distinctions. The "strong" view, in contrast, takes the specific form of the Confucian *dào* as already implicit in and defined by human nature.[4] For example, Mencius lists the sprout of rightness as a heart of shame and aversion (*xiūwù zhī xīn* 羞惡之心).[5] Taken weakly, Mencius claims that human beings naturally feel shame, and thus we feel motivated to conform to moral codes. The feeling of shame itself would not determine the details of this moral code, so while a culture with no morality could be rejected as unnatural, particular moral systems could not. On the strong view, human beings tend naturally not only to develop *morality* but to develop *Confucian morality*, which would express or realize human nature most fully. The moral systems of other cultures would be more or less deficient. The sprout of wisdom, a heart that affirms and negates (*shìfēi zhī xīn* 是非之心), can be interpreted along a similar divide.[6] On the weak view, Mencius simply claims that human beings naturally make distinctions. This ability, if supported, naturally leads to some body of wisdom, *zhì* 智, but since human beings can make sense of the world in many different ways, this basic tendency would not suffice for choosing among different bodies of wisdom. On the strong view, the heart innately knows what is so and not-so, even if that takes time to develop.

Hansen summarizes the dilemma in the two positions:

> So we may read Mencius' moral psychology of innate morality in two ways: (1) the weak version, which is empirically plausible, widely shared in China, and compatible with Mohism or traditional Confucianism; and (2) the strong version, which is empirically implausible but necessary for Mencius' naturalistic, innatist, internalist response to Mòzǐ. (2000, 172)

To see the power of this dilemma, one must consider two aspects of what would be required for an adequate response to the Mohist challenge. First, a good person for Mencius is not simply a person with virtues like bravery, moderation, reverence, compassion, and so on, virtues that the Mohists shared. Mencius must justify things like three years of mourning or large state orchestras. It was these specifics that were challenged by the Mohists, so if an appeal to human nature is to provide an adequate defense, it must justify such details.[7] Second, to respond to the Mohist challenge, Mencius needs not just to say that human nature is most fulfilled by the Confucian *dào* but that human nature allows us to *know* this. Human nature must provide a standard for evaluating practices, something like a "compass and square." Keeping these two requirements in mind, Hansen seems right in asserting the implausibility of a view of human nature strong enough to justify the Confucian *dào* against others.

Emphasizing *development* over *innatism* does not lessen the problems but makes them less apparent. The issue is whether or not human nature alone can justify things like the three years of mourning (rather than a simpler Mohist funeral). If the answer is yes, then one is committed to the strong view, even if the superiority of the Confucian *dào* only becomes apparent after years of nourishment. Hansen addresses this point in a note referring to Wáng Yángmíng 王陽明:

> I believe Wáng got Mencius right. I find this assumption the most coherent way to make sense of Mencius. P. J. Ivanhoe has argued that the two Confucians have quite different views of natural morality. Wang's, he says, is a discovery model and Mencius' is a development model. But Mencius does think there is a correct path for developing the seeds. And his normative position is that correct means, "in accord with innate dispositions." So if there is a correct way to develop, it must be *in* the seeds as much as in the end state. (2000, 397–98, n. 31)[8]

Something must determine the correct way the "seeds" should develop; if this standard comes from human nature itself, one is committed to the strong view. Development may provide a different model of self-cultivation, but it does not change the basic normative theory. Finally, we might note that any appeal to human nature as an ultimate justification for the Confucian *dào* results in the problem intrinsic to the "innatist" defense of tradition: If the Confucian *dào* is programmed into my nature, why do I need to rely on that tradition? (Hansen 2000, 173). This is just the charge that Xúnzǐ makes against Mencius (*Xúnzǐ*, "Xìng è," 549).

Having discussed the difficulties with the strong view, we can turn to explore the other horn of the dilemma. The "weak" version of human nature merely claims that human beings have tendencies toward compassion and concern, reactions of shame and aversion, feelings of reverence and yielding, and an ability to make distinctions and learn. These four sprouts would naturally lead any group of human beings to develop bonds of care (*rén* 仁), moral rules (*yì* 義), rituals (*lǐ* 禮), and some body of wisdom (*zhì* 智). The content of these, though, would not be determined, which is why the sprouts provide no direct basis for judging that the moral code or the rituals of the Confucians are superior to those of the Mohists.[9]

An extensive argument for the weak version as the correct interpretation of the *Mencius* would exceed the scope of this chapter. Philosophically, it has the advantage of being a plausible account of human nature, and it can explain and accept cultural diversity. The textual evidence is ambiguous. Passage 6A:7, in which Mencius says that the superiority of the food cooked by Yì Yá is determined by the nature of the human mouth, is difficult to read in any way other than the strong position. In contrast, the weak reading is supported by the claim in 3A:4 that human beings had to be taught social relations as basic as care between father and son or distinction between husband and wife.[10] Ultimately, the decision of interpretation depends on broader questions of context and purpose. On this, two points should be noted. First, there is little evidence that Mencius intends his conception of *xìng*, human nature, as a way of justifying the Confucian *dào*. Explicit appeals to *xìng* or the sprouts are consistently raised in relation to the process of becoming good. They show that it is possible for anyone to become good (3A:1, 1A:7), that we become good by tapping into and extending our natural reactions (2A:6, 7B:31), and that becoming good requires no violence to our natural feelings (6A:1, 6A:2). If we turn to the broader context, the Guōdiàn Confucian texts discuss *xìng* in relation to the Confucian tradition but show no indication of using the former to justify the latter. It makes the most sense to read Mencius's use of *xìng* as continuous with that context. Second, the *Mencius* advocates a traditionalist position. On the strong view, Mencius believes that we have a natural a-cultural guide that allows us to evaluate tradition, but there is no emphasis on such an ability in the text. On the contrary, becoming good is sometimes presented as no more than imitating the sages:

> Shùn was a person, I am also a person; Shùn was a model which the world could transmit to later generations, but I still cannot avoid being a plain fellow. This is a proper concern. What kind of concern? To be like Shùn, that is all. (4B:28; cf. 6B:2)

Unlike Mòzǐ, Mencius never lays out specific criteria by which to use our judgment or intuitions to evaluate claims or practices. His most important statement on criteria takes up but crucially modifies the Mohist metaphor of the square and compass: Mencius does not say that our *heart* is the compass and square but rather that the *sages* are our compass and square (4A:1, 4A:2).[11] Tradition is the yardstick by which we measure, which means that the tradition itself cannot be measured.

Justifying the Confucian *Dào*

The problem that remains with the weak version of human nature is with justifying the Confucian *dào*. Mencius was aware of and desperately concerned about the threat from the Mohists (3B:9, 7A:26). Surely he realized the challenge was not just about how one becomes good but rather about what itself counts as good. Thus, we rightly expect Mencius to offer a defense of the Confucian *dào* against rival *dào*s. It is this expectation that leads Hansen to attribute the less plausible "strong" view to Mencius. Can the "weak" view make sense as a response to the Mohist challenge?

The key to understanding Mencius's defense is to consider the offense to which he responds. Mòzǐ's arguments for reform presuppose two things:

(1) The criteria of goodness are fairly simple, namely, benefit (*lì* 利), taken as food for the hungry, clothing for the cold, and rest for the weary (*Mòzǐ*, 253), or as a population that is larger, more prosperous, and more orderly (*Mòzǐ*, 169).

(2) Human beings have some intellectual capacity which allows us to analyze institutions and cultural change. This ability must be sophisticated enough to trace out the consequences of cultural changes and free enough of prejudice as to allow us to compare and evaluate different practices.

Consider an example. The Mohists demonstrate that large, costly orchestral performances with dancing and banquets generate more harm than benefit, wasting the resources of the people and forcing them to neglect the work they need to survive (*Mòzǐ*, 253–63). In making this argument, the Mohists (1) do not attend to other possible goods that would complicate the analysis, such as aesthetic pleasure, and (2) they are confident they can predict the outcome of abandoning this practice. Similarly, to show that drastic prolonged mourning causes more harm than benefit, they (1) eliminate consideration of other goods such as the expression of feeling, and (2) they trust their ability to predict the consequences of this change, and even to objectively compare practices from different cultures (*Mòzǐ*, 171–90).

We might take Mencius as setting up a counter-position that (1) defines what is good by the moral tendencies in human nature and (2) explains the intellectual ability through a heart that intuitively knows what to *shì* and *fēi*. These together would show that three years of mourning and big orchestras are necessary for the full realization of human nature. We have already seen, though, that such a response requires a view of human nature that is implausibly strong and ultimately eliminates the need for tradition. The weak version of human nature opens up a route more suitable to a traditionalist position by undermining both points presupposed in Mohist standard-based criticisms.

First, on Mencius's view of human nature, there is no simple criterion for what is good. Mencius allows for the importance of benefit. The people need a stable livelihood and it is natural for us to hate death (6A:10). Benefit is even spread across the senses: we want things like bear paws to eat, beautiful people to gaze at, and good music to listen to (6A:10, 6A:14). Family feeling adds a greater depth of complexity in analyzing human needs, because it suggests that people cannot be counted equally in any calculus of benefit. Finally, the four sprouts point to even more complex human needs. Since many of these needs/desires can be strengthened, weakened, or redirected, it is unlikely that even in theory one could claim that a single set of cultural practices maximally fulfilled human needs. Mencius's account of human nature also throws into question assumption (2) in the Mohist position. On the weak reading, we have only a bare tendency to make distinctions, something that takes form through culture and education. We have no innate knowledge that would allow for wholesale evaluation of that tradition itself. Thus even if there were cultural practices that were *the best* in expressing all the needs of human nature, we would have limited ability to recognize those practices as such.

If I am correct, then Mencius takes up a skeptical position in relation to the Mohists, but this skepticism cannot be pushed too far, lest we make Mencius into Zhuāngzǐ. Mencius does not say that human beings have no natural needs or that those needs are infinitely flexible. Similarly, the heart that affirms (*shì*) and negates (*fēi*) must have some ability to recognize more or less natural distinctions. Together, these allow cultivated people to engage in some cultural tinkering — for example, modifying a ritual to substitute a silk hat in place of a linen one (*Lún Yǔ* 9:3) — and they explain the abilities needed to interpret and apply any tradition. These aspects of human nature also provide a potential way to justify the tradition itself: with thousands of years of organic development, with adjustments here and there and a couple of great sages every millennium, even our limited abilities should produce workable practices.[12] Mencius does not explicitly take this position, but it would be a mainstream Confucian view, appearing most clearly in the *Xìng zì mìng chū* 性自命出, in which rituals are initiated by spontaneous human feelings (*qíng* 情) but take specific shape through the deliberate and cumulative work of sagely people.[13] Moreover, there is evidence that such a view is assumed in the *Mencius*, as in the connection between the heart and mourning practices. In a discussion with the Mohist Yí Zhī 夷之, Mencius explains the origins of funerals by appeal to a natural feeling of revulsion at seeing a parent's decaying corpse, which leads people to get shovels and return to bury the bodies (3A:5). Since the natural reactions of the heart here lead the people to have a simple, Mohist-style funeral, the passage clearly assumes that such natural reactions do not suffice to establish proper ritual practices. A second discussion of funeral practices also brings in the heart:

> The ancients had no set measure for the inner and outer coffins. In mid-antiquity, the inner coffin was seven inches and the outer coffin suited it, from the son of Heaven to the common people. This was not just to look at its beauty, but to fully express the people's hearts. (*Mencius* 2B:7)

Mencius takes funeral practices as becoming more refined over time, which would not be required if human nature directly enabled us to know what was correct. Yet this development does not happen blindly — the feelings of the heart (and the judgments of people) have guided the process. This is why we can assume the tradition works fairly well. We cannot *know* this, and there is little reason to think these practices are perfect. But there is even less reason to think that the suggestions of a couple of Mohists would function better. Who knows what consequences might follow from eliminating orchestras? Perhaps the people would feel less awe toward their rulers, making them more likely to rebel. Perhaps the ruling class, lacking the ability to express their martial spirit through music, would channel more of their energy into real wars. Of course, maybe only good would result, but can we be sure enough? The connection between power and music has withstood the test of time. Wouldn't it be more sensible to follow Mencius and just encourage rulers to have more public concerts (1B:1)?

Thus far I have emphasized the contrast between Mencius and the Mohists, but it is important to see the continuity between their positions. The Mohists are far from the radical rejection of tradition that one finds in someone like Descartes. The *Mòzǐ* itself frequently cites traditional sources as support, and the views of past sages constitute part of its criteria for evaluating claims.[14] While Mencius says that an individual in his time should make judgments using the tradition embodied by the past sages as the "compass" and "square," this tradition itself is justified because it emerged from cumulative human judgment. Thus both the Mohists and Mencius allow significant roles for tradition and human judgment. One could say that the contrast lies in how they balance these two factors, the Mohists giving more priority to individual judgment and Mencius giving that priority to the tradition. A more accurate characterization, though, is that Mòzǐ puts more emphasis on the judgment of the individual person, while Mencius subordinates individual judgment to the judgment of the community, taking that community as constituted through history and expressed in tradition. In general, contemporary philosophers' thinking in the wake of the European Enlightenment strikes the balance in a way closer to the Mohists, although the Mohists are probably still more conservative.[15]

On this interpretation, the philosophy of Mencius has clear intersections with some traditionalist positions in Europe, such as the conservatism of Edmund Burke, who writes: "We are afraid to put men to live and trade each on his own private stock of reason; because we suspect that the stock in each man is small, and that the individuals would do better to avail themselves of the general bank and capital of nations and ages" (1999, 415).[16] In fact, this "conservative" reading of Mencius aligns with that of the great Qíng Dynasty commentator Jiāo Xún 焦循 (1763–1820). Jiāo Xún takes Mencius's claim that human nature is good in a weak sense to mean only that human beings, unlike animals, are able to learn and so to become good (*Mencius* 1987, 316). According to Jiāo Xún, the fundamental problem with Mòzǐ (or Yáng Zhū) was not ill intention but simply that he tried to think for himself and make judgments without relying on tradition. Jiāo Xún writes:

Some do not practice and study the six classics, but emptily rely on their heart and thoughts and use this to approach the first sages. Such people say they defend the *dào*, they say they protect the models of the sages. With this, each stands at a gate or window, fighting amongst themselves, not knowing they themselves are Yáng's and Mò's, but all calling each other Yáng's and Mò's. The world's states and families follow negativity and receive its harm, but do not know the reason for all this is not practicing. Mencius's disputes with Yáng and surely have their original root in practicing the *dào* of the first sages, which is practicing the six classics, not emptily relying on the heart's enlightenment. (*Mencius* 1987, 457–58)

On Jiāo Xún's reading, Mencius's response to Mòzǐ is not a counterargument taking human nature as a standard but rather an analysis of human nature that shows that we lack the ability to make such judgments at all.

No Need for Hemlock: The Failure of the Mohist Challenge

For those of us who hear the words "Socratic challenge" and feel warm inside, the implausibility of the Mohist view may not immediately strike us. Yet it displays considerable arrogance, made less so only by contrast to someone like Socrates or Descartes. To a Mòzǐ or a Socrates or a Descartes who thinks he has a standpoint from which to evaluate tradition, Mencius can reply: Why do you think you know better than the sages, that you as a single person can stand in judgment of a system developed by your ancestors over thousands of years? A Platonized Socrates might answer: I have access to eternal truths, ideas that exist independently of the order of this particular culture. I can use those ideas, of the good or of justice or of beauty, to evaluate what we do.[17] Socrates imagines a critique of the shadows in the cave based on an analysis of the shadows themselves, but he rejects this skill; rather, the philosopher ascends from the cave, accesses "the intelligible realm," and then returns to the cave with an independent perspective.[18] Descartes goes further, explicitly claiming an ability to free himself from culture through years of travel and then systematic doubt.[19] From this neutral standpoint, he can determine the truth for himself, an ability he has because his mind contains a rational capacity grounded in God. For both Socrates/Plato and Descartes, the universe is structured according to the same categories in which we human beings think, either because we can recollect those structuring ideas or because our ideas are modeled on those of God, who designed and created the structures. Plato/Socrates and Descartes do display a remarkable arrogance in relation to the traditions in which they are embedded, but this is hardly surprising, as their theories are grounded in the divine.

How could Mòzǐ respond? He could say: "I have Heaven's intention [*tiān zhì* 天志], like the wheelwright has the compass and the woodworker has the square" (*Mòzǐ*, 197, "Heaven's Intention I"). It may not be coincidence that the most philosophical and radically critical early Chinese philosopher also relies most directly on a divine force that transcends particular cultures. Mòzǐ explicitly links his ability to criticize cultural institutions to his access to Heaven, *tiān* 天, as we see in the passage from the "Models and Standards" chapter mentioned earlier. After explaining that parents, teachers, and sovereigns cannot provide reliable models for rightness, Mòzǐ concludes:

> Thus fathers and mothers, studies, and sovereigns, of these three none can be the model. So then what can be a model for governing? Thus it is said, there is no model like *tiān*. (*Mòzǐ*, 21–22, "Models and Standards")

This passage demonstrates skepticism of any human authority, basing this skepticism and its alternative on something superhuman, *tiān* or Heaven.

There is no denying a certain similarity between Descartes and Mòzǐ in this movement, but the critical standpoint granted by appeal to *tiān* is much weaker than that taken by Descartes. Descartes' position requires both a God who thinks like us *and* some access to the mind of that God, but there is no evidence that the Mohists believe we have direct access to the way *tiān* thinks. There is nothing like innate ideas that work in parallel to the ideas of *tiān*, nor are there explicit commandments or scriptures from *tiān*.[20] As a consequence, the will of *tiān* is known through the world, by observing natural and historical patterns. In spite of their anthropomorphic language, the position of the Mohists is closer to the attempt to reform culture by appeal to natural laws than it is a direct appeal to the divine. Following Descartes, we might say that Mòzǐ lacks the "the natural light [*lumine naturali*]" and so can only rely on what he is "taught by nature [*doceri a natura*]" (Descartes 1984, 57).

The problem for justifying radical cultural critique in an early Chinese context is that it is much more difficult to distill patterns of nature and apply them to social and political problems than it is to appeal directly to God's ideas as recorded in books or inscribed in our own minds. The Mohists argue that, according to the laws of nature, people who benefit others are benefited and people who harm others are harmed, and although they support this claim with empirical evidence, it is far from convincing.[21] Furthermore, if we do not give some divine status to human thought, it is not clear why we should grant so much trust to individual judgment, particularly if we also view those judgments as socially formed. In such a context, a view that a human being (or a small group) can make correct judgments about their own tradition seems unlikely. While this position dominates the Western philosophical tradition, it was there bolstered by ultimately bizarre views of an anthropocentric world structured according to the categories of human thought.

Of the various labels one might use to characterize philosophy as a contemporary discipline, "opposition to authority" is one of the more obvious. It is simply unacceptable to explicitly appeal to tradition or authority in a philosophical discussion. If you doubt this, imagine I explained to my freshmen students that there is no God and the self is just a heap of perceptions, and I told them that unless they want to spend ten or fifteen years researching it, they should just trust my authority. Or imagine I gave my students some work of Kant (or Aristotle or Heidegger or Wittgenstein) and told them to read it, understand it, and believe it, noting that if they are gifted and work hard, perhaps in twenty or thirty years they can start to make some criticisms.[22] Such approaches would somehow betray what it means to practice philosophy; one might even say they would violate the dignity of my students. To rely on tradition or authority without demanding a justification is not only unphilosophical but almost shameful. Of course, philosophy has not always been this way. For about half of the history of philosophy in Europe, Mencius's skepticism of individual judgment and his reliance on tradition would have seemed quite reasonable — but we call that the "middle" or "dark" half.

If we take philosophy in this modern European sense of reliance on individual judgment, then we can say that there is little classical Chinese philosophy, but such a view is misleading and simplistic. It would be better to broaden our definition and consider what philosophy might be if it emerged in a context that lacked the anthropocentric assumptions that nourished Western trust in individual reason. Such a perspective is all the more important, since, while our views of human reason have shifted away from Descartes or Socrates to something closer to those of Mòzǐ, Mencius, or Zhuāngzǐ, our *practice* of philosophy has not. It is important to emphasize this point, because I am *not* arguing that philosophers still believe individuals have an independent and a-cultural ability to reason; my point is that, while the foundation has changed, the practices lag behind. Of course it might still be possible to justify the practices of modern European philosophy without the assumption of divine reason or even individual autonomy, even if such practices would have been unlikely to have emerged without those assumptions. In closing, though, we can borrow a statement that Hansen makes regarding individualism and ethics in a global context:

> I do not insist, however, that a naturalistic conception of human nature, together with an awareness of the way in which human nature is shaped by culture, is incompatible with individualism or with a strong sense of the dignity of the individual. But it remains to be shown how we could justify Western moral attitudes given such difference in background conceptions. Reasonable people sitting down together in a disciplined dialogue should be able (in principle and in the long run and so forth) to reach agreement on fundamental moral principles. But the case for some of our favorite moral principles may not be found particularly compelling by genuinely moral and reasonable discussants from the Chinese philosophical tradition. (1985, 380)

In such a dialogue, philosophy as consisting solely in the judgment of the individual also might not fare so well. Perhaps the most radical form of philosophy to emerge would be that of the Mohists; perhaps even that would demand too much, leaving us to decide only between Confucian traditionalism and Zhuangist skepticism.

Notes

1. Bryan Van Norden has a nice discussion of the importance of tradition and a partial defense of its use in early Chinese philosophy (2007, 134–35, 154–57).
2. This position is also clear in *Mòzǐ*, 454 (48:4), where Gōng Mèngzǐ uses phrasing very similar to Mencius 6B:2 to say that one should imitate the words (*yán* 言) and clothing of the ancients. Mòzǐ responds that not all of the ancients were good, and so one cannot simply imitate them.
3. For Xúnzǐ's views on how opposing opinions should be treated, see "Fēi shí èr zǐ" (*Xúnzǐ*, 102) and "Róng rǔ" (*Xúnzǐ*, 60).
4. Most scholars do not explicitly mark the difference between the two interpretations. Kwong-loi Shun seems to take the "strong" interpretation, writing that part of Mencius's view is the claim that "the heart/mind of human beings already contains an ethical direction, so that human beings do not need to seek ethical guidance from outside the heart/mind" (1997, 212). James Behuniak's emphasis on the role of history and culture in the formation of a person are closer to the weak view (2005). Bryan Van Norden claims that "Mencius argues that human nature places constraints on what Way humans can and should follow" (2007, 198), which seems more like the weak view (depending on how narrowly one takes the constraints), but his claims that the Confucian *dào realizes* human nature (rather than just working within its constraints) suggests the strong view (215, 257).
5. For excellent discussions of these terms, see Shun (1997, 58–63) and Van Norden (2007, 257–70).
6. For a discussion of the sprout of wisdom, see Perkins (2007) and Shun (1997, 71).

7. Obscurity on this point may go back to Mencius himself. Robert Eno argues that Mencius responds to the Mohist challenge with a "rhetorical device," switching emphasis from ritual (*lǐ*) to rightness (*yì*) while covertly identifying the two (1990, 112). This move shifts attention away from the specificity of the Confucian *dào*. It is striking that both Shun and Behuniak concentrate only on giving a justification for rightness, leaving aside the specificity of the rituals (Shun 1997, 56–58, 84–85; Behuniak 2005, 79).
8. Shun describes Mencius's position in similar terms: "to live a proper life, all one needs to do is to manage and develop these predispositions in the direction indicated by the predispositions themselves" (1997, 135). For P. J. Ivanhoe's argument that Mencius follows a development model in contrast to Wáng's discovery model, see Ivanhoe (2000).
9. It is possible to caricature the Mohists into a position that would be rejected even by the weak position on human nature, for example by taking them as utterly eliminating ritual or all particular (familial) relationships of care. Both readings are obviously false, the first shown perhaps most clearly by the fact that the Mohists argue for restraining (*jié* 節) rather than eliminating (*fēi* 非) funerals, the second by the frequent use of filial piety (*xiào* 孝) as a virtue. On the latter point see Robins (2008a, 386–88; 2008b).
10. For an excellent discussion of this passage and its implications against a strong innatist interpretation, see Behuniak (2005, 74–78).
11. For a discussion of how Mencius inherits the metaphor of the compass and square from the Mohists, see Dīng (2008, 407–9).
12. James Behuniak and Dan Robins both point out the Confucian view that institutions must develop gradually (Behuniak 2005, 90; Robins 2008b). In fact, Robins argues that the main conflict between the Confucians and the Mohists was on how institutions should change. One consequence of the necessary gradualness of institutional change is that little change can be made by any one person.
13. See slips 15–20 of the *Xìng zì mìng chū* (Liu 2003).
14. Each of the "Against fate" chapters begins with criteria for evaluating doctrines, and each includes the authority of the sages as one of the criteria (*Mòzǐ*, 265–66, 273–74, 278).
15. This point is clear if we take a contemporary example like same-sex marriage. Most academics (including myself) feel confident enough that we can judge the consequences of such a significant change in custom, and although the actual Mohists would surely oppose that specific change, they would in the abstract allow for such kinds of change. Mencius would surely oppose it.
16. Contrast Descartes: "My plan has never gone beyond trying to reform my own thoughts and construct them upon a foundation which is all my own" (1985, 118).
17. The Socrates of the early dialogues (and probably Socrates himself) would not say such things, and the relationship between the divine and the conventional in Plato's works is more nuanced than serves my purposes here. Nonetheless, consider, for example, the *Symposium*. Diotima begins by telling Socrates, "But how would it be, in our view, if someone got to see the Beautiful itself, absolute, pure, unmixed, not polluted by human flesh or colors or any other great nonsense of mortality, but if he

could see the Beauty itself in its one form? … [I]n that life alone, when he looks at Beauty in the only way that Beauty can be seen — only then will it become possible for him to give birth not to images of virtue (because he is in touch with no images), but to true virtue (because he is in touch with the true Beauty)" (Plato 1997b, 494, *Symposium*, 211e–12a).
18. Plato (1997a, 1132–34, *Republic*, 514a–17b).
19. Descartes writes regarding his years of travel, "In fact the greatest benefit I derived from these observations was that they showed me many things which, although seeming very extravagant and ridiculous to us, are nevertheless commonly accepted and approved in other great nations; and so I learned not to believe too firmly anything of which I had been persuaded only by example and custom. Thus I gradually freed myself from many errors which may obscure our natural light and make us less capable of heeding reason" (1985, 115–16).
20. The later Confucian view that the heart contains the *lǐ* 理 (patterns/order) of the universe could function critically like innate ideas. Wáng Yángmíng writes: "In study, the most valuable is attaining from the heart. If it is negated by seeking in the heart, then even if the words come from Confucius, I would not dare affirm them — how much less if from one not as good as Confucius! If it is affirmed by seeking in the heart, then even if the words are common sayings, I would not dare negate them — how much less if the words comes from Confucius!" (Wáng 1967, 167). I am grateful to Peng Guoxiang for suggesting this quotation.
21. Such arguments appear throughout the *Mòzǐ*, but for an example, see *Mòzǐ*, 204–7 ("Heaven's Intention II").
22. As strange as such approaches might appear for a contemporary philosopher in North America, they are probably what the Confucians would have recommended. For a partial defense of a similar tendency in contemporary China, see Bell (2008, 107–27).

References

Behuniak, J. 2005. *Mencius on becoming human*. Albany: SUNY Press.
Bell, D. 2008. A critique of critical thinking. In *China's new Confucianism: Politics and everyday life in a changing society*. 107–27. Princeton, NJ: Princeton University Press.
Burke, E. 1999. Reflections on the revolution in France. In *The portable Edmund Burke*, ed. I. Kramnick. New York: Penguin Books.
Descartes, R. 1984. Meditations on first philosophy. In *The philosophical writings of Descartes, volume II*, ed. and trans. J. Cottingham, R. Stoothoff, and D. Murdoch. Cambridge: Cambridge University Press.
———. 1985. Discourse on method. In *The philosophical writings of Descartes, volume II*, ed. and trans. J. Cottingham, R. Stoothoff, and D. Murdoch. Cambridge: Cambridge University Press.
Dīng Xéixiáng 丁為祥. 2008. Mengzi's inheritance, criticism, and incorporation of Mohist thought. *Journal of Chinese Philosophy* 35 (3): 403–21.
Eno, R. 1990. *The Confucian creation of heaven*. Albany: SUNY Press.

Hansen, C. 1985. Punishment and dignity in China. In *Individualism and holism: Studies in Confucian and Daoist values*, ed. D. Munro. 359–84. Ann Arbor: University of Michigan Press.

———. 2000. *A Daoist theory of Chinese thought*. New York: Oxford University Press.

Ivanhoe, P. 2000. *Confucian moral self-cultivation*, rev. ed. Indianapolis, IN: Hackett Publishing.

Liú Zhāo 劉釗. 2003. *Guōdiàn chǔjiǎn jiàoshì* 郭店楚簡校釋. Fúzhōu: Fújiàn Rénmín Chūbànshè, 2003.

Lún Yǔ. 2002. In 論語譯註 (Interpretation and annotations on the *Lúnyǔ*), ed. Yáng Bójùn 楊伯駿. Beijing: Zhōnghuá Shūjú.

Mencius. 1987. In 孟子正義 (Orthodox interpretation of Mencius), ed. Jiāo Xún 焦循. Beijing: Zhōnghuá Shūjú.

Mòzǐ. 2001. In 墨子閒詁 (Interlineated commentary on *Mòzǐ*), ed. Sūn Yíráng 孫詒讓. Beijing: Zhōnghuá Shūjú.

Perkins, F. 2007. The sprouts of wisdom and the love of learning in *Mengzi*. In *Liebe – Ost und West/Love in Eastern and Western Philosophy*, ed. H. Möller and G. Wohlfart. 89–98. Berlin: Parerga Verlag.

Plato. 1997a. *Republic*, trans. G. Grube, rev. C. Reeve. In *Plato: Complete works*, ed. J. Cooper. 971–1223. Indianapolis, IN: Hackett Publishing.

———. 1997b. *Symposium*, trans. A. Nehamas and P. Woodruff. In *Plato: Complete works*, ed. J. Cooper. 457–505. Indianapolis, IN: Hackett Publishing.

Robins, D. 2008a. The Moists and the gentlemen of the world. *Journal of Chinese Philosophy* 35 (3): 385–402.

———. 2008b. The roots of Mohism. Unpublished draft.

Shun, K. 1997. *Mencius and early Chinese thought*. Stanford, CA: Stanford University Press.

Van Norden, B. 2007. *Virtue ethics and consequentialism in early Chinese philosophy*. Cambridge: Cambridge University Press.

Wáng Y. 王陽明. 1967. 傳習錄 (Records of teachings and practices), ed. Yè Shàojūn 葉紹鈞. Taipei: Táiwān Shāngwú.

Xúnzǐ 荀子. 1979. 荀子集釋 (Collected commentaries on Xúnzǐ), ed. Lǐ Díshēng 李滌生. Taipei: Xuéshēng.

4

Mohism and Motivation

Chris Fraser*

Mòzǐ and his followers saw themselves largely as social and political reformers, dedicated to eliminating war, eradicating poverty, and promoting prosperity and social order. The aim of Mohist ethical and political thought thus was not just to elucidate the *dào* 道 (the right way or norms) but to lead society as a whole to follow it. Despite this practical orientation, however, the Mohists are widely regarded as having only a thin, crude view of human motivation — one so simplistic as to leave them without a plausible account of how to lead people to practice their *dào*.[1] The purpose of this chapter is to elucidate the Mohist view of motivation and to defend it against this criticism. I will show that in fact the *Mòzǐ* presents a rich, nuanced picture of a variety of sources of moral and prudential motivation that the Mohists can reasonably view as sufficient to guide people to practice the core tenets of their ethics. The widespread opinion to the contrary is probably due mainly to two factors. One is a misunderstanding of just what Mohist ethics demands, which I address briefly in the first section below. The other is a failure to understand the Mohist conception of action and motivation, which I address in the subsequent section. One reason for this failure may be a tendency in the literature to focus on ideas prominent in Mencian and Xunzian discussions of motivation, such as the role of spontaneous affective responses or that of desires arising from people's nature (*xìng* 性). Because the Mohist approach does not center on affects or desires, it is considered simplistic. As I will show, however, once the Mohists' conception of action and motivation is elucidated, they can be seen to have a sophisticated, defensible approach to motivation.

---

* I am grateful to Bill Haines, Loy Hui Chieh, Dan Robins, Timothy O'Leary, and an anonymous referee for very helpful comments on earlier versions of this chapter.

Let me begin by clarifying the conceptual and methodological basis of my discussion. By "motivation," I will refer broadly to psychological states and dispositions that play, or potentially play, a direct causal role in producing action. For the purposes of this chapter, I will include beliefs and analogous cognitive states among an agent's motivating states, since, as we will see below, the Mohists themselves seem to do so. Besides such states and dispositions, a treatment of motivation will typically touch on a range of other psychological traits and capacities less directly connected to action. I take it that, to be justified, claims about motivation or about these other aspects of human psychology need not state exceptionless, universal truths, but only credible generalizations about how people tend to think, feel, and act. The features they describe need not be innate or spontaneous, nor aspects of human *xìng* or nature, however understood. For my present purposes, it is enough that they obtain regularly and widely, and thus count among the conditions that a moral theory or reform program such as the Mohists' can or must work with — what features such a theory or program can take for granted, for instance, and what obstacles or constraints it faces. Thus I take the Mohists' depiction of certain features as widely observed in people as grounds for including them in my interpretation of their view of motivation.

Unlike the three major classical Confucian anthologies — the *Analects* 論語, *Mencius* 孟子, and *Xúnzǐ* 荀子 — the *Mòzǐ* contains relatively few passages that focus specifically on motivation. A likely explanation is that the core Mohist essays are roughly the equivalent of political reform pamphlets, aimed mainly at convincing rulers and officials to adopt Mohist policies. They are neither theoretical treatises (as much of the *Xúnzǐ* is) nor records of a master's day-to-day coaching or instruction (as much of the *Analects* and *Mencius* seems to be). Still, in the course of presenting and defending their ethical and political doctrines, the Mohists frequently make claims about human traits, dispositions, or behavior that bear on the topic of motivation. Other claims they make seem best explained by attributing to them certain implicit assumptions about motivation. My approach here is to draw some of these explicit claims and implicit assumptions together into a sketch of their view of how to motivate people to practice their *dào*.

In the next section, I outline the nature and content of the Mohist ethical and political project, since we cannot evaluate their view of motivation fairly without understanding just what they hoped to lead people to do. In the following section, I reconstruct their conception of action and contrast it with familiar conceptions based on the practical syllogism and the belief-desire model. I then explain how their understanding of action affects their approach to motivation. The following two sections survey the major motivational techniques the Mohists employ and the sources of motivation on which they rely. The chapter concludes with a brief critical evaluation.

The Mohist Reform Program

The Mohists' approach to motivation is intertwined with their ethical and sociopolitical reform program. To understand and evaluate their approach to motivation, then, we need to understand the nature of this program and the normative ideals that they hope people will pursue. In this section, I highlight three aspects of Mohist ethics that are crucial to understanding their practical aims.

First, the Mohists are concerned primarily with social reform, and only secondarily with the individual moral life (Hansen 1992, 108).[2] This is not to suggest that personal moral development is unimportant to them; their doctrinal essays do address individual moral agents, particularly officials of various ranks. But their theoretical and practical focus is social and collectivist. The central question for them is not "How can I be good?" but "What is the *dào*, and how can we collectively lead everyone to follow it?" In their doctrinal essays, at least, their approach to guiding people to practice the *dào* emphasizes political policy and social interaction rather than individual reflection and self-improvement.[3] One reason for this orientation lies in the nature of moral discourse in their time. Their primary audience, as they saw it, was not individual members of society, but government officials, from rulers of states down to low-level officers, who they hoped would lead society to follow the *dào*. Another reason is that the Mohists, like most early Chinese thinkers, tended to employ a communitarian, rather than individualist, conception of what it is to be human. They regarded people primarily as members of social groups — specifically, the family or clan and the political community — and not as atomic individuals. A further reason is that central Mohist normative ideals presuppose collective practice of the *dào*. The Mohist ideal of social order (*zhì* 治), for instance, requires collective adherence throughout society to a unified set of moral norms. The norm of inclusive care (*jiān ài* 兼愛) is explicitly reciprocal: people are to "care inclusively about each other and in interaction benefit each other" (15/10–11).[4] Hence a single agent alone cannot practice inclusive care; for the norm to be realized, it must be practiced by the majority of a community. A corollary is that some of the motivational resources the Mohists invoke to explain how people can practice inclusive care — such as people's tendency toward reciprocity — are contingent on others' practicing it as well. For all of these reasons, the Mohist approach to motivation is oriented mainly at leading communities to follow the *dào*. This orientation helps to explain, among other features of their position, why they assign a central role to encouragement and enforcement by political authorities.

A second point is that the ethical norms by which the Mohists seek to reform society are not exceptionally demanding. One factor driving the impression that Mohist moral psychology is untenably simplistic is the assumption that Mohist ethical norms are heroically difficult — so much so that no one could live up to them without elaborate, extensive training (Nivison 1996, 131). Many writers assume, for instance, that Mohist ethics demands complete impartiality toward others, in the sense that we have an equal obligation to benefit all people, regardless of their relationship to us.[5] The Mohists themselves clearly do not regard their *dào* as especially demanding, however. Though they acknowledge that opponents perceive inclusive care as difficult, for instance, they insist that this is a misconception. Compared with genuinely difficult feats, they claim, inclusive care is actually quite easy to practice (16/81, 15/19). In fact, as I have argued previously, Mohist ethical norms appear to be only moderately stringent, amounting roughly to what many people today would consider basic moral decency (Fraser 2002, sect. 7; cf. Loy 2006, ch. 6).

A few distinctions will help to clarify this point. A famous passage in the *Zhuāngzǐ* indicates that some Mohists sought to emulate the laborious altruism of the mythical sage-king Yǔ (*Zhuāngzǐ* 1956, 33/27ff). Other early sources make it clear that, by the middle of the third century BCE, Mohist militias were renowned for fanatical devotion to their cause (Knoblock and Riegel 2000, 487–88; Hé 1998, 1406). However, these texts describe committed Mohist followers, who had dedicated their lives to their moral ideals. Contemporary analogues would be members of an elite military unit, ascetic religious order, or other organization committed to a demanding code of conduct. Just as we do not expect everyone to join the Marines or the Jesuits, the Mohists give no indication that they expect the entire populace to pursue moral sagehood or enlist in a Mohist militia.

The general norms that the Mohists do apply to everyone are those of *rén* 仁 (moral goodness) and *yì* 義 (moral rightness). There is an important distinction between these, however. As a normative ideal, *rén* is more demanding than *yì*. Yet it is probably *yì*, not *rén*, that constitutes the minimal moral standard the Mohists expect everyone to meet. *Yì* is the standard that, according to the Mohists, *Tiān* 天 (Heaven, Nature) intends that people comply with. To fall short of *yì* is to do something wrong and so to be blameworthy. By contrast, to be *rén* is to achieve a degree of moral goodness that goes beyond the threshold of *yì*. A person whose conduct conforms to *yì* yet falls short of *rén* has room for moral improvement, yet may not be blameworthy.

The criterion of *yì* for the Mohists is what *Tiān* intends (27/73), and what *Tiān* intends is only that each individual conform to norms that, if generally followed, would promote the benefit of all. The norms the *Mòzǐ* specifies include inclusive care (26/22); refraining from war, theft, oppression, and exploitation; sharing labor, knowledge, and resources; performing one's social role conscientiously, thus contributing to social order and economic prosperity; helping to provide for orphans and the childless elderly; and exercising the relational virtues of kindness toward subordinates, loyalty toward superiors, compassion toward one's children, filial devotion toward one's parents, and fraternal love toward siblings (27/14–20, 26/36–38, 28/35–39). By today's standards, all this adds up roughly to being a caring and considerate family member, a responsible member of society, and a decent neighbor willing to offer others a helping hand and to contribute to charity for those with no other means of support. The Mohist conception of *yì* may be more demanding than a minimalist conception of morality on which we have only negative obligations to others. But I suggest it is at most only slightly more demanding than the generally accepted morality of most citizens of contemporary liberal societies.

The third point is that people's natural tendency to feel special affection for and obligations toward family and friends presents no obstacle to the practice of Mohist ethics, because the Mohists endorse distinctive concern for and treatment of those closest to us. As noted above, the Mohists are often taken to hold that we should be impartially concerned for everyone, regardless of their relationship to us, and so should devote no special attention or treatment to our family, friends, or community. The main grounds for this interpretation are that the *Mòzǐ* characterizes inclusive care as being "for others as for oneself" (16/10) and as viewing others' states, families, and persons "as one views one's own" (15/11–12). Let's grant that these formulations depict a form of equal consideration for all. Even so, given what else the Mohists say about inclusive care, it clearly is not only compatible with, but actually requires special caring attitudes and treatment toward those with whom we have close personal relationships. For the Mohists justify inclusive care by arguing that it promotes, among other goods, the practice of the relational virtues — virtues they associate with the core social relationships of ruler and subject, father and son, and elder and younger brother (Fraser 2002, sect. 7). They hold that inclusive care is right partly because, for example, it leads sons to exercise filial devotion to their fathers and subjects to exercise loyalty toward their rulers (15/13, 16/85). Virtues such as filiality and loyalty are normally understood to entail distinctive emotions, obligations, and treatment toward those to whom we stand in the relevant relationships, and nothing suggests the Mohists think otherwise.

In advocating that we be committed "for others as for oneself," then, the Mohists do not intend to displace traditional kinship and political relationships from the center of social and ethical life. What they probably mean is that we should have the same degree of consideration for others' welfare as we do for our own. "Inclusive care" amounts to a label for the attitudes and conduct of an agent who has such equal consideration for all and accordingly has internalized a *dào* that promotes the welfare of all. It contrasts not with special concern for the welfare of one's family and associates — people simply could not be filial or loyal without special concern for their parents and associates — but with the attitude that others can be disregarded and freely harmed in pursuit of our interests (15/12–15).

The Mohist Conception of Action and Motivation

A key to understanding the Mohists' approach to motivation is to grasp their conception of practical reasoning and the psychological antecedents of action. This conception is the basis for their view of how to prepare people psychologically to act in a normatively correct way — that is, how to educate and motivate them to follow the *dào*.

The conception of action in the Western tradition has been deeply influenced by argument-like models of practical reasoning. Aristotle's practical syllogism is one such model; the belief-desire model is another.[6] Such models inspire the view that the psychological antecedents of action are states whose content corresponds to premises in pieces of practical reasoning. According to the belief-desire model, for instance, action springs from a combination of a cognitive state — a belief — represented by one premise in a practical argument and a conative state — a desire or other pro-attitude — represented by another.

The Mohists are similar to Aristotle, Hume, and other Western thinkers in tying their conception of the structure of action to their conception of the structure of practical reasoning. However, their conception of the structure of reasoning is significantly different from Aristotle's and from the sentential, deductive models that inspire the belief-desire model. The Mohist conception of reasoning is not syllogistic, or even deductive. It is analogical and concerns mainly terms, not sentences. The Mohists understand reasoning as a process of discrimination or distinction-drawing, which they call *biàn* 辯. Discrimination typically proceeds on the basis of comparisons of similarity to a model or standard (*fǎ* 法), resulting in an attitude of deeming something *shì* 是 (this, right) or *fēi* 非 (not, wrong) (35/6). These attitudes are typically indexed to a contextually specified kind (*lèi* 類) of thing, denoted by a general term, such as "ox" or "horse." They correspond functionally to the judgment that an object is or is not of that kind, and thus that the term for the kind can correctly be predicated of it. The kind may be an aggregate of similar concrete objects, such as oxen or horses, or an aggregate of events or situations that share some abstract status, such as being *yì* (morally right). Examples of particular *shì* or *fēi* attitudes, then, include the attitude, directed at some animal, that it is or is not an ox, and the attitude, directed at some course of conduct, that it is or is not morally right. Besides alluding to a contextually specified kind, *shì* and *fēi* can be used to refer generally to anything that is correct, right, or prudent, on the one hand, or incorrect, wrong, or imprudent, on the other. Thus they can also be construed as general "pro" and "con" attitudes.

Consistent with this model of reasoning and judgment, the Mohists apply what I call a discrimination-and-response model of action.[7] The structure of action, as they understand it, is that the agent discriminates an object, a situation, or a course of conduct as *shì* or *fēi*, typically with respect to some kind, and then responds to it according to norms appropriate for interacting with things of that kind. For example, an agent might distinguish an animal as *shì* with respect to the kind *ox* and then respond to it by calling it "ox" or using it to pull a cart. Or the agent might distinguish some course of conduct as *fēi* with respect to the kind *yì* (morally right) and respond by condemning or refraining from it. What drives action is a combination of *shì-fēi* 是非 attitudes and the norm-governed responses to various kinds of things that these attitudes prompt. Some of these responses may be innate, such as an infant's response to food. Most are probably acquired in roughly the same way we learn manners or skills. At the highest, most abstract level, when no specific kind is invoked by the context, *shì* and *fēi* themselves can directly prompt action via their role as generic pro and con attitudes (Hansen 1992, 120). Aside from occasional instances of akratic thought or action, then, to deem something *shì* is to be motivated to do, endorse, or promote it, while to deem it *fēi* is to be motivated to avoid, condemn, or eliminate it.

Shì and *fēi* are not the only motivating attitudes the Mohists recognize. They also see action as sometimes following from a state they call "desire" (*yù* 欲). For instance, they claim that *Tiān*'s (Heaven's) conduct provides evidence of its desires (4/10–13), and they assume that people who desire to do what is right will act on the conclusions of cogent normative reasoning (19/62–64, 25/86–88). They also sometimes refer to action as following from the attitudes of "intention" (*yì* 意) or "commitment" (*zhì* 志) (46/14–15, 49/59). When discussing their ethical and political proposals, however, the motivating attitudes they generally focus on are those of deeming things *shì* or *fēi*.

The conception of action I have been sketching is illustrated by the Mohists' hypothetical account of the state of nature that obtained before the advent of political society. According to the Mohists, people in the state of nature are strongly, even obstinately, committed to their personal conception of *yì* 義, or what is right. Since different people's conceptions of *yì* disagree, however, this commitment leads to conflict and eventually violent disorder. The Mohists describe people's attitudes by saying that they "*shì* their *yì* and on that basis *fēi* others' *yì*, and thus *fēi* each other" (11/2). That is, they each deem their *yì* to be *shì*, on those grounds deem others' *fēi*, and thus fall into a cycle of reciprocal condemnation. A key observation is that people's attitude of deeming their *yì* to be *shì* and others' *fēi* is accompanied by a strong motivation to act on their convictions, which ultimately leads to social turmoil. This correlation between *shì-fēi* attitudes and conduct is underscored by the tight link Mohist political theory draws between emulating the *shì-fēi* attitudes and statements (*yán* 言) of political superiors, who serve as moral role models, and emulating their conduct (*xíng* 行).

The Mohist position that *shì-fēi* attitudes are typically sufficient to move agents to act converges in some respects with the views of influential contemporary writers who argue that rational or moral agents normally tend to do what they believe there is most reason to do (Nagel 1970, 27–32; Korsgaard 1986; Scanlon 1998, 33–36). Other things being equal, moral agents do not need some further motivation to move them to act beyond their discrimination (*biàn*), based on what they hold are compelling grounds, that something is right or *shì*.[8] That they sometimes fail to act as they deem best shows only that a breakdown has occurred between motivation and action, not that they lack sufficient motivation.

The theoretical role of *shì* and *fēi* attitudes corresponds at least partly to that of judgment or belief, and the Mohists apparently hold that these attitudes alone can be sufficient to motivate action. Hence their position can to some extent be characterized as anti-Humean.[9] However, they do not necessarily hold that purely cognitive attitudes alone are sufficient for motivation, without the influence of conative or affective attitudes. Without question, *shì-fēi* attitudes generally have a cognitive aspect or component. The Mohists see them as shaped by cogent reasoning, and indeed they play a central role in the Mohist conception of cognition. To recognize a square object as square or an ox as an ox is to distinguish it as *shì* with respect to the kind *square* or *ox*. In some contexts, *shì-fēi* attitudes may verge on being purely cognitive. But in ethical contexts, they can express approval or disapproval (e.g., 17/1), and so they may also have a conative aspect, intertwined with their role as general pro and con attitudes. They may have an affective aspect as well. When the Mohists condemn as *fēi* such conduct as theft, murder, war, and exploitation of the poor, their words ring with moral indignation (e.g., 32/22–23). Conversely, when they approve a practice as *shì*, their claims often carry a tone of moral satisfaction, even exultation (16/15). In their account of the state of nature, they envision people's *fēi* attitudes toward others as motivationally so potent that they lead to violence. Family members' *fēi* attitudes toward each other spark resentment intense enough to overwhelm familial love and respect, driving them to split up (11/3).[10] Given the passion apparently associated with *shì-fēi* attitudes in morally fraught contexts, they probably either incorporate affective elements or are closely associated with affective states.[11] Most likely, they are neither purely cognitive, conative, nor affective, but, depending on the context, may incorporate all three aspects.[12] In focusing on the motivational role of *shì-fēi* attitudes, then, the Mohists are probably not overlooking conative and affective attitudes. Rather, they may subsume these within the scope of *shì-fēi* attitudes.[13]

The Mohists consider the ability to draw and act on *shì-fēi* distinctions properly a form of competence or know-how (*zhī* 知), akin in some respects to the ability to perform a skill. Hence their primary explanation for an agent's failure to act properly is that the agent lacks the relevant know-how. As they understand it, such failure is typically due not to insufficient motivation but to ignorance or incompetence in distinguishing *shì* from *fēi* and responding accordingly. Mohist texts depict three overlapping types of cases of such ignorance or incompetence. The first occurs when the agent simply does not know how to distinguish *shì* from *fēi* properly, as when people fail to distinguish wars of aggression as *fēi* and even deem them *yì* (morally right) (17/9–13, 28/50). The texts especially call attention to cases of partial incompetence, in which people distinguish *shì* from *fēi* properly in some but not all relevant instances — as when they rightly condemn theft and murder but wrongly support unprovoked warfare aimed at seizing the wealth and slaughtering the people of other states. Another is when they apply a norm such as "employing the capable" properly in some cases, as when hiring a professional bowyer to repair a bow or veterinarian to cure a sick horse, but not others, as when they appoint an inexperienced relative to an official post (10/10–20). Such cases represent a failure "to know (*zhī*) the distinction (*biàn*) between right (*yì*) and not-right" (17/13).

The second type of case is when an agent verbally draws distinctions correctly but then fails to act properly. The agent may mouth the right words about morality, yet lack the practical know-how to reliably distinguish and choose what is right and reject what is wrong (19/4–6, 47/23–26). These are cases in which agents' conduct (*xíng*) fails to conform to their statements (*yán*). To count as having moral know-how, the agent must respond to *shì-fēi* distinctions, not just by making the appropriate sort of statements, but by reliably performing appropriate actions.

A third type of incompetence is when an agent endorses the *dào* and undertakes to act on it yet fails to do so. The agent commits to the *dào*, and presumably has some grasp of the distinctions and responses it entails, but falters in carrying it out, perhaps because of doubt or confusion about what to do, a lack of self-confidence, or motivational inertia. In the Mohist theoretical scheme, this sort of failure to follow a *dào* one endorses is comparable to akrasia, or weakness of will, since it amounts to a failure to do what one intends or deems best. However, rather than framing the problem as a failure to act on one's best judgment or to carry out one's intention to perform some discrete act, the Mohists view it as a lack of ability or competence in carrying out a *dào* one has embarked on. One *Mòzǐ* passage addresses the issue as follows: "If you undertake to do *yì* (right) but are not able, you must not abandon the *dào*. To give an analogy, a carpenter who saws [a straight edge] but is not able does not abandon the marking line" (47/20–21). The emphasis on ability (*néng* 能), paired with the carpentry analogy, suggests that — as in the second type of case above, when people say the right things but then fail to act properly — the Mohists ascribe this sort of akratic failure to a form of incompetence, not insufficient motivation. This incompetence is analogous to a deficiency in performing a skill, such as sawing a straight edge. So they probably see the remedy for akratic failure as analogous to that for ineptitude in a skill: the agent should continue training himself to recognize and act on evaluative distinctions properly, with the *dào* as his guide, until he can do so reliably — just as the novice carpenter should keep practicing his sawing technique, with the marking line as his guide, until he masters his craft. For the carpenter, the eventual outcome is skill mastery; for the moral agent, it is virtue.[14]

The discrimination-and-response model should not be confused with psychological behaviorism, the view that action can be explained without appeal to mental states and controlled simply through conditioning. The model does not imply that the Mohists see agents as capable only of primitive, unreflective pro/con attitudes and conditioned responses. The point is that their conception of the psychological states and processes that produce action is different from conceptions associated with the practical syllogism or the belief-desire model. On their model, our most basic psychological operation is one of distinguishing different kinds of things and adopting *shì* or *fēi* attitudes toward them accordingly. The content and consequences of these attitudes vary depending on the context. Reasoning lies in adopting further *shì* or *fēi* attitudes on the basis of perceived analogical relations between things. This model of cognition and reasoning is at least initially plausible, given that discriminating between kinds is simply pattern recognition, a basic cognitive process that underlies many more complex processes.

Nor does the Mohist approach to action entail a concern only with outward conformity to the *dào* rather than character development aimed at following the *dào* spontaneously, from virtuous motives.[15] The Mohists are clearly concerned not simply to modify what people say and do, but to have them develop the underlying *shì-fēi* attitudes that motivate proper statements (*yán*) and conduct (*xíng*) (11/9–22). To suggest they are concerned only with behavior, and not motives or character, would be to overlook the role of *shì-fēi* attitudes. Having the right *shì-fēi* attitudes just is having the right motives, and developing reliable moral know-how just is developing a virtuous character. The Mohists' aim is for people to internalize the relevant *shì-fēi* distinctions and normative responses so that they acquire a reliable disposition to respond, smoothly and directly, to morally pertinent situations according to the *dào*. Of course, pending development of the appropriate *shì-fēi* attitudes, the Mohists might provisionally settle for behavioral conformity, partly as a second-best outcome and partly as a means of habituating agents into the right attitudes.[16] Thus in some contexts, as we will see below, they appeal to prudential, nonmoral considerations either to help motivate people or to show that those who do not yet endorse their *dào* on moral grounds nevertheless have other good reasons to follow it (or at least not to oppose it). But the fundamental aim is to win people's moral approval of the Mohist *dào* and to bring their evaluative and motivating attitudes fully in line with it. This stance is clearly reflected in *Mòzǐ* passages that tie moral worth to action-guiding attitudes such as intentions (*yì* 意) and commitments (*zhì* 志) and to robust, stable aspects of agents' character (see, e.g., 46/12–15, 48/84, 49/36–38).[17]

Framing the Practical Project

The Mohists' model of action and motivation affects how they frame the practical project of leading people to follow the *dào*. Because they see *shì-fēi* attitudes as the key form of morally relevant motivation, they view this project as one of guiding people to distinguish *shì-fēi* correctly and to act accordingly.

The overall project can be divided into two parts. The primary task is to use education, including persuasion and training, to modify how people distinguish *shì-fēi*. In some respects, education can be regarded as a process of redirecting existing motivation rather than developing new motivation. It aims to redirect people's existing general motivation to do what they deem *shì* by convincing them that courses of action they previously did not endorse are indeed *shì*. It also appeals to motivating attitudes the Mohists assume are shared by all — such as valuing social order (*zhì* 治) — and seeks to redirect these toward practicing the Mohist *dào*. In other respects, however, education can be regarded as producing new motivating attitudes, as it may lead people to acquire entirely new habits of distinguishing *shì-fēi*, some of them perhaps in areas of conduct that they previously did not attend to. It may also reshape people's motivational structure in various ways. For instance, it may eliminate inappropriate motivation by helping people see that certain of their *shì-fēi* attitudes are mistaken, as when the Mohists seek to show warmongering rulers and their supporters that wars of aggression are in fact *fēi*, not *yì* (morally right) (17/12–14). Or it may remove motivational obstacles by showing people that certain apparently conflicting attitudes actually converge with the *dào*, as when the Mohists seek to show that filial devotion is consistent with inclusive care (16/64–72).

Because *shì-fēi* attitudes are normally sufficient to produce action, successful persuasion and education will be sufficient to lead most people to conform to moral norms with some degree of reliability. People occasionally fail to act on their *shì-fēi* attitudes, however. So the second major part of the practical project is to improve the reliability with which people translate *shì-fēi* attitudes into action. This task can be conceived of abstractly as one of strengthening people's character. More concretely, the aim is to improve their moral competence or know-how so that they more smoothly and reliably perform the actions that follow normatively from their *shì-fēi* attitudes. This part of the project is carried out through concrete practice in acting properly, backed by moral coaching in the form of instructions and encouragement, presentation of role models, praise and material incentives for success, and criticism and disincentives for failure (11/9–22, 12/12–31). Such coaching may come from social superiors, peers, or oneself.[18] The Mohists recognize that the process of strengthening people's character and moral competence is gradual, not instantaneous. They claim only that leading people to practice inclusive care would be much easier than getting them to perform more difficult practices — such as dieting to the point of starvation or wearing uncomfortable clothing — that rulers in the past nevertheless led their subjects to adopt "within a generation" (16/80).[19]

Given this conception of their practical project, the central question to ask in evaluating the Mohist approach to motivation is whether they offer a plausible account of how people can acquire the discrimination-and-response dispositions — that is, the virtues — needed to practice their *dào* reliably. The next two sections aim to show that they do.

Motivational Techniques

The Mohists either employ or propose to employ at least five interrelated techniques for educating and training people to distinguish *shì-fēi* properly and act accordingly. All five, I think, are widely agreed to be effective methods of guiding and modifying people's conduct.

The most prominent of these techniques is probably normative persuasion and explanation. Since *shì* and *fēi* attitudes have motivational force, a convincing argument or explanation that some practice is *shì* or *fēi* will generally be sufficient to move agents to perform or avoid it. This point partly accounts for the emphasis on normative argument throughout Mohist ethical writings. It is also reflected in the concluding summaries of many Mohist essays, which urge people who desire to do what is morally good and right, or who desire the goods that Mohist ethics takes to be criteria of morality, to carefully "examine" Mohist doctrines (e.g., 10/46, 19/63, 25/86). The underlying assumption is probably that if people evaluate for themselves the grounds for Mohist teachings, seeking to understand them and distinguish whether and why they are *shì* or *yì* (morally right), they will generally be led to practice them.[20]

A second, interrelated technique is to establish explicit verbal teachings or statements (*yán* 言) and verbal or non-verbal models (*fǎ* 法) by which people can direct their conduct. By committing to a statement or model as a guide to conduct, people become motivated to act in line with it, and repeatedly doing so trains them to act on the values it articulates. The Mohists allude to this technique when they remark that statements (*yán*) that are effective in guiding conduct should be repeated frequently (46/37–38, 47/18–19).[21] It is reflected in their concern with evaluating whether particular statements (*yán*), such as those of fatalists (35/5) or of advocates of rich burials and prolonged mourning (25/12), are right or wrong, and thus whether they should be taken as a guide to conduct. It is also reflected in the emphasis throughout the *Mòzǐ* on guiding and evaluating conduct by comparison with clear, measurement-like models (*fǎ*), akin to the carpenter's setsquare or wheelwright's compass (26/41ff.).[22] Among the models the Mohists introduce are general goods, such as "the benefit of the state, clan, and people" (35/9); general norms of conduct, such as "inclusively caring for each other and in interaction benefiting each other" (15/10); concrete guidelines, such as detailed specifications for burial practices (25/83); and exemplary figures or role models, such as the historical sage-kings (35/8) and the "superior person" (16/26). Guiding and checking one's performance by such models amount to a training process that habituates agents to follow the *dào*.

A third approach to motivating people to act according to the *dào*, intertwined with the preceding, is model emulation. The Mohists seek to harness people's tendency to emulate admired role models, including political leaders, exemplary historical figures such as the sage-kings, and ideal types such as the "morally good person" or the "filial son." They explicitly employ forms of model emulation to justify their doctrines (25/1–16), demonstrate their feasibility (16/47–63), and educate people to follow them (11/9–22). I suggest that in all three of these sorts of cases they also implicitly invoke the motivational power of model emulation. People are likely to become motivated to follow the Mohist *dào* because it is the *dào* of respected leaders, heroic historical figures, and paradigmatic archetypes.

A fourth method of motivation is social encouragement and pressure, from both superiors and peers. Mohist political theory proposes a society-wide scheme for moral education and training in which virtuous political leaders serve as moral teachers, instructing people to conform to a unified set of moral norms and setting a good example for them to follow, while members of society provide positive and negative reinforcement by praising each other's good conduct and criticizing transgressions (11/9–13).

A fifth, final technique is material incentives and disincentives. To help ensure conformity to the *dào* even among those who are not motivated by normative considerations or social pressure, the political system also incorporates material rewards and penalties for proper or improper conduct. The Mohists expressly state that the aim of criminal punishment is not retribution, but to bring into the fold those who will not identify with political leaders in following unified moral norms (11/24–25, 12/48–49).

Sources of Motivation

The Mohists identify at least six distinct sources of motivation that they seek to bring into play through the techniques just described. All six may contribute to a particular agent's overall motivation to practice the *dào*.[23]

Perhaps the most prominent source of motivation for the Mohists is people's normative attitudes. As we have seen, the Mohists take *shì-fēi* attitudes to be inherently motivating. Since whatever people deem *yì* (morally right) they will normally also deem *shì*, the motivational force of *shì-fēi* attitudes carries over to the distinction between *yì* and not-*yì*: people are normally motivated to do, endorse, or defend what they deem *yì* and to avoid, condemn, or prevent what they deem not-*yì*. The motivational role of the *rén* 仁 versus not-*rén* (morally good versus bad) distinction is similar, though perhaps more complex. Conceivably, the attitude that something is *rén* may motivate people to endorse and defend it, without feeling compelled to pursue it themselves. However, Mohist argument strategies make it clear that people are expected to find the *rén* person's deeming something *shì* or *fēi* convincing grounds for deeming it *shì* or *fēi* themselves and becoming motivated accordingly (15/1–15, 32/1–7).

Numerous passages in the *Mòzǐ* illustrate the assumption that distinguishing something as *yì* or not-*yì* normally motivates agents to act accordingly. Most prominent is the account of the hypothetical state of nature, discussed above.

Other examples include a passage claiming that people will fight to the death over a statement (*yán*) because they value *yì* over everything else and another claiming that anyone would give a hand up to a worker struggling with a heavy load, because doing so is *yì* (47/1–3, 47/43–44).[24] Particularly telling is the Mohists' explanation of why warmongering rulers and their supporters wage immoral wars of conquest: they do not know that doing so is morally bad and wrong, but instead take their actions to be *yì* (17/9–14, 19/4–6, 28/50–55). The rhetorical strategy of the Mohists' central moral argument against such wars rests on the assumption that how people distinguish *yì* from not-*yì* determines their conduct. The argument aims to show that, like robbery and murder, such wars are not-*yì* (immoral), for if rulers were to deem them not-*yì*, they would desist from them.

Besides a formal commitment to doing what they deem *yì*, according to the Mohists, people share substantive beliefs about *yì* that can be expected to help motivate them to follow the *dào*. Mohist political theory assumes, for instance, that people share the conviction that *yì* comprises public, objective norms of conduct to which everyone should conform, that such a unified *yì* is a prerequisite for social order, and that a unified *yì* can be achieved only by having everyone in society obey the leadership of morally worthy political authorities (Fraser 2008, 440–44).

A second source of motivation to which the Mohists appeal is widely shared values that they contend are promoted by their *dào*. They assume that most people value social order, economic prosperity, and sufficient population, the goods they identify as constituting "the benefit of the world," their criterion of what is morally right. One component of social order, as they understand it, is the exercise of the relational virtues, goods that again they assume most people value. Hence they plausibly hold that people's pre-existing motivation to promote these goods carries over into motivation to practice the Mohist *dào*.

A third important source of motivation is prudential self-interest, in the broad sense of an interest in both one's own welfare and that of one's immediate kin. That self-interest is a common, even universal, motive is presupposed by the "Caretaker" and "Ruler" arguments defending the "applicability" of inclusive care (16/22ff, 16/35ff) (Fraser 2008, 449–51).[25] Self-interest also grounds the Mohists' belief in the power of social and material incentives and disincentives to modify people's attitudes and conduct — though only, they specify, if these are perceived as distributed fairly (12/52–55), with equal opportunity for all (8/9–14), and in a way that makes people feel cared for rather than merely used as means (9/23–24). The Mohists expect self-interest to converge with, and perhaps contribute to, people's motivation to practice their ethics, since they hold that their *dào* is consistent with and even tends to promote self-interest. One's own interests count among "the benefit of all," the Mohists' basic criterion of morality. So morally right practices are expected to promote one's own interests as much as everyone else's.

A further source of motivation engaged by Mohist ethical norms is people's general tendency to reciprocate beneficial or detrimental attitudes and conduct (15/18–19, 16/70–71). The abstract phrasing the Mohists use to describe this tendency — "Those who care about others will surely be cared about" — suggests they expect not only those with whom we have previously interacted directly but people in general to treat us as we treat others. This tendency is thus a potentially powerful source of motivation that converges with the norm of inclusive care. As we saw earlier, inclusive care is a reciprocal ideal: it calls for us each to care about everyone else such that we interact in ways that benefit each other. A tendency toward reciprocity thus means that people are predisposed to just the sort of attitudes and conduct that constitute the practice of inclusive care. Of course, this tendency is only a formal inclination to respond to others in kind, whether they have treated us well or badly. It is not a substantive inclination to care about and benefit each other. Still, it does predispose people to sustain the sort of virtuous cycle of care and benefit that the Mohist *dào* calls for.[26]

A fifth important source of motivation is people's inclination to respect and follow leaders (16/72–81). According to the Mohists, an effective political leader can motivate people to carry out difficult, even life-threatening, acts, let alone follow moral norms that are not particularly stringent and promote the benefit of all. They emphasize, however, that such motivation is conditional on people's confidence that the leader governs fairly and in the public interest. If people perceive that their ruler fails to meet these criteria, they will ally themselves in resistance against him (12/53–55). The motivational force of a leader's influence is thus constrained and, when the political system functions properly, reinforced by a sixth and final source of motivation, people's tendency to seek peer approval. The Mohists emphasize that people live together in communities, and community approval or disapproval ultimately has a greater influence on their conduct than any reward or penalty from a ruler whose judgment the community rejects (12/56–59).

In the ideal Mohist political society, the ruler employs the techniques sketched in the preceding section to govern in such a way that all six of these sources of motivation converge to support practice of the *dào*. He explains, exemplifies, and enforces unified norms of conduct grounded in values people either already share or find it easy to endorse, thus winning their respect and support. He sets forth explicit statements and models as guides to the norms and brings into play people's tendency to conform to authority and seek peer approval. By fairly and reliably enforcing the norms, he gives miscreants and free riders an incentive to co-operate and prevents them from harming the interests of the morally conscientious. He thus helps to ensure that conformity to the *dào* converges with self-interest and that people's tendency toward reciprocity is engaged in a beneficial rather than harmful direction.[27]

Concluding Remarks

Is the Mohist approach to action and motivation plausible? I think the Mohists' understanding of the structure of action is at least initially plausible, and indeed it may provide rich material for comparative work in the philosophy of action. Their conception of *shì-fēi* attitudes as inherently motivating is highly plausible, as is the view I have tentatively ascribed to them, that such attitudes can comprise both cognitive and conative or affective aspects. The five motivational techniques identified from their texts I think are widely agreed to be effective. Of course, we might question whether some are as powerful as the Mohists claim. For educated adults, for instance, model emulation and encouragement from political leaders may be less compelling than the Mohists think. But commonsense experience strongly suggests that all of these methods do work, within certain constraints (some of which the Mohists explicitly recognize).

The sources of motivation to which the Mohists appeal probably are indeed genuine features of the typical agent's motivational system. People do tend to be motivated to act on what they endorse as right.[28] They do tend to share at least some of the values the Mohists appeal to, and they obviously tend to pursue self-interest at times. Respect for authority and peer pressure can indeed play a role in motivating action, and people probably do tend to reciprocate others' attitudes and treatment, though perhaps less consistently than the Mohists envision. Even if none of these sources of motivation by itself is perfectly reliable, jointly they could add up to a powerful, reliable inclination to follow the Mohist *dào*. I think we can conclude that the Mohist approach to motivation is rich, nuanced, and reasonably plausible, even if in some respects incomplete.

Difficulties in motivating people to practice the Mohist *dào*, I suggest, probably would not arise from defects in the Mohist approach to motivation, nor from any failure to provide for the character development that agents need to become virtuous, reliable performers of the *dào*. Mohist texts sketch a thorough, sophisticated program for character development. Motivational obstacles would be more likely to stem from weaknesses in the Mohists' normative conception of the *dào*. Without question, many aspects of Mohist ethics are compelling. There are good reasons to think that unprovoked wars of aggression are indeed wrong, that others' welfare should count in determining how we act, that society should help provide for the care of orphans, and that impoverished farmers should not be taxed to buy luxuries for despots, to cite just a few Mohist ethical views. But other aspects of the Mohist *dào* — such as their extreme parsimony — are much less convincing. By the Mohists' own lights, the most serious motivational obstacle to practicing an ethical teaching is a cogent argument that it is unjustified. My contention is that the normative justification for some Mohist doctrines is not wholly persuasive, and thus people may reasonably lack the motivation needed to practice them.

Notes

1. See, e.g., Nivison (1996, 96), Shun (1995, 515), Ivanhoe (1998, 451–55), and Van Norden (2007, 309).
2. I am pleased, in this volume dedicated to Chad Hansen, to acknowledge that this and other points cited below are developments of seminal ideas introduced in his work. Of particular relevance is his discussion of the structure of "*dào* ethics" and the Mohist conception of agency (1992, 140–43).
3. Personal moral development is a more prominent theme in the Mohist "Dialogues" (Books 46–49 of the *Mòzǐ*), especially Book 47, "Valuing Morality."
4. References to the *Mòzǐ* cite chapter and line numbers in *Mòzǐ* (1986).
5. See, for instance, Nivison (1996, 133), Táng (1986, 115), Cài (1978, 44), Wong (1989, 251), Liu (2006, 110), and Van Norden (2007, 179).
6. Arguably, the belief-desire model is itself an extension or generalization of the practical syllogism.
7. I have discussed this model in Fraser (2009).
8. In this respect, the Mohist position seems to converge with what Shafer-Landau calls "motivational judgment internalism," the view that, if an agent judges an action to be right, the agent is thereby (defeasibly) motivated to perform it (2003, 142–45).
9. Here I am construing Humeanism as the view that beliefs and desires are mutually independent types of states, that desires are necessary for motivation, and that beliefs are not sufficient to motivate. I construe anti-Humeanism as the view that beliefs — or in the Mohists' case, states with a theoretical role largely comparable to that of beliefs — can be sufficient to motivate.
10. Kwong-loi Shun sees the breakup of families in the Mohist state of nature as evidence that the Mohists think people lack affection for kin (1997, 34). But to explain the breakups, they need assume only that people's commitment to conflicting norms can overpower their affection for kin, not that they lack affection.
11. Hence I think the Mohists would reject the distinction David Nivison draws between doing something one recognizes as morally right and doing it "with the inner *feeling* that it just is the thing to do" (1996, 131, his emphasis). For them, the conviction that something is *shì* or *yì* probably carries with it the sort of feeling Nivison alludes to. The role of *shì-fēi* attitudes also makes it question-begging to criticize the Mohists for neglecting "the problem of my ability to feel the way I would have to to be genuinely moved" to do what is right (Nivison 1996, 96). To have the appropriate *shì-fēi* attitudes just is to be "genuinely moved."

12. In contemporary ethics, James Griffin has articulated a related position, arguing that cognitive recognition and affective reaction are inextricably intertwined (1996, 20–36).
13. The Mohists are thus unlikely to advocate guiding action by "dispassionate intellect," as David Wong suggests they do (2002, 453), for they draw no clear distinction between intellect and the passions. The passage Wong cites as emphasizing intellect over emotions in fact instructs followers to guide their conduct by objective norms of moral goodness and rightness rather than their personal emotions and preferences, because the latter are too easily biased (47/19–20). Intellect is not mentioned.
14. This brief account should be sufficient to rebut Nivison's claim that the Mohists have no explanation of akrasia beyond "sheer perversity" on the agent's part (1996, 84).
15. For the claim that the Mohists advocate a "wholly outer-directed" ethics and are unconcerned with whether agents act from the right motives, see Wong (2002, 454) and Schwartz (1985, 147).
16. I thank Loy Hui Chieh (personal communication) for suggesting I include this observation.
17. For a fuller discussion of these points, see Fraser (forthcoming).
18. A practitioner of inclusive care is depicted engaging in a bit of self-coaching at 16/26–27.
19. Nivison holds that, for the Mohists, there is "*no* problem of inner psychic restructuring or nurturing needed to make a person morally perfect" (1996, 83, his emphasis). Similarly, Wong suggests that, for them, "no transformation of human character is needed to act on the right values" (2008, sect. 3). I suggest that, on the contrary, the Mohists' emphasis on education and practice indicates that they consider a process of "nurturing" or "transformation" crucial to ensuring correct performance of the *dào*. They seek to transform how people distinguish *shì-fēi*, the norms they follow in acting on these attitudes, and the reliability with which they do so.
20. According to Nivison, the Mohists' assumption that people will respond to normative arguments by modifying their attitudes and conduct commits them to a form of voluntarism, namely, the view that agents have direct, voluntary control over their motivational states (1996, 130; cf. 83, 93). This interpretation is shared by Ivanhoe (1998, sect. 2) and Slingerland (2003, 128–29). In fact, voluntarism is probably inconsistent with the role the Mohists assign to normative argumentation. Were they voluntarists, the Mohists could not assume that cogent arguments are a reliable means of influencing what people deem *shì* or *fēi* and how they act, for if people's *shì-fēi* attitudes were under their voluntary control, they could at will ignore the force of any argument. Nivison's view seems premised on the assumption that the Mohist reform program is aimed primarily at changing people's affections (1996, 130), which he seems to regard as the only reliable source of morally worthy motivation (1996, 99, 142–45). I am arguing that the Mohists are instead concerned mainly with changing people's *shì-fēi* attitudes and associated patterns of conduct. Note that, in calling for people to "examine" their doctrines, the Mohists implicitly allow that conversion to their *dào* may take time and psychological effort.
21. For further discussion, see Fraser (forthcoming).
22. On this point, see too Hansen (1992, 99–100).

23. This section thus rebuts the view that the Mohists take self-interest to be people's predominant source of motivation. For versions of this view, see Nivison (1996, 83), Schwartz (1985, 145), Ivanhoe (1998, sect. 4), and Shun (1997, 35). For a detailed discussion, see Fraser (2008).
24. Passages such as these also refute skepticism about whether the Mohists ascribe to people any sort of morally worthy motivation. Nivison (1996, 83) and Ivanhoe (1998, sect. 4), for instance, seem to think that for the Mohists there is no such thing as virtuous motivation. Contemporary New Confucian writers have expressed similar views (Cài 1978, 83).
25. Briefly, both arguments contend that inclusive care can be applied in practice as a social *dào*, because agents concerned about choosing a caretaker or a ruler to protect their own or their family's interests would choose a candidate who practices inclusive care over one who disregards others. For detailed discussion, see Fraser (2008).
26. Thus I suggest that the Mohists' claims about reciprocity answer a worry raised by Kwong-loi Shun, namely that, because they do not regard their *dào* as "the realization of certain inclinations that human beings already share," they may have difficulty explaining how people can come to practice it (1997, 34–35). A tendency toward reciprocity is a shared inclination that is realized in the practice of the Mohist *dào*.
27. As this section indicates, the Mohist reform project does not require wholesale changes in people's motivation but mainly seeks to build on existing motivation, particularly people's commitment to *yì* (right) and values such as social order, filiality, and self-interest. The widely repeated claim that the Mohists see human nature as "extremely plastic" (Ivanhoe 1998, 451) or "highly malleable" (Van Norden 2007, 195) is thus unsustainable.
28. Of course, people's substantive beliefs about *yì* — such as their view on whether *yì* must be unified — may diverge from the Mohists' assumptions, thus potentially reducing their motivation to practice the Mohist *dào*.

References

Cài, R. 蔡仁厚. 1978. 墨家哲學 (Mohist philosophy). Taipei: Dōng Dà.
Fraser, C. 2002. Mohism. In *The Stanford encyclopedia of philosophy*, ed. E. Zalta. http://plato.stanford.edu/archives/win2002/entries/mohism. Stanford, CA: The Metaphysics Research Lab.
———. 2008. Moism and self-interest. *Journal of Chinese Philosophy* 35 (3): 437–54.
———. 2009. Action and agency in early Chinese thought. *Journal of Chinese Philosophy and Culture* 5: 217–39.
———. Forthcoming. The ethics of the Mohist "Dialogues." In *The many faces of* Mòzǐ, ed. C. Defoort and N. Standaert. Leiden: Brill.
Griffin, J. 1996. *Value judgement*. Oxford: Oxford University Press.
Hansen, C. 1992. *A Daoist theory of Chinese thought*. New York: Oxford University Press.
Hé, N. 何寧, ed. 1998. 淮南子集釋 (Collected explications of *Huáinánzǐ*). Běijīng: Zhōnghuá.

Ivanhoe, P. 1998. Mohist philosophy. In *Routledge encyclopedia of philosophy*, vol. 6, ed. E. Craig. 451–55. London: Routledge.
Knoblock, J., and J. Riegel, trans. 2000. *The annals of Lü Buwei*. Stanford, CA: Stanford University Press.
Korsgaard, C. 1986. Skepticism about practical reason. *Journal of Philosophy* 83:5–25.
Liu, J. 2006. *An introduction to Chinese philosophy*. Oxford: Blackwell.
Loy, H. 2006. *The moral philosophy of the* Mozi *core chapters*. Ph.D. dissertation. University of California, Berkeley.
Mòzǐ. 1986. 墨子引得 (*A concordance to Mòzǐ*). Harvard-Yenching Institute Sinological index series, supplement no. 21 (reprint). Shànghǎi: Shànghǎi Gǔjí.
Nagel, T. 1970. *The possibility of altruism*. Princeton, NJ: Princeton University Press.
Nivison, D. 1996. *The ways of Confucianism*, ed. B. Van Norden. La Salle, IL: Open Court.
Scanlon, T. 1998. *What we owe to each other*. Cambridge, MA: Harvard University Press.
Schwartz, B. 1985. *The world of thought in ancient China*. Cambridge, MA: Harvard University Press.
Shafer-Landau, R. 2003. *Moral realism: A defense*. Oxford: Oxford University Press.
Shun, K. 1995. Mo Tzu. In *The Cambridge dictionary of philosophy*, ed. R. Audi. 515. Cambridge: Cambridge University Press.
———. 1997. *Mencius and early Chinese thought*. Stanford, CA: Stanford University Press.
Slingerland, E. 2003. *Effortless action*. New York: Oxford University Press.
Táng, J. 唐君毅. 1986. 中國哲學原論導論篇 (*Sources of Chinese philosophy: Introduction*). Taipei: Xuéshēng.
Van Norden, B. 2007. *Virtue ethics and consequentialism in early Chinese philosophy*. Cambridge: Cambridge University Press.
Wong, D. 1989. Universalism vs. love with distinctions: An ancient debate revived. *Journal of Chinese Philosophy* 16 (3/4): 251–72.
———. 2002. Mohism: The founder, Mozi (Mo Tzu). In *Encyclopedia of Chinese philosophy*, ed. A. Cua. 453–61. London: Routledge.
———. 2008. Chinese ethics. In *The Stanford encyclopedia of philosophy*, ed. E. Zalta. http://plato.stanford.edu/archives/spr2008/entries/ethics-chinese. Stanford, CA: The Metaphysics Research Lab.
Zhuāngzǐ. 1956. 莊子引得 (*A concordance to Zhuāngzǐ*). Harvard-Yenching Institute Sinological index series, supplement no. 20. Cambridge, MA: Harvard University Press.

5
"It Goes beyond Skill"

Dan Robins*

> To be human is to be in a reality viewed as open invitations to ways to "carry on."
>
> Chad Hansen (2003, 221)

> You have heard of knowing by means of knowing something, but you have not heard of knowing by means of knowing nothing.
>
> *Zhuāngzǐ* (Book 4)

In early Chinese discourse, a *dào* 道 was most often a norm-governed way of doing something, such as filling a role, engaging in an activity, or achieving some goal. The *dào* promoted by the various masters were of this sort, for example. But there are also texts according to which *dào* is prior to and gives rise to the cosmos. For example, Book 6 of the *Zhuāngzǐ* tells us that "*dào* . . . [is] from the basis, from the root, when there were not yet heaven and earth, since ancient times it has persisted . . . it produces heaven and produces earth" (*Zhuāngzǐ* 6:230/81). The aim of this chapter is to give an account of how these two uses of the term "*dào*" relate, of what it might mean for ways of acting to give rise to the cosmos.

---

* I presented earlier versions of this chapter at the Midwest Conference on East Asian Thought (Indiana University, Bloomington, April 2008) and at "Dao, Mind, and Language: A Conference in Honour of Chad Hansen" (University of Hong Kong, May 2008); the trip to Hong Kong was generously funded by the Richard Stockton College of New Jersey. I have received helpful comments from Tongdong Bai, Chris Fraser, Chad Hansen, Brian Hoffert, Don Munro, Timothy O'Leary, Hagop Sarkissian, Ted Slingerland, Stephen Walker, and Lee Yearley. The chapter is dedicated to Chad.

The two uses certainly relate somehow. The *Zhuāngzǐ* passage quoted above tells us not only that *dào* produces heaven and earth but also that it "can be passed on but cannot be received." The word "*dào*" is not repeated, so we cannot explain this incongruity by positing shifts in meaning or reference: according to this passage, the very *dào* that produces heaven and earth is *dào* that can be passed on but not received. The latter *dào* are probably ways of acting, though there are other possibilities.[1] My question, then, is how the author or authors of this passage made sense of the claim that a way of acting produces heaven and earth.

The opening line of the *Dàodéjīng* may raise a similar puzzle. It reads, "*Dào* can be *dào*ed, it is not constant *dào* (道可道非常道)."[2] If one *dào*s something, it cannot be constant *dào*, but it is nonetheless in some sense *dào*, presumably the *dào* mentioned first in the line. We thus have a contrast between *dào* that can be *dào*ed and constant *dào*. To *dào* something might be to treat it as a way of acting, which is to say to follow it, or it might be to teach it. Either way, the *dào* that can be *dào*ed is most likely a way of acting. The constant *dào*, however, is often equated with the beginning of heaven and earth or the mother of the ten thousand things, both of which are mentioned later in the same verse. Read this way, the line presents ways of acting that we can follow and the cosmic origin as incompatible alternatives; but they do not sound like alternatives at all, unless, perhaps, the claim is that the cosmos has its origin in a way of acting that cannot be followed. The puzzle is what this could mean.

Throughout the chapter I frequently help myself to the term "Daoist." Even restricting attention as I do to the late Warring States period (roughly, 320–221 BCE), the term gives scholars a great deal of leeway in the selection of both texts and points of reference, and this leeway raises serious methodological difficulties. The difficulties are all the more pressing because Warring States thinkers themselves seem not to have recognized a distinctive intellectual or religious tradition encompassing just the figures, ideas, and practices that now pass as Daoist. Here I avoid some common pitfalls because I am trying to reconstruct not a single Daoist theory or worldview but a network of concepts. This allows me to recognize a variety of ways in which Daoists put these concepts into play. Still, in a chapter of this length it is impossible to do justice to the methodological issues that remain. In particular, I cannot provide an explicit defense of my implicit claim that the texts I discuss represent something that can usefully be classified as Daoist.

Situational *Dào*

I take as my point of departure some recent attempts by Chad Hansen to give an account of what he calls the metaphysics of *dào*.[3] These attempts extend his earlier arguments that *dào* never plays a role in classical Daoist thought analogous to that of an ultimate reality or a creator (Hansen 1983; 1992, ch. 6 and 8). Hansen instead takes classical Daoists to have been engaged in a sort of metaethics, reflecting on the nature of norms of action. In the more recent work, he takes questions about the metaphysics of *dào* to concern the metaphysics of normativity.

Central to the account that Hansen develops is the idea that norm-governed ways of acting can be real features of a situation. Consider a way to get through a forest. That it is a way to get through the forest is determined by such factors as the physical geography of the area, the weather conditions, and any local threats. If there is a path, its formation likely altered these factors, and if so, its formation helped constitute the way that it traces. However, this is not necessary. There can be a way through the forest even without a path, if conditions are right. And even if there is a path, its significance is largely epistemological: it indicates a way that would exist even in the absence of the path. (Markers of other sorts normally have just this epistemological role.)

Or consider Huìzǐ's enormous gourd (*Zhuāngzǐ* 1:32–33/34–35).[4] Huìzǐ can see no use for it, so he smashes it, whereupon Zhuāngzǐ asks why he did not tie the gourd to his waist and float along the rivers and lakes. That there is such a way to use the gourd depends on the nature of the gourd itself together with relevant bits of context (such as the availability of rivers and lakes). But given that there is such a way, it exists as a real feature of Huìzǐ's situation.

A way through a forest exerts a kind of normative pull on those who want to get through the forest: given their goal, they have a reason to follow that way. Similarly with Huìzǐ's gourd: Huìzǐ attracts Zhuāngzǐ's criticism precisely because he fails to recognize a way of using the gourd. In this second case, the way does not owe its normative pull to the agent's existing goals or desires; the criticism may even imply that Huìzǐ's goals are too limiting. Still, the criticism likely assumes that floating down the rivers and lakes would give Huìzǐ an especially valuable sort of satisfaction. If this is right, then the way exerts a normative pull on Huìzǐ because of how things are with Huìzǐ.

Following a way may also require skills, sensitivities, and fortitudes that not all people share. A particular way through the forest might require the ability to clamber over fallen trees, for example, and the way that Zhuāngzǐ suggests for using Huìzǐ's big gourd requires the ability to set aside one's other goals and find contentment floating along the rivers and lakes. If Huìzǐ did not have this ability, he could be pitied, but it would be unfair to fault him. A way has normative pull only on those who have what it takes to follow it.

Some of the aptitudes required for following a way are epistemological in nature: we have to be able to recognize that there is such a way in the first place. I noted above that paths and markers address this epistemological requirement, but it is an answer that Daoists are likely to find suspicious. This, I take it, is the point of the provocative statement that the sages "do not follow *dào* (不緣道)" (*Zhuāngzǐ* 2, 85/46); they do not follow *dào* because the *dào* according to which they act are not marked out in advance. Elsewhere we read of the utmost person who "wanders where there are no signs (遊無朕)" (7:300/97).[5] Paths and markers can be misleading if conditions have changed, or if the route they indicate was poorly chosen in the first place. Though they normally indicate what worked in the past (or anyway what worked well enough), they cannot guarantee that what worked then will still work now, or that no other way would work better. Largely for this sort of reason, classical Daoists tended to prefer a different sort of account of how we are able to recognize ways of acting that are built into situations.

The Swimmer and the *Dào* of Water

The swimmer who appears in Book 19 offers one of the *Zhuāngzǐ*'s most important accounts of how we are able to know *dào* (19:702/204–5).

Confucius is visiting the waterfall at Lǚliáng. The water is so turbulent that even turtles, lizards, and fish cannot swim there. But a man jumps in. Confucius assumes his aim is to kill himself, but he soon emerges downstream and starts singing. Confucius asks him, "Does swimming have a *dào*?" The swimmer answers, "It does not. I have no *dào*. . . . When it is settled I enter, when it is choppy I emerge, following the *dào* of the water and not acting on my own behalf." He goes on to explain these claims in terms of his *xìng* 性, or spontaneous character. As Graham notes, the swimmer here contrasts his *xìng* with his *gù* 故, the character he had from birth (1990, 8). The apparent point is that growing up in water developed his *xìng* in such a way that now he can spontaneously find a way through the water. But he specifically denies that, as a result, he acquires a *dào* of swimming, saying instead that he swims according to the *dào* of the water, which is to say a *dào* built into the situation. What he has acquired, then, must be a sort of spontaneous attunement to the ways that water flows.

What would it mean for the swimmer to have his own *dào* of swimming? This would have to be a *dào*, a way of acting, that he has already mastered when he enters the waters. Such a *dào* could be highly sophisticated and could take account of many of the ways in which different waters flow differently. Still, someone who swam simply by following such a *dào* would be sensitive only to those differences that are somehow anticipated in her *dào*. A Daoist might worry that she would overlook the subtle particularities of unique situations and be entirely unprepared for situations that are truly novel.

Of course no one actually swims this way. An ordinary skilled swimmer relies not only on her prior mastery of ways of swimming, but also on her sensitivity to just the water she is currently swimming in, and she is often able to adjust to its particularities even when they have not been anticipated in her training. This, indeed, is part of the skill of swimming: not just applying techniques one has already mastered, but adjusting those techniques to the needs of the current situation. And much the same could be said of any skilled activity.

When the swimmer says that he has no *dào*, what he means is that the adaptiveness that accompanies any skill is not merely necessary for effective action, but it is also sufficient. To use language we find elsewhere in the *Zhuāngzǐ*, he is saying that the truly skilled swimmer is empty, responding like a mirror but not storing anything up (see especially 7:300/97): nothing he has previously learned interferes with his ability to adapt to the flow of the water that he currently faces (cf. Cline 2008, 338–41; Oshima 1983, 74–79). Generalized, his claim is that someone who is sufficiently sensitive to the *dào* built into situations needs no *dào* of her own. Apparently we acquire this sensitivity by allowing our spontaneous character to develop naturally or, as the passage from Book 7 puts it, by exhausting what we have from heaven. But this does not require us to master any *dào* of our own.

Riding *Dào* and *Dé*

Book 20 of the *Zhuāngzǐ* opens with a passage that advances similar ideas (20:719–20/209–10). This passage takes up an argument we find twice in Book 4, that useless trees are able to survive while more useful ones are cut down and used (4:150–58/63–66). The argument implies that it is in a way useful (to us) to be useless (to others) — because when we are useful to others, they are liable to use us, and that is unlikely to be good for us. (In Book 20, the argument is put in terms of worthlessness rather than uselessness.)

But Book 20 does not allow the argument to go unchallenged. After Zhuāngzǐ praises worthlessness to his followers, he goes to dine with an old friend. The friend asks that a goose be prepared for dinner, and when asked whether to kill the goose that can sing or the goose that cannot sing, he says to kill the one that cannot sing. Zhuāngzǐ's followers later point out that this meant killing the worthless goose, and ask him whether to side with worth or with worthlessness.[6] Zhuāngzǐ's mysterious answer is that we should not constantly fix on either one. Instead, we should float along, riding *dào* and *dé* 德, transforming along with the seasons, without holding to any particular preference. He describes this as floating along within the ancestor of the ten thousand things and contrasts it with acting according to social or ethical traditions.

When the passage tells us to ride *dào*, it clearly does not mean we should follow a *dào* that we bring with us. That would imply a fixed preference, one not sensitive to the particularities of the situation. Rather, it means that we should ride the *dào* built into the situations we find ourselves in. In some situations, we are better off if worthy, because we will be kept around; in others, we are better off if worthless, because no one will try to use us in ways that are bad for us. But no *dào* that we can master in advance will always be able to distinguish the situations that call for being worthy from the ones that call for being worthless. And similarly with *dé*. This, I take it, comprises the particular dispositions and sensitivities we act on in following a *dào*. To follow a *dào* built into the current situation, we must act from *dé* that is also situational.[7]

Kitchen Dīng's *Dào*

The *Zhuāngzǐ*'s most famous example of someone who flourishes while being useful is, of course, Kitchen Dīng, the butcher who appears in Book 3 (3:102–5/50–51).[8]

Kitchen Dīng is butchering an ox, and he is doing it with remarkable skill. His lord comments on this, and Dīng replies by saying, "What I love is *dào*, it goes beyond skill (進乎技矣)."[9] Here is how he explains this reply:

> Nowadays, I encounter it with my spirit and do not use my eyes to see. Sensory knowledge stops and spirit desires proceed. I depend on the natural structure (*tiān lǐ* 天理), attack the great cracks, and take guidance from the great openings. I adapt to what is inherently so (因其固然).

In other words, Dīng goes beyond skill by acting according to *dào* built into the ox's body. But this is not the *dào* that he says he loves, for the *dào* built into the ox's body do not in any sense go beyond skill, they just exist independently of it. Rather, the point must be that the skill he brings to the encounter is not precisely adapted to the body of the particular ox he is unraveling, so in order to butcher this ox effectively he must make adjustments. "*Dào*" is his word for the way he does this.

Dīng also seems to recognize a more straightforward sense in which *dào* goes beyond skill. In ordinary skilled butchering, he must adjust to the particularities of this ox, but he is able to do so as if automatically, without interrupting the flow of his action. But something more happens when he comes to what he describes as a knotty (*zú* 族) part, a part where it is difficult for him to go forward: he cautions himself, proceeds slowly, stills perception, and is able to get the knife through the joint.[10] The ox's flesh then falls apart "like earth crumbling to the ground." This is an intensification of the state he is already in, required presumably because he must now do more than simply adjust his existing skill. His problem here is that his existing skill simply is not up to the intricacies of this particular joint, so he must acquire the ability to deal with the joint by actually dealing with it. *Dào*, as we read elsewhere, are made by acting (*Zhuāngzǐ* 2:61/40).

The *dào* that Kitchen Dīng loves is not, however, the various ways he acquires of cutting up oxen. It is rather a *dào* of adaptation and flexibility. The swimmer from Book 19 also has this sort of *dào*: though he has not mastered a fixed way of swimming, his ability to recognize and adapt to the *dào* of the water is precisely what Dīng is here calling *dào*.

We can distinguish three kinds of *dào* in these passages. First, a *dào* can be a fixed way of doing something, a way that one masters prior to the situations in which one puts it into practice. Daoist texts are in general suspicious of this sort of *dào*, and the swimmer from Book 19 of the *Zhuāngzǐ* right out says he has none. Second, *dào* can be built into the situations we encounter, into, for example, the forests we hope to get through, the waters that we hope to swim, and the oxen we hope to butcher. Third, there is the way we adapt to the situation at hand, going beyond any *dào* we have previously mastered. Daoists seem to have differed over whether the way we do this can legitimately be called *dào*: the swimmer says no, the butcher says yes.

Kitchen Dīng and the swimmer differ over more than terminology. In Dīng's terms, the swimmer denies having skill and claims to act entirely on the basis of *dào* that goes beyond skill. Dīng's account is less extreme. In saying that *dào* goes beyond skill, he acknowledges that, without his existing skills, he could not butcher oxen effectively, so though mastering skills is not sufficient, it is necessary. As noted above, going beyond one's existing skills and doing what one is not yet able to do is part of ordinary skilled activity, and Dīng stays close to this view. The swimmer, by contrast, abstracts our ability to go beyond skill from the skills we go beyond, claiming in effect that, given the ability to go beyond our skills, we do not need skills in the first place. This is a much more extreme view — though I have found that people who grew up by and in water often appreciate his description of a spontaneously developed sensitivity to its ways.

Going beyond Skill

Kitchen Dīng explains how he is able to go beyond skill by describing the state he puts himself into while butchering. Throughout the *Zhuāngzǐ* we find numerous other attempts to characterize similar states.

Consider, for example, Qìng the woodworker (19:706–7/205–6). He prepares himself to make a bellstand by fasting, putting himself in a state in which he forgets all thought of praise and blame and of skill and clumsiness, forgetting even his own body. After seven days of this, he goes into the forest and begins carving from a tree only if he can see a bellstand already somehow in it as part of its heavenly character (*tiān xìng* 天性). Like the swimmer and Kitchen Dīng, he is not simply applying a skill he has previously learned. Like them, he explicitly denies this. Rather, he puts himself into a state in which he is sensitive to the *dào* in the trees he encounters. As a result, people wonder if the bellstands he makes have been produced by spirits (*shén*). Spirit is also important in Kitchen Dīng's account: he claims that he encounters the ox with spirit and proceeds according to spirit desires, in both cases drawing a contrast with ordinary perception.[11]

Consider also Confucius's advice to Yán Huí when the latter is preparing for a mission to Wèi 衛, during which he will try to reform that state's wicked ruler (*Zhuāngzǐ* 4:117–34/54–58). After arguing at length that it is a mistake even to try, Confucius dismisses the two plans Yán Huí has come up with and then tells him how he will have to proceed. This involves listening with his *qì* (rather than his ears or his heart), because *qì* "is empty and waits on things (虛而待物)"; *qì* here plays the same role that spirit played for Kitchen Dīng. Confucius sums up his advice by saying, "I only advise, collect emptiness (唯道集虛)" (4:130/57–58).[12] Yán Huí is to enter the ruler's court without depending on any plans worked out in advance, and simply respond to the situation before him. Confucius later says, "You have heard of knowing by means of knowing something, but you have not heard of knowing by means of knowing nothing" (4:134/58). The point is that he is going to have to act according to *dào* that he has not yet acquired.

The most interesting attempts to characterize our ability to go beyond skill come in Book 2 of the *Zhuāngzǐ*.[13] Much of this book addresses the problem of how to choose between the many *dào*s available to us and of how to avoid settling so firmly on a particular *dào* that one becomes blind to alternative ways of doing things. The text advocates a state it calls *míng* 明, or illumination, which enables one to shift between *dào* as the situation demands. This state is described at one point as the pivot of *dào*, a point at which various *dào* come together but which privileges none of them. In such a state, there is no limit to the ways in which we can respond to the situation, but we are not (yet) committed to any of them. To achieve this state is to go beyond skill, to be ready to take up any of the various skills one might have mastered while also adapting to the *dào* built into the current situation.

The story of the monkey keeper illustrates these ideas nicely (*Zhuāngzǐ* 2:61/41). The monkey keeper disappoints his monkeys by giving them each three nuts in the morning and four nuts in the evening, but they become pleased when he instead gives them four in the morning and three in the evening. The anecdote is introduced with the line, "Working one's spirit to illuminate (*míng*) as one but not knowing their sameness, call it three in the morning." This is usually taken to mean that there is no difference between the two distributions of nuts (since either way it is seven nuts each day), and that the monkeys are confused because they do not realize this. The monkey keeper, by contrast, is a sage who recognizes the oneness of all things.

But the monkeys are not confused: there is nothing irrational about wanting the bigger meal in the morning. And the monkey keeper does not regard the two distributions of nuts as the same, for if he did, he would have no reason to switch from the first to the second, and he might as well continue giving the monkeys three in the morning.[14] But this is precisely the error that the passage's opening warns against: to insist on three in the morning would be to illuminate as one without seeing the true sameness. Sameness here cannot be identity. The two distributions may be the same in all respects that matter to the monkey keeper, but they differ in other respects that matter to the monkeys, and this is precisely what the monkey keeper notices. Realizing the sameness of the two distributions must then be realizing the respects in which they are the same, a realization that also requires noting the respects in which they differ. The passage goes on to comment, "The sage harmonizes them . . . and rests on the potter's wheel of heaven (*tiān*). This is what is called practicing both of them." The monkey keeper harmonizes his *dào* with the *dào* of the monkeys by finding a way to act that is compatible with both. Though his own *dào* does not distinguish between the two distributions, the monkeys' does. Their *dào* is not built into his situation as a way through a forest is, but recognizing it and acting according to it require a similar adaptiveness. Elsewhere the same point is made with the statement that "from the others' points of view one cannot see, but from knowledge one can know them (自彼則不見，自知則知之)" — know (or understand) others' *dào*, that is, despite not being able to see things from their perspective (2:58/39).

The metaphor of the potter's wheel of heaven recalls an image found in both the *Mòzǐ* and the *Guǎnzǐ*, of trying to determine the directions of sunrise and sunset on a spinning potter's wheel.[15] Both texts present this as an analogy for operating without fixed norms, an approach they oppose. The monkey keeper anecdote uses the same metaphor to insist that we must go beyond fixed norms in order to adapt to the various *dào*s of those we deal with. The reference to heaven here is interesting: it figures heaven as a source of disruption for any fixed *dào*.[16] The lesson is that we cannot rely on any particular fixed way of acting but must instead go beyond skill.

Much of Book 2 deals with language, and especially with the action-guiding distinctions we draw in language. The text uses the abstract pair *shì-fēi* to stand for any such distinction. It treats them as indexicals whose applicability can only be judged on the basis of one or another fixed *dào*. This treatment exploits the fact that "*shì*" could mean *this* as well as *right* (Graham 2003, 109–11; Hansen 1983, 33–34). A concern throughout is that we tend to become attached to particular ways of drawing distinctions and being guided by them, attributing to them an ultimacy they cannot truly possess. Language is perhaps especially suspect, because when distinctions are put in linguistic form they can be passed on and then used to guide action even in situations to which they are poorly adapted. Having been taught to be useful, for example, we respond poorly to situations in which being useful will get us into trouble. Still, the text seems to acknowledge that there are uses of language that avoid this problem, at least partially. This is, for example, a natural way to interpret the distinction that A. C. Graham finds in the text between *yīn shì*, a sort of adaptive judgment, and *wéi shì*, which is fixed, "deeming" judgment (see Graham 2003, 110–11; and see *Zhuāngzǐ* 27:1089–90/303–5).

None of these arguments can justify the claim that we are better off not drawing any distinctions at all, and I doubt they were intended to. Having reached the center of the circle, the pivot of *dào*, we are not committed to any particular way of drawing distinctions and being guided by them, but to respond is precisely to adopt such a way, albeit only provisionally. Action would be impossible in an undifferentiated world. (Imagine the consequences if Kitchen Dīng did not distinguish between ox and non-ox.) The hope that seems to animate these texts — when they are hopeful — is that we can find the appropriate distinctions somehow built into the situations we face and not let our responses be fixed by previously internalized linguistic guidance.

Skill itself becomes a problem: practicing a *dào* brings it to completion, and this completion is also an injury or a loss (*Zhuāngzǐ* 2:61, 66/40–42). This worry gets raised most directly in the difficult passage about the three masters (2:66/41–42). The musician Zhāo Wén represents completion and loss when he strums his *qín* 琴 zither and their lack when he does not strum it. Completion here involves commitment to a particular tune, loss the ruling out of the other tunes he could have played instead. But completion immediately takes on a second sense. The three masters are complete, if they are, because they have mastered their skills, but this very mastery closes them off from other people: they want to get others to understand their skill and perhaps also to share their love for it, but this proves impossible.[17] As a result, Huìzǐ engaged in pointless philosophizing, and Zhāo Wén was unable to teach his skill to his son.[18] We could put the point this way: when we master skills, we tend to get locked into particular ways of doing things, and this makes it all the more difficult to interact successfully with others — precisely the difficulty that the monkey keeper manages to avoid.

The Great Ancestor

When the passage about the worthless goose says that we should float along, riding *dào* and *dé*, it describes this as floating along with the ancestor of the ten thousand things and as taking part in the thinging of things (20:720/210). An ancestor is a kind of source. Here, it is the source of things, and presumably of the *dào* built into those things, the *dào* one is supposed to ride.

Dàodéjīng 4 makes a similar connection. It opens, "*Dào* pours out, but in using it something is not filled. An abyss! Like an ancestor to the ten thousand things."[19] Here it is explicit that the ancestor produces both things and *dào*. We use the *dào* that pours out of it but are not thereby filled, which is to say that we adjust to the *dào* that pours out without storing any up. We retain the emptiness that will allow us to adjust to future *dào*.

Neither of these passages characterizes the ancestor as *dào*.[20] There are, however, other texts that present *dào* as a kind of ancestor. For example, the passage from Book 6 of the *Zhuāngzǐ* that I quoted at the beginning of the chapter says that *dào* produces heaven and earth. Presumably *Dàodéjīng* 42 is appealing to similar ideas when it says, "*Dào* produces the one, the one produces the two, the two produce the three, the three produce the ten thousand things." And *Dàodéjīng* 25 introduces "*dào*" as a style name for "a thing formed in confusion, born before heaven and earth" which "can be considered the mother of heaven and earth."

Some of the language in these passages could be taken to imply that the ancestor produced heaven and earth in an act of creation that took place, and was concluded, in the distant past. However, the dominant impression they give is of an ongoing process whereby the ancestor continues to give rise to heaven and earth, the ten thousand things, and *dào*. This is the only way I can see to make sense of the idea of floating along with the ancestor of the ten thousand things, for example, and if I am reading it correctly, *Dàodéjīng* 4 is referring to an ongoing production of *dào*. Similarly, when Zǐyú takes ill and says, "The maker of things is making me all crookedy like this," the implication is that the maker's generative activity continues (6:241/84; the translation of "*jūjū* 拘拘" as "crookedy" is Watson's). If some texts do posit an absolute cosmogonic beginning, the dominant impression they give is that any such beginning can at least be repeated.

It can be repeated especially by those adepts who have mastered the various psychophysiological techniques hinted at in Daoist texts, such as the heart fasting (心齋) that Confucius advocates for Yán Huí (*Zhuāngzǐ* 4:130/57–58). I side with those scholars for whom these techniques provide an essential point of reference for many Daoist texts (see especially LaFargue 1994; Roth 1999). In particular, the techniques provide essential context for early Daoist appeals to cosmogony, which gain much of their point from attempts to reenact cosmic beginnings through a return to the source of things. For example, we read in *Dàodéjīng* 52, "The world has a beginning, we take it to be the mother of the world. Having attained the mother one thereby knows the children. Having known the children, one returns to guard the mother." The children here are presumably the ten thousand things. By returning to the cosmic mother, one knows these things and is thus able to respond to them appropriately. The return is what makes it possible to float with the ancestor, and thus to practice *dào* that goes beyond skill. In effect, the adept joins in the *dào* of the mother or of the ancestor, the *dào* whereby the ten thousand things emerge.

If this would be a literal joining, and the aim was to merge with the mother's or ancestor's *dào*, then *dào* that goes beyond skill just is the *dào* by which things arise. That these are the same *dào* is independently plausible both from the language of passages describing a return to the source of things and because of obvious analogies between them: their spontaneity, appropriateness, and so on. We have thus found a clear sense in which a way of acting produces things.

Dào as a Thing

If it made sense for early Daoists to think of the ancestor's *dào* or the mother's *dào* as a way of acting, then what about the ancestor or mother herself? This would be an entity distinct from and somehow responsible for the cosmic process, a true maker of things (*zào wù zhě* 造物者).[21] Such a maker could not itself be a way of acting, yet there is reason to think that some Daoists nonetheless thought of it as *dào*.

This is plainest in *Dàodéjīng* 25 and 21, which explicitly refer to *dào* as a thing (*wù* 物), the first certainly in a cosmogonic context. We cannot explain these usages by identifying *dào* with the cosmic process, because as a thing *dào* would have to be distinct from that process; it would have to be not the mother's *dào* but the mother herself.

One way to address this issue is to deny that "*wù*" means "thing" in these passages. Ames and Hall take this approach in their translation of the *Dàodéjīng* (2003, 107 and 115), arguing that *Dàodéjīng* authors privileged continuity over discreteness, did not take *wù* to be static, and did not conceive of *wù* in terms of substance. They infer that, in these passages, *wù* are processes or events rather than things (2003, 67).

This argument is weak. The continuity/discreteness distinction is irrelevant to the process/thing distinction (though it may be relevant to the mass/count distinction). Things are rarely, if ever, static (though *Dàodéjīng* 25 seems to say that one *wù*, namely *dào*, "does not change"). And unless Ames and Hall use "substance" simply as a synonym for "thing," it is by no means obvious that things should be accounted for in terms of substance (they certainly have not always been accounted for that way in the Western tradition). Early Chinese uses of "*wù*" actually match those of "thing" very closely, with two main differences: "*wù*" could be used specifically of living things, and when individuation was not implied "*wù*" meant "stuff" rather than "thing" (Robins 2000, especially 168–69).[22]

The passages that call *dào* a thing must instead presuppose a reification. The way things take shape would count naturally as *dào*, the cosmic *dào*. Reifying this way, the *Dàodéjīng* comes to use "*dào*" also as a term for a thing somehow responsible for the course taken by the cosmic *dào*. The result was a shift in meaning, but an intelligible one. The shift would have been all the more intelligible if, as is likely, some Daoists independently believed in a cosmic mother. Such a belief could have derived from religious cosmology or from meditative experience (likely both) and would have made it easier to think of *dào* as mother: the reification would have involved a reconceptualization but would not have required belief in anything new.

Reified, *dào* could no longer be identified with a way of acting. It would instead have to be something that sustains a way of acting, perhaps an agent of some sort. This does not undermine the conclusions reached above, however, for the passages that equate ancestral *dào* with a way of acting are not among those that call ancestral *dào* a thing, and can easily be read as describing the process of cosmic generation and not a thing distinct from and somehow responsible for that process. For example, Book 6 of the *Zhuāngzǐ* tells us about the process that gives rise to heaven and earth (and says, quite reasonably, that this process has been taking place since before there were heaven and earth). This is *dào* that goes beyond skill, and it is distinct from any mother or ancestor.

Thinging Things

If there is a cosmic mother or ancestor distinct from and responsible for the cosmic process, then the cosmic process does not itself proceed spontaneously (*zìrán* 自然, of itself). Daoists who believed in a cosmic mother therefore faced a tension. *Dàodéjīng* 25 acknowledges the tension when it says that "*dào* models itself after spontaneity": to model oneself after something is precisely not to be spontaneous, and it can only be as a thing distinct from the cosmic process that *dào* is not already spontaneous.

This may be why the texts are so hesitant about calling *dào* a thing. The author of *Dàodéjīng* 25, admitting that he does not know what to call the mother of heaven and earth, introduces "*dào*" as a formal style name, a 字 *zì Zhuāngzǐ*, rather than as a more familiar *míng* 名. This, then, was not a standard use of "*dào*," and it does not put us on familiar terms with the cosmic mother.[23] *Dàodéjīng* 21 is more direct, saying, "*Dào* as a thing — unclear! indistinct!" In other words, we risk confusion when trying to think of *dào* as a thing. But this is precisely what *Dàodéjīng* 25 attempts when it refers to the cosmic mother as *dào*.

A passage from Book 22 of the *Zhuāngzǐ* registers this issue in a particularly interesting way. It says, "There something produced before heaven and earth. Is it a thing? What things things is not a thing" (22:844/246). We find similar language in Book 4, in which the great tree says to Carpenter Shí, "You and I are both things, what can we do about thinging one another?" (4:151/64). And when the passage about the worthless goose from Book 20 describes floating along with the ancestor, it asks, "Thinging things but not being thinged by things, how could one then manage to get entangled?" (20:720/210). These passages imply that it is a mistake to think of ancestral *dào* as a thing, because ancestral *dào* is what produces things in the first place.

Or more precisely, ancestral *dào* is what things things. This is most naturally read as a causal use of the word "*wù* 物." To thing something, then, is to cause it to be a thing. We might think of this as more a shaping than a creating, but we must be careful. The issue is unlikely to be individuation, a separating off of individual things from the cosmic stuff, since *wù* functions here as a mass noun: no individuation is implied. (I suppose "stuffing stuff but not being stuffed by stuff" would be more literal, if even more confusing.)

A more promising way forward is suggested by the passages from Books 4 and 20. In both, the worry is that if we get entangled in the *dào* of other creatures, then we will end up getting used in ways that are bad for us. It is this entanglement that they describe as being thinged. To thing something, then, is to fit it into a *dào* for using it; things emerge as things by becoming resources for different ways of acting. This complicates the idea, discussed above, that ways of acting are built into situations, because it makes things and ways mutually dependent. As we join in with ancestral *dào*, we take part not only in the production of things but also in the pouring out of *dào*.

Given that what things things is not itself a thing, in joining with ancestral *dào* we cease being things. This is an ideal of going beyond skill that surpasses anything claimed by Kitchen Dīng or even the swimmer, because it involves more than just adaptation to ways that are already present. Among people, perhaps this amounts to a kind of charismatic power that enables one to shape other people's ways. This indeed is the sort of power in which Confucius instructs Yán Huí in Book 4 of the *Zhuāngzǐ*, and we might even see an echo here of the idea (from *Analects* 2:12) that the gentleman does not serve as an implement (*qì* 器). Perhaps when applied to things more generally, the ideal implies a kind of creativity that allows one to find new ways of using things, as with Zhuāngzǐ's advice to Huìzǐ about how to use the enormous gourd. But it is hard to believe that the ideal does not call for something more than this, something much harder to swallow.

Whatever we make of it, it is one of a family of Daoist views all centered on the idea of *dào* that goes beyond skill. This idea has a clear basis in our everyday experience of skilled (and even not-so-skilled) behavior. It appears to have fascinated many Daoists, as witness (for example) the many depictions of skilled behavior in the *Zhuāngzǐ*, most of which I have not mentioned here. And I hope I have shown that focusing on this idea helps make sense of a variety of otherwise puzzling Daoist texts and views.

Notes

1. The *dào* that can be passed on but not received might be, for example, teachings about the *dào* that produces heaven and earth or mystical union with that *dào*. Neither

possibility avoids the sort of puzzle raised in the main text, however, for it remains unclear how a teaching or a mystical union could produce heaven and earth.

2. The line is often parsed as if "可道 (can be *dào*ed)" were a relative clause ("[*dào*] that can be *dào*ed"), but there is no relative clause in the Chinese (that would be "可道之道" or, perhaps, "道之可道者").
3. See especially Hansen (2003) and Hansen's chapter in this volume.
4. Citations to the *Zhuāngzǐ* provide the book number and page references to Wáng (1988) and Watson (1968).
5. Contrast *Xúnzǐ* 荀子 17.11/379. Citations to the *Xúnzǐ* provide section numbers within Knoblock (1988–94) and page references to Lǐ (1979).
6. This is, then, an objection by counterexample to the arguments of Book 4. Intriguingly, the objection is associated with Zhuāngzǐ himself, who is not mentioned in Book 4. Indeed, in all other passages that depict Zhuāngzǐ discussing uselessness, he argues that something (such as Huìzǐ's big gourd) that seems useless given conventional expectations and goals actually does have a use (see 1:32–37/34–35, 26:1071/299) (and Huìzǐ smashes his big gourd precisely because he considers it useless). This is a rather different view of uselessness from the one defended in Book 4. Superficially, at least, the two views are actually inconsistent. Could the passage from Book 20 be an attempt by one Zhuāngist author or group to show that another holds a mistaken view about uselessness? Certainly nothing we know about the textual history of the *Zhuāngzǐ* contradicts this conjecture.
7. I raise a complication for this reading in the section below entitled "The Great Ancestor."
8. "*Dīng* 丁" may be an indication of rank ("fourth grade") rather than a proper name.
9. Hansen mistranslates this line (1992, 287) as "What I care about is a *dao* which advances my skill." This misconstrues the syntax of the Chinese, which incorporates no relative clause, and "*jìn hū* 進乎" means *go beyond*, not *advance, move forward*. This mistranslation is essential to Hansen's treatment of the passage, but not, I think, to his broader interpretive claims.
10. My translation of "*zú* 族" as "knotty" is based on Guō Xiàng's gloss of it as "交錯聚結 (things interlocking and getting knotted together)." See Wáng (1988, 108 n.14).
11. See also Xúnzi's statement that "with spirit, none is greater than transforming to *dào*" (*Xúnzǐ* 1/2:2). (Of course, Xúnzǐ has in mind a very different sort of *dào*.)
12. This sentence is difficult to parse. An alternative translation would be, "Only *dào* collects emptiness," which perhaps also yields sense. For discussion, see Fraser (2008, 143–44 n.13).
13. My discussion of this book owes a great deal to Hansen (1983) and to many conversations with Hansen and with Chris Fraser.
14. If he really were treating all things as the same, it could not matter to him whether the monkeys are pleased or angry, or how many nuts each monkey gets each day. Why not four in the morning and four in the evening?
15. See *Mòzǐ* 35:394/182–83, 36:406/189, 37:415/195, and *Guǎnzǐ* 6:29. Citations to *Mòzǐ* provide the book number and page references to Wú (2006) and Mei (1973). Citations to *Guǎnzǐ* provide the book number and page references to Dài (1954).

16. Compare the use of the expression "heavenly *ní* (天倪)" at *Zhuāngzǐ* 2:91/48 and 27:1089–90/303–5. (It is a difficult question how exactly to understand the "*ní* 倪." Watson gives "equality"; Chén Gǔyìng gives "*fēnjì* 分際 [divisions, borders].")
17. The Chinese here reads, "唯其好之也以異於彼其好之也欲以明之彼非所明而明之." This is difficult to parse, and the whole passage is odd on literary grounds (for example, in its lack of any closing comment about Master Kuàng, the conductor); we may be dealing here with fragments. The interpretation in the main text is common. See, for example, Liú (1999, 53–54) and Guō (1961, 77 n. 12–14).
18. Contrast the anecdote about Wheelwright Biǎn (*Zhuāngzǐ* 13:498–99/152–53). Biǎn takes his inability to teach his skill to his son to show that true skill cannot be passed on in language and therefore that we should not try to learn from the transmitted words of ancient sages: he questions the value of language but not of skill. In the passage from Book 2, however, the fact that one cannot communicate one's understanding to others motivates pessimism precisely about skill.
19. "*Chōng* 沖 (pour out)" is often read as "*zhōng* 盅 (cup)" here, and taken to refer to the emptiness within a cup and mean *empty*. (This interpretation goes back at least as far as the *Shuōwén jiězì* [see Xǔ 1963, 104].) This is hard to square with the next clause, which is usually taken to say (with some grammatical awkwardness) that when we use *dào* it does not get filled or does not need refilling — but then *dào* would not be at all like an empty cup.
20. On the alternative reading sketched in note 19, *Dàodéjīng* 4 probably does characterize the ancestor as *dào*.
21. Though this expression, taken out of context, could refer to the making of things rather than their maker, it is consistently used for a being of some sort. See *Zhuāngzǐ* 6:241/84, 6:250/87, 6:264/90, 7:281/93, 32:1259/355.
22. Might the frequent use of "*wù*" as a mass noun be significant here? Certainly "*dào*" must be a mass noun when *Dàodéjīng* 42 tells us that *dào* produces the one, and thus that *dào* itself is not individuated. That passage does not, however, refer to *dào* as *wù*, and I cannot see how thinking of *dào* as stuff would raise fewer or even different puzzles than thinking of it as a thing.
23. Angle and Gordon interpret the use of "*zǐ*" here by analogy with nicknaming, "*dào*" making sense as a nickname because the cosmic mother "is something on which one can model, something that one can, in a sense, follow," even though it is not literally *dào* (2003, 20). This implies that some passages (notably the first line of the *Dàodéjīng*) move back and forth between literal and nicknaming uses of the word "*dào*" (Angle and Gordon 2003, 24–25). However, this strategy will not work with the passage from Book 6 of the *Zhuāngzǐ* quoted at the beginning of this essay, in which "*dào*" occurs only once. Nonetheless, Angle and Gordon's conclusions are in broad agreement with my own.

References

Ames, R., and D. Hall, trans. 2003. *Daodejing: A philosophical translation*. New York: Ballantine Books.

Analects 論語. Citations provide standard section numbers, as in, for example, Lau 1979.

Angle, S., and J. Gordon. 2003. "*Dao*" as a nickname. *Asian Philosophy* 13 (1): 15–27.

Chén G. 陳鼓應. 1999. 莊子今註今譯 (Contemporary notes and glosses on *Zhuāngzǐ*), rev. ed. Taipei: Commercial Press.

Cline, E. 2008. Mirrors, minds, and metaphors. *Philosophy East and West* 58 (2): 337–57.

Dài W. 戴望, ed. 1954. 管子校正 (Comparative and corrected edition of *Guǎnzǐ*). Beijing: Zhōnghuá Shūjú.

Dàodéjīng 道德經. Citations provide verse numbers according to the traditional ordering, as in, for example, Lau 1963.

Fraser, C. 2008. Psychological emptiness in the *Zhuāngzǐ*. *Asian Philosophy* 18 (2): 123–47.

Graham, A. C. 1990. The background of the Mencian theory of human nature. In *Studies in Chinese philosophy and philosophical literature*, 7–66. Albany: State University of New York Press.

———. 2003. Chuang Tzu's essay on seeing things as equal. In *A companion to Angus C. Graham's Chuang Tzu*. 104–29. Honolulu: University of Hawai'i Press. (Originally published 1969–70.)

Guō Q. 郭慶藩, ed. 1961. 莊子集釋 (Collected explanations of *Zhuāngzǐ*). 4 vols. Beijing: Zhōnghuá.

Hansen, C. 1983. A *tao* of *tao* in Chuang-tzu. In *Experimental essays on Chuang-tzu. Asian Studies at Hawaii* 29, ed. V. Mair. 24–55. Honolulu: University of Hawai'i Press.

———. 1992. *A Daoist theory of Chinese thought: A philosophical interpretation*. Oxford: Oxford University Press.

———. 2003. The metaphysics of *dao*. In *Comparative approaches to Chinese philosophy*, ed. B. Mou. 205–24. Aldershot: Ashgate.

Knoblock, J., trans. 1988–94. *Xunzi: A translation and study of the complete works*. 3 vols. Stanford, CA: Stanford University Press.

LaFargue, M. 1994. *Tao and method: A reasoned approach to the Tao Te Ching*. Albany: State University of New York Press.

Lau, D. C., trans. 1963. *Tao te ching*. London: Penguin.

———. trans. 1979. *The Analects*. London: Penguin.

Lǐ D. 李滌生, ed. 1979. 荀子集釋 (Collected explanations of *Xúnzǐ*). Taibei: Xuesheng.

Liú W. 劉武, ed. 1999. 莊子集解內篇補正 (Expanded and corrected edition of collected explications of the *Zhuāngzǐ* inner chapters). With 莊子集解 (Collected explications of the *Zhuāngzǐ*), ed. Wáng Xiānqiān 王先謙. Beijing: Zhōnghuá Shūjú.

Mair, V., ed. 1983. *Experimental essays on Chuang-tzu. Asian Studies at Hawaii* 29. Honolulu: University of Hawai'i Press.

Mei, Y., trans. 1973. *The ethical and political works of Motse*. Reprint. Westport, CT: Hyperion Press. (Originally published 1929).

Oshima, H. 1983. A metaphorical analysis of the concept of mind in the *Chuang-tzu*. In *Experimental essays on Chuang-tzu. Asian Studies at Hawaii* 29, ed. V. Mair. 63–84. Honolulu: University of Hawai'i Press.

Robins, D. 2000. Mass nouns and count nouns in classical Chinese. *Early China* 25: 147–84.

Roth, H. 1999. The *Laozi* in the context of early Daoist mystical praxis. In *Religious and philosophical aspects of the Laozi*, ed. M. Csikszentmihaly and P. Ivanhoe. Albany: State University of New York Press.

Wáng S. 王叔岷, ed. 1988. 莊子校詮 (Comparative interpretations of *Zhuāngzǐ*). Taibei: Institute of History and Language, Academia Sinica.

Watson, B., trans. 1968. *The complete works of Chuang Tzu*. New York: Columbia University Press.

Wú Y. 吳毓江, ed. 2006. *Mòzǐ jiàozhù* 墨子校注 (Comparative annotations to *Mòzǐ*). 2 vols. Beijing: Zhōnghuá Shūjú.

Xǔ S. 許慎. 1963. 説文解字 (Explanations of words and phrases). Beijing: Zhōnghuá Shūjú.

6
The Sounds of *Zhèngmíng*:
Setting Names Straight in Early Chinese Texts

Jane Geaney

In early Chinese texts, straightness often indicates correctness, hence many things are said to be *zhèng* 正.[1] But among them, only *zhèngmíng* 正名 emerged as a rhetorical slogan promising the production of order and elimination of human confusion and fakeness.[2] In scholarship on Chinese ethics, the slogan is usually understood as working toward these goals by making behavior accord with names or by making "names" (norms or social roles) accord with behavior. By contrast, on the assumption that uses of the term "*míng*" (name/title/fame) involved what something is *called* or what is *heard* about it, the chapter focuses on interpreting *zhèngmíng* in light of ideas about speech, music, tones, and sound in general — items that are distinct from, but related to, *míng* 名.[3] The chapter considers *zhèngmíng* as part of a textual tradition wherein recurring poetic "sound-effects" appear in a variety of genres. In light of this context, it argues that the power of the sovereign's *zhèngmíng* stems from participating in such effects.

The "*zhèngmíng*" chapter of the *Xúnzǐ* 荀子 provides a useful starting point for this investigation, with its claim that *míng* have "certain goodness" (*yǒugùshàn* 有固善). The chapter notes that *míng* that are good (and presumably "straight") are, among other things, non-contrary (*bùfú* 不拂).[4] Because the same chapter also asserts that the relation of names to their *shí* 實 is based on conventions — rather than some "certain" (*gù*) relation (*wúgùshí* 無固實) — it is not possible to interpret this as a claim that names' goodness consists of not being contrary to *shí*.[5] Moreover, mere compliance with conventions cannot be what makes names good, because the text calls for the rejection of some (presumably conventional) names on the grounds that they were not authorized (*shàn* 擅).[6] Hence this chapter explores the unanswered puzzle:

What makes names good or straight? It argues that the factors that make names straight include being limited in sonorous quantity (in relation to their visible counterparts) and being in accord with other name-sounds.[7] As a result, much as sovereigns concern themselves with selecting the music to which they expose their subjects, so too they must choose suitable *míng* that can be readily heard and obeyed. This interpretation of *zhèngmíng* makes the slogan part of the obligation to rule, not through active force but through harmonious "influences of air" — songs, winds, and virtue (*dé* 德) — that penetrate human subjects through hearing and smelling (*wén* 聞).[8] This apparently forceless, yet commanding, form of governance is the context in which a good ruler might hope to use *zhèngmíng* to eradicate falseness and confusion, thereby producing an orderly society.

Míng and Writing

This interpretation builds on the idea that early Chinese texts tend to use the term "*míng*" for something that is spoken or heard, a position that I argue for elsewhere.[9] In addition, this chapter presupposes arguments I have made elsewhere regarding balanced aural/visual contrasts as being a constant and crucial feature of early Chinese conceptions about the world. Thus, assuming that *míng* is aural means that it is aligned with other aural aspects of the cosmos in the context of a powerful tendency to seek aural/visual balance.[10]

Interpreters since Zhèng Xuǎn 鄭玄 (127–200 CE) have sometimes taken early uses of *zhèngmíng* as pertaining to writing per se, with the result that *zhèngmíng* is understood to mean doing something to graphs.[11] If indeed uses of *zhèngmíng* in early Chinese texts can be interpreted as being about graphs, then the slogan could concern establishing appropriate orthography, i.e., writing the standardized graphs might be *zhèngmíng*. Currently that interpretation of *zhèngmíng* is rarely applied specifically to the *Analects*, but it is employed for understanding the slogan generally in early Chinese texts.[12] In the interests of brevity, I will introduce a single, but decisive, piece of evidence that the term "*míng*" was normally understood in early China to be oral/aural.[13] This evidence comes from among references to the physical process of writing, which are uncommon in early texts but emerged with the greater expansion of literacy. (As later texts indicate, straightening out writing is one thing; straightening out names [*zhèngmíng*] is another.)[14] The example occurs in the *Kǒngcóngzǐ*'s memorial of Jì Yàn 季彥 (d. 124 CE), the ideal descendant of Confucius. As soon as Jì Yàn lets his brush drop to the page, his writing achieves form, falling into a state of completion. So, too, what he "spews" (so to speak) into speech are *míng* that are *zhèng*.

The very moment he lowered his brush, his writing took shape in perfectly formed injunction and the speech he uttered could not but straighten out names and embody principles.[15] (*Kǒngcóngzǐ* 7.2, ch. 23)

In this physical description, *zhèngmíng* does not involve writing. That is, the movements by which the brush drops do not produce *míng* in this passage.[16] On the contrary, these *míng* spring from the genuineness of "spit out" speech. With such evidence in mind, this chapter proceeds with one assumption about uses of "*zhèngmíng*": the term is understood to be oral/aural and does not concern doing anything to graphs.

Overlaps in Discursive and Musical Sonority

The prestige with which early Chinese texts regard music is well known, but it is less often noted that the potency of *yuè* 樂 ("music") is rooted in the way sound enters the body. In other words, the transformative power of music stems from its peculiarly penetrative capacity, which belongs to sound in general.[17] As Roel Sterckx argues, the "performative effects of music" are part of a cosmology centered on reciprocal reactions, wherein music moves on air to transform the wilds into civilization (2000, 30). In this conception, all sound moves on air and penetrates bodies. As Sterckx puts it, early Chinese texts "associate human sagacity with the ability to penetrate (*tōng* 通) the masses through the medium of sound, an idea also reflected in the occurrence of the term *shēng* 聲 ('sound,' 'reputation,' or 'aura') as a paronomastic gloss for *shèng* 聖 'human sage'" (2000, 4). This power of sonority explains why in some cases animals are described as transformed by music (*yuè*), even though they only "know" sounds (*shēng*), according to the "*Yuèjì*" 樂記. This general feature of sound also explains why the repeated claims about sound "entering" and "penetrating" are not limited to claims about *yuè*. For example, the *Xìngzìmìngchū* 性自命出 notes that sound (*shēng*) enters and stirs people's heartminds "thickly" (*hòu* 厚). The *Xúnzǐ* argues that "sound and music" (*shēngyuè* 聲樂) enter deeply, while the *Shuō Yuàn* 說苑 contends that "sound and tones" (*shēngyīn* 聲音) enter more deeply than anything else.[18] If these graphs from the *Xúnzǐ* and the *Shuō Yuàn* were reversed, we might conclude that the subject is only "musical sound" or "tonal sound," but instead it seems deliberately broader. Hence when Confucius advocates banishing the music of Zhèng 鄭, it is not *yuè* per se but sounds that he indicts as "overflowing" (*yín* 淫).[19]

> As for music (*yuè*), adopt the Sháo 韶 and the Wǔ 舞. Banish the sounds (*shēng*) of the Zhèng and keep glib people at a distance. The sounds of Zhèng are overflowing (*yín* 淫) and glib people are dangerous. (*Analects* 15:11)

Steven Van Zoeren interprets this criticism as aimed at the musical performance itself, as opposed to the lyrics.[20] Indeed, the passage's denunciation is explicitly directed at sound (*shēng*). But one need not posit that "sound" excludes lyrics or discursive sound in this context, since the use of the graph *shēng* can encompass both the sound of speech and that of music. Moreover, the passage's shift in topic from the *shēng* of the Zhèng to the danger of glibness — a shift that recurs in the condemnation of Zhèng sounds in *Analects* 17:18 — indicates that the target of Confucius's concern is sound in a broad sense. Improper sonority in general is damaging to human character because of its penetrative capacity. A series of semantic overlaps in the use of terminology related to hearing reinforces the breadth of this concern: *yīn* 音 and *shēng* 聲, as both "music" and "voice"; *fēng* 風, as both "wind" and "song"; and *wén* 聞, as both "hear" and "smell." That is, in a general way, music, voice, and song are all items that travel on air or wind to penetrate deeply through the body's holes by means of hearing and smelling. A rigid demarcation between musical and discursive sound is not likely, since both of them penetrate bodies through the same means.

Moreover, insofar as comments in early Chinese texts about sonorous penetration reflect a general pattern of aural/visual couplets, they do not exclude discursive sound. In the case of sound penetration, the relevant aural/visual pattern is that sound operates on the inside of the person as distinct from visual items, like ritual, operating on the outside. The *Lǐjì* 禮記 makes this claim about music (*yuè*), which it contrasts to ritual emerging from a person's inside.[21] But the claim in the *Shuō Yuàn* is more expansive: "sounds and tones" (*shēngyīn*) are best for straightening out the inside. As the aural/visual contrast entails, the *Shuō Yuàn* also mentions that ritual is appropriate for straightening the outside.

> Of the things that enter from outside, none penetrates more deeply than sounds and tones, and none affects people more extremely . . . Therefore the gentleman uses ritual to straighten the outside and music to straighten the inside (以禮正外，以樂正內).[22] (*Shuō Yuàn* 19:43)

The logic of this passage seems to be that, because sounds and tones in general penetrate deeply, musical sound is useful for transforming human interiors. In other words, the reason music is associated with the inside is that it operates aurally. This is borne out by the aural/visual contrast in the *Fǎ Yán* 法言. In its explanation of the nature of seeing and hearing, the *Fǎ Yán* says:

> In giving birth to people, heaven makes their eyes and ears able to see and hear. Thus, what people look at is ritual and what people listen to is music.[23] (*Fǎ Yán* 4)

In light of the contrasts between interiority and exteriority discussed above, the implication of this statement that music epitomizes sounds sensed by the ears helps clarify that it is specifically because it is audible that music pertains to interiority. Thus the contrast that the texts seem to emphasize is between (inwardly operative) sound and (outwardly operative) vision, not between music and some other form of sound.

It is because sound pertains to interiority that early Chinese texts present moral instruction as a matter of aural internalization. Learning is a process of hearing, internalizing, and embodying in action. For example, the *Shuō Yuàn* (16:179) and the *Xúnzǐ* (Book 1) describe instruction as something entering the ears, being stored in the heartmind, and then manifested in action. While such passages are vague about the extent to which the sonorous education entering the ears is musical, the instruction is explicitly musical when rulers initiate music-making in early Chinese texts. Rulers take an exceptional interest in the socially regulative function of music, installing music directors and commanding that music be created. According to Kenneth DeWoskin, in early China, the five tones required a fixed pitch, and "control over the moment and pitch at which music began was control of the entire performance" (1982, 44, 48). Hence, ethical rulers authorized music and thereby metaphorically established the pitch (*Lǔshì Chūnqiū* 呂氏春秋 22.6, 5.4). It is not surprising that their instruction was musical since, as Michael Nylan points out, the visual pun connecting music (*yuè* 樂) to joy (*lè* 樂) is a reminder that studying through music is a most palatable way of imbibing instruction (2001, 100). But this means that, even if the ethical learning described as entering the ears in the *Shuō Yuàn* and the *Xúnzǐ* is best understood as discursive or argument-based, it was likely to have capitalized on the benefits of sonorous rhetorical devices. With internalizing sound as the optimal method for moral instruction, it would be neither necessary nor useful to posit any firm distinction between musical and discursive instruction.

The odes (*shī* 詩) are a compelling example of the difficulty of positing a rigid distinction between discursive and musical sonority.[24] As implied by Confucius's "refined speaking" (*yǎyán* 雅言) of the odes, their sonorous effects were important. Indeed, Van Zoeren argues that, at an early stage, Chinese texts understood the odes primarily in terms of their sonority (1991, 28–35). This is plausible not only because the odes were metered and rhythmic but also because they were performed to music and perhaps even sung with special pronunciation and in a special key (Nylan 2001, 91). Moreover, the claim in the *Shū Jīng* 書經 that, from its very inception, the sovereign's music (*yuè*) involved *shī*, counters any presumption that early Chinese texts strictly differentiate *yuè* from sound that involves speech. In the *Shū Jīng*'s story of the appointment of Kuí 夔 as music master, it is metered, rhymed, and sung speech that is at issue. The passage emphasizes the role of speaking by noting that the music master will operate via the method of making *shī* "speak" (*yán* 言) the heartmind's aims:

> Kui! I appoint you Overseer of Music (*yuè*) and to teach our sons. . . .
> The odes speak (*yán* 言) of aims, singing elongates this speech (*yán*), sound (*shēng* 聲) relies on that elongation, and pitch-pipes harmonize sound (*shēng*). (*Shū Jīng* 2)

Thus, the odes, as "measured songs," are inextricably linked to "music" (Picken 1977, 88–89). Moreover, "musical conversation" is part of what the *Zhōulǐ* 周禮 presents as the task of the Music Master:

> [The Grand Music Master shall] employ "musical *dé*" (*yuèdé* 樂德 musical virtue? musical charisma?) to instruct the sons of people of rank in uprightness, harmoniousness, respect, constancy, filial piety, and friendship. [He shall] use "musical conversation" (*yuèyǔ* 樂語) to teach them stimulus (*xīng* 興), exposition (*dào* 道), admonition (*fèng* 諷), praise (*sòng* 誦), speech (*yán* 言), and conversation (*yǔ* 語).[25] (*Zhōulǐ* 3)

The passage attests that musical conversation is a technology that can be used to teach a variety of other discursive skills: speaking (*yán*) being only the most obvious.[26] Thus, as these uses of the odes indicate, moral instruction appears likely to include a combination of musical and discursive aspects.

The freedom with which early Chinese texts interpret the odes also indirectly points to the importance of their sound. When excavated texts cite the odes, they frequently use homophonous sounds but different graphs, which leads Martin Kern to conclude that "the highly archaic and poetic language of the Odes was . . . open to numerous possibilities of understanding" (2007, 783). Because the writing system was unstable, while the sounds of the words were not, the auditory aspects of the words could easily have seemed more important than any particular semantic aspect. This could explain why specific semantic content does not seem to have been the criterion for appropriate usage of the odes. Many early Chinese texts show the odes being interpreted in ways that are suited to whatever point needed to be made.[27] In spite of stories about the odes originating in folk songs and being adapted by blind musicians in the service of rulers, there seems to be no presumption that successful use of them required reconstructing those "original meanings." As Haun Saussy puts it, the odes served as a "poetics of quotation" — a means by which to express one's *own* intent by properly reciting the words of others (1993, 64). Thus, to the extent that early Chinese texts seem unperturbed by attributing varying semantic content to the odes, it does not appear that a lot hinged on any specific semantic content. Perhaps what mattered more was how they were, in Van Zoeren's words, "crooned or chanted in a rhythmic and singsong fashion" (1991, 40), which contributed to whatever they were thought to express (or betray).[28]

The "Musical" Aspects of *Míng*

Taking this a step further, sonority might have been important in other genres besides *shī* 詩. If, as the *Zhōulǐ* puts it, "musical conversation" facilitates teaching both speech (*yán* 言) and conversation (*yǔ* 語), then it does not seem far-fetched to posit that sound would be relevant in ostensibly argument-based texts. Wolfgang Behr contends that "aurally effective devices" figure heavily in pre-Qin philosophical prose. While "rhyming nets" and "assonance chains" characterize earlier texts, he notes that, by the fourth century BCE, texts like the *Lǜshì Chūnqiū* also began to feature "paronomastic cadence" and "symmetrical arrangements of lexical roots" (2005a, 26). Behr describes paronomasia as becoming "extremely popular in late Warring States and Han philosophical discourse" (2005a, 28). He even sees a link between the use of paronomasia and musical metaphors for rulership:

> Musical metaphors such as the pitch pipe standards (*lǜ* 律) for the rule of law or the notes on the pentatonic scale for the basic social relationships abound. But it is not only through metaphors and more commonly, metonymy, that such arguments [about music as a means of appropriate rulership] are enhanced. Equally frequent is the device of paronomasia. (2005a, 28)

If, as Behr argues, rhymes, assonances, and paronomastic cadences appear in all sorts of texts that are not, strictly speaking, "musical," sonorous techniques of rulership need not be limited to music per se.

Indeed, wherever aurally effective devices appear in early Chinese texts, there is no reason to expect they were not seen as pertaining to the *míng* in the text. Meaningful utterances were seen as containing *míng* (although it is not clear whether every minimal signifying unit of an utterance was understood to be a *míng*).[29] Insofar as *míng* are relatively short, by themselves they cannot be described as having rhythm or creating rhyme, assonance, or paronomastic cadences, but through their use in sound-correlated figures they can echo other *míng*. (For example, the slogan "*zhèngmíng*" itself is used to resonate through associations of that sort. The *Analects* 12:17 explicates *zhèng* 政 through *zhèng* 正, and *míng* 名 is often written with *míng* 命, while the *Zhuāngzǐ* 4 and

Zhuāngzǐ 5 write it as *míng* 鳴.)³⁰ This may shed light on the recommendation of *Analects* 17:9 to study the odes for greater knowledge of the *míng* of birds, animals, grasses, and trees. Since the odes were in an archaic language, it is unlikely that they would be employed to teach students the current names of entities with which they were unfamiliar. Instead, learning *míng* by reciting the odes would foster acquisition of refined pronunciation. Such knowledge would enhance one's ability to manipulate the poetic devices required to incisively "cap" a situation (whether in official service or at home, as the passage notes). Thus, it would be important to listen and reproduce proper ancient *míng* in order to enhance one's skill in wielding resonant sounds.

Implied in this phenomenon of learning ancient pronunciations is the possibility that actual features of linguistic usage might help to account for the texts' repeated suggestion that sounds that were once *zhèng* in ages past have now become confused. This declension narrative applies to *míng* as well as to music — an impression reinforced by a shared use of terminology to describe them. For instance, *Xúnzǐ* 20 explains that "corrupt tones" (*xiéyīn* 邪音) have made refined sounds "chaotic" (*luàn* 亂), just as *Xúnzǐ* 22 notes that "corrupt spoken explanations" (*xiéshuō* 邪說) have made *zhèngmíng* "chaotic." *Lǚshì Chūnqiū* 6.3 contrasts the gentleman's emission of music through *zhèngdé* (正德以出樂) with "music that has overflowed" (*yuèyín* 樂淫), which it associates with the sounds of Zhèng and Wèi (鄭衛之聲). Using similar rhetoric, the *Lǚshì Chūnqiū* employs the term "*yín*" 淫 to depict the form of speech that has destroyed *zhèngmíng*. If *míng* are *zhèng* then there is order.

> If *míng* are destroyed then there is chaos. What causes *míng* to become lost is overflowing (*yín*) "spoken explanations" (*shuō* 說). With overflowing spoken explanations, the acceptable can be unacceptable, what is so can become not so, and what is this can become not this. (16.8)

In the contexts of both music and *míng*, the perception is that overflowing sound blurs proper boundaries — a concern that might reflect historical changes in the use of sound.³¹ Laurence Picken speculates that the new repertory of Zhèng exhibited greater than usual irregularity in line rhythms (1977, 107), while DeWoskin, working with more recent archeological evidence, hypothesizes that Zhèng music featured a new scale that exceeded five tones (1982, 45). Like these musical innovations, the sound changes that occurred in linguistic usage in early China were not insignificant. The *Lǚshì Chūnqiū* indirectly notes this in its complaint that between the past and the present, speech has become different and legal statutes have diverged. Hence it adds:

The *míng* 命 (commands? terminology?) of old mostly do not communicate (不通) in the speech (*yán* 言) of today. (15.8)

Indeed, such linguistic confusion may have occurred. Analysis of phonological reconstructions, phonetic series, and *Shī Jīng* 詩經 rhymes have led historical linguists to posit that Old Chinese featured derivational morphologies wherein grammatical morphemes combined with lexical morphemes to convey certain aspects of meaning. Although it is impossible to determine when exactly the derivational affixes of Old Chinese disappeared from the language, Behr suggests that at least some would have still existed in the Warring States period and a memory of them would have persisted up to the Western Han.[32] Thus what might have been felt to be disappearing from the language were sounds that to some degree contributed to understanding *míng*. Moreover, the increasing use of paronomasia observed by Behr might constitute one attempt to compensate for this change in linguistic sound. While puns in the *Zhuāngzǐ* seem to celebrate the slippery play of meaningful sound, the puns in most early Chinese texts are generally presented as if they confirm its reliability. In light of this history, the *míng* that appeared to be "non-contrary" (*bùfú* 不拂) could have been those that resonated with other *míng* used in similar ways.

Another factor that might have been perceived as causing a decline into acoustic confusion was the mere proliferation of sound. In terms of confusion in music, whereas Picken's and DeWoskin's accounts focus on irregular rhythm and tone, the *Zuǒzhuàn* 左傳 (B10.1) implicates a quantitative form of sonorous excess: its example of *yínshēng* (淫聲) is playing the same music more than five times.[33] Something like this quantitative type of sonorous excess might be the target of the choice of "directness" (*jìng* 徑) as a criterion for goodness in names in *Xúnzǐ* 22. In fact, both the discussions of *zhèngmíng* in the *Xúnzǐ* and the *Lǚshì Chūnqiū* imply that the production of *míng* should be limited. This limit appears to be set by adherence to the visual *shí* 實 that they are supposed to match. *Xúnzǐ* 22 addresses the application of *míng* to appearance (*zhuàng* 狀) and location (*suǒ* 所), both of which pertain to visual perception. The number of names to be used depends on what the visual elements indicate about how many entities should be counted, as if for every (visible) action, event, or thing, there should be one *míng* and no more. The discussion of *zhèngmíng* in *Lǚshì Chūnqiū* 16.8 also notes that *míng* match "forms" (*xíng* 形), another visual term. Since the *Lǚshì Chūnqiū* discussion of *zhèngmíng* also emphasizes limiting the extension of *míng* (providing "only enough" [*zúyǐ* 足以] speech to accomplish particular goals), the concern seems to be that, unless otherwise checked, the number of *míng* tends to exceed that of their visual counterparts. From this perspective, keeping in mind that *zhèngmíng*'s failure is caused by an "overflowing" (*yín* 淫) form of speech, a *míng* that is *zhèng* is one that is "direct," that is, restrained by the count of visible entities. In its depiction of *zhèngmíng* as saying little while having one's orders enacted (言寡而令行，正名也), *Shīzǐ* 尸子 1.5 is a variation on this. (Since *Xúnzǐ* 27 describes *xíng* 行, in contrast to sound, as that which can be seen, *Shīzǐ* 1.5 can be read as an assertion that *míng* are *zhèng* when orders consisting of concise sounds produce visible actions.)[34] But it is worth noting that an emphasis on brevity in *zhèngmíng* need not imply a preference for silence. For instance, when *Lǚshì Chūnqiū* 16.8 presents *zhèngmíng* as the opposite of the ruler's inclination to use the name "*shì* 士" (gentleman) without knowing its "referent" (其所謂士), his ignorance about how to use "*shì*" is exposed no less by his repeated silence in "response" (*yìng* 應) to questions about "*shì*" than by his misuse of it. Thus, *zhèngmíng* implies responsive brevity, not silence, reflecting a tendency toward parallelism of aural and visual things. The required restraint in the apparently ever-proliferating amount of sound is supposed to be achieved through *zhèngmíng* being "direct" in relation to their visual correlates.

This analysis of *míng* as sound is equally applicable to its use as "fame." The fact that both *shēng* 聲 (sound) and *míng* are employed to mean "fame" signals that fame entails hearing sound. In this sense, the ruler's *míng* is expected to be as broadly audible as possible. References to a virtuous person's widespread *míng* rarely bother to qualify it with mention of its ethical status: the assumption is that it matches virtuous deeds.[35] When *míng* functions in this way as "long-distance sound," the implication is that it has power to create positive transformations in those who hear it. This feature of sound is epitomized by the sympathetic resonance in stringed instruments, which DeWoskin calls "a splendid example of accomplishment through nonaction" (1982, 74). As the initiator of sound, in setting the pitch, the ruler's reputation causes responsive actions. Being the source of his own *míng* (fame), he "sets the tone" that implicitly informs the world of his virtue and thereby transforms it.

These ways in which *míng* 名 participate in "sound effects" also help explain the role of *mìng* 命 (command, fate) in discussions of *zhèngmíng*. The interchanging of *míng* 名 and *mìng* 命 emphasizes that, in the process of instituting names and titles, the ruler also performatively commands. The "*Zhèngmíng*" chapter of the *Xúnzǐ* elaborates on this, both by asserting that the ruler's aims and intentions must be made clear so that his *mìng* 命 can be obeyed, and by suggesting that *míngcí* 名辭 (*míng* in conjunction with phrases) are capable of conveying these commands.[36] Hearing is a fitting metaphor for how such commands operate, because one cannot shut or even tighten one's ears. The penetration of sound through the ears suggests inescapable obedience.[37] One might say that the commanding tones of the ruler's naming penetrate the ears deeply enough so that the hearers must "listen" (*tīng* 聽) and obey their fate (*mìng* 命).[38] (Perhaps this explains the otherwise puzzling portrait in *Mencius* 7B:33 of the ideal "gentleman" as simply awaiting orders/fate.)[39] In

The Sounds of Zhèngmíng: *Setting Names Straight in Early Chinese Texts*   **135**

the same way that rhythm, melody, rhyme, and paronomasia create harmonious and orderly patterns, so too a tone of voice that is suitable for giving commands might facilitate rulership. Indeed, there are repeated references to the ruler himself being "quiet" (*jìng* 靜) as he issues *zhèngmíng*.[40] The implication might be that the ruler needs to avoid, for example, the impression of vehemence or brashness. Speaking his commands from tonal quietude might allow greater control of how his intentions are heard.

In a context where music is valued precisely because humans are susceptible to the sway of airs/winds, there is no reason to expect the resonant power of what enters the ears to be limited to non-discursive sounds. Sound in general penetrates human inwardness deeply. The degree to which early Chinese texts are structured by means of sound-based rhetorical devices suggests the measure of their awareness of these aspects of speech *as sound*. In such a context, the "straightening out" of discursive sound would be a potent force for prompting responses in both speech and action. Thus, the ethical ruler might simply be still and straighten out *míng*, because instruction that penetrates the body through air has the effect of gentle inevitability, like the wind bending the grass, or like fate itself.

NOTES

1. I am not proposing the "core meaning" of *zhèngmíng* in early Chinese texts, since that notion implies that meanings exist independent of the context of use and interpretation. Nevertheless, focusing on one consistent thread from early Chinese texts — the transformative potency of resonant sound — highlights something that is part of the relevant background for our (necessarily limited) attempts to reconstruct tendencies in the use of the slogan in the early Chinese period. The appropriateness of "straight" as a tentative translational equivalent of *zhèng* is suggested by the spatial metaphors for *zhèngmíng* and *zhèngyán* that emphasize the difference between direct fit and indirection through "leaning" (*yǐ* 倚) and "crookedness" (*wǎng* 枉). For the implications of standard translations of *zhèngmíng*, see Defoort (1997, 168–77). For other discussions of *zhèngmíng*, see Im (2008), Moeller (2000, 91–107), Makeham (1994), Defoort (1998, 111–18; 2003, 217–42), Creel (1974, 106–24), and Loy (2008).

   The source for my analysis is passages in early Chinese texts predominantly dating from the fourth century BCE to the first century BCE. Unless otherwise noted, all chapter numbers for Chinese texts in the original follow the Chinese University of Hong Kong CHinese ANcient Texts "CHANT" database. Unidentified translations are my own.

2. The significance of *zhèngmíng* for Confucius's own thought might be exaggerated, as Bryan Van Norden (2007, 82–96) argues, but these claims occur outside the *Analects*. Examples of such assertions about order include: "If names are straight, there is order" (名正則治, *Lǚshì Chūnqiū* 16.8); "straighten the names and [thereby?] order the things" (正名治物, *Sīmǎfǎ*

司馬法 1); "if names are straight and portions are clear, the masses will not be confused about the way" (名正分明則民不惑於道, *Guǎnzǐ* 管子 10); "Huángdì straightened the names of the hundred things to enlighten the masses to share the wealth" (黃帝正名百物以明民共財, *Lǐjì* 24); "Therefore in making the laws, the sages needed to render them clear and easy to understand, and with names straightened, the stupid and the knowledgeable were all able to understand them" (故聖人為法, 必使之明白易知, 名正, 愚知毲能知之, *Shāngjūnshū* 商君書 26); "with preservation of attentiveness and straightening out of names, falsity and deceit will cease" (守慎正名, 偽詐自止, *Guǎnzǐ* 15).

3. Given the broad range of understandings of "word," it is important to avoid using it as a translation of *míng*. It would be surprising if *míng* had been employed in early China in a way that resembles any understanding of "word" in modern linguistic theory or even in ordinary parlance. Moreover, uses of *yī yán* 一言 ("one unit of speech") as what we might call "one word" also complicate that reading. Hence, instead of treating "*zhèngmíng*" as something done to "words," this chapter approaches the slogan from a perspective that foregrounds *míng*'s most common uses: name, fame, and title. In addition to its use as names of persons broadly (including *xìng* 姓 and *hào* 號), and its use as "title" and "fame," "*míng*" is used to talk about names in the sense of special "terminology" or "technical terms." Evidence that *zhèngmíng* has implications for speech is famously apparent in the *Analects* 13:3, where it results in smooth speech.

4. The other things are "directness" (*jìng* 徑), which is discussed below, and "easiness" (*yì* 易), which I do not discuss because it is not specific enough to be informative about what constitutes goodness in names.

5. Standard translations of *shí* (實 (objects, actuality, reality, stuff) inevitably seem to present misleading implications about what it is that names name. They invoke what Bruno Latour (2004) calls "matters of fact," whose composition is unaffected by the very power of naming that this chapter explores. Hence I leave *shí* 實 untranslated.

6. *Xúnzǐ* 22 also notes that the appropriateness of naming conventions is not "certain" (*wúgùyí* 無固宜), so the conventions alone seem unlikely to produce "certain" goodness.

7. Roger Ames (2008) argues that, insofar as the production of meaning involves non-referential associations among names, *zhèngmíng* is a matter of regulating the way meaning operates through the associative power of language. In ethics, such an interpretation of *zhèngmíng* is an affirmation of relationality: just as the "meaning" of *míng* emerges through the context of echoed relationships with other *míng*, so too "meaningful" lives are created through particular relationships in resonance with their discursive communities.

8. "Influences of air" is Kenneth DeWoskin's expression (1982, 92). For a note on the significance of "smelling," see Nivison (1996, 24).

9. My argument is that the few uses of "*míng*" as meaning "graph" in early Chinese texts are aberrations that occurred as a result of the need to develop a term to indicate a single graph. See Geaney (2010).

10. For the argument that early Chinese texts feature an oral/aural conception of *míng*, see Geaney (2002, 109–35; 2010).

11. See Geaney (2010) for the limitations of Zhèng Xuǎn's interpretation of *míng* as "graph."
12. For instance, Chad Hansen maintains that what Confucian philosophers called the "rectification of names" was "following the sage's instructions, which were written in . . . characters" (1993, 393). Henry Rosemont reaches a similar conclusion regarding the use of *míng* to mean "graph" in the "*Zhèngmíng*" chapter of the *Xúnzǐ* on the basis of the idea that "good" names are graphs that look like what they signify (personal communication, Spring 2006).
13. See Geaney (2010) for a more detailed version of this argument.
14. The phrase "*zhèngzǐ* 正字" is not common, but it does occur in the first century *Hànshū* 漢書 and the second century *Tàipíng Jīng* 太平經, meaning something like "standard graphs."
15. Yoav Ariel translation, slightly modified (1996, 137).
16. This is not to claim that *míng* cannot be written, but the fact that *míng* are recorded does not mean that *míng* are graphs, any more than the graph for "action" refers to writing because "actions" can be written about.
17. The conception of music in the "*Yuèjì*," while not necessarily characteristic of the whole of the early Chinese period, seems to fit the broad definition proposed by John Blacking (1973, 3): "humanly organized sound." The "*Yuèjì*" explains that *yuè* is the first level in a hierarchy of sound that appears to be based on degrees of complexity — higher than *yīn* 音 (tone or tune) and *shēng* 聲 (sound or voice). Nevertheless, my interpretation of *yuè* as the highest form of humanly organized sound might need to be supplemented by the suggestion in the "*Yuèjì*" that visual elements that emerge after sound (shields, axes, plumes and ox tails) are also part of the technical requirements of *yuè*.
18. For the *Xìngzìmìngchū* examples, see *Guōdiàn Chǔmù Zhújiǎn* (Beijing: Wenwu, 1998), strips 23, 30–31, and 36; 180. See also *Xúnzǐ* 20 and *Shuō Yuàn* 19.43.
19. I gloss the term *yín* 淫 in note 33.
20. Van Zoeren (1991, 31). See also Nylan (2001, 90). Van Zoeren's claim is part of a thesis about the historical development from an early treatment of the odes as music to the Hàn 漢 habit of interpreting the *Odes* through textual exegesis. Although the development is undeniable, his argument does not notice the ways in which the term *yán* (which he calls "language") is presented as if its qualities were similar to, rather than opposed to, those of music.
21. The *Lǐjì* says, "Music emerges from the inside; ritual acts from the outside" (樂由中出, 禮自外作). It also says, "Therefore music is something that acts on the inside; ritual is something that acts on the outside" (故樂也者, 動於內者也; 禮也者, 動於外者也) (*Lǐjì* 19.1, *Shǐjì* 3.2).
22. My choice of a male-gendered translation for *jūnzǐ* is a deliberate historical reminder that the focus of concern about the *jūnzǐ* in early Chinese texts is generally not on female-bodied persons.
23. See also a slightly different comment in *Huáinánzǐ* 淮南子 1: "[His] eyes have never seen ritual and etiquette, and his ears have never heard the ancients or the past" (目未嘗見禮節, 耳未嘗聞先古).

24. I use the formula "the odes" to mean their pre-canonical state, as distinct from their later form as "The *Odes*."
25. Translation modified from Saussy (1993, 62).
26. A number of factors related to how *yán* 言 ("speech") functions make plausible the idea that speech and music intersect. The fact that animals are credited with the ability to speak (*yán*) is one hint that a fairly wide range of sonorous communication must count as *yán*. (See *Lǐjì* 1.6 and *Zhōulǐ* 5.24 and 5.26.) Moreover, that which *yán* seems to communicate — *yì* 意 — appears to involve something like the sounds of the heartmind (as suggested by its entry in the *Shuōwén Jiězì* and by the fact that it interchanges with *yīn* 音 ["tone"] in excavated manuscripts). As Chad Hansen argues, *yì* does not resemble mental concepts (1992, 76). The use of *yì* as well as *zhì* 志 in relation to *yán* makes speech resemble other means of expression, suggesting something along the lines of an overall "intent" or "aim," such as can be said of music and dance.
27. While the hermeneutic principles implied in *Mencius* 5A:4 and 5B:8 might be an exception, for the most part the interpretation of odes in the *Mencius* also seems fitted to suit the occasion. Moreover, in spite of calling the *Odes* a "classic," the *Xúnzǐ* treats determining their meaning as requiring little effort, with an attitude that suggests that questions about how to interpret them are not particularly complex or pressing. For the *Xúnzǐ*, it *is* a problem that the writings and rhythms of the very ancient sages are lost. Nevertheless, the contemporary gentleman seems to have no trouble manifesting the way of the Zhōu 周 through what he prizes in his behavior (*Xúnzi* 5).
28. Through an interpretation of *Zuǒzhuàn* B9.27.5 and B9.29.13, Martin Svensson Ekström posits that the difference between an iteration of the odes qua music and qua coded message is this:

    > As music, the *Odes* are transparent, non-manipulatable and reveal the corruption or virtue of their makers like a Freudian slip reveals the innermost secret of the neurotic. By contrast, when a person recites the *Odes* to "express his intentions" (言志 *yánzhì*), he is in full control of both himself and the poems that serve both to veil and disclose, whereas music presents him "warts and all." (2006, 84–85)

29. See note 3. In early Chinese texts, surnames, personal names, nicknames, and titles (not to mention reputations and terminology) are not necessarily monosyllabic. Still, "*míng*" generally seems to refer to smaller units of discursive sound than "*yán*," except perhaps some uses of "one *yán*" (*yīyán* 一言).
30. For a listing of some early Confucian uses of paronomasia, see Ames (2008, 37–43).
31. As DeWoskin notes (1982, 92), this corruptive "influence of airs" might account for the analogy in *Analects* 17:18 between the sounds of Zhèng and the way the color purple robs from vermillion.
32. However, Behr maintains that consciousness of language change is only a rare undercurrent in pre-Qín discourse about *zhèngmíng* (2005b, 17, 20–21).
33. These observations from Picken and DeWoskin are helpful because, while in the context of music, "*yín* 淫" has often been taken to mean licentious sexuality, that

reading is not plausible for explaining its effects on discursive sound. Indeed, it probably is not apt for music either. In *Zuǒzhuàn* B10.1, *yínshēng* (overflowing sound) is not sexual excess, but it fosters that excess through something like contagion.
34. "Speech can be heard and action can be seen" (言為可聞 行為可見) (*Xúnzǐ* 27).
35. The modification of *míng* by *yín* 淫 in *Guóyǔ* 7.7 is a rare and illuminating exception. The *yínmíng* 淫名 that is heard (*wén* 聞) throughout the world belongs to a power-usurping ruler who oversteps boundaries.
36. The chapter's distinction between *míng* 名 and *cí* 辭 is similar to that of the "Neo-Mohist Canons" 11.2 ("With names, pick *shí*; with *cí*, sift intentions" 以名舉實, 以辭抒意), as well as that of *Lǔshì Chūnqiū* 18.4.
37. By contrast, it might have been thought that even the pores can be tightened. See Kuriyama (1994, 37).
38. According to post-phenomenologist Don Ihde, such assessments of sound as penetrating appear in other languages, in which they are also linked to the notion of sound-as-command. Ihde writes:

> [H]earing and obeying are often united in root terms. The Latin *obaurdire* is literally meant as a *listening* "from below." It stands as a root source of the English *obey*. Sound in its commanding presence *in-vades* our experience . . . one's train of thought is likely to be upset by the "command" of the sound which is so penetrating or loud that he can't "hear" himself think. (1976, 81)

39. "Speech and conversation must be trustworthy, but not for the sake of correcting actions. The *jūnzǐ* enacts models in order to await orders/fate, and that is all" (言語必信, 非以正行也. 君子行法, 以俟命而已矣) (*Mencius* 7B:33).
40. *Hánfēizǐ* 韓非子 5, *Hánfēizǐ* 8, and *Shīzǐ* 1. See also *Jiǎyì Xīnshū* 賈誼新書 8.3. The term *jìng* 靜 is used to mean both "quiet" and "still," but, in light of the interchange of *yì* 意 with "tone" (*yīn* 音, see note 26), its use in conjunction with "empty" (*xū* 虛) in this formula also evokes the quiet tone of an empty heartmind.

References

Ames, R. 2008. Paronomasia: A Confucian way of making meaning. In *Confucius now: Contemporary encounters with the* Analects, ed. D. Jones. 37–48. Chicago, IL: Open Court.

Ariel, Y., trans. 1989. *K'ung-ts'ung-tzu: The K'ung family master's anthology*. Princeton, NJ: Princeton University Press.

Behr, W. 2005a. Three sound-correlated text structuring devices in pre-Qin philosophical prose. *Bochumer jahrbuch zur Ostasienforschung* 29: 15–33.

———. 2005b. Language change in premodern China: Notes on its perception and impact on the idea of a "Constant Way." In *Historical truth, historical criticism, and ideology: Chinese historiography and historical culture from a new comparative perspective*, ed. H. Schmidt-Glintzer, A. Mittag, and J. Rüsen. 13–52. Boston, MA: Brill.

Blacking, J. 1973. *How musical is man?* Seattle: University of Washington Press.

Creel, H. 1974. *Shen Pu-Hai: A Chinese political philosopher of the fourth century B.C.* Chicago, IL: University of Chicago Press.

Defoort, C. 1997. *Pheasant Cap Master: A rhetorical reading.* Albany, NY: SUNY Press.

———. 1998. The rhetorical power of naming: The case of regicide. *Asian Philosophy* 8 (2): 111–18.

———. 2001. Ruling the world with words: The idea of *zhèngmíng* in the *Shīzǐ*. *Bulletin of the Museum of Far Eastern Antiquities* 73: 217–42.

DeWoskin. K. 1982. *A song for one or two: Music and the concept of art in early China.* Ann Arbor: Center for Chinese Studies, University of Michigan Press.

Geaney, J. 2002. *On the epistemology of the senses in early Chinese thought.* Honolulu: University of Hawai'i Press.

———. 2010. Grounding "language" in the senses: What the eyes and ears reveal about *míng* 名 in early Chinese texts. *Philosophy East and West* 60 (2): 251–93.

Hansen, C. 1992. *A Daoist theory of Chinese thought.* New York: Oxford University Press.

———.1993. Chinese ideographs and Western ideas. *Journal of Asian Studies* 52 (2): 373–99.

Ihde, D. 1976. *Listening and voice: A phenomenology of sound.* Athens, OH: Ohio University Press.

Im, M. 2008. "Rectification of names." Posted at http://warpweftandway.wordpress.com/2008/01/28/rectification-of-names-zhengming-正名/.

Kern, M. 2007. Excavated manuscripts and their Socratic pleasures: Newly discovered challenges in reading the "Airs of the States." *Études Asiatiques/Asiatische studien* 61 (3): 775–93.

Kuriyama. S. 1994. Imagination of winds. In *Body, subject and power in China*, ed. A. Zito and T. Barlow. 23–41. Chicago: University of Chicago Press.

Latour, B. 2004. How to talk about the body? The normative dimension of science studies. *Body and Society* 10.2/3: 205–29.

Loy, H. 2008. *Analects* 13.3 and the doctrine of "correcting names." In *Confucius now: Contemporary encounters with the* Analects, ed. D. Jones. 233–42. Chicago, IL: Open Court.

Makeham, J. 1994. *Name and actuality in early Chinese thought.* Albany, NY: SUNY Press.

Moeller, H. 2000. Chinese language philosophy and correlativism. *Bulletin of the Museum of Far Eastern Antiquities* 72: 91–109.

Nivison, D. 1996. *The ways of Confucianism*, ed. B. Van Norden. Chicago: Open Court.

Nylan, M. 2001. *The five "Confucian" classics.* New Haven, CT: Yale University Press.

Picken, L. 1977. The shapes of the *Shi Jing* song-texts and their musical implications. *Musica Asiatica* 1: 85–109.

Saussy, H. 1993. *The problem of a Chinese aesthetic.* Stanford, CA: Stanford University Press.

Sterckx, R. 2000. Transforming the beasts: Animals and music in early China. *T'oung pao* 86: 1–46.

Svensson Ekström, M. 2006. On the hybrid origins of Chinese "literature." In *Literary history: Towards a global perspective, Vol. 1*, ed. G. Lindberg-Wada. 70–110. Berlin: Walter de Bruyter.

Van Norden, B. 2007. *Virtue ethics and consequentialism in early Chinese philosophy.* New York: Cambridge University Press.

Van Zoeren, S. 1991. *Poetry and personality: Reading, exegesis and hermeneutics in traditional China.* Stanford, CA: Stanford University Press.

7
Embodied Virtue, Self-Cultivation, and Ethics

Lisa Raphals

Virtue ethics, one of the three major contemporary approaches to normative ethics, places emphasis on virtue or moral character. Within the Greek context on which it draws, it is centrally concerned with the key concepts of virtue (*aretê*), practical wisdom (*phronesis*), and the "good life" (*eudaimonia*).[1] In this chapter I offer a view of the first two, *aretê* and *phronesis*, that differs from the prevailing approaches of virtue ethics. I explore Chinese and Greek views of virtue and character derived from self-cultivation practices based on notions of ethics and virtue as specifically embodied and of selves that are "cultivated" by physical practices with an explicitly physical dimension. The immediate occasion for this chapter was the 2008 Summer Olympic Games in Beijing and the implicitly comparative problems they raise about the role of virtue in athletic competition. These problems provide a useful framework for examining broader ethical aspects of embodied Chinese self-cultivation practices. I discuss notions of embodied virtue and self-cultivation in three contexts: early Confucian texts, Daoist and technical works, and finally in a comparative perspective.

An important role of the Olympic Games in Greece was the mediation of inter-polis relations.[2] Needless to say, the problem of harmonizing, pacifying, or aligning various *poleis* through periods of war and peace did not occur as such in imperial China and arguably did not occur during the periods of non-imperial control, especially the Warring States. So we may speculate at the outset that there is nothing in China that we could, or arguably should, attempt to compare to the Games as a set of sociopolitical and cultural institutions. I argue against that speculation in order to look in a different direction, namely, how self-cultivation was understood. The context of the Games and athletic competition offers an opportunity to consider the role of embodied self-cultivation practices in Warring States and Hàn China. It also offers an interesting comparative prospect. How do we compare athletics or physical self-cultivation between a tradition that is monistic in the sense that body, mind, and spirit form a continuum with an aggressively dualistic tradition that posits a complete separation between mind and body? Finally, it offers an interesting alternative to both virtue ethics (as it is usually construed) and to consequentialism as a way of looking at early Chinese philosophical thought.

Self-Cultivation and Athletic Performance

"Sport" is something that has an enduring and transnational appeal, and it might be said that we "recognize it when we see it." But what do we mean by sport or athletics? Among theorists of the origin of sport, there are three basic approaches, each with its problems: ethological, Marxist, and religio-ritual.[3] Ethologists view sport as a manifestation of instinctive behavior. Marxists derive sport from the processes of labor and production. More interesting for present purposes is the view that all sport is based on ritual, sacrifice, and religion; sport has even been defined as "the ritual sacrifice of physical energy" (Sansone 1992, 37). But what does that "sacrifice" involve or presuppose? I want to suggest that, at least in early China, three practices form a continuum:

1. "Athletic" contests that involve skilled and possibly competitive specialized athletic performance, possibly derived from, or assimilated to, combat.[4]

2. Physical exercise, "self-cultivation" regimens, and other related practices understood to "transform the qi 氣" for purposes of health and longevity.

3. Ritual performance that was viewed as a fundamental aspect of the cultivation of virtue and ethics.

It could be argued that these practices had different purposes: competition, moral development, health, and so on. Where they form a continuum is in the nature of the techniques used and the ethical, religio-medical, and metaphysical assumptions behind them.

I argue that Chinese "athletic performances" are based on notions of virtue and self-cultivation. I use these terms beyond the trivial point that athletic excellence, like any other, requires great effort and cultivates, at the very least, the physical self. Aristocratic competitions in archery, charioteering, and the like were judged not by victory but by quality of performance. They were linked to broadly Ruist ("Confucian") notions of ethics and virtue. But they are also part of a broader set of "embodied virtue" traditions, based on: (1) the tacit and unexpressed view that mind and body are a continuum rather than a duality, and (2) the explicit view that embodied self-cultivation practices can transform the *qì*. These include, but are not limited to, athletic performance properly undertaken. This view of embodied virtue is grounded in late Warring States physiognomy and medicine. It was also closely linked to "Daoist" texts, to southern schools (nowadays most visible in excavated texts from the state of Chǔ 楚), and in "moralized" views of health in the traditions that culminated as the *Huángdì Nèijīng* 黃帝內經.

A Ruist View

Archery Contests in the Analects, Mencius, *and* Lǐjì

Chinese athletic performances included court competitions in archery and charioteering, but in some accounts at least, competition was not their primary purpose. Archery appears indirectly in Chinese ritual and historical texts through ritual hunts. The emperor and his officials personally shot game and sacrificed the meat at imperial tombs.[5] But archery as a manifestation of the virtue of the athlete first appears in the *Analects* (*Lúnyǔ* 論語). The *Analects* refers to ritual archery contests of the nobility, but Confucius praises less the skill of archery than the character of the *jūnzǐ* 君子 (gentleman), expressed in noncompetitive behavior. For example, in *Analects* 3:7 Confucius says, "The *jūnzǐ* has nothing over which he contends." He uses the example of archery; the archer behaves with ritual courtesy and, although in contest with others, remains a *jūnzǐ*. Elsewhere Confucius remarks that, in archery, the important point is not hitting the target, because people's strength is not equal (3:16).

For Mencius (3A:3), archery was one of four traditional institutions that make the people understand human relationships: *xiáng* 庠 (rearing), *xù* 序 (archery), *xué* 學 (learning), and *xiào* 校 (teaching). The "*Zhōngyōng*" 中庸 chapter of the *Lǐjì* 禮記 also ascribes to Confucius the view that archery revealed moral superiority:

> In archery there is something like the *jūnzǐ*. When the archer misses
> the center of the target, he turns round and seeks for the cause in his
> person.[6]

A *Lǐjì* chapter devoted to archery describes the conduct and meaning of ceremonial archery contests and explicitly links archery style to character. After describing the general conduct of the archers, it states that "in this way it is possible to observe the virtue (*dé* 德) of their conduct (*xíng* 行).[7] The *Shèyì* 射義 makes an explicit link between archery and benevolence, which elaborates on the previous passage: "Archery is a *dào* 道 of benevolence (*rén* 仁). The archer seeks to be correct in himself and then discharges the arrow. Again, if he misses, he is not angry with a superior archer, but seeks the cause of failure in himself."[8]

Cultivating Radiant Qì

Nonetheless, the picture presented of ritual athletic activity in explicitly Ruist texts is idealized. We may question whether the archer was not primarily trying to win. But even if he was, the physical practice of archery to describe virtue mirrors other passages in which Mencius emphasizes the importance of embodied virtue. Ritual and other physical performances entail a view of material virtue grounded in the transformation of *qì*. Let me mention two examples.

In 2A:2, Mencius famously describes *qì* as filling the body and moved by the will:

> The will is commander over the *qì*, while the *qì* is that which fills the body. The *qì* halts where the will arrives.

When Gōngsūn Chǒu 公孫丑 asks Mencius about his own particular strengths, he replies:

> I understand language, and I am good at nurturing my radiant ("flood-like") *qì*.[9]

He emphasizes that the radiant *qì* is difficult to describe but nonetheless gives hints for how to nurture it:

> This is a *qì* which is, in the highest degree, vast and unyielding. If you are straightforward in nourishing it and never harm it, it will fill all the space between heaven and earth. It is a *qì* that puts together righteousness (*yì* 義) and *Dào* 道. Without these, it starves. It is what is born from accumulating righteousness; you cannot win righteousness by luck or grasp it in your hand. (2A:2)

Physiognomy

Given Mencius's view that virtue arises in part from physical self-cultivation of the *qì*, we might expect the results also to be visible in the body. In several passages, Mencius does seem to say that self-cultivation transforms the body and its appearance. It is visible in a jade-like countenance and in the appearance of the eyes. In 7A:21, he describes the four virtues of the *jūnzǐ* (*rén* 仁, *yì* 義, *lǐ*

禮, and *zhì* 智) rooted in the heartmind and visible in the body. They produce a glossy coloration visible in the face and visible in the limbs. "The four limbs do not speak, but they convey it."

But if virtue is visible in the body, it should be possible to "read" it, and Mencius effectively defends the practice of physiognomy:

> In examining others, nothing is more effective than the pupils. The pupils cannot conceal evil. If that within the chest is upright [*zhèng* 正], the pupils are clear and bright; if it is not, they are clouded. If you listen to their words and examine their pupils, how can people hide anything?[10]

Xúnzǐ 荀子, by contrast, rejected physiognomy as based on endowments received at birth and thus not an indicator of self-cultivation. In a similar vein, the Hàn iconoclast Wáng Chōng 王充 explicitly attacks Mencius's physiognomy on the grounds that clarity or cloudiness of the eyes is determined at birth and does not depend on character.[11] In summary, for Mencius, this theory of *qì* linked the development of ethics and virtue and the transformed appearance of a sage.[12]

Embodied Virtue: A Broader Chinese Perspective

Now I turn to a more broadly Chinese view of embodied self-cultivation practices. Mencius's views about *qì* conform to and probably draw on a culture of embodied (bodily based) self-cultivation practices, aptly described in a recent book by Mark Csikszentmihalyi. These practices and the concepts behind them structured much of early Daoism, medical theory, and, more broadly, important areas of early Chinese ethics and metaphysics.[13] Such "material virtue" traditions held that the body-mind was constructed of *qì* and that embodied self-cultivation practices could transform *qì*. Such views informed Warring States accounts of dietary practices, exercise regimens, breath meditation, sexual cultivation techniques, and other technical traditions associated with *fāngshì* 方士 (masters of recipes). Material virtue traditions also had important links with "Daoist" texts and southern schools, as well as potential links to the "moralization" of health in the traditions that culminated as the *Huángdì Nèijīng*. Accounts of these practices appear in passing in the texts of the received tradition. Many more come from texts excavated from tombs.

Daoist "Virtue" Traditions

Several early Daoist texts describe what happens when a sage transforms the *qì* that constitutes the body. Here the emphasis is not visible virtue but actual power.

The *Nèiyè* 內業 clearly refers to cultivation of *qì*, *jīng* 精 (vital essence), and *shén* 神 (spirit), specifies that the cultivation of *dé* 德 or "power" must be worked on each day, and describes *Dào* as pervading the person of a sage.

> Respectful and cautious, and avoiding excesses, he daily renews his power (*dé*). He comes to understand everything in the world and thoroughly examines its four extremities.[14]

The *Zhuāngzǐ* 莊子 and other texts refer to the figure of the *shén rén* 神人 (spirit-person) as someone who has effectively transformed the physical body and the *qì* that constitutes it. *Zhuāngzǐ* 1 describes the *shén rén* of Gūyè 姑射, who concentrates his *shén*, avoids the five grains, rides the clouds, and, through the concentration of his *shén*, "protects creatures from sickness and epidemic and makes the yearly harvest ripen."[15] This passage suggests that a realized sage can have a nurturing effect even on the world at large, by acting at a distance. The *Zhuāngzǐ* does not indicate that these effects are intended; they may be simply a by-product of self-cultivation practices.

Zhuāngzǐ 22 clearly identifies *qì* as the basis of the physical constitution of the body: "Human birth is caused by the gathering together of *qì*" (*Zhuāngzǐ* 22: 733). A related strand of fourth-century BCE thinking about embodied virtues stresses the need to regulate the *qì* of one's constitution in order to achieve emotional balance. Passages of this kind occur in the *Zuǒ Zhuàn* 左傳 and the *Guǎnzǐ* 管子.[16]

The *Lǚshì Chūnqiū* 呂氏春秋 describes how the sages "made their numinous essence (*jīng shén*) tranquil, and preserved and lengthened their longevity."[17] The *Zhuāngzǐ* also describes harmonizing or taking charge of the six *qì*:

> The *qì* of heaven is out of harmony, the *qì* of earth is tangled and snarled. The six *qì* are out of adjustment, the four seasons are out of order. Now I want to harmonize the essences of the six *qì* in order to nurture life. (11:386)

There are many other passages that could be adduced. The point is that a sage or numinous person achieves that status through physical as well as meta-physical means, which are not distinguished. Similarly, a broad category of *yǎngshēng* 養生 ("self-cultivation" or "nurturing life") techniques sought physical self-cultivation and longevity. These included therapeutic gymnastics, dietetics, breath cultivation, and sexual cultivation.

Medicine, Fāng Arts, and Physiognomy in Excavated Texts

Now I turn to technical texts of a slightly different orientation: health, longevity, and the assessment of the "virtues" of people and objects. For example, many titles of medical manuscripts excavated from tombs describe techniques for self-cultivation through dietary, exercise, and sexual practices. These fragments and titles suggest the extent to which early self-cultivation techniques were linked to magico-medical and technical expertise traditions.

Most of these texts do not survive in the received tradition, but we can get some idea of their contents from the titles of lost texts in the *Hànshū* 漢書 *Yìwénzhì* 藝文誌.[18] It lists the titles of texts in the imperial library under six categories in an explicitly descending hierarchy that created a paradigm used by subsequent compendia to classify texts.[19] So, even though many of the titles are no longer extant, they provide a guide to categories of knowledge used by Hàn thinkers. Most useful here are the last two of the six sections of the treatise, "Numbers and Techniques" (*Shùshù* 數術) and "Recipes and Methods" (*Fāngjì* 方技).

The "Recipes and Methods" section includes the *Huángdì Nèijīng* as well as the titles of other medical works concerned with physical cultivation, health, and longevity. For example, the *jīngfāng* 經方 subsection includes "Recipes for Married Women and Infants" and "Food Prohibitions of Shén Nóng 神農 and Huáng Dì 黃帝" (*Hànshū* 30.1777–78).

The sexual arts section includes five texts titled "The *Yīn* Way" (*yīn dào* 陰道), ascribed to *Yáo* 堯 and *Shùn* 舜 and other putative masters.[20] It also includes a "*Yīn* and *Yáng* of [the star god] Tiān Yī 天一," "Recipes for Nurturing *Yáng* of Huáng Dì and the Sage-Kings," and "Inner Chamber Recipes of the Three Schools for Having Children."

Other sections describe physical exercises and therapeutic techniques, such as "Stepping and Pulling Book of *Huáng Dì* and Other Masters," "Massage of *Huáng Dì* and *Qí Bó* 岐伯," and several titles on fungi and mushrooms and household recipes (*jiāfāng* 家方).

The subject matter of these texts is borne out by medical and esoteric texts excavated from Mǎwángduī 馬王堆 (Chángshā, Húnán, 168 BCE).[21] For example, "Eliminating Grain and Eating Vapor" concerns dietetics and breath cultivation.[22] "Drawings of Guiding and Pulling" is a series of forty-four drawings of human figures performing exercises, some with captions. Some are described in another excavated text, the *Yǐnshū* 引書 or "Pulling Book" from Zhāngjiāshān 張家山 (Jiānglíng, Húběi). Both exemplify a tradition of exercise for both therapy and health known as *dǎoyǐn* 導引 (pulling and guiding). "Recipes for Nurturing Life" consists of eighty-seven recipes, including food, drugs, and beverages, along with several sexual cultivation exercises. "Various

Restricted Recipes" is a series of charms, including remedies for marital problems and crying babies and love charms to secure the affections of another. "Harmonizing *Yīn* and *Yáng*" and "Discussion of the Culminant Way of All under Heaven" refer to the movements and postures of animals as whole-body metaphors for sexual techniques.[23] The *Yǐnshū* also describes exercises that refer to or are named after animals, including inchworms, snakes, mantises, wild ducks, owls, tigers, chickens, bears, frogs, deer, and dragons.

In summary, most of the above texts can be described as part of a "*yǎngshēng* 養生 culture," which offered and emphasized control over the physiological processes of the body and mind, understood as transformations of *qì*. These transformations were understood as self-cultivation in the coterminous senses of moral excellence, health, and longevity (rather than medical pathology) and physiological transformation through the manipulation of *qì*.[24]

Physiognomy

If the transformed *qì* of a cultivated individual was visible in the body, the corollary was that a skilled individual could "read" these transformations. In theory at least, the ability to physiognomize persons and things allowed a skilled reader to assess the merit, not only of individuals but of animals and plants used in agriculture, and even of material used in warfare.

Within the transmitted tradition, titles of texts on physiognomy appear in the "Numbers and Techniques" section of the *Hànshū Yìwénzhì*. All the texts are lost, but their titles give an indication of their concerns, including a range of titles on practical physiognomy: "Military Prohibitions and Physiognomizing Clothing and Material," "*Shén Nóng*'s Cultivations of Fields, Physiognomizing the Earth, and Plowing and Planting," "Planting Trees, Storing Fruit, Physiognomizing Silkworms," "Physiognomizing People," "Physiognomizing Precious Swords and Knives," and "Physiognomizing Six Kinds of Animals" (*Hànshū* 30: 1773–75).

These titles suggest the practical and technical uses to which these skills were put. Physiognomy could be used to assess the economic worth of objects (clothing, equipment, swords), animals (domestic animals, silkworms), and people. Excavated texts on physiognomy emphasize these practical contexts, for example, a text from Yínquèshān 銀雀山 (Línyí, Shāndōng c. 140–118 BCE) on the physiognomizing of dogs, a Han sword physiognomy text from Jūyán 居延 (Gānsū), and a text on the physiognomy of horses from Mǎwángduī. All share the view that internal *qì* is reflected in appearance and makes it possible to judge character or potential. In economic and military contexts, this meant judging the "character" of an animal or weapon.

A Comparative Perspective

In conclusion, I turn to the problem of comparing Greek and Chinese views of what, in both cases, look like athletic performance.[25] In Greek views of sport as competitive, there are clear winners and losers but also a morality of competition that puts virtue ahead of victory. In the Chinese case, what on the surface looks like competitive sport may be something very different.

There is an apparent incommensurability between Greek and Chinese sport. Greek sport was centralized, democratic, competitive, external, and aesthetic (in some contexts erotic). Chinese sport was local, hierarchical, non-competitive, internal, and in some contexts imitative of the whole body movements of animals.[26] Needless to say, very different social structures and institutions underlie these differences. Both are linked to ritual and sacrifice, but in different ways. Although a definition of sport as the sacrifice of energy may apply to Chinese sport, it is not clear that it has the same purchase in China as in Greece.

In Greece the connection between athletic contests, competition, and sacrifice (including the sacrifice of animal victims, libations, and feasts) is much older than the establishment of the Olympic Games in 776 BCE.[27] For example, the Homeric poems devote the better part of a book of the *Iliad* to the funeral games for Patroclus and describe at length the ad hoc games held in honor of Odysseus at the court of King Alkinoos.[28] The heroic ethos of competition became a part of such games: "always to be best and to surpass others" (*Iliad* 6.208). Such excellence was encouraged by the perceived approbation, or even active participation, of a divine audience.

There is also a "dark side" of Greek sport, involving its attitudes toward cunning and deception, the morally ambiguous quality of "practical and cunning intelligence" the Greeks called *mêtis*.[29] In *Iliad* 23, Nestor advises his son Antilochus to use *mêtis* in the chariot race, because Antilochus is disadvantaged by slow horses that will mar his chances of victory. He urges his son to fill up your spirit with every kind of *mêtis*, which will enable him to prevail.

> The horses of these men are faster, but they themselves do not
> understand this art any more than you.
> But come my dear son, fill up your spirit with every kind of *mêtis*
> so that the prize may not elude you.
> The woodman does more by *mêtis* than by force;
> by *mêtis* the helmsman holds his swift ship on course,
> though torn by winds, over the wine-dark sea,
> and so by *mêtis* one charioteer can outpace another. (*Iliad* 23.311–18)

Nestor instructs his son to make a tight turn at the post, potentially cutting off another driver. This strategy will give him a clear shot, even with slower horses. This example illustrates a second characteristic of *mêtis*: its close links to physical action.

The "deceptions" of the *Sūnzǐ* 孫子 general or the wily Odysseus are a far cry from the "virtues" and ethics advocated by Confucius or Plato. But all are models of sagacity, very differently understood. Interestingly, each case has its counterpart in sport (and also in metaphors that compare sport to wisdom or moral excellence). These accounts show very different moralities of competition, along with complex relations between virtue, victory, performance, and entertainment. They also draw on very different metaphysics.

How much must we be put off by these? Can we reconcile an apparent Greek mind-body dichotomy with a Chinese metaphysics in which mind and body are a continuum, or even inseparable? Do we find ourselves in a glen of incommensurables?

I would argue that we do not. Both Greek athletics and Chinese-embodied self-cultivation practices (and their athletic aspects) are based on notions of ethics, virtue, and self-cultivation. The social and institutional contexts for their expression differ greatly, as do Greek and Chinese epistemologies and metaphysics.

Greek sport is based on notions of virtue and self-cultivation in several senses, beginning with its ancient connections with sacrifice, in which the athlete is a willing offering. Any sacrificial victim must be the best of its kind, and an athlete achieves this status through competition. A second sense of self-cultivation is the wholehearted effort and concentration that victory requires, in which human virtue or *aretê* is understood as a unitary whole of which athletic eminence is a part. Thus understood, athletic competition is a demonstration of the virtue of the athlete, rather than a form of technical expertise. That virtue is expressed in effort, in the discipline of training, in the sacrifice of time and money, and in the willingness to risk defeat and disgrace (Fränkel 1975, 487–88). A third notion of virtue derives from the Greek ideal of balance between the two modes of excellence of mind and body (in which the two are viewed as profoundly different).

The Chinese evidence also urges us to reconsider conventional accounts of Greek philosophy that treat mind and body as profoundly separate. Such views may derive in part from accounts of the mind-body problem in Plato and Aristotle.[30] However, other Greek traditions unite mind and body in ways that warrant further exploration, for example, the view that that moral virtue could and should manifest *through* the body as *kalos kagathos* (good to look at and good in action).³¹ Another example is the linkage of health with virtue and ethics, for example in a fragment by Sophocles:

> Most beautiful of all is to be just; best is to live without disease, and sweetest the means to seize each day what one desires.³²

To conclude, as we have seen, the classical Confucian representation of archery stressed the expression of the character of the *jūnzǐ*, despite the fact that bow and arrow were also military weapons with a long history of use in combat. But archery was also part of a spectrum of embodied practices which expressed, and transformed, the virtues of the practitioner. Other self-cultivation practices included gymnastics, longevity practices, and arguably the quotidian activities of cooking and medicine. In these practices, mind and body are a continuum that warrants comparison to Greek views, dualist and otherwise.

NOTES

1. This in contrast to deontology and consequentialism. For virtue ethics, see Hursthouse (2009).
2. Two Panhellenic institutions, the Olympic Games and the oracle of Apollo at Delphi, were particularly important for co-operation in inter-polis relations in ancient Greece. See Tod (1913).
3. The Marxist definition does not account for the pursuit of health or longevity. The ethological view is better suited to play (with its biological or evolutionary functions) than to sport. The religio-ritualist approach has suffered from methodological problems, but the prevalence of religious and ritual aspects of sport has been widely noted. See Sansone (1992, 15–28).
4. The present discussion focuses on archery because of its specific association with Confucian virtue. It was one of several modes of athletic competition associated with military training, including charioteering, jumping and throwing, wrestling, swimming, boating, ball kicking (*cùjú* 蹴鞠), and chess. Other recreational athletic activities included lifting heavy objects, acrobatics, dancing, and games of accuracy (such as throwing arrows into a wine bottle or hitting a wood pack). Yet other activities were linked to seasonal festivals, such as lion dances, walking on stilts, and flying kites. Finally, some broadly athletic procedures were exercises for health, including "exercises for pulling" (*dǎoyǐn*, discussed below) and "martial arts" (*wǔshù* 武術), including both hand and sword methods. Both *dǎoyǐn* and *wǔshù* were linked to the movements of animals. See Ren (1988, ch. 2, 55–90).
5. These sacrifices are described in the *Zuǒ Zhuàn* 左傳 and systematized in the *Zhōulǐ* 周. See Lewis (1990, 145–51).
6. *Lǐjì* 31, "Zhōng yōng," 884, cf. Legge (1885, vol. 2, Book 28, 307).
7. *Lǐjì* 46, "Shè yì," 1014–15, cf. Legge (1885, vol. 2, Book 43, 446).
8. *Lǐjì* 46, "Shè yì," 1020; cf. Legge (1885, vol. 2, Book 43, 452).

9. For discussion of "floodlike" and "radiant" as translations for *haòrán* 浩然, see Csikszentmihalyi (2004, 152–56, especially note 122).
10. *Mencius* 4A:15, trans. Csikszentmihalyi (2004, 101).
11. *Lùnhéng* 論衡 3, "Běn xìng" 13, 135 (Forke 1911, 1.385).
12. Mark Csikszentmihalyi argues that a "material virtue" tradition of "embodied" virtues developed as a response to criticisms of Ruist ritual, initially in the *Mòzǐ* 墨子 and *Zhūangzǐ* 莊子. At issue was whether these "archaic" (and expensive) practices were a genuine element in self-cultivation and the creation of social order. One *Rú* 儒 defense against this critique was a claim for an authentic practice. See Csikszentmihalyi (2004, 59).
13. For an excellent summary of some of these, see Lo (2005).
14. *Guǎnzǐ* 管子 XVI, 49, 4a–b, trans. Rickett (1985, 48).
15. *Zhuāngzǐ* 1:28, cf. Graham (1986, 46).
16. "People have love and hate, pleasure and anger, sorrow and joy. These are born from the six *qì*. Therefore be careful to choose your models from the fitting categories in order to regulate the six intentions" (*Zuǒ Zhuàn* Zhào 25.3, 1458). A similar fourth-century BCE passage from the *Guǎnzǐ* describes the responses of the sage-kings to the six emotions: "Love and hate, pleasure and anger, and sorrow and joy are the transformations of life. Clear perception and appropriate responses to things are the virtues of life. Therefore the sage kings were moderate in satisfying their tastes and timely in their movement and repose. They rectified and controlled the transformations of the six *qì* and prohibited excess in sound and color" (*Guǎnzǐ* X, 26, 2a). This translation is based on the *Sìbù Bèiyào* text but is indebted to Rickett 1:379. I follow Rickett's practice of using Roman numerals for *juàn* 卷 and Arabic numerals for *piān* 篇 and page numbers (see Rickett 1985, 1:47).
17. *Lǚshì Chūnqiū* 3.2, 3b–4a.
18. The thirtieth chapter of the *Hànshū* (Hàn history) is a "Bibliographic Treatise" (*Yìwénzhì*), compiled in the first century CE by Bān Gù 班固 (32–92), based on earlier compilations by the Hàn court bibliographers and exegetes Liú Xiàng 劉向 (79–8 BCE) and his son Liú Xīn 劉歆 (46 BCE– 23 CE). Liú Xiàng's "Separate Listings" (*Biélù* 別錄) was initiated by Hàn Chéng Dì 漢成帝 (r. 32–7 BCE) in 26 BCE. Liú Xīn abridged it under the title of *Seven Epitomes* (*Qīluè* 七略). The *Shùshù* 數術 section was compiled by the grand astrologer Yǐn Xián 尹咸; and, not surprisingly, gives precedence to the astrocalendric divination methods that fell within the purview of his office.
19. *Hànshū* 30.1701–84. The categories are: (1) the "Six Arts" (*Liùyì* 六藝) or "Six Classics" (*Liùjīng* 六經); (2) the "Masters" (*Zhūzǐ* 諸子); (3) poetry (*Shīfù* 詩賦); (4) military works (*Bīngshū* 兵書), (5) "Numbers and techniques (*Shùshù*), and (6) "Recipes and methods" (*Fāngjì*).
20. Other putative authors include Róng Chéng 容成, Wù Chéngzǐ 務成子, Tāng Pángēng 湯盤庚, and Tiān Lǎo and other masters 天老雜子.
21. The Mǎwángduī 馬王堆 medical corpus consists of eleven medical manuscripts written on three sheets of silk. They reflect Warring States medical traditions of the third and second centuries BCE, before the cosmological correspondence theories of the

Huángdì Nèijīng. Several reflect embodied self-cultivation traditions. The importance of this site is well known for its two versions of the *Lǎozǐ* 老子 and its medical texts on *yīnyáng* 陰陽 theory and acumoxa.

22. Eliminating grain is accomplished with the aid of both breathing exercises performed at morning and evening, and by eating the herb *shíwéi* 石韋. The text also contains a seasonal regimen of breath cultivation through consuming six *qì* and avoiding another five. For translations of these texts see Harper (1998). For a survey of the corpus, see Harper (1998, 25–30).

23. For example, the description of the "Ten postures" in "Harmonizing *yīn* and *yáng*": the first is "tiger roving"; the second is "cicada clinging"; the third is "measuring worm"; the fourth is "river deer butting"; the fifth is "locust splayed"; the sixth is "gibbon grabbing"; the seventh is "toad"; the eighth is "rabbit bolting"; the ninth is "dragonfly"; the tenth is "fish gobbling" (Harper 1998, 418).

24. For an excellent summary, see Lo (2001).

25. Most Greek terms are transliterated according to the third edition of the *Oxford Classical Dictionary*. Unless otherwise indicted, Greek texts are from Loeb Classical Library editions. Translations are my own unless otherwise indicated.

26. For the history of Chinese sport, see Ren (1988).

27. For an overview of the history of the relation between religion and Greek sport, see Scanlon (2002), especially ch. 1.

28. For the funeral games, see *Iliad* 23.256–897. For the games for Odysseus, see *Odyssey* 8.97–384. There is also a spontaneous boxing match between Odysseus and the beggar Iros (18.66–897).

29. For *mêtis* in a Greek context, see Detienne and Vernant (1978). For a comparative context, see Raphals (1992).

30. Plato first poses the problem as the connection between an immortal soul and a mortal body in the *Phaedo* (82e, 85e–86d), *Phaedrus* (246ad, 253c–254c), and *Republic* (439c–441b). For an overview, see Robinson (2002). Aristotle's position on the nature of the soul is more difficult to characterize, and there is no scholarly agreement on this subject. See van der Eijk (2002) and edited volumes by Lloyd and Owen (1978) and Nussbaum and Rorty (1992).

31. See Dover (1974), 41–45. Dover emphasizes that (like *jūnzǐ*) this term denotes an elite social class as well as a moral elite.

32. Sophocles fr. 356, quoted by Aristotle at *Nicomachean Ethics* 1, 9 1099a 25 (cf. Pearson 1917, vol. 2, 28).

References

Csikszentmihalyi, M. 2004. *Material virtue*. Leiden: Brill.

Detienne, M. and J.-P. Vernant. 1978. *Cunning intelligence in Greek culture and society*, trans. J. Lloyd. Atlantic Highlands, NJ: Humanities Press. Originally published as *Les ruses d'intelligence: la métis des Grecs* (Paris: Flammarion, 1974).

Dover, J. K. 1974. *Greek popular morality in the time of Plato and Aristotle*. Oxford: Blackwell. Reprint, Cambridge and Indianapolis: Hackett Publishing, 1994.

Forke, A., tr. 1911. *Lun Heng: Essays of Wang Chong*. 2 vols. Reprint, New York: Paragon Books, 1962.

Fränkel, H. 1975. *Early Greek poetry and philosophy*, trans. M. Hadas and J. Willis. New York: Harcourt Brace Jovanovich.

Graham, A. 1986. *Chuang-tzu: The inner chapters*. London: George Allen & Unwin. Reprint, Hackett Publications.

Guǎnzǐ 管子. Sìbù Bèiyào edition.

Harper, D. 1998. *Early Chinese medical literature*. London and New York: Kegan Paul International.

Hursthouse, R. 2009. Virtue ethics. In *The Stanford encyclopedia of philosophy*, ed. E. Zalta. http://plato.stanford.edu/archives/spr2009/entries/ethics-virtue/.

Legge, J. 1885. *Li chi: Book of rites. Sacred books of the East*, vols. 27 and 28. Oxford: Oxford University Press. Reprint, New York: University Books, 1967.

Lewis, M. 1990. *Sanctioned violence in early China*. Albany: SUNY Press.

Lǐjì zhùshū 禮記注疏. 1815. In *Shísānjīng zhùshū* 十三經注疏, comp. Ruán Yuán 阮元. Facsimile reprint, Taipei: Yìwén, 1980.

Lloyd, G. E. R. and G. E. L. Owen, eds. 1978. *Aristotle on mind and the senses*. Cambridge: Cambridge University Press.

Lo, V. 2001. The influence of nurturing life culture. In *Innovation in Chinese medicine*, ed. E. Hsu. Needham Research Institute Studies. Cambridge: Cambridge University Press.

——. 2005. Self-cultivation and the popular medical traditions. In *Medieval Chinese medicine: The Dunhuang medical manuscripts*, ed. V. Lo and C. Cullen. 207–25. London: RoutledgeCurzon.

Lùnhéng jiàoshì 論衡校釋. Wáng Chōng 王充. 1990. Běijīng: Zhōnghuá.

Lǚshì Chūnqiū jiàoshì 呂氏春秋校釋, ed. Q. Chén 陳奇猷. 1984. Shànghǎi: Xuélín.

Nussbaum, M. and A. O. Rorty, eds. 1992. *Essays on Aristotle's De Anima*. Oxford: Oxford University Press.

Pearson, A. 1917. *Sophocles: Fragments*. 3 vols. Cambridge: Cambridge University Press.

Raphals, L. 1992. *Knowing words: Wisdom and cunning in the classical traditions of China and Greece*. Ithaca, NY: Cornell University Press.

Ren, H. 1988. *A comparative analysis of ancient Greek and Chinese sport*. Ph.D. dissertation. University of Alberta.

Rickett, W. A. 1985 and 1998. *Guanzi: Political, economic and philosophical essays from early China*. 2 vols. Princeton, NJ: Princeton University Press.

Robinson, T. M. 2002. The defining features of mind-body dualism in the writings of Plato. In *Psyche and soma: Physicians and metaphysicians on the mind-body problem from antiquity to Enlightenment*, ed. J. Wright and P. Potter. 37–56. Oxford: Oxford University Press.

Sansone, D. 1992. *Greek athletics and the genesis of sport*. Berkeley: University of California Press.

Scanlon, T. 2002. *Eros and Greek athletics*. Oxford: Oxford University Press.

Tod, M. 1913. *International arbitration amongst the Greeks*. Oxford: Clarendon Press.

van der Eijk, P. J. 2002. Aristotle's psych-physiological account of the soul-body relationship. In *Psyche and soma: Physicians and metaphysicians on the mind-body problem from antiquity to Enlightenment*, ed. J. Wright and P. Potter. 57–78. Oxford: Oxford University Press.

Zhuāngzǐ jīshì 莊子集釋, ed. Q. Guō 郭慶藩. 1961. Běijīng: Zhōnghuá.

[*Chūnqiū*] *Zuǒzhuàn zhù* 春秋左傳注, ed. B. Yáng 楊伯峻. 1991. Gāoxióng: Fùwén.

Part Two
New Departures

8
Moral Tradition Respect

Philip J. Ivanhoe*

In "The Normative Impact of Comparative Ethics: Human Rights," Chad Hansen develops and employs the notion of *moral tradition respect* (hereafter MTR) to argue for a particular view about the role of comparative ethics in moral philosophy (Hansen 2004). His immediate aim in developing a conception of MTR is to describe criteria for respecting other moral traditions, by which he means "taking seriously" a moral tradition, foreign or domestic, outside the mainstream of a broadly liberal view of rights.[1] Such "respect" is based upon three conditions concerning the distinctiveness, structural complexity, and ethical success of a moral tradition, and these are presented as a way to make clear the proper aims and approach for comparative ethics.

Upon first glance, the phrase "moral tradition respect" easily lends the impression that Hansen is concerned with a particular kind of respect: the kind owed to moral traditions. His account of MTR, though, shows that his goal is to describe the conditions for offering respect to a moral tradition; to be more precise, his goal is to describe the conditions that warrant *moral* respect for (purportedly) moral traditions.[2] He further claims that when we understand the proper conditions for according moral respect to a tradition we will be able to see how such respect functions in the project of comparative ethics. While the project of analyzing the concept of MTR is both original and potentially insightful, there are good reasons to question Hansen's account of MTR and his related claims about its role in comparative ethics. In order to facilitate an

---

* This essay is offered with gratitude to Chad Hansen for his many contributions to the field of Chinese and comparative philosophy. Thanks to Erin M. Cline, Eric L. Hutton, Michael R. Slater, Justin Tiwald, and the editors for comments and suggestions on earlier drafts.

exploration of these questions, I shall consider some things one *might* mean by MTR and use these possibilities to illuminate the nature and function of Hansen's distinctive account.

Among the first questions one might ask about MTR is what exactly do we mean by *respect*? There are quite a few issues to sort out here. For example, we might understand MTR on the model of respect for persons. As such, MTR would be an initial stance from which we view other traditions, one that commands us to recognize that they are entitled to and people can claim for them certain rights, and we must treat them with some as yet unspecified level of dignity. The challenge for such a view would be to describe what it is about the nature of moral traditions that could possibly warrant such respect.[3] In the case of persons, religious justifications for fundamental respect provided the earliest answers to this question. In more modern, secular moral theory, Kantian ideas about the nature of moral agents serve as the basis for such respect. One might argue that such a view about what we owe each other's traditions entails not only some minimal level of respect for the tradition but also provides a warrant to ask other traditions to justify their moral claims, the idea being that at least part of what it is to respect a given moral tradition is to hold it to the same standards we expect from any viable moral system. Understood on the analogy of respect for persons, MTR would accord traditions certain fundamental rights, perhaps the right to be "taken seriously," but it would also open them up to praise and blame according to the standards of Western liberal morality. On such a view, respecting a moral tradition would not entail agreeing with it any more than respecting persons requires us to abstain from criticizing and when warranted resisting what they believe, say, and do. Let's call this understanding of MTR the *traditions as persons* interpretation.

A second and related understanding of MTR most closely resembles Kant's views about aesthetic judgments. Kant famously argued that the beautiful is a symbol of the moral, by which he meant, among other things, that the former shares certain features with the latter and engages some of the same human capacities and responses. The general idea is that judgments about what is beautiful are actually quite complex: they involve a felt response to certain formal features of an object and thereby lie somewhere between pure emotion and cognition. Such judgments involve the recognition that an object of beauty is the product of a free will working to express itself but in the absence of any clear and distinct end. While not fully under the command of our rational nature, and hence not quite moral, artistic creativity displays a free and autonomous will striving to express itself under some general notion of an object. These formal features of a work of art are the ultimate basis of our appreciation; we respond to the creative activity, which some have argued led to the related but quite different notion of *art for art's sake*. If we take this view of aesthetic judgments as our model, we might understand MTR as a sense of respect for the creative effort to form a moral system or found a way of life. Such respect would not be fully moral, but it would be special and important because of the particular nature of moral traditions and their significance for human lives. As is true of the *traditions as persons* interpretation, such a view does not commit us to fully accepting or appreciating every aspect of a given moral system, but even the worst moral system, like the worst example of art, merits some level of respect as an expression of unique human capacities and aspirations. We take a tradition seriously not only when we study and admire it but also when we sincerely engage and criticize it. Let's call this understanding of MTR the *traditions as art* interpretation.

A third possibility is to understand MTR not as an initial stance toward other traditions but a judgment we come to concerning the moral value of other traditions and perhaps indirectly their value as a goad or guide to help us understand more about what is good and become better ourselves. Seen in this way, MTR is similar to what Steve Darwall calls "appraisal respect" as opposed to the kinds of respect discussed earlier, which are forms of what he calls "recognition respect."[4] On such an understanding of MTR, there is no command or obligation to respect another tradition per se; respect is contingent and something we grant or come to have only after finding that we appreciate a given tradition or at least enough of it to treat the whole tradition, however defined, as worthy of respect.[5] Let's call this understanding of MTR the *traditions as values* interpretation.

All three of the alternatives I have described above construe MTR as in some sense normative; each requires that we show other moral traditions some measure of dignity and deference, but the justification, extent, and nature of "respect" is quite different in each case. All these ways of respecting a moral tradition express, to some degree, ethical attitudes[6] and in this way differ from some other forms of "recognition respect." For example, we might respect a moral tradition and decide to show it some level of deference because we recognize its resiliency and longevity. We have a type of respect for things that simply manifest the ability to survive. Anything that is tough, clever, or adaptable enough to hang in there in the struggle for existence warrants such recognition. Taking appropriate account of these qualities and facts, giving them proper deliberative weight, and acting in light of such recognition are important parts of what it is to have a reasonable view of and response to the world. We respect certain creatures in this way; we even have such respect for many diseases. If something is formidable and a threat, that adds something to our sense of respect, but fear need not be present for us to respect a creature's resiliency and ability to hang tough. Many of us, perhaps grudgingly, might admit to having a certain amount of respect for cockroaches. After all, they have been here long before we came on the scene, and it is probably they — and not the meek — that shall inherit the earth. Such "grudging respect," though, entails no ethical judgment or appraisal, and so it is not a viable interpretation for MTR. In order for MTR to live up to its name, it must represent an ethical response to moral traditions. This appears to be what Hansen intends, for the larger purpose of MTR is the role it plays in explaining the "normative relevance of comparative studies" (Hansen 2004, 79).

Hansen describes MTR in terms of "three conditions" that a moral tradition must meet (2004, 79):
1. The rival moral tradition is significantly different in its conceptual or theoretical approach.
2. It is an intellectually rich, reflective, hierarchical system of norms.
3. It satisfies some plausible condition for substantive rightness (e.g., has been historically successful or leads to correct moral judgments).[7]

It will be useful to explore each of these three conditions in turn and see how they function collectively to constitute a proper standard for MTR.

The first condition is needed to ensure that the moral tradition under consideration is indeed something "other" than what we already know and accept. Of Hansen's three criteria, only this one has no ethical dimension. Its purpose is to distinguish something as a moral tradition distinct from one's own. The second condition functions to guarantee that the moral tradition is indeed a system not only of norms, but norms that have higher-order justifications and that are held in light of reflection and argumentation, broadly construed. Such a condition rules out purely traditional codes of conduct that are followed without question, coerced behavior, and the like. This too seems like a reasonable stipulation for MTR. The third condition is the most substantial, ethically speaking, for it requires a moral tradition to yield "correct moral judgments." A moral tradition must get things right in the sense of offering us "moral insights that impress us from our present moral point of view" (2004, 79).[8] Other moral systems must produce judgments about what people should and should not do that cohere closely, at least in enough cases, with our own sense of right and wrong, no matter how differently they may arrive at and justify such judgments. The general thrust of this condition seems initially plausible, but it generates several substantial questions that require further elaboration.

First, it is not clear how much agreement there must be or whether such agreement must cover certain core issues or problems. It certainly seems right to say we cannot respect a tradition that rejects *all* of our moral beliefs — one might even argue that traditions that could not accommodate any of our moral beliefs would not be seen as *moral* traditions at all — but it is not clear how much and what kind of overlap there must be in order to generate MTR.[9] One might think there *must* be overlap concerning certain basic and general features of moral theory. For example, we can only have MTR for traditions that recognize there is a special category of creatures called persons, moral agents who are free to choose and act and thereby are responsible for the things they do. However, such a requirement could not accommodate traditional forms of Buddhism, which deny the reality of persons along with most of the phenomena we associate with the real world. One need not look beyond the Western tradition or back in time to find moral traditions that pose such problems; as is famously argued by Rawls, most forms of utilitarianism do not take the status of persons seriously (1971, 27).[10] This should make clear that there is much more work to be done specifying just what is meant by "correct moral judgments" and "moral insights that impress us from our present moral point of view." On a very minimal sense of these ideas, almost any moral tradition would qualify: a tradition that did not agree with any of our moral judgments would not strike as a moral tradition at all. On a more stringent reading, and the one that is implied by Hansen's goal of eventual global consensus, almost no other moral tradition would qualify; for example, most forms of Buddhism (and utilitarianism) seem to have a principled disregard for the rights and fundamental dignity of persons.

The most charitable way to understand this aspect of Hansen's view is that MTR must be based on an all-things-considered judgment about the moral value of another tradition. This is an important issue if MTR is going to offer a distinctive sense of respect for moral *traditions*. We cannot just "cherry pick" one or two features of a tradition and on the basis of these alone say we respect *the tradition*. Admiring individual *features* of a tradition is not enough for moral *tradition* respect. In such cases, the right thing to say is: I respect or admire feature "X" about tradition "Y" (even though I might have no respect for the tradition as a whole). For example, I might admire the dedication and commitment that certain politically motivated terrorists show to their cause and each other. I might agree with some of their claims and reasons for fighting a reigning political or economic order, but I can regard such people, their methods, and the lives they lead as morally wicked and despicable.[11] Such individuals or groups might live according to an ideology that fulfills the first two conditions Hansen sets. It would fail to meet the third condition, but only if the third condition is spelled out in a clearer, more robust, and all-things-considered way.[12]

If this is a fair account of Hansen's conception of MTR and how one might try to answer some challenges he did not specifically address, we can move on to ask how it compares with the three interpretations of MTR with which we began. We can move quickly across the first two possibilities, the *traditions as persons* and the *traditions as art* views, for both of these construe MTR as an ethical stance or attitude based upon and responding to *formal features* of moral traditions themselves. In other words, on such views, anything that is a moral tradition of inquiry and practice would, on the basis of that fact alone, warrant respect. But, as noted earlier, contrary to what one might assume when first encountering the phrase "moral tradition respect," Hansen is not talking about anything even remotely like a Kantian form of moral respect for traditions, a kind of respect we owe to any and all traditions of moral reflection and practice. He is setting down criteria that any tradition that purports to be moral, and thereby worthy of respect, must meet.

We can explore these first two conceptions of MTR a bit further, before leaving them, if we modify the third of Hansen's three conditions slightly, for then the three conditions can serve jointly as criteria for what a *moral tradition* might be. Leaving conditions one and two as stated, condition three can be changed to require not getting things *right* by arriving at correct moral judgments but simply as *being concerned with* the kinds of issues we think describe the core and range of moral philosophy.[13] According to the *traditions as persons* and the *traditions as art* views, any tradition that fits our modified set of three conditions qualifies as another moral tradition and as such would merit our respect. This, though, clearly is not Hansen's view, for unlike the modified version suggested above, his original third condition establishes an ethically demanding standard.

Hansen's conception of MTR is most like the *traditions as values* interpretation. It is a form of appraisal respect; it rests upon a conditional judgment about the moral value of a given tradition of moral inquiry: how successful the tradition is in getting things right. Given this understanding of MTR, it has nothing to do with the kind of respect that Kantians accord to persons or even to art. It is not something traditions or their advocates can expect from us in virtue of their being moral traditions of inquiry and practice or demand from us based upon their very nature. We are the ones who do the demanding; they have to meet our moral standards in order to qualify for respect and be "taken seriously." Hansen's conception of MTR involves a normative, ethical attitude, and in this regard it is unlike the kind of respect we might give to a tradition based upon its resiliency and longevity or the kind we might admit we have for lethal and virulent diseases. On such an understanding of Hansen's view, it does not make much sense to talk about *grudging* MTR.

Let us now turn to the second aspect of Hansen's account: the role that MTR is to play in comparative ethics. Hansen develops and deploys the notion of MTR in order to analyze the "role of comparative ethics in normative reasoning" (2004, 72). As I understand him, his view is that MTR opens the door to rival traditions sharing information with one another in an atmosphere of tolerance. Such mutual sharing will cause us to "adopt a mildly skeptical attitude toward our own morality"; this, in turn, will stimulate richer moral discourse within each tradition and may eventually lead to a desired synthesis (2004, 79). The first thing to note is that not all interest in or respect for other traditions must follow the path that Hansen describes. In more than a few cases, people come to find their own traditions unfulfilling, develop skepticism about the adequacy of the answers their home traditions provide, or even come to reject and wholly disavow their home traditions *before* they encounter any alternative. More than a few people *turn to* and seek to learn about other traditions after losing confidence in their home tradition.[14] Given this fact, MTR often does not play anything like the role Hansen insists it does in the project of comparative ethics.

Hansen insists that any movement toward what he sees as the eventual synthesis of moral traditions would have to be "bottom-up, gradual change." Within a given tradition, it would "have to be motivated mainly by its own norms with the addition only of the mild skepticism induced by granting moral tradition respect to the other" (2004, 81). This description of how comparative ethics can facilitate a grand moral synthesis of traditions will sound familiar to anyone acquainted with the writings of Alasdair MacIntyre.[15] As is well known, MacIntyre argues that there is no tradition-neutral perspective from which an ideal, ahistorical conception of rationality can adjudicate between competing conceptions of morality. Rival traditions must make their case by showing how their beliefs make *better* sense of moral problems in terms the competitors themselves can accept and endorse. This describes a process very similar to what Hansen presents by appealing to such things as tradition-specific norms and bottom-up change, and in his claim that comparative philosophers can "inform traditions about each other . . . but may not otherwise 'guide' or adjudicate the shape of the final synthesis" (2004, 72).

What Hansen's account adds is the notion of MTR and an argument about the role it plays in this process. He suggests that members of rival traditions must first develop MTR for one another's tradition and as a result entertain at least mild skepticism toward their own beliefs in order to embark upon the work of coming to understand one another's views. As noted above, this is not the only way one might become interested in and even devoted to another tradition, but it does describe one way such interest might emerge. Something like MTR could make an interesting and plausible addition to MacIntyre's general scheme that would make it more amenable as an approach to comparative philosophy. Unless they start out simply with the aim of overcoming and converting their rivals, *no matter what they might think*, it is hard to see why people would make the effort that can lead to a moral synthesis unless they are motivated by *some* common moral beliefs or attitudes and open to the possibility that they do not already know *everything* worth knowing. Nevertheless, even in such cases, it is not clear that a person will necessarily follow the neat plan and trajectory that Hansen describes. For example, skepticism about one's ethical beliefs is not at all required in cases where other traditions offer ideas or ideals that build upon aspects of one's home tradition. Another tradition simply might augment, enhance, extend, and reinforce views we already hold. Contrary to what Hansen claims, rather than relying on skepticism, such cases presume a commitment to the fundamental values of one's home tradition and a desire to see them developed and understood further. If skepticism simply means entertaining *some* doubt that one already knows everything, it loses sense. Even the mildest "skepticism" must entail more than the denial of omniscience.[16]

I would like to conclude by raising one further question about Hansen's views about the nature, relevance, and role of comparative ethics and another about his notion of a grand moral synthesis, which, for the most part, he shares with MacIntyre. Hansen claims that the normative relevance of comparative ethics lies in "inducing moral tradition respect and warranting a kind of excuse (tolerance) for continued disagreement" (2004, 82).[17] I have argued that there are several good reasons to reject this claim, at least in its present form. In addition, I doubt whether "tolerance" and "continued moral disagreement" are the right ways to describe the general view he defends. Tolerance differs not only from skepticism but also from the kind of mutual interest in another tradition's views that Hansen rightly sees as necessary for shared inquiry and mutual enrichment to take place. In order for people to make the effort that is required to explore and learn from other traditions, they need something more robust than tolerance. Tolerance does not imply interest in what another believes, much less a commitment to understanding why another might hold and live by such beliefs, nor does it connote or encourage being open to appreciating another's point of view. At best, tolerance is a way to halt mutually destructive attempts to coerce agreement. Historically, it owes it origins to European religious wars. As a contemporary liberal virtue, it strikes me as too weak and complacent to play any significant role in comparative ethics.[18]

Hansen sees the ultimate goal of comparative ethics as a kind of grand moral synthesis. While he insists that each and every viable moral tradition must come to such a synthesis under its own steam and according to its own lights (what he describes as its own norms), in the end, there will be a single moral order. This is quite similar to MacIntyre's view. The latter more clearly models his view of the interaction of rival moral traditions on views about competing theories or paradigms of science, and of course MacIntyre owes a clear and acknowledged debt to Hegel's philosophical approach and method. MacIntyre's view is more clearly a conquest model, which describes one moral tradition triumphing over and absorbing another; Hansen prefers the more neutral language of synthesis, though judging from the things he says in this and other work, it seems clear that he believes the Western liberal tradition of morality will serve as the substantial core of any viable future ethics.[19] My final comment, though, does not turn on whether one prefers the language of conquest or synthesis; I want to question the very idea of a unified moral order that these two views seem to share.

One of the most impressive features of MacIntyre's view is how he manages to engage and bring to bear three distinctive aspects of contemporary Western culture. In *After Virtue*, he tells a story about the history of modern Western moral theory that purports to provide *an account of the actual course of events*, which also seeks to *explain why contemporary moral philosophy is in conceptual disarray*, which, in addition, analyzes the source of *contemporary social decay* (MacIntyre 1984, 1990). True to his own Hegelian principles, his analysis of these problems is grounded in a historical process and not some abstract set of principles and norms. After diagnosing the maladies of modern Western ethics and their effects on society, he prescribes a cure: we need to abandon appeals to abstract, disembodied reason and engage in the tradition-based dialogue that he and Hansen so eloquently describe. MacIntyre assures us that such dialogue will lead to consensus, just as it tends to do in science; Hansen points toward the "final synthesis" of East and West. The problem is that neither has given us any good reason to expect such an outcome.

One might contend that MacIntyre's project runs aground on this issue. While it is true that traditions of inquiry in the natural sciences tend to operate in the way he suggests rival moral traditions should and that this tends to lead to one winning out in the end and disposing of or absorbing its rivals, there is little historical evidence that this is how things work when it comes to moral traditions. Judaism, Christianity, and Islam have been in conversation for quite some time but show no sign of coming to consensus, and these three rival traditions share many fundamental commitments and even scriptures. For that matter, single traditions such as Christianity seem to show more splintering and sharp disagreement than they do a trend toward consensus and unity. When we expand the circle and ask whether Buddhists, Hindus, Daoists, and Confucians — of various and often conflicting opinions — are likely to *help* these Western traditions work toward a comprehensive moral synthesis, it is hard to see a case for optimism.[20] Any such optimism clearly cannot be grounded in historical precedents or tendencies; it seems more an expression of hope or faith.

If the response is that only secular moral traditions can participate in such a dialogue, one might be tempted to think there is a greater possibility for consensus. The cost, though, is rather high, for secular liberal moralists will exclude from the discussion the beliefs, practices, and history of the vast majority of humankind. More important, secular liberal moral theorists do not seem any more inclined or likely to agree among themselves; deontology, utilitarianism, and virtue ethics constitute three rival versions of moral theory within, and in many forms cutting across, the category of secular liberal ethics. When it comes to comparative ethics on a global scale, such an ad hoc limit is a non-starter.

All, though, is not lost! In fact, we will be better off when we stop thinking of ethics as closely modeled on the natural sciences. As splendid and powerful as the natural sciences are, they do not offer a helpful model for — though they have a great deal to contribute to — discussions about moral traditions. Moral traditions involve invention as well as discovery and have histories that are not reducible to abstract principles or brute facts. They are constituted as much by practices as they are by norms. For these and other reasons, we should not expect them to reach consensus in some grand synthesis. This, though, should be a source of joy, not disappointment. A world in which irreducibly different forms of moral life stand up on their own two feet, shoulder to shoulder, is immensely more interesting and a greater testament to humanity than any homogenized conception of morality ever could be. I would like to suggest that one of comparative philosophy's most important contributions is not to show the way toward a grand moral synthesis but to make clear the many aspects of different ethical forms of life, show how they hang together to constitute appealing ways to live, and demonstrate that we all are better off when we work to understand and appreciate the wide variety of good lives that are available and yet to come.[21] We should no more expect or work toward a comprehensive synthesis in ethics than we should work toward a single global cuisine or a unified tradition of landscape painting. That would diminish — not respect — our fundamental humanity.[22]

I have presented my interpretation of Hansen's conception of MTR and the role it can play in comparative moral theory. My aim was first to present a clear and charitable account of his view. I attempted to do this by offering three alternative ways one might construe the notion of MTR and using these to highlight some of the distinctive features of Hansen's view. I concluded by describing how Hansen thinks MTR can help us to understand what comparative ethics can contribute to contemporary moral theory. Along the way, I offered a few criticisms and raised some questions about Hansen's conception of MTR and its role in the project of comparative ethics, in the hope that he and others will further develop this helpful and fascinating line of inquiry in future work. If I have shown anything definitively, it is that Hansen and his work continue to offer powerful and productive ways to think about the nature, role, and value of Chinese and comparative philosophy.

Notes

1. In some places, Hansen describes a moral tradition as a "reflective moral culture" (2004, 94) or "a broadly defined moral community with all its divisions and disagreements" (2004, 89). At other times, though, he talks about specific traditions such as "the teachings of a Navajo shaman or the polygamous prophet of some rural mountain community" (2004, 80). While an important issue for his overall argument, the question of what constitutes a moral tradition does not directly affect my discussion of MTR. Later, I shall suggest one possible way to define a moral tradition as part of a conception of MTR.
2. It is important to get clear about these issues in order not to be misled from the start about the nature of the project. Hansen's essay is about the proper conditions for according an ethical tradition moral respect and what this implies for the role of comparative ethics.
3. Advocates of "group rights" face a similar challenge justifying what it is about certain groups that warrants granting them special rights. In general, they tend to argue that the special nature of certain social groups, for example, ethnic groups that have suffered sustained and systematic prejudice, warrants such distinctive status (Shapiro and Kymlicka 1997). Tom Regan offers another example, when he seeks to extend a Kantian view of moral worth to non-human animals. He seeks to establish that non-human animals have certain fundamental rights because of their inherent worth, which is predicated on their status as "moral patients" and being "subjects of a life" (Regan 2004).
4. Appraisal respect requires that one both understand and truly appreciate some other value: one must *value* it as opposed to simply being able to evaluate it. Of course, this does not entail that one wants what is valued for oneself (Darwall 1992).
5. The question of how good a tradition has to be to warrant respect is a difficult issue and one to which we shall return below.
6. Some might insist that the *traditions as art* interpretation describes a "merely aesthetic" point of view. There is room for argument here concerning the importance an aesthetic sense has for any good human life, but since such a conception of our response to the beautiful is so similar to a full moral attitude, it seems to be at least quasi-ethical, and that will suffice for the task at hand.
7. It is not clear what Hansen means by "has been historically successful." This might imply criteria defining the kinds of nonmoral recognition respect discussed above. This, though, would not fulfill Hansen's intended aim: to describe a form of MTR that plays an important role in explaining the "normative relevance of comparative studies." Since Hansen goes on to explain the third criterion as "yields moral insights that impress us from our present moral point of view," I will take this to be the content of his third criterion.
8. A further issue concerns whether Hansen intends only beliefs that we already have or beliefs that we judge to be true once we come to understand them. Thanks to the editors for raising this point.
9. Bryan W. Van Norden defends a similar claim; his point, though, is that too much similarity or too much difference threatens to undermine the reasons for Western

philosophers to study Chinese philosophy, while my point concerns the need for overlap as a basis of respect (Van Norden 1996). It is conceivable that some new moral tradition could *convert* us wholesale to its form of life. We then would respect it but not our old moral point of view. This, though, is not the kind of scenario Hansen has in mind.

10. This aspect of traditional utilitarianism is made most explicit and defended by Derek Parfit (1986). Parfit notes the similarities between his views and those of classical Buddhism.
11. For example, Theodore John Kaczynski surely showed admirable dedication, pluck, and commitment and offered an impressive and systematic set of reasons for pursuing a policy of murder and terror, the latter most clearly and cogently presented in his essay "Industrial Society and Its Future."
12. Justin Tiwald has noted that the all-things-considered judgment of a tradition as valuable is a kind of absolute measurement rather than a measurement relative to other traditions. While one will want to be able to judge that one tradition is ethically *better* than another, there is some threshold of value that warrants MTR. For Hansen, MTR is best thought of as "taking another tradition seriously" as a conversation partner about morality.
13. What I am suggesting is a rough parallel between these cases and a Kantian conception of moral agency. One can dramatically fail to come to *correct* moral judgments and still possess chapter and exercise the capacities that establish one as a moral agent. This is why even the most despicable people have the right to be treated with dignity: they may make terrible choices, but the fact that they choose testifies to their status as moral agents.
14. Thanks to Justin Tiwald for pointing out and helping me to develop these points in comments on an earlier draft of this chapter.
15. Hansen acknowledges some similarity to MacIntyre's views in note 23 of his essay. The structure of their respective views, though, strikes me as more similar than this note would lead one to think.
16. Thanks to Erin M. Cline for pointing out and helping me to develop these points in comments on an earlier draft of this chapter.
17. I take it that "tolerance" and "continued disagreement" describe an interim period between the establishment of MTR and the grand synthesis that Hansen goes on to describe.
18. I offer a defense of these claims and argue for the more robust notion of "ethical promiscuity" in Ivanhoe (2009).
19. Michael R. Slater has suggested that such a view could helpfully be described as "ethical inclusivism," which would offer a parallel to inclusivism in the philosophy of religion. Just as there are religious exclusivists, inclusivists, and pluralists, there can be ethical exclusivists, inclusivists, and pluralists.
20. As Hansen has argued in many of his other works, Daoists and Confucians have managed to disagree for thousands of years about fundamental ethical issues.
21. For a defense of these claims, see Ivanhoe (2009).
22. In much of his work, Hansen agrees with David B. Wong in presenting Daoists as defending "moral relativism," and on this basis finds them philosophically interesting. In his most recent book, Wong describes his preferred view as "pluralistic relativism,"

but it purports to remain a form of relativism. I agree that Daoists are of immense importance and interest, though I think they express a robust form of "pluralism" — one that regards plurality as valuable rather than regrettable — not relativism. I also think this is a better way to describe Hansen's own view, at least as expressed in his later writings. Among other things, I do not see how relativists of any stripe can tend toward the grand moral synthesis Hansen describes in "The Normative Impact of Comparative Ethics: Human Rights." In any event, I defend what I regard as a Daoist-inspired form of pluralism and explicitly respond to Wong's latest work in "Pluralism, Toleration, and Ethical Promiscuity."

References

Darwall, S. 1992. Two kinds of respect. In *Ethics and personality*, ed. J. Deigh. 65–78. Chicago, IL: University of Chicago Press.

Hansen, C. 2004. The normative impact of comparative ethics: Human rights. In *Confucian ethics*, ed. K. Shun and D. Wong. 72–99. Cambridge: Cambridge University Press.

Ivanhoe, P. 2009. Pluralism, toleration, and ethical promiscuity. *The Journal of Religious Ethics* 37 (2): 311–29.

Kaczynski, T. 1995. *Industrial society and its future.* http://en.wikisource.org/wiki/Industrial_Society_and_Its_Future.

MacIntyre, A. 1984. *After virtue: A study in moral theory.* Notre Dame, IN: University of Notre Dame Press.

———. 1990. *Three rival versions of moral enquiry: Encyclopaedia, genealogy, and tradition.* Notre Dame, IN: University of Notre Dame Press.

Parfit, D. 1986. *Reasons and persons.* Oxford: Clarendon Press.

Rawls, J. 1971. *A theory of justice.* Cambridge, MA: Harvard University Press.

Regan, T. 2004. *The case for animal rights*, rev. 2nd ed. Berkeley: University of California Press.

Shapiro, I. and W. Kymlicka, eds. 1997. *Ethnicity and group rights.* New York: New York University Press.

Van Norden, B. 1996. What should Western philosophy learn from Chinese philosophy? In *Chinese language, thought and culture: Nivison and his critics*, ed. P. Ivanhoe. 224–49. Chicago, IL: Open Court Press.

9
Piecemeal Progress: Moral Traditions, Modern Confucianism, and Comparative Philosophy

Stephen C. Angle

What relevance do alternative moral traditions, such as early Chinese ethical thinking, have for people in the contemporary world? For example, suppose that we can find in early Confucian ethics particular values that are distinctively different from Western notions. How important would such a finding be today? According to three influential accounts of comparative ethics, the presence (or absence) of any given concept is not, on its own, of much significance. Chad Hansen, Alasdair MacIntyre, and Thomas Metzger all emphasize the importance of holistic units of analysis like "traditions and discourses" rather than focusing on individual ideas; all would suggest that trying to form any normative conclusions based on apparent facts about a single word or concept is likely to be highly misleading. In many ways they are correct. The initial section of this chapter focuses on the positive things we learn from their holistic emphases. One lesson of this analysis is the importance of a critical spirit to the flourishing of a tradition. The second section therefore addresses the long-standing idea that the expression of Confucian ethical truths is governed by a quasi-genealogical transmission, or *dàotǒng* 道統, since the *dàotǒng* idea is often taken to fit poorly with genuine critical rationality. I argue to the contrary, showing that the function of *dàotǒng* in modern Confucianism does not undermine its status as a vital and developing tradition. Finally, in the last section I show that, despite the value of the holistic approaches canvassed in the first section, each risks significantly misconstruing the nature of cross-tradition philosophical learning. Contemporary reflection on a tradition like early Confucianism can be critical to fruitful philosophical creativity, but the resulting philosophical practice, which I call rooted global philosophy, depends on piecemeal progress, not on wholesale judgments of the superiority of one tradition to another.

Traditions and Discourses

In an essay called "The Normative Impact of Comparative Ethics," Chad Hansen explores the relevance that alternative moral traditions have to moral debate today. Distinguishing "comparative ethics" from anthropology or history, Hansen suggests that "philosophers evaluate the motivation or warrant of different normative positions against the background of the entire philosophical and conceptual system" (2004, 73). Unlike "first-order" moral discourse — people within a moral community debating moral questions in accord with their shared norms of reasoning — comparative ethics operates at the level of the broad moral tradition: its role is "the rather 'academic' one of exhibiting and illuminating the rich complexity and coherence of the background assumptions, concepts, and norms of reflection" (2004, 82). Comparative ethics, thus understood, can contribute to normative debates today, but only in an indirect way. When our comparative inquiries lead us to see a given alternative tradition as internally robust in certain ways, we should then accord it "moral tradition respect."

Moral tradition respect accrues to an alternative tradition when we come to see that adherents of a tradition pay serious attention to objections and to rival positions — and especially if they provide "sound responses" to these objections (2004, 92). Keep in mind that Hansen is looking for second-order normative effects of comparative philosophy, quite independent of the degree to which one might simply find what some other group says to be attractive. Suppose that, upon learning that Confucians place more value on funeral rituals than one's own tradition does, one decided, "I see the point of the Confucian practice, and think it's better than what we have been doing; I henceforth embrace the value they place on mourning and funerals." This is not a matter of moral tradition respect but simply a first-order moral judgment. Hansen's focus is on cases when first-order disagreement persists. If the rival tradition is just a series of unsupported assertions, Hansen says that comparative philosophy gives us no *further* reason to respect or tolerate these beliefs, beyond our own first-order moral beliefs in toleration. However, when the tradition is positively engaged in defending its positions in light of reasoned critiques from its rivals, then we respect it as a philosophical tradition. Hansen suggests as an analogy the way in which we "positively excuse" someone for his or her good intentions and principled behavior, over and above the more normal case of "negatively excusing" when we simply withhold blame after someone makes a predictable mistake. Similarly, he argues that when a tradition exemplifies high epistemic or philosophical standards by seriously engaging with rival positions, we respect that tradition in such a way that we have an additional (or stronger) reason for the tolerance of continued disagreement.

Moral tradition respect can lead to something else as well. When, notwithstanding its significant conceptual or theoretical differences from our own tradition, the alternative tradition "satisfies some plausible condition for subjective rightness (e.g., has been historically successful or leads to correct moral judgments)," Hansen argues that this can "mildly destabilize" our own moral confidence (2004, 79). If we learn about a rich, systematic tradition that agrees with our own judgments in some ways but disagrees in others, this might make us slightly unsure whether there is not some defect in our own thinking. I will wait until the third section of the chapter to pursue Hansen's few comments about how we might follow up on this kind of destabilization, because Hansen (correctly, in my view) sees that the follow-up has what I will call a disaggregated character. The attribution of moral tradition respect, in contrast, functions at the holistic level. The holistic level of analysis also dominates Alasdair MacIntyre's influential conception of comparative ethics, to which we now turn.

The concept of tradition has been at the core of much of MacIntyre's writing on both the history of ethics and its present plight. As he uses the term, traditions exist only when a community engages in enquiry in accord with standards that they collectively recognize, and they do so self-consciously: "A tradition of enquiry is more than a coherent movement of thought. It is such a movement in the course of which those engaging in the movement become aware of it and in self-aware fashion attempt to engage in its debates and carry its enquiries forward" (MacIntyre 1988, 326). The idea that the enquiries move "forward" is also key to tradition. Even though he is content with the idea that traditions may be (and see themselves as) intrinsically open and unfinished, he insists that traditions are capable of progress.[1] In several writings, MacIntyre uses the inability of certain coherent movements of thought conclusively to answer their own questions as central evidence for concluding that they are not traditions.[2] At least in broad outline, this conception of tradition is similar to Hansen's sketch of those moral discourses that deserve moral tradition respect. In each case, the traditions are viewed as responsive to reasoning; as Hansen says, challenges are "seriously address[ed]" (2004, 78). For MacIntyre, and I believe also for Hansen, what counts as a robust or sound response to the objection is determined by standards internal to the tradition itself.

Hansen says that the mere fact that another tradition endorses a given norm does not give us a reason to believe it, though moral tradition respect leads to strengthened tolerance for the others and potentially to a mild destabilization of our own views. MacIntyre agrees that the mere fact of others' different views does not give us any reason to change our own. Indeed, because he stresses the different (and even incommensurable) standards by which adherents of different traditions reason, he puts even more emphasis on this point than Hansen does.

Be this as it may, MacIntyre argues that it is possible for adherents of one tradition to see that their tradition is inferior to another, and to rationally choose to adopt the alternative tradition. One tradition can defeat another. Roughly, the story goes like this: (1) if we perceive our tradition to be in crisis, because it is repeatedly failing by its own standards; and (2) we come to understand the norms and reasoning of a different tradition, perhaps by learning it as a "second first language";[3] and (3) we furthermore see that the alternative tradition is not in crisis; and finally (4) we see how the alternative tradition can explain in its terms why our own tradition had failed — if all these happen, then we can rationally choose to adopt the new tradition.[4] Because my interests lie elsewhere, I will not delve into the details of this process; suffice it to say that perhaps such a transition can take place.[5]

For present purposes, what is striking is that, while MacIntyre regularly talks about encounters between whole traditions and the possibility that one or the other may turn out to be superior, he almost never discusses a more piecemeal process of learning from others. When he does treat philosophers who explicitly draw on ideas or problematics from outside their tradition, MacIntyre typically argues that the results are bad. For example, he discusses certain nineteenth-century thinkers who sought to develop Thomism in response to what they saw as challenges from Kant. MacIntyre says that this led one such philosopher to "absorb into his own system a good deal of Kant and thereby, seemingly unwittingly, distort those older positions by reworking them in Kantian terms" (1990, 70). Of course, MacIntyre may be right that this particular philosopher's work failed both philosophically and theologically; my intention is not to defend this particular effort but rather to highlight the lack of recognition on MacIntyre's part that good can come from working across traditions — unless, he thinks, it is the good of coming to see another whole tradition as superior to one's own. Perhaps the clearest sign that MacIntyre views things this way comes in the way he sketches a possible replacement for the liberal arts university. He takes the current situation to be a pastiche of different books and viewpoints presented "neutrally," shorn of their connections to traditions. He proposes to replace this with a "post-liberal university of constrained disagreement." It would seek to advance enquiry within various particular traditions, and to "enter into controversy with other rival standpoints" (1990, 231). Comparison with others serves two purposes: it can help us understand ourselves better, by setting our views in relief against theirs; and it can, in extreme cases, lead to the conversion process discussed above. But nowhere in his discussion of the new university does MacIntyre reflect on other ways we might learn from others.

The reasons for MacIntyre's lack of interest in piecemeal learning from others are not hard to find. He emphasizes the ways in which concepts and standards of reasoning are interdependent, embedded not just in discursive traditions but also in particular social structures and community activities. In this context, he takes a "piecemeal" approach to mean separating an issue out from the tradition and setting it up as a "problem" that can be identified and perhaps solved independently of the system of thought out of which it emerged. The "problem of free will" and the "mind-body problem" are good examples. MacIntyre worries that once attention is focused on "problems" existing separately from a particular tradition of enquiry, they will become irresolvable. Whether he is discussing late-medievals like Duns Scotus or contemporary Anglo-American philosophy, once the focus is on problems, any purported solution will be ad hoc and always subject to an equally ad hoc rebuttal (1990, 152, 159). We will see in the final section that MacIntyre occasionally shows some interest in what I call "piecemeal progress," which will help us connect his holistic insights with what I will characterize as the more routine work of comparative philosophy. There is no question, though, that MacIntyre's main focus is on whole traditions, and he is worried about what happens when we step outside the framework of a tradition.

The third perspective to be canvassed here belongs to Thomas Metzger. Especially in his recent book *A Cloud across the Pacific: Essays on the Clash between Chinese and Western Political Theories Today*, Metzger has emphasized the continuities between and among various strands of pre-modern and modern Chinese political thinking. Because he wants to articulate deep continuities even where there appear to be dramatic differences — for instance, between contemporary Marxists, Liberals, and Confucians — he relies on the concept of discourse rather than tradition. It would be hard to argue that the core texts of the Marxists, Liberals, and Confucians are the same, or even have much in common. Each might count, in MacIntyre's terms, as a tradition, but they surely do not collectively constitute a single tradition. Metzger's analysis, however, seeks to show that they share a range of "rules for successful thinking" and various "indisputable" premises, such that they all belong to a single discourse. In a manner reminiscent of both Hansen's and MacIntyre's treatment of traditions, Metzger views discourses as dynamic conversations aimed at addressing unresolved or controversial issues, as defined by the framework of indisputables. Discourses are "on-going arguments," rather than "static sets of mass belief" (2005, 77).

In order to make his case, Metzger insists that we look not at individual concepts or statements, but work out whole fields of meaning: to see which discourse a given thinker is operating in, we must tease out his or her epistemological and ontological presuppositions. On the basis of this type of analysis, Metzger demonstrates that broad patterns of similarity exist among many Chinese political thinkers and that these are systematically different from many Western political thinkers. One example is the way in which participants in "Discourse #1" (in China) consistently resist, reject, or simply are blind to the results of what Metzger terms the Great Modern Western Epistemological Revolution (GMWER) and its resulting "epistemological pessimism." In a complementary way, Metzger argues that Western theorists who participate in the GMWER-permeated "Discourse #2" have difficulty articulating the grounds for resolute moral progress. A major thesis of *Cloud across the Pacific* is that Discourse #1 and Discourse #2 are saddled with complementary strengths and corresponding weaknesses, which he calls the "Seesaw Effect" (2005, 118). These contrasting perspectives undergird the mutual misunderstandings Metzger observes in the political world today.

Metzger is ultimately interested in finding a way off the "seesaw." He hopes that adequate mutual understanding and the application of "critical rationality" will enable us to collectively identify some synthetic position that is better than the current plight of either discourse. The overwhelming emphasis of his book, though, is on applying holistic analysis to show the pervasiveness of the two discourses. Metzger stresses that only when holistic description comes first can we identify the difference between "indisputables" and ideas that are genuinely up for grabs in a given context. He describes a disagreement with a colleague over whether a particular pair of ideas played an important role for a specific thinker, on whom the colleague had recently written a well-regarded book. Metzger suggests that his broader view enabled him to see that the mental process depicted by the pair of ideas "was logically integral to the whole structure of reality" as articulated by the text in question. As Metzger sees it, his own "desire to describe a body of thought as a whole" clashed with his colleague's "intention to pull out those ideas in a text that shed light on certain issues important to him."[6] I dwell on this incident because it anticipates the comments I will make in the third section about the obstacles that Metzger's penchant for holistic analysis places in the way of more piecemeal progress. Still, I believe that Metzger's broad reading of Discourses #1 and #2 contains a great deal of insight. Holistic interpretation, as practiced by Hansen, MacIntyre, and Metzger, is vital to the work of comparative ethics, even if it is not the only thing that comparative ethicists should do.

Dàotǒng

On both Hansen's and MacIntyre's accounts, a genuine tradition — worthy of our respect and perhaps of our allegiance, if our own tradition breaks down — is partly constituted by the activity of reasoning. Metzger has also emphasized the centrality of reasoning to well-functioning discourses. The discourse's or tradition's own standards help to determine what counts as reasoning within its framework, but the mere fact that adherents claim their tradition to be robust may not settle the issue. All three of our analysts believe that critics can legitimately challenge whether adequate reasoning is actually taking place. In slightly different ways, Hansen, MacIntyre, and Metzger have each argued, in particular, that modern Confucians have (so far) failed to shoulder the responsibility to defend and develop their tradition in light of various contemporary challenges. For example, Hansen strongly suggests that modern Confucianism may be either "a scholastic tradition (one that accords religious status to classical scriptures)" or else a tradition whose cultural dominance was rooted in "a political orthodoxy chosen by an emperor for its worth in sustaining his and his family's dynasty" (2004, 88). If either of these is the best description of Confucianism, then it does not merit moral tradition respect. For his part, MacIntyre asserts that a principal obstacle to opening up philosophical conversation with Confucian moral theorists is "the failure of modern Confucians to debate adequately among themselves the crisis within Confucianism that should have been and sometimes has been generated by its encounter with modernity" (2004, 210). Metzger, finally, emphasizes the ways that modern Confucians persistently fail to grapple with the challenges raised by the GMWER and Discourse #2.[7]

My question in this section is whether these characterizations are correct, and more specifically whether modern Confucians have essentially admitted that they are not interested in taking external challenges seriously because of their commitment to a certain *dàotǒng*. John Makeham nicely captures the surface meaning of *dàotǒng* by translating it as the "interconnecting thread of the way"; Makeham remarks that the idea has "been employed since Song times as a powerful tactic in the retrospective creation of lineages and 'schools' and also in the promotion of certain thinkers and the exclusion of others from privileged versions of just who and what constitutes orthodoxy."[8] In the twentieth century, *dàotǒng* has been used in both broad and narrow senses (Zhèng 2001, 138–43). The former stresses the many continuities in China's scholarly, philosophical, and/or spiritual traditions; its main point is to contrast the richness and value of China's culture with failings in the political realm. The narrower use — which in at least some ways has more in common with pre-twentieth century uses of *dàotǒng* — pays more attention to specifying which specific thinkers in the tradition grasped the Way. This narrower meaning of *dàotǒng* thus bears comparison to the traditional idea of "*pànjiào* 判教" or "distinguishing teachings," according to which the views of different thinkers or even schools of thought are arranged hierarchically, depending on how closely they come to the full truth. Our main concern hereafter will be with how best to understand this narrower use of *dàotǒng*, especially as seen in the philosophy of leading twentieth-century Confucian Móu Zōngsān 牟宗三 (1909–95) and in the insightful reading of Móu's views offered by the contemporary scholar Zhèng Jiādòng 鄭家棟.

As is well known, Móu Zōngsān argued at considerable length that both the standing interpretation of Neo-Confucianism into two main schools, as well as the tendency to valorize Zhū Xī 朱熹 as the tradition's greatest figure, were mistakes. Móu favored a reading of the tradition that stressed the insights of a series of thinkers he grouped into a third strand; on this view, Zhū Xī and his followers represented a subsidiary and partly wrongheaded direction of development. Móu's version of the *dàotǒng* passes through Zhāng Zǎi 張載, Hú Hóng 胡宏, and Liú Zōngzhōu 劉宗周, in particular, before being picked up in the early twentieth century by Xióng Shílì 熊十力. Zhèng Jiādòng explains that Móu found it important to trace the *tǒng* 統 or "interconnecting thread" through these different thinkers, rather than to explicate the *dào* directly, because of the great difficulty of stating clearly and simply the meaning of the Way. Still, Zhèng makes clear that Móu was not focused on the literal transmission of the Way from teacher to student; his interest is with those who got things right — who saw the same truth (2001, 186).[9]

A second, important aspect of Zhèng's reading of Móu's view of *dàotǒng* is what we can loosely — and subject to the caveats below — call its religious dimension. Zhèng and other commentators have noted that Móu's greatest priority was carrying on and teaching the Confucian Way (*dào*); his historical scholarship (*xué* 學) itself was of secondary importance. As historian Yu Yingshi puts it, "In accord with the *Doctrine of the Mean*'s statement that 'Cultivating the Way is called teaching (*jiào* 教),' that which the New Confucians advocated was in fact 'teaching (*jiào*)' rather than what we commonly mean by 'scholarship (*xué*).'"[10] Yu elaborates his understanding of this distinction between *jiào* and *xué* by linking the former with the "highest truth" and viewing departures from *jiào* as heterodoxy, whereas he connects the latter with pluralism, relativism, and dependence on perspective. In other words, whereas a historian might acknowledge that there are a variety of illuminating perspectives on what took place in an earlier era and not insist that we choose only one as manifesting the whole truth, for the New Confucians their scholarship played a different role. They sought, through their construction of a *dàotǒng*, to get at a deep and universal truth. This idea is connected to the stress one sees in figures like Xióng Shílì and Móu Zōngsān on the universal truth that can be seen in subjective moral experience: moral experience serves as a kind of personal witnessing of moral truth.[11] Cultivating the *dào* is about attending to and properly understanding these experiences. As they understood both the Confucian tradition and their own work, articulating the route to experiencing this truth lies at the core; figures who had correctly seen this were to be studied as guides and taken as points of departure for further efforts to explicate and defend the tradition's insights. Such an approach to the task of a Confucian contrasts with those who stress classical scholarship as an end in itself. "Classical commentary (*jīngxué* 經學)," "Hàn learning (漢學)," and philology — like the historical scholarship to which Yu Yingshi referred — were, according to Móu and other like-minded thinkers, of a decidedly secondary importance (Zhèng 2001, 190–91).

I said at the beginning of the last paragraph that I would be addressing the "religious" dimension of Móu's *dàotǒng*. Readers may be wondering, though, where the "religious" appeared in the balance of that paragraph. Móu cares about *dào* more than about *xué*, even though he engages in a great deal of *xué*; does that make his concerns "religious"? Even the word "teaching (*jiào*)" is itself open to various interpretations, although we might say it has a practical, rather than abstract or academic, meaning.[12] To some degree, it is apt to talk about Confucian doctrine and about the "beliefs (*xìnyǎng* 信仰)" of individual Confucians.[13] However, I think the previous paragraph makes clear that, when Zhèng Jiādòng refers to *dào* and *jiào*, as opposed to *xué*, he is not emphasizing doctrine and beliefs.[14] Instead, his focus is on lived moral experience: witnessing it, cultivating it, and theorizing it. Because *xué* points in the direction of scholarship for its own sake, Móu pushes in a different direction. Because "philosophy" in the present world is primarily an academic enterprise with little connection to lived moral experience, Zhèng Jiādòng calls Móu's central concern "religious" (or "spiritual") (2001, 194). But I think that a strong distinction between "philosophy" and "religion" is not particularly helpful here. After all, at various times in its past, "philosophy" has been more connected to people's lived experience than it is at present.[15] The priority that Móu puts on *dào* over *xué* may well suggest a critique of the way philosophy is understood and practiced — both in China and in the West — but it should not lead us to conclude that Móu is only interested in religious doctrine rather than philosophical reasoning. Móu's concern with *dàotǒng* is not a "mere academic" interest in tracing genealogies; he believes that a proper understanding of *dàotǒng* is integral to arriving at philosophical truth and personal transformation.

Let us return now to the questions that opened this section. We are tracking the ways in which distinct moral traditions — and early Chinese ethics in particular — can be relevant today, and are worried that modern Confucianism may poorly exemplify this relevance because it fails to merit moral tradition respect. Its attachment to a *dàotǒng*, the argument goes, means that neither non-Confucian Chinese nor any other outsiders have the extra reasons we discussed in the first section to respect or tolerate Confucianism. In fact, is the emphasis on *dàotǒng* that I have used Móu Zōngsān to exemplify actually inconsistent with others granting his tradition moral tradition respect?

A balanced assessment of the following four points leads, I think, to the conclusion that moral tradition respect is in fact warranted. First, we should certainly grant that sometimes, and to some degree, the intensity with which Móu and others worked to establish their understanding of the *dàotǒng* served precisely the ulterior motives that Makeham identified: "the retrospective creation of lineages and 'schools' and also . . . the promotion of certain thinkers and the exclusion of others from privileged versions of just who and what constitutes orthodoxy" (2008, 149). Not only were pre-twentieth century thinkers promoted and excluded, but so, too, were figures from more recent times. Xióng Shílì and his students were given priority over Féng Yǒulán, for example. The reasons for this are complex; some are well in keeping with the legitimate uses of *dàotǒng* to which I am about to turn. At other times it is harder to be sure, but let us keep in mind that Móu was no sage: he was a flawed human subject to mixed motives. This should not impugn the very idea of concern with *dàotǒng*. Turning then to the second point, it is important to note that modern Confucians have been more engaged with the challenges raised or revealed by modernity than Hansen or MacIntyre are aware. Even Metzger, who has written extensively on modern Confucianism, may not give them their full due. Elsewhere I have argued that Móu's notion of "self-negation (*zìwǒ kǎnxiàn* 自我坎陷)" is a constructive way to respond to the tension between a virtue-based tradition like Confucianism and the need for democracy and human rights (Angle 2009, chs. 10–11). This is not the place to pursue that question, but suffice it to say that we can find considerable engagement between modern Confucians and both the theory and reality of modernity.[16]

My third point takes on the practice of *dàotǒng*-construction more directly. I believe that the general *pànjiào*-style appropriation of tradition is part and parcel of what philosophers do the world over. Consider the difference between the approach a contemporary Confucian philosopher might take to explaining the significance of a central concept like "coherence (*lǐ* 理)" in Neo-Confucianism, and the approach an intellectual historian would take.[17] The philosopher is in dialogue with earlier thinkers in the tradition; rather than trying to say just what they said — as a historian might, in order to communicate his or her ideas to today's audience — the philosopher may correct what an earlier figure said. The philosopher will not be beholden to actual genealogies but may find some voices to be clearer and more insightful than others and will emphasize those. To be sure, there is an aspect of historical understanding that is important here, if the philosopher is actually to be — and to be understood by others to be — developing the tradition rather than inventing out of whole cloth. This relates to one of Móu's disagreements with Féng Yǒulán 馮友蘭. Móu endorses Féng's idea that modern Confucians can and must "continue (*jiēzhe* 接着)" the tradition rather than just "follow (*zhàozhe* 照着)," but Móu believes that Féng goes too far in leaving behind the core categories and problematic of Neo-Confucianism.[18] In any event, whether one finds one's point of departure in Plato, Aquinas, Locke, or Zhū Xī, all of this counts as constructing a *dàotǒng* — a conversation with earlier thinkers aimed at better articulating the truth.

Fourth and finally, modern Confucianism is not, as Hansen worries, "a scholastic tradition (one that accords religious status to classical scriptures)." Móu's *dàotǒng* does express a commitment to a certain kind of religiosity, namely, what matters above all is encouraging people to understand and experience the Way. Thus understood, though, religiosity is no bar to reasoning. Indeed, much of MacIntyre's work on the rationality of traditions focuses on reasoning within traditions that have a significant theological and religious component.[19] Hansen's suspicion about modern Confucianism should perhaps serve as a warning to us not to jump too quickly from the discovery that a tradition is not "pure" philosophy to the conclusion that it does not merit moral tradition respect. Both his and MacIntyre's views on modern Confucianism also suggest the difficulties attending a judgment about another tradition. Modern Confucian writings are often dense and difficult and, as is especially relevant for a non-sinologist like MacIntyre, mostly unavailable in translation. This makes the work of comparative philosophers in facilitating mutual understanding all the more important.

Disaggregation

In the first section we saw a variety of ways in which holistic approaches to traditions and discourses have been mobilized by comparative philosophers. The second section explored a Confucian idea that bears some relation to the idea of a "tradition" and found that, in the case of modern Confucian Móu Zōngsān, at least, his concern for a *dàotǒng* should not stand in the way of our seeing him as a philosopher, engaged in criticism and argumentation and open to cross-tradition engagement. It is now time to ask what comparative philosophers who emphasize holistic comparison might be missing. We will see that each of our main subjects has at least something to say about more piecemeal comparative work, but each also leaves us short of a full-fledged understanding.

Recall that Chad Hansen argued that, when we come to have "moral tradition respect" for an alternative tradition, it can mildly destabilize our commitment to our own norms. He adds that when this happens, we will wonder whether, working together with thinkers in the other tradition, we might be able to generate a moral view that synthesizes the insights of the two traditions and which would seem, from both our perspectives, to be superior to our starting points. Hansen suggests that this kind of thought undergirds the cherished ideal of universal moral synthesis. He adds, though, that he doubts that comparative philosophers have a major role to play in this process. They cannot serve as "moral prophets" who declare the truth based on their familiarity with both traditions. Instead, Hansen writes:

> The move to synthesis must take place as each moral community gradually shifts. It would have to be motivated mainly by its own norms with the addition only of the mild skepticism induced by granting moral tradition respect to the other. In effect, it would have to be a bottom-up, gradual change. That is, a Chinese theorist would have to make arguments that convince other Chinese given their existing norms, experiences, and assumptions. Similarly, a Western advocate has to make first-order normative arguments. (2004, 81)

I believe that this is extremely well said. When moral growth takes place in response to stimulus from another tradition, it is typically through this kind of bottom-up, gradual change, throughout which we continue to feel beholden to our own norms, even if they themselves are gradually changing. However, Hansen downplays the importance of comparative work in facilitating just the kind of piecemeal progress he has just sketched. For example, a few lines later he says:

> *Let us suppose that each is aware of and appreciates the other moral tradition.* Still, I suggest, it is improbable that these comparativists will successfully convince other members of their home community to reject an existing moral attitude simply by citing its status in the foreign scheme. That may count as a reason for initiating a moral debate about it, but not a reason for accepting the moral attitude in question. (2004, 81, emphasis added)

Again, this is very persuasive, except for the implausible first sentence. One of the upshots of the second section of the present chapter is that Hansen himself has quite a shallow understanding of modern Confucianism, and thus is not well positioned to appreciate its values and arguments. As we proceed, I will draw on what Hansen says about the requirement that people be convinced by their own norms but resist the idea that comparative philosophers have little role beyond the holistic project of identifying when moral tradition respect is warranted.

Our discussion of MacIntyre in the first section uncovered very little interest on his part in discussions that involve one aspect of a tradition engaging with one aspect of another tradition. Instead, his attention is focused on cases in which all the values and concepts of a tradition, taken as an aggregate, are compared to another whole tradition. Now I want to acknowledge that there are occasional moments when he suggests other possibilities. In particular, consider the following passage that comes well into his book *Whose Justice? Which Rationality?* — a book that explores the conceptions of justice found within several different Western traditions. After having wended his way through many developments in each of these traditions, MacIntyre says:

> A tradition becomes mature just insofar as its adherents confront and find a rational way through or around those encounters with radically different and incompatible positions which pose the problems of incommensurability and untranslatability. An ability to recognize when one's conceptual resources are inadequate in such an encounter, or when one is unable to frame satisfactorily what others have to say to one in criticism and rebuttal, and a sensitivity to the distortions which may arise in trying to capture within one's own framework theses originally at home in another are all essential to the growth of a tradition whose conflicts are of any complexity or whose mutations involve transitions from one kind of social and cultural order to another and from one language to another. (1988, 327)

This seems to be open to the idea that encounters between traditions need not be all or nothing; a specific challenge from another tradition can lead to "growth." The trouble is that I do not find the sentiments expressed here to be fully exemplified in MacIntyre's lengthy exposition of the developments of the traditions themselves. What happens when one recognizes an inadequacy in conceptual resources? We need to hear more about how "growth" can take place as a response to such a realization.[20]

In the first section above I highlighted Thomas Metzger's stress that holistic understanding must be prior to particular comparisons or challenges. Unless we base our understandings on broad interpretations of whole discourses, he argues, we may well miss some of the key "indisputable" premises that lie behind more innocuous-sounding statements. To some degree this mirrors MacIntyre's concern about "problem"-based philosophical argument. MacIntyre charges that problem-based argument is ad hoc and unending, because it has lost its framework of tradition-based reasoning; similarly, Metzger worries that attention to specific problems, without attending to the background discourses, results in interminable "clashes" rather than genuine understanding. As indicated above, there is much to learn from such holistic perspectives. Indeed, although I cannot pursue the matter here, I am persuaded that the correct theory of meaning is holistic in nature.[21] However, holism comes with costs. Three are worth our noting here.[22] First, holism makes it relatively difficult to talk about, or even to recognize, differences among thinkers who participate in a single discourse. Second, there is a related tendency to dichotomize rather than seeing a spectrum of differences, since the analyst will try to fit each figure into one or another full system of meaning. Finally, the holistic approach makes it somewhat harder to do justice to changes to discourses. To be sure, one can still talk about self-criticism within the confines of a given discourse, which I would call "internal criticism." The most significant changes, however, often occur at the margins between discourses or communities. Critical encounters with other traditions tend to be much more piecemeal, partially mediated through existing language and concepts, and have more ambiguous results. For all the explanatory power of Metzger's or MacIntyre's inclusive, holistic approaches, the changes that have taken place — and the room for future changes — are obscured.

To counteract an excessively single-minded emphasis on holism, I recommend we consider the value of partially disaggregating a tradition or discourse. As one sets about interacting with people from other backgrounds, thinking about one's own values in a disaggregated way can help one to arrive at a certain level of mutual understanding or agreement. Michael Walzer has put this in terms of "thin" values; unlike "thick" values, when we talk in terms of thin values we do not concern ourselves with their underlying justification, full meaning, or broad inferential connections. We just seek to find superficial common ground with others (Walzer 1994). This strategy was put into practice by the drafters of the Universal Declaration of Human Rights and made explicit by Jacques Maritain, a philosopher charged with summarizing the views of the world's philosophers on human rights. He famously wrote, "Yes, we agree about the rights, but on condition that no one asks us why" (1949, 9). We can in fact go farther than this, and say that when, from a disaggregated stance, an agent comes to value something that is given more weight in other groups than in his or her own — for instance, when a Muslim political thinker comes to embrace the value of human rights — he or she may be prompted to re-examine his or her own traditions and see if they can be revised so as to give the value in question a firmer footing in the local tradition.[23] In addition, the disaggregated stance allows more room for minority voices to come to the fore. To be sure, one cannot push disaggregation too far. After all, it relies on temporarily resisting many of the inferential connections that give our words their meaning. Alternatively, we might see it as an effort to temporarily step away from some of the social norms whose "inertia" exerts a mighty influence on what we are able to say to one another, and even understand. As such, the disaggregative perspective is fragile and prone to error. So, both as agent engaged in cross-cultural dialogue, and as analyst seeking to understand such conversations, we must cautiously balance the holistic and disaggregative perspectives.

As a way to flesh out what I mean, let us consider a recent essay in which Metzger quite explicitly thinks about a kind of disaggregation and its relation to moral progress (Metzger 2008). Metzger's essay is a response to a keynote lecture delivered in 2004 at a conference on New Confucianism by the eminent scholar Láo Sīguāng (Láo 2006), which itself is concerned with the possibilities for the future relevance of Confucianism. Very briefly, Láo asks whether the New Confucian model of developing (*kāichū* 開出) an internal Confucian response to the challenges of modernity is likely to succeed, and answers in the negative. He believes that, if Confucianism is to have a constructive role in the future, it must first be "disaggregated (*dǎsàn* 打散)" so that its "open" ideas having "universal value" can be used to solve certain existing problems, thus contributing to "world culture" (2006, 12–13). Before turning to Metzger's reaction, three quick items. First, if we were to ask Hansen what he thought of Láo's suggestion, he would probably respond that Confucianism does not appear to be playing any significant role. Láo apparently does not view it as possessing viable responses to current challenges, and so it probably does not warrant moral tradition respect. Insofar as it contains ideas that are of universal significance, furthermore, Láo suggests that the source of these ideas in Confucianism has no particular importance; people working out of another tradition could just as well come up with them. Second, for his part, MacIntyre would insist that, in abandoning any framework of tradition-based reasoning, Láo has lost whatever footing would enable him to make judgments about which ideas are "open" and which "closed." Within the context of the development of a tradition, it may be possible to identify and discard "closed" elements of the tradition that are leading to problems (Láo 2006, 7), but if we set this process outside of all traditions, MacIntyre would anticipate interminable disagreement. Third, I want to emphasize that Láo's idea of disaggregation is different from mine. Where I am suggesting a need for tentative and temporary disaggregation, Láo's idea leans more in the direction of breaking open the Confucian tradition once and for all, and then rummaging within it for ideas that can be used elsewhere.

Metzger is friendlier to Láo's vision than MacIntyre would be. Metzger approves of the general idea of working toward a "philosophical unification" (2008, 69). He rejects what he calls the ideal of a "multiphilosophical" world, "each culture parochially developing its own philosophies, uninterested in philosophies being developed elsewhere" (2008, 67). This is not to say that he views such a conception as unintelligible; indeed, Metzger says that "many Chinese philosophers today see themselves as pursuing the development of 'Chinese philosophy,' not as pursuing 'philosophy' to determine how Chinese culture should be revised" (2008, 67). Like Láo, though, Metzger believes that such a parochial approach is closed-minded and doomed to irrelevance. Metzger wants philosophers to recognize that a grounding in historical texts and traditions is necessary as a "first step methodologically required by the pursuit of any philosophically critical understanding," but he simultaneously demands "a multicultural, comparative intellectual history, instead of assuming . . . that one ancient segment of intellectual history included a somehow perfect or 'natural' understanding of the norms all humans should follow (*dàotǒng*)" (2008, 63–64). He says that the identification "of inherited cultural premises with universal truth" is central to the New Confucians' idea of *dàotǒng*, but we must resist this identification because others equally have their *dàotǒng* (2008, 71). If the pursuit of "open" ideas is to mean anything, we cannot exempt any culturally inherited content from critical scrutiny. Metzger's main criticism of Láo, in fact, ends up being that Láo's critique of New Confucian ideas does not run deep enough. Láo speaks of "learning to achieve virtue (*chéngdé zhī xué* 成德之學)" as a core, valuable, and potentially "open" Confucian orientation. Metzger contends that, in so doing, Láo fails to distance himself adequately from Confucian "epistemological optimism" (2008, 75).

Metzger's belief that we are faced with a choice between a "multiphilosophical world" and "philosophical unification" suggests to me that his dichotomization of holism and disaggregation is too stark. We can also see this in his treatment of Láo: on the one hand, he not only embraces Láo's quite extreme notion of disaggregation but also suggests that Láo himself is still stuck with problematic Confucian ideas; in other words, Láo's view is not disaggregated enough. On the other hand, Metzger's evidence for this characterization of Láo is (roughly) that Láo speaks of "learning to achieve virtue" as a valuable thing. Metzger leaps from this to the conclusion that Láo is guilty of epistemological optimism. This would only follow, though, if the only way to think about "learning to achieve virtue" required a problematic kind of optimism. Here we see Metzger's radical holism at work. If there is any hint of Confucian "sage" talk, he convicts the speaker of being a card-carrying Neo-Confucian. But this is too fast. Between extreme epistemological pessimism and extreme optimism, there is considerable space. Ideas of virtue and sagehood are also compatible with many different metaphysical and epistemological views. A key to pushing a tradition forward is that, even while we are conscious of the many entailments among the concepts and values of the tradition, we can resist some of those entailments — we can temporarily disaggregate some of the concepts — in order to explore what happens if we respond to old challenges in new ways, or come to see new challenges to which the tradition had made our predecessors blind. Although MacIntyre says very little about such activity — which requires working both within and across traditions — it may be what he had in mind when he talks about growth in response to challenges from another tradition. Unlike Metzger's quest for philosophical consensus, this kind of growth is driven by the quest for the *dào*, for truth and goodness, as viewed from within a given tradition.[24] It is nonetheless dependent on openness to other philosophical traditions and so does not collapse into a polarized multiphilosophical world. In other words, to work in this mode is to do what I have started calling "rooted global philosophy."

Hansen's talk of moral tradition respect and the possibility that it can mildly destabilize us fits in well with this way of thinking. In conclusion, it remains only to comment again on Hansen's lovely assumption that, in a given context, "each is aware of and appreciates the other moral tradition." If that were true, then we would all be comparative philosophers. I think this is precisely the goal toward which we should be working: all philosophical activity should be at least implicitly comparative. For the foreseeable future, specialized skills and background will often be needed to facilitate such openness. Still, all of us can strive to learn to balance holism and disaggregation so that we can promote local, piecemeal progress within our home traditions.

NOTES

1. MacIntyre offers Thomism as an example of a tradition that is fundamentally open (1990, 74, 124).
2. See, for example, MacIntyre (1990, 158–60), where he refers to both late-medieval scholastics and twentieth-century Anglo-American philosophers. MacIntyre makes an exception for Liberalism, which he says has become a tradition that self-consciously revolves around "perpetually elusive debate" (1988, 343–44).
3. MacIntyre suggests that in some cases one can "become a child all over again and learn [a] language — and the corresponding parts of the culture — as a second first language" (1988, 374). Something like this can happen with anthropologists who live in the society of another culture. MacIntyre also says it is possible for "those with the requisite linguistic and historical skills" to use textual and other materials to become "surrogate participants" in earlier cultures and so to acquire ancient languages in a corresponding way.
4. MacIntyre discusses this kind of encounter between traditions in numerous writings. See especially *Whose Justice? Which Rationality?* (1988) and "Relativism, Power, and Philosophy" (1989).
5. In fact, I am rather skeptical. MacIntyre (1990) uses this model to try to explain Aquinas's synthesis of Aristotelianism and Augustineanism, but it is hard to see how

this can work, since Thomism was not a pre-existing tradition. (Indeed, given the lack of uptake in generations immediately following Aquinas, I am not sure that Thomism counts as a tradition at all, at least prior to the nineteenth century; compare MacIntyre [1990, 151].) Another possible example is the switch of Chinese intellectuals from Confucianism to Liberalism (or Marxism) in the early twentieth century. Two challenges to this view are first, whether whatever they switched to counts as a tradition; and second, whether a neat "switch," rather than a messier (and less discontinuous) learning-from/appropriation model, best explains what happened. As we will see below, Thomas Metzger has argued for a great deal of continuity between Confucianism and both Chinese Liberalism and Chinese Marxism.

6. Metzger (2005, 70). The pair of ideas in question is "not yet issued (*wèifā* 未發)" and "already issued (*yǐfā* 已發)," which figure importantly in Metzger's analysis of Neo-Confucianism in *Escape from Predicament: Neo-Confucianism and China's Evolving Political Culture* (1977).
7. Metzger and MacIntyre, at least, are also highly critical of the modern Western moral discourse, but that is a separate issue from our present concern.
8. Makeham (2008, 149). Makeham has also discussed the *dàotǒng* idea in "The new *daotong*" (2003), and see more generally Wilson (1995).
9. We should not exaggerate the difference between the earlier mode of *dàotǒng* and Móu's approach, since earlier accounts of *dàotǒng* have always included huge temporal leaps: from Yǔ to Tāng, Tāng to Wén, the Duke of Zhōu to Confucius, and (the biggest leap of all) from Mencius to whichever early Sòng Dynasty figure one prefers.
10. Quoted in Zhèng (2001, 188).
11. This is an important theme in several of their major writings. One accessible discussion is Móu (1983, ch. 2). See also Yu (2002) and Tang (2002).
12. "*Jiào*" is part of the Chinese compound term that has been used for the last hundred years to translate "religion"; "*xué*," by contrast, is part of the compound term used to translate "philosophy." "Confucianism" has several flavors in Chinese, including both "*rújiào*" and "*rúxué*." The former is typically used when focusing on ritual or institutional practices; the latter typically covers academic discussions. See Makeham (2008). In contrast, in both classical and Neo-Confucian times, *xué* was by no means a purely intellectual or academic notion: "learning" to become a sage was understood to be a concrete, if life-long, task.
13. Yu Yingshi says that his teacher Qián Mù's attitudes toward Confucianism can be divided into two levels: the level of views about historical facts and the level of belief (Zhèng 2001, 191). Thomas Metzger's extended discussion of Táng Jūnyì's Confucianism likewise stresses certain tenets to which he held fast throughout his life (2005, ch. 2).
14. John Makeham is thus mistaken when he says that Zhèng "invests the term *daotong* with a new sense to mean a core moral doctrine or set of teachings and ideals that forms the basis for a system of belief" (2008, 142).
15. See Hadot (1995) and MacIntyre (1988, 1990), which emphasize the embeddedness of genuine philosophical (and theological) traditions in communal structures and various facets of people's lives.

16. I pursue this issue specifically with regard to Metzger's main argument in Angle (2008). Another example is Móu's extensive and detailed encounter with Kant. For a particularly good discussion, see Bunnin (2008).
17. I confess that I have in the back of my mind here the approach that I myself take toward "coherence," on which see Angle (2009, ch. 2).
18. Féng introduces the distinction at Féng (2001, 4); Móu's disagreement is discussed in Zhèng (2001, 142).
19. The only exception I find is the Liberal tradition. MacIntyre explicitly argues that Liberalism has become a tradition, but it is an odd one, characterized by continuous, perpetually inconclusive, but nonetheless socially effective debate about the principles of justice (1988, 343–44).
20. An indication of MacIntyre's actual ambivalence about the idea that encounter with another tradition can spur piecemeal growth is his treatment of Aquinas. In his 1988 book he treats Aquinas as emerging from a single tradition that encompasses Aristotle, Augustine, and others (1988, 205). That sounds like growth within a tradition. In his slightly later *Three Rival Versions* book, however, Aquinas founds a new tradition that synthesizes the pre-existing, and incompatible, traditions of Aristotelianism and Augustinianism (MacIntyre 1990, 120). Another hint that MacIntyre recognizes that piecemeal progress is possible comes in an essay on comparative approaches to Confucian ethics. He raises a series of challenges to modern Confucians — and many of them are insightful, notwithstanding his lack of knowledge about modern Confucianism, as noted above — and then goes on to acknowledge an area in which contemporary Thomist moral theorists (that is, those working within the moral tradition that MacIntyre himself finds most congenial) need to learn from Confucians. He says: "About the relationship between respect for ceremonial forms and the practice of virtues . . . , we (Thomistic) Aristotelians do have a good deal to learn from Confucians, and I hope that we are duly grateful" (MacIntyre 2004b, 158).
21. See Angle (2002, ch. 2; 2008; and especially 2006).
22. The remainder of this paragraph, and the next one, draw on Angle (2008).
23. For an important instance of this process, see An-Na'im (1990). Charles Taylor explores some similar ideas in "Conditions on an Unforced Consensus on Human Rights" (1999).
24. As we saw in section two, the notion of *dàotǒng* need not be inimical to openness and growth.

References

An-Na'im, A. 1990. *Toward an Islamic revolution: Civil liberties, human rights, and international law*. Syracuse, NY: Syracuse University Press.

Angle, S. 2002. *Human rights and Chinese thought: A cross-cultural inquiry*. New York: Cambridge University Press.

———. 2006. Making room for comparative philosophy: Davidson, Brandom, and conceptual distance. In *Davidson's philosophy and Chinese philosophy: Constructive engagement*, ed. B. Mou. 73–100. Leiden: Brill.

———. 2008. How serious is our divergence? A reply to Thomas A. Metzger. *China Review International* 14 (1): 20–32.

———. 2009. *Sagehood: The contemporary significance of Neo-Confucian philosophy.* New York: Oxford University Press.

Bunnin, N. 2008. God's knowledge and ours: Kant and Mou Zongsan on intellectual intuition. *Journal of Chinese Philosophy* 35 (4): 613–24.

Féng, Y. 馮友蘭. 2001. 三松堂全集 (Collected works of Féng Yǒulán). Zhengzhou: Hénán Rénmín.

Hadot, P. 1995. *Philosophy as a way of life: Spiritual exercises from Socrates to Foucault.* Cambridge, MA: Blackwell.

Hansen, C. 2004. The normative impact of comparative ethics: Human rights. In *Confucian ethics: A comparative study of self-autonomy and community*, ed. K. Shun and D. Wong. 72–99. New York: Cambridge University Press.

Láo, S. 勞思光. 2006. 從當代思潮看儒家 (Seeing Confucianism from the perspective of modern thought). In 香港中文大學的當代儒者 (Contemporary Confucians of Chinese University of Hong Kong), ed. C. Cheng 鄭宗義. 1–15. Hong Kong: Chinese University of Hong Kong Press.

MacIntyre, A. 1988. *Whose justice? Which rationality?* Notre Dame, IN: University of Notre Dame Press.

———. 1989. Relativism, power, and philosophy. In *Relativism: Interpretation and confrontation*, ed. M. Krausz. 182–204. Notre Dame, IN: University of Notre Dame Press.

———. 1990. *Three rival versions of moral enquiry: Encyclopedia, genealogy, and tradition.* Notre Dame, IN: University of Notre Dame Press.

———. 2004a. Questions for Confucians. In *Confucian ethics: A comparative study of self-autonomy and community*, ed. K. Shun and D. Wong. 203–18. New York: Cambridge University Press.

———. 2004b. Once more on Confucian and Aristotelian conceptions of the virtues: A response to Professor Wan. In *Chinese philosophy in an era of globalization*, ed. R. Wang. 151–62. Albany: SUNY Press.

Makeham, J. 2003. The new *Daotong*. In *New Confucianism: A critical examination*, ed. J. Makeham. 55–78. New York: Palgrave.

———. 2008. *Lost soul: "Confucianism" in contemporary Chinese academic discourse.* Cambridge, MA: Harvard University Asia Center.

Maritain, J. 1949. Introduction. In *Human rights: Comments and interpretations*, ed. UNESCO. 9–17. New York: Columbia University Press.

Metzger, T. 1977. *Escape from predicament: Neo-Confucianism and China's evolving political culture.* New York: Columbia University Press.

———. 2005. *A cloud across the Pacific: Essays on the clash between Chinese and Western political theories today.* Hong Kong: Chinese University of Hong Kong Press.

———. 2008. Limited distrust of reason as a prerequisite of cultural convergence: Weighing Professor Lao Sze-kwang's concept of the divergence between "the Confucian intellectual tradition" and "culture." *The Journal of Chinese Philosophy and Culture* 3: 22–75.

Móu, Z. 牟宗三. 1983. 中國哲學十九講 (*Nineteen lectures on Chinese philosophy*). Taibei: Xuéshēng.

Tang, R. 2002. Mou Zongsan on intellectual intuition. In *Contemporary Chinese philosophy*, ed. C. Cheng and N. Bunnin. 327–46. Malden, MA: Blackwell.

Taylor, C. 1999. Conditions on an unforced consensus on human rights. In *The East Asian challenge for human rights*, ed. J. Bauer and D. Bell. 124–44. New York: Cambridge University Press.

Walzer, M. 1994. *Thick and thin*. Notre Dame, IN: University of Notre Dame Press.

Wilson, T. 1995. *Genealogy of the way: The construction and uses of the Confucian tradition in late imperial China*. Stanford, CA: Stanford University Press.

Yu, J. 2002. Xiong Shili's metaphysics of virtue. In *Contemporary Chinese philosophy*, ed. C. Cheng and N. Bunnin. 127–46. Malden, MA: Blackwell.

Zhèng, J. 家棟. 2001. 斷裂中的傳統：信念與理性之間 (Fractured tradition: Between belief and reason). Beijing: Zhōngguó Shèhuì Kēxué.

10

Agon and *Hé*: Contest and Harmony

David B. Wong*

In this chapter, I consider two values that are usually taken to be in tension with each other: the value of *agon* or contest, a central value of Greek classical culture, and the value of *hé* 和 or harmony, a central value of Chinese classical culture. The association of these values with the Greek and Chinese traditions respectively leads to contrasts between the "combative individualism of the West" and the "harmonious social humanism of China." *Agon* and *hé* are often taken to be mutually exclusive. However, I shall argue in this chapter that contest and harmony co-exist in both the Greek and Chinese moral traditions, because these values not only exist in tension with one another but also mutually imply one another. The Greek and Chinese traditions differ in the prominence given to contest in the former and to harmony in the latter, but the other value given less prominence is still present in each tradition. Each tradition, I argue, can learn from the way that the two values are related in the other tradition. This learning does not require the assumption that only one of these traditions can have the "right" answer about how to approach conflicts between these values. My approach in arguing for these conclusions is guided by (1) my "naturalistic" conception of morality as a set of norms that human beings develop partly to

---

* I dedicate this chapter to Chad Hansen with great respect, who will no doubt disagree with much of what I say here, especially the parts that are sympathetic to Confucianism; but I hope he will see how much we have in common in our appreciation for the Chinese philosophical tradition and the ways it can be brought into fruitful interaction with the other great philosophical traditions. I have benefited from and am grateful for comments on an initial version of this chapter at the Běijīng Forum at Běijīng University in November 2007 by my colleagues at the National Humanities Center for 2007–08, Amélie Rorty and Stephen Salkever, and also by the editors of this volume.

promote and regulate social co-operation; and (2) my interpretation of Zhuāngzǐ 莊子 as welcoming the conflict of perspectives and urging us to incorporate new insights from perspectives that do not fit with our old ones. Under my naturalistic conception, moralities can be judged more or less adequate to the extent that they are successful in channeling and shaping the drives of human nature for the sake of promoting social co-operation. Guided by the Zhuangist philosophy of learning from different perspectives, I discuss what we may learn from the ways that the values of contest and harmony help to accomplish this function in different traditions.

Agon and Why it Must Presuppose Some Dimension of *Hé*

Friedrich Nietzsche's observations on the role of *agon* in Greek culture, contained in the short essay "Homer's Contest," are illuminating and surprising for their subtle conception of the relation between human nature and culture. They are surprising because of Nietzsche's widespread reputation for *opposing* nature and culture, the latter as the lid that must be clamped over the boiling pot of the will to power — the drive to overcome and to take delight in destroying. In fact, Nietzsche presents culture not only as repressing but also as *harnessing* and thereby channeling the pleasure of destroying toward constructive outlets. He draws from Hesiod's notion that there are two Erises, two goddesses of discord and strife. The elder Eris encourages unrestrained war and feud, whereas the younger Eris spurs human beings through the emotions of hatred, envy, and jealousy to surpass each other and set new standards of excellence. The younger Eris spurred Militiades, for example, to rivalry with the distinguished Aristides; and as reported by Thucydides, Militiades went on to demonstrate a purely instinctive genius for grasping the nature of an emergency at the shortest notice and a far foresighted appreciation for probable future developments.

Nietzsche claims that the goal of agonal education was the welfare of the whole. In contrast to the "unmeasured and unmeasurable" ambition of modernity, every Athenian's ambition was both kindled and restrained by the desire to be an instrument for the good of the city, and they were freer than modern individuals because their goals were "closer and more tangible" (Nietzsche 1997, 40). In discussing the implications of Nietzsche's claim, Christine Acampora has pointed out that rising above one's opponents in excellence means first appreciating the excellence they have achieved. The greater the competition, the more significant the victory is (2002, 27). Recognizing how an opponent spurs one to new achievement brings out another unexpected consequence of Nietzsche's conception of *agon*: the relational nature of the individual. Who we are implicates and depends on whom we oppose. H.

W. Siemens observes that many have been blinded to Nietzsche's sociological insights into the social origins of the individual by "his individualistic gestures and anti-communitarian pathos" (2002, 90). This is not to say that Nietzsche dismissed the claims of autarkic individualism but to recognize that for him "the perfectionist task of individual genius can only be performed in *a non-coercive community that accommodates the freedom of genius to break with established mores and create a new law or standard of evaluation*" (Siemens 2002, 90).

Nietzsche has put forward important insights into the nature of Greek culture, revealing why it is a mistake to characterize it simply as celebrating a "combative" or "autarkic" individualism. Through his distinction between the two Erises, Hesiod teaches the Greeks that nature and culture are not opposed but rather work together, that envy is not something to be despised but something to be valued because it can weave together the individual's and community's striving for excellence (Sax 1997). While Achilles may certainly be taken as an exemplar of the combative Greek warrior, the *Iliad* is a story of how his pride and his temper lead him to fail his friend Patroclos and to mistreat the body of Hector. Hector, before his death, is the other tragic hero of the *Iliad* and is moved at key points in the poem by an acute sense of shame arising from his awareness of what Troy expects of him. His tragic fall is to temporarily subordinate his bond to the community for the sake of personal glory. He brushes aside pleas to retreat temporarily within the walls of Troy, in order to meet Achilles in combat. The fact that he loses his courage at the initial moment of confrontation with Achilles signifies that he has cut himself off from the source of his strength — his community — his isolation signified by his choice to stay outside the walls.[2]

The presence of *agon* in Greek culture is most apparent in the wrestling match and other athletic contests, but as Nietzsche points out, it is also the basis of Greek pedagogy. The sophist, who is the "advanced educator of antiquity," meets other sophists in a rivalry (Sax 1997, 51). Even the instruction of art in music and drama is imparted to the people in the form of a colossal wrestling match. And in philosophy, Plato in effect declares to the sophists, orators, and dramatists of his time, "I can do what you do, only better! I can devise more beautiful myths (the Cave), more gripping dramas (as in the *Symposium*), and great orations (as in the *Gorgias*), and then I can show how your imitative art should be despised!"

Nietzsche's criticisms of the Socratic *elenchus* are interesting from the perspective of *agon* as ultimately serving the welfare of the whole.[3] The *elenchus* is a form of contest between one who defends an initial thesis, say, about the meaning of piety or justice, and an examiner, Socrates, who poses to the defender a series of questions to which the answers can only be "yes" or "no." The series ends with the compelled assent of the defender to a conclusion that contradicts the initial thesis. Though Nietzsche (2004) declares that the *elenchus* is a new form of contest, fascinating in its appeal to the competitive impulse of the Greeks, he is unimpressed by its purpose and ultimate effect. Socrates saw the anarchy of instincts all around him, and his cure was to employ reason as the tyrant to master the instincts. For Nietzsche, the instincts are the source of life, so fighting them with the clear, cold daylight of reason is another form of the disease, not the cure. Its ultimate effect is nihilistic: it is used to destroy the confidence of those who think they know and who often defend the traditional values that are in the process of eroding, but the Socratic *elenchus* cannot establish anything positive and life-affirming in their place.

Plato might have agreed that the Socratic *elenchus* cannot establish positive conclusions. In Book 1 of the *Republic*, Plato portrays Socrates as demolishing conventional definitions of *dikaiosune* (often translated as "justice" but with the understanding that its scope is closer to something like "rightness") as truth-telling and respect for the property of others. Socrates then proceeds to demolish arguments of Thrasymachus, who claims to know the underlying deflating reality behind conventional conceptions of justice. However, Socrates' companions, Glaucon and Adeimantus, are not persuaded by his arguments for nonskeptical conclusions about justice. After Book 2, the philosophical methodology is very different and can be taken as conveying Plato's alternative to the Socratic *elenchus*. There are no longer formidable opponents such as Thrasymachus. The posing of questions to which there can only be a "yes" or "no" answer is put to the service of lengthy expositions of theory concerning the nature of justice in the city-state and the individual's soul. Knowledge of the forms is claimed to be genuine knowledge, but there is no demonstration that such knowledge can be given through Socratic *elenchus*. Those who are capable of attaining this knowledge are presented as emerging from a specific political and economic structure that provides them with the requisite nurturance, training, and education. Moreover, those who seek knowledge of the forms must undertake a process of inquiry, and such a process cannot be replicated through following a chain of refutations of a thesis, at least as could be presented in a text such as the *Republic*.

Whatever the nature of this quest for knowledge of the forms, to engage in it is to have a shared commitment to inquiry, the outcome of which cannot be known. To prepare people for such inquiry is a joint undertaking by a community, and the inquirers who put forward their arguments to one another must be genuinely open to the possibility of having their minds changed by their fellow participants, just as a competitor in an athletic contest must acknowledge the possibility of defeat by others who demonstrate excellence that he or she has not been able to master. To do philosophy may be to engage in contest, but as in the other forms of Greek contest, it requires shared commitment and a willingness to subordinate personal ends to those that are shared with one's fellow competitors. When Critias, in the dialogue named after him, accuses Socrates of trying to refute him instead of pursuing the argument, Socrates replies that he pursues the argument primarily for his own sake and in some degree also for the sake of his friends, and that the discovery of things as they truly are is a good common to all humankind (Plato 1953, 22/166d).

Self-Regarding Drives in Human Nature and Their Relation to Morality

In this section I seek to relate Nietzsche's insights into the relationship between human nature and the value of *agon* to a theory of morality I have developed, most recently in *Natural Moralities* (Wong 2006). Nietzsche is exactly right in holding that nature and culture work together. The long period of the Pleistocene during which human beings evolved social instincts overlapped considerably with the period in which people began living in social groups with cultural institutions. If culture was a partner in this biological evolution, then it is plausible to hypothesize that some of our biological traits, as anthropologists Robert Boyd and Peter Richerson have suggested, might prepare us to regulate ourselves through culture: for example, the disposition to follow the majority or to emulate the most successful members of one's group.[4] Such traits could have conferred an evolutionary advantage on members of a group by enabling them to adopt satisfactory solutions to problems that were worked out by other members. Individuals do not need to "reinvent the wheel" on their own but can instead follow cultural norms established over some period of time, provided that the group's environment changes slowly enough so that the solutions embodied in those norms remain satisfactory.

Moral norms, on my view, culturally evolved to promote beneficial social co-operation, not simply through requiring behavior that is co-operative and considerate of the interests of others but also through encouraging, strengthening, re-channeling, and directing the sorts of feelings and desires that make people promising partners in social co-operation.[5] An ancestor of this functional view of morality is defended by the Confucian philosopher Xúnzǐ 荀子. A virtue of this functional view is that it helps to organize and systematize many of the most central moral beliefs that appear across cultures and historical periods: beliefs that specify the conditions for permissibly killing or conducting aggression against other human beings, beliefs about the right to assign and distribute the basic resources needed to sustain life, and beliefs that require reciprocation of good for good. There is a lot of variation in how these beliefs are filled in with specific content and in the nature of the particular restrictions and distributions, but a common end these beliefs serve is the regulation and promotion of social co-operation.

Some prominent functionalist accounts of morality claim that the primary purpose for which morality is invented is to counteract socially destructive motivations (e.g., Thomas Hobbes) or the limitations they impose on our sympathies for others (e.g., G. J. Warnock, J. L. Mackie).[6] I favor a more complex functional picture. Moral norms need to take into account the strength of such motivations in order to *accommodate* them and to encourage their *integration* with motivations that more directly lead to acting on behalf of others. Effective moralities, then, do not merely restrain actions from motivations such as self-interest, hatred, envy, and the desire for revenge, nor do they merely encourage the development of opposing motivations. Effective moralities also provide outlets for the expression of such motivations that are consistent with the expression of other-regarding motivations. Self-regarding motivation, for example, can clearly have undermining effects on social co-operation when it prompts non-co-operation and unrestrained aggression against others. However, in the right circumstances self-regarding motivations can support, rather than oppose, other-regarding motivations (Gintis 2000). To return to Nietzsche's point about Greek *agon*, the energies of the individual can be turned towards benefiting the group and away from purely destructive strife. Rather than saying that an effective morality should always constrain potentially anti-social motivations and reinforce other-concern, I would suggest that it should often attempt to accomplish a productive balance or reconciliation between the different types of human concern.

Let me roughly characterize the value of harmony as the value that promotes reconciliation and congruence between the individual's interests, the interests of others, and the group's common projects (ends that members are striving to achieve qua members of that group). The harmonization holds between three items and not just two, because the interests of others do not necessarily coincide with the group's projects, anymore than the self's interests coincide with the group's projects. To seek to harmonize, then, is to try to render compatible and whenever possible mutually supportive the self's interests, others' interests, and the group's projects.

Conceived in this way, harmony is implicated in the value of *agon* as it was realized in Greek culture, and that is to be expected if morality's function includes the channeling of potentially destructive motivations for the sake of promoting social co-operation. The contest in its various cultural forms brings together interests of the competitors in striving for and achieving distinction in the relevant kind of excellence, and the relevant kind of excellence is conceived in such a way as to blend with or contribute to the group's projects. Thus conceived, harmony is realized in a continuous process, and there will continuously arise during this process various possibilities for failures of judgment and mismatch between the individual's most keenly felt interests and those of others and the projects of the group. Achilles' anger and pride lead him into conflict with the Greeks' project of winning the Trojan War; Hector's preoccupation with personal glory right before the climactic confrontation with Achilles also leads him into conflict with the project of Troy to prevail against the Greeks.

There is another reason for seeing a connection between contest and harmony. The sorts of contest we see in Greek culture are practices in Alasdair MacIntyre's sense. They are socially established co-operative activities through which certain goods are pursued. These goods are "internal" to the practice in the sense that the meaning of these goods is dependent on standards of excellence that partly define the activity (MacIntyre 2007, 187). For example, the good of having wrestled well cannot be understood apart from the standards of excellence that partly define what wrestling is. Internal goods contrast with goods external to a given practice that can be defined independently of that practice. Thus one might receive material reward for having wrestled well, but the material reward is external in the sense that it can be understood independently of the practice of wrestling. The viability of a practice depends on sufficient commitment from its participants to the achievement of its internal goods. That is why there is so much anxiety over the money and notoriety that so often accompanies success in professional sports in the United States. Americans fear that dedication to achieving the standards of excellence in these sports has eroded and been replaced by obsession with money and notoriety.

The competitive ambition that motivates contenders can easily slide into a willingness to evade or violate the rules of contest when one can get away with doing so. The attractions of external goods can contribute to such willingness. The relationship between rivals can easily degenerate into a hatred that overflows the rules of contest and its standards of excellence. On such occasions, *agon* as a social value slides into *agon* as individualistic combat, where victory is achieved by suspension of mutually agreed-upon constraints and standards for what a legitimate victory is. *Agon* as a social value yields moral hazards because it requires sublimation, a channeling, of competitive and self-assertive motivations. There is danger that these motivations, once stimulated and cultivated within a culture that prizes contest, will overrun the channels set for them by shared ends. The "bad" Eris can replace the "good" Eris as the individual's competitive ambition becomes more intense. A culture might take the path of giving a great deal of weight to this caution and emphasize non-competitive ways of advancing compatibility between the interests of different individuals and the group's common projects. This leads me to ancient China and its value of *hé*.

Hé and Why It Must Presuppose Some Dimension of *Agon*

Analects 3:7 reflects the theme of de-emphasizing competition for the sake of harmony: "The exemplary person [*jūnzǐ* 君子] does not compete. If necessary he should do so in archery. Yielding to others while ascending the hall; saluting with drinks after descending. This is how the exemplary person competes." A text compiled during the Hàn period, the *Ceremonies and Rites* (*Yí lǐ* 儀禮) gives us an intricately detailed set of procedures for conducting the District Archery Ceremony, including the winners of the contest hastening to prepare drinks for the losers. Winning or losing are goods that are subordinated to the good of a certain desired set of relationships and attitudes cultivated by the ritual. In the *Records of Ritual*, the *Lǐ jì* 禮記, contestants are described as regulating their shooting by thoughts of the duties appropriate to their station. It is also significant that archery is a contest in which the contestants do not face each other, as in wrestling, but shoot towards a common target. The contest is at least as much with oneself as it is with others, and victory is the self's achievement of excellence.

This fits with one of the central themes of the *Analects*. *Analects* 1:1 suggests that a mark of the exemplary person is the ability to go unacknowledged by others without becoming frustrated. Or consider 4:14, where the Master says not to worry about having an official position but to worry about what it takes to have one. Do not worry about others acknowledging you, but strive to do what makes you worthy of their acknowledgment. The period of the composition of the *Analects* was full of ambitious men striving to become noticed and chosen for political office. Then, as now virtually everywhere, it is tempting to cultivate the qualities that will gain notice, but these are not the qualities that make one worthy. As 1:3 puts it, "Clever speech and ingratiating demeanor rarely go along with Goodness (*rén* 仁)." That a genuine and worthy character is not the same as having superficially attractive qualities is a theme that also runs through the Daoist text *Dàodéjīng* 道德經. Chapter (or section) 24 (Wáng Bì text) says that "Those who tiptoe do not stand; those who stride do not walk." The image is of someone who is straining to stand tall in order to become noticed, who strides with big steps and therefore does not walk steadily. These suggestions are confirmed by what follows: "He who displays himself will not shine; he who is self-righteous will not be distinguished; he who brags will not achieve; he who boasts will not endure."

There is another theme running throughout both the *Dàodéjīng* and the other great Daoist text of the classical period, the *Zhuāngzǐ*, that shows a keen awareness of the hazards of competition with others, and these hazards exist even if the competition is over the worth of one's character. Chapter 4 of the *Zhuāngzǐ* playfully articulates this theme in an imagined dialogue between Confucius and his favorite student, Yán Huí 顏回. Yán Huí tells Confucius that he is going to the state of Wèi 衛, where the ruler is very young, thinks little of how he rules, and fails to see his faults. Yán Huí says he is going to restore this state to health. Confucius expresses fear that Yán Huí is rather going to his execution. He says,

> Power (*dé* 德) is dissipated by that which gives birth to knowledge, and it is competition that gives birth to knowledge (*zhī* 知). To make a name for oneself is to compete with others. Knowledge is a tool in that competition. To insist in the presence of a tyrant on Goodness (*rén*) and righteousness (*yì* 義) amounts to taking advantage of someone's ugliness to make one look handsome.[7]

In reading Confucius's warning to Yán Huí, we are invited to put scare quotes around "knowledge," for it is not anything genuine but simply a tool for lording it over others. It is "knowledge" Socrates would accuse the sophists of having. It is "knowledge" that his detractors would accuse Socrates of having. On the Zhuangist perspective, moreover, preaching moral ideals is counterproductive because people resent the implied assertion of superiority over them. Therefore, in these Daoist texts, competition not only leads one to acquire the flashy qualities that get one noticed, but it also perverts the very ideals one tries to realize. Chapter 19 of the *Dàodéjīng* expresses this theme by associating the elimination of "sageliness" and throwing away of "knowledge" with benefiting the people a hundredfold, the elimination of *rén* and throwing away of *yì* with the return of filial piety and compassion. The denigration of these values is completed with the association of eliminating craftiness and throwing away profit with the absence of robbers and thieves.

I take these themes from the Confucian and Daoist texts as reflecting a cultural path that emphasizes non-contentious forms of harmony, in contrast to the Greek theme of contest for the sake of the common good. The advantage of non-contentious harmony is that it avoids the hazards that come from encouraging and cultivating the motivations of competitive ambition. But a more complex view about the relation between harmony and contest emerges upon further inquiry into Chinese thought. Consider *Analects* 13:23: "The exemplary person seeks harmony rather than agreement (*hé ér bù tóng* 和而不同); the small person does the opposite (*tóng ér bù hé* 同而不和)." What does harmony mean if not agreement? In their translation of the *Analects*, Roger

Ames and Henry Rosemont point to extended commentary on this passage from the *Zuǒ Commentary to the Spring and Autumn Annals* (Zhào 20), where Master Yàn 晏 says harmony is like making congee. The cook blends the various ingredients harmoniously to achieve the appropriate flavor. When it is too bland, the cook adds flavoring. When it is too concentrated, he dilutes it with water. In the relationship between ruler and minister, harmony requires an analogous adjustment. When the ruler considers something right and yet there is something wrong about it, the minister should point out what is wrong as a way of achieving what is right. When the ruler considers something wrong and yet there is something right about it, the minister should point out what is right as a way of setting aside what is wrong. For the minister to say that whatever the ruler says is right is like seasoning water with water or playing the same note on your lute. This is the inadequacy of "agreement" (Ames and Rosemont 1998, 254–55). In another work, Ames points to a passage in *Discourses of the States* (*Guó Yǔ* 國語 16/4a–b) that explicates harmony in terms of things accommodating each other on equal terms. Examples include harmonizing the five flavors to satisfy the palate, strengthening the four limbs to protect the body, and attuning the six notes to please the ear (Ames 1993, 60–61).

What harmony means in practice requires further clarification. The passage about the minister pointing out what is wrong in what the ruler considers right could be interpreted as equating harmony with the type of agreement that is reached through a thoughtful and respectful expression of each party's perspective, rather than slavish or obsequious parroting of a superior's point of view. The minister reflects on what is right and wrong in what the ruler holds, and attempts to bring the ruler around to his point of view. This interpretation of harmony emphasizes the necessity for an airing of divergent views so as to maximize chances for identifying the best, most well-founded view. It suggests that a frank airing of differences is necessary for harmony because a society cannot be guided wisely unless its leaders confront truths that may be inconvenient, unpleasant, or downright ugly for them to confront.

The *Zǐ dào* 子道 (The Way of the son) chapter of the *Xúnzǐ* emphasizes the necessity for the subordinate in an unequal relationship to be frank with the superior (Xúnzǐ 1978, 347–48; tr. Knoblock 1999, 949). Remonstrating servants make their states stronger and their families' ancestral shrines safe from being overturned. A remonstrating son enables his father's conduct to be fully in accord with ritual principles. A minister cannot maintain integrity by merely following his lord. Consider also that Mencius once responded to the charge that he was fond of disputing by pointing to the popularity of Yangism and Mohism. He disputes these doctrines by necessity, he says, not because he is fond of disputation (*Mencius* 3B:9). My point here is that, while there is this difference in the way that the contest of views is valued between Greek and Chinese cultures, there is considerable contestation in Chinese thought, and recognition of the need for it. Other examples in the classical tradition are not hard to find. Mencius and Xúnzǐ departed dramatically on how to develop Confucianism in more theoretical directions, and the *Xúnzǐ* explicitly criticizes Mencius's position on the goodness of human nature. Mòzǐ criticized the Confucian love for music and ritual. The *Dàodéjīng* and *Zhuāngzǐ* contain implicit or explicit criticisms of Confucian values.

The discussions of harmony without agreement, and in particular the reference to the blending of ingredients and things accommodating each other on equal terms, suggests something in addition to the need for debate and a diversity of views. It suggests that harmony requires the mutual adjustment of *interests*. In fact, disagreement over what promotes the common good is often difficult to disentangle from disagreement over how the interests of different parties are to be weighed or how they are to be reconciled in case of apparent conflict. The story of sage-king Shùn's 舜 marriage, as told in the *Mencius*, is a dramatic and surprising example of how harmony requires adjustment and reconciliation of interests. When the time came for Shùn to marry, he knew that his father would refuse permission if asked. So, Shùn did not ask. One of the reasons given for this surprising decision by the ultimate filial son is that letting his parents prevent his marriage would have prevented him from having the most important of human relationships, and that would have caused bitterness toward his parents (5A:2). That is, the satisfaction of one of Shùn's most vital interests is crucial for the viability of his relationship to his parents. It would have been foolish for Shùn simply to have swallowed his bitterness and submitted to what he knew his parents' wishes to be, foolish in terms of his own interests in marriage, and foolish for his relationship to his parents. Shùn's action contradicts the stereotype of the Confucian individual who subordinates himself to others. It rather illustrates that the welfare of the self is bound up with the health of its relationship to others entering into its identity. A self that consistently denies its own interests, even for the sake of those others, cannot maintain the health of its relationships to them.

Xià Yǒng 夏勇 (1992), of the Chinese Academy of Social Sciences, expresses a related theme in differentiating between harmony and unity. Harmony, he says, is a proper balance between separation and connection. He believes that the West has overdeveloped separation in the form of competition and conflict, whereas China has erred in the direction of too much connection (*hé yī* 合一 and *yītóng* 一同).[8] To illustrate the kind of harmony that is compatible with the recognition and acceptance of a degree of separation, Stephen Angle asks us to imagine a married couple, each partner with a career. What they need to do for success in their respective careers puts a strain on their family life. The ideal of unity would require something like the entire family placing a priority on either the husband's or wife's career. When he gets a good job offer in another city, for example, there is no question as to what ought to be done. However, the ideal of harmony would rely less on the idea of there being a fixed priority upon which everyone agrees in advance, but rather on balancing, negotiating, tweaking, and cajoling. For example, suppose she gets an especially compelling offer, but rather than simply deciding to move the family solely on the grounds of her career, the couple may work very hard at finding him a good opportunity in the new city, and decide to move only after they find such an opportunity. Or another way of negotiating may be "taking turns." This time her career gets advanced, next time, his.

This interpretation of the ideal of harmony fits with the Confucian value of relationships. At the center of the Confucian ethic is the idea that human beings are profoundly social beings. It means our identities, our senses of who we are, are bound up with our social roles and our relationships with particular people, and it also means that our sense of what our legitimate interests are is bound up with our judgments about what is needed to sustain our most important relationships. The husband and wife in Angle's example have interests in their own careers, but they also have interests in the flourishing of each other's careers, and they have interests in their relationship and their family life that influence their senses of how far their career interests can go and still be legitimate. It would not just be "whatever it takes to advance my career." Rather, the "harmonization" of each partner's interest in a career would involve weaving it into the nexus of all the other interests that matter to the family members.

Does this kind of mutual adjustment between the interests of individuals and the group require contest? Let us say that it requires confidence in the worth of one's interests and the ability to assert and defend their worth when they come into conflict with the interests of others. When the husband and wife negotiate about how to reconcile their potentially conflicting interests, each must have an appropriate degree of confidence in the worth of his or her interests. Perhaps their negotiation need not be called a contest. But it *may* involve contest and argument as each member of the family defends the worth and legitimacy of his or her interests, or as is often the case, his or her own conception of what those interests are. No one can claim to be infallible as to what the interests of others really are and the proper weight to be given their interests. Each should be prepared to admit that he or she has failed to give adequate consideration to others. Sometimes that takes an argument. It can be a gentle disagreement in which a son, for example, remonstrates (*jiàn* 諫, as in 4:18 of the *Analects*) with his father and mother. The Chinese value of harmony, even in its non-contentious version, sometimes requires the readiness to contend.

Chapter 10 of the *Zhōngyōng* 中庸 (usually translated as the *Doctrine of the Mean*) contains an exchange between Confucius and his student Zǐ Lù 子路 that conveys this point about the necessity of readiness to contend. Confucius distinguishes between two kinds of strength. The strength of the northerners is constant readiness to fight to the death for what is right. The strength of the southerners is flexibility and not responding in kind to injustice. The exemplary person combines both these kinds of strength, standing at the center without leaning to one side or the other (*lì zhōng ér bù yǐ* 立中而不倚). To me this means that the exemplary person stands ready to exhibit either kind of strength as the occasion demands.

It may be objected that contest is so devalued in Chinese culture that it has not ever received significant institutionalization.[9] I reply that, on the contrary, the civil service examination, which for most of the 1,300 years of its existence served as the basic institution of Chinese political life, was designed to harness the ambitions of talented men for the sake of the country. As Miyazaki states at the beginning of his classic study of the "examination hell" that stood before entry into the Chinese civil service bureaucracy, competition began in one sense before birth, in the hopes of a young man's family to have male children who could begin to be prepared for the examinations as early as possible by memorizing the Confucian classics, composing poetry, and writing essays in the prescribed, highly stylized forms. As the pool of potential candidates grew, the examinations grew in number and in stringency (Miyazaki 1981). Indeed, the examinations stimulated competition ambitions to such a degree (and with a focus on the external goods to be gained, such as patronage, prestige and wealth) that Zhū Xī 朱熹 was led to propose their reform in order to make them tests of moral character rather than of writing skills.[10] Furthermore, China to this day employs highly competitive examinations for entrance to its elite schools.

Other-Regarding Drives in Human Nature and Their Relation to Morality

Whereas the value of contest (when it is a moral value) harnesses and channels self-regarding and competitive motivations in human nature for the sake of promoting social co-operation, harmony draws directly from other-regarding motivations in human nature that directly support co-operation. It has always been pretty clear why self-regarding and competitive motivations could have been selected to become part of human nature. Such motivations are good instruments for promoting the individual's survival and subsequent reproduction, therefore spreading his or her genes through the human gene pool. The more puzzling question is how other-regarding motivations could have been selected during the biological evolution of the human species. But recent theory has begun to explain how other-regarding motivations could have evolved to become part of human nature.

It is apparent that family members do act for the sake of each other at a significant cost to themselves, and the widely accepted hypotheses of inclusive fitness and kin selection have been forwarded to explain this phenomenon. These hypotheses add up to the idea that evolution favors maximization of reproductive fitness not of individuals, but of their genes and their copies in kin. From the perspective of maximizing such "inclusive fitness," individuals who sacrifice themselves to save a sufficient number of relatives will be doing better than individuals who save themselves (Hamilton 1964). Elliott Sober and David Sloan Wilson (1998) argue that direct concern for one's kin evolved because ultimate desires for the welfare of kin constitute the most efficient and reliable way of ensuring that individuals benefit their kin. More controversially, Sober and Wilson defend the idea of group selection to explain co-operation and altruistic behavior between non-kin. The idea of group selection is that natural selection can operate not only on genes and individual organisms, but also on hives, herds, and other aggregations of organisms, including groups and tribes of human beings. Some groups may acquire a competitive advantage over other groups because they have a greater proportion of members who are prepared to sacrifice for the sake of others in the group. Other-concerned individuals find each other forming successful groups, and this may have aided in the genetic transmission of other-regarding motivations. Culture may also have worked hand in hand with the evolution of genetically based altruism. Groups with a greater proportion of other-regarding individuals may also have evolved cultural norms that require punishment and ejection of those who fail to adequately consider the interests of others. If human genes and culture co-evolved, as suggested earlier, it is plausible that genetically based other-regarding tendencies evolved together with cultural norms that reward such tendencies and punish their absence, and that the genetically based tendencies and cultural norms evolved together and mutually influenced their specific content.

If something like this story is correct, then human beings evolved to become creatures with a complex array of motivations. They were equipped with motivations to benefit self and others, to compete with others, and motivations to conform with and imitate others that enabled them to guide themselves with cultural norms. Such norms, depending on their content, can reinforce, de-emphasize, and channel the other motivations and strike different balances between them. Given this picture, it is no surprise that there could be significant variations in the emphasis given to the value of contest relative to the value of a non-contentious harmony. The Greek-Chinese comparison provides an exemplar of such a difference in relative emphasis. Yet I have argued that contest as a moral value requires a certain degree of harmony and that harmony requires a readiness to contest when necessary. I have supplied some rough explanations of why there should be connections between values that are in important respects opposed to each other. Contest as a moral value is not just about the individual striving for victory but also about promoting the shared ends of the group. Contest as a moral value harnesses the energies of the self-regarding drives for the sake of those shared ends. On the other hand, harmony as a moral value also requires the readiness to contest because the group functions well when the self-regarding interests of its individual members are integrated with the group's ends. If individual members perceive their urgent self-regarding interests to be in conflict with the group's ends, there is less possibility for their investing their energies into promoting those ends and more possibility of their undermining those ends if they can get away with it. The integration of individual and group interests is a continuous process that requires individuals to be ready to present and defend whatever they believe to be their legitimate interests, whatever they believe ought to be acknowledged by the group as worthy of satisfaction and protection.

Cultural Pluralism and Mutual Learning

To counter the expectation that there needs to be a single correct answer as to how to balance the values of contest and harmony, let me introduce my reading of the *Zhuāngzǐ*. This formidably complex text expresses the thesis that no one moral perspective is uniquely correct, but it does not dismiss moral values. In Chapter 5, men who have lost feet as punishment for crime are scorned, but not by their Daoist masters, who see what is of *worth* in them. In Chapter 1, Zhuāngzǐ chastises his friend Huìzǐ 惠子 for failing to see beyond the ordinary, humdrum uses of some large gourds. Huìzǐ tried using one of the gourds for a water container, but it was so heavy he could not lift it. He then tried to make dippers from them, but they were too large and unwieldy. He deemed the gourds of no use and smashed them to pieces. Zhuāngzǐ asks why he did not think of lashing the gourds together into a great tub so he could go floating around the rivers and lakes, instead of worrying because they were too big and unwieldy to dip into things! "Obviously you still have a lot of underbrush in your head!" concludes Zhuāngzǐ. Note that Zhuāngzǐ does not deny that the more ordinary uses are genuine uses for the gourds, and clearly, they are. Rather, Zhuāngzǐ's point is to clear the underbrush from our heads and get an *enlarged* view of what is of value.

Zhuāngzǐ undermines the assumption that our own perspectives are uniquely correct not by discrediting them but by undermining their claim to have exhausted what there is to see, and this involves opening our eyes to perspectives other than our own. We are not disabused of the notion that our moralities embody real values. We are compelled to recognize that others embody real values just as ours do. In this strain of argument I am highlighting, then, Zhuāngzǐ's appreciation for diversity is a *moral* stance at the same time as it constitutes a distancing from one's own original moral commitments.

On my view, moral values are human inventions that answer to compelling human needs and desires (as noted earlier, a predecessor in defending this view is Xúnzǐ), and are subject to the constraints derived from human nature and the function of facilitating and promoting social co-operation. I have argued, for example, that given this function of morality, the value of contest must include an element of harmony, and that harmony must include an element of contest in order to integrate properly the individual's self-regarding and competitive motivations with shared ends of the group. Within such constraints, the Zhuangist vision encourages us to recognize that there is no uniquely best way to satisfy important needs. Instead, there are plural ways to satisfy those needs, none of them the best because each succeeds in emphasizing certain basic values only by paying a cost in other values. Every coherent moral code loses something of genuine value. Every coherent code, in defining what is right, also requires what is wrong. Zhuāngzǐ's constructive skeptical argument holds that typical normative perspectives go astray in claiming an exclusive and comprehensive insight into value, and it encourages us to retain our own commitments as commitments to genuine values, but also to expand our view of what other commitments have a similar status.

A culture can encourage the competitive ambition of individuals and attempt to harness the considerable resulting energies for the common good. But it must also be prepared to deal with the hazards of encouraging competitive ambition — all the different ways that such ambition can undermine the common good. A culture can encourage non-contentious harmony and thereby avoid many of the hazards of encouraging competitive ambition, but then it must be prepared to deal with the hazards of sliding into an enforced unity that stifles the creative energies of individuals and thereby impoverishes and stultifies the common good or ultimately engenders rebellion by those members whose interests are systematically subordinated. Cultures that emphasize one or the other value must be prepared to pay a price for doing so, and though they can avoid some of the cost by recognizing the necessity of the other value in that pair, it is difficult for me to believe that there is a single perfect point of balance between these values. At the perfect midpoint between the Greek celebration of *agon* and the Chinese prizing of *hé*, there may lie not perfect balance but bland mediocrity, with neither the zestful individuality that emerges in cultures that emphasize contest nor the heartening gathering of spirits that emerges in cultures that emphasize non-contentious harmony.

The Zhuangist perspective also encourages us to learn from other moralities. Recognizing the worth of other ways of life can and often should have a deeper and wider effect on one's original moral commitments. If one genuinely appreciates the use of gourds as tubs to float around in, one is unlikely to remain the sort of person who smashes them when one fails to use them as water dippers. If one opens up one's mind to new sources of value, one should sometimes go beyond acceptance of the new towards incorporating it into one's commitments. One need not try to incorporate an entirely different way of life into one's commitments. Alternatively, one seeks to affirm certain values underlying that other way of life by balancing one's efforts to realize them in relation to values one already affirms. In other words, our moral commitments should remain open-ended and flexible, to a certain degree indeterminate with respect to what values it affirms and what the relationship of priority is among those values in case of conflict. We must remain ready to affirm values and priorities that are not presently encompassed by our current commitments.

For example, many in the United States have forgotten about the kind of harmony that is required to harness the energies of self-regarding and competitive motivations for the sake of shared ends. They could learn from the Confucian notion of ritual (lǐ 禮) as fostering a sense of community and shared ends.[11] On the other side, Chinese might consider with interest a changed attitude toward contest not only as a sometime necessity but also as a joy for its own sake. This would not only encourage the readiness to articulate and defend one's legitimate interests but also reap the benefits of the exuberant energies that come along with delight in competition. If the originally American game of basketball can become the hugely popular sport it is now in China, then other forms of contest may come to be accepted to enliven and encourage the harmony that is not necessarily agreement.

NOTES

1. This wording is taken from Keightley (1990, 54). It should be noted, however, that Keightley qualifies the contrast as one of "emphasis or nuance" and not an "absolute distinction" (1990, 53).
2. For an extensive discussion of the character of Hector in the *Iliad*, see Redfield (1975).
3. See Nietzsche (2004), especially paragraphs 8–12, pp. 11–13.
4. The latter strategy requires people to be selective imitators and to have at least an inkling of what good solutions to common problems are. See Boyd and Richerson (1985, 2005).

5. This does not mean that directly facilitating social co-operation is the only function of morality. Some moral norms take the form of character ideals and conceptions of the good life specifying what is worthwhile for the individual to become and to pursue. This intrapersonal function of morality comprehends what has been called the "ethical," as opposed to what might be called the "narrowly moral." Morality in the broader sense used here comprehends the ethical. This part of morality helps human beings to structure their lives together in a larger sense, i.e., not just for the sake of co-ordination with each other but also for the sake of co-ordination within themselves.
6. See Hobbes (1994), Warnock (1971), and Mackie (1977, ch. 5). Xúnzǐ's view is ambiguous. He wavers between claiming that inculcation of moral norms can actually create other-regarding behavior, claiming that moral norms strengthen and channel other-regarding impulses that naturally exist alongside the self-regarding ones. See Wong (1996).
7. My rendering of this passage is adapted from the translation by Graham (2001, 67).
8. An excerpt of this work is translated under the title "Human rights and Chinese tradition" in Angle and Svensson (2001, 372–89). For Stephen C. Angle's discussion of harmony, see Angle (2002, 231–33).
9. A point that was raised at the Beijing Forum.
10. Zhū Xī (1996) (c.1245). See De Weerdt (2006) for a discussion of Zhū Xī's proposed reforms of the examination system.
11. I have written about the possibility of democratized ritual in Wong (2000) and chapter 9 of Wong (2006).

References

Acampora, C. 2002. Nietzsche contra Homer, Socrates, and Paul. *Journal of Nietzsche Studies* 24: 25–53.

Ames, R. 1993. *Sun-Tzu: The art of war.* New York: Ballantine Books.

Ames, R., and H. Rosemont, Jr. 1998. *The Analects of Confucius: A philosophical translation.* New York: Ballantine Books.

Angle, S. 2002. *Human rights and Chinese thought: A cross-cultural inquiry.* Cambridge: Cambridge University Press.

Angle, S., and M. Svensson, eds. 2001. *The Chinese human rights reader: Documents and commentary 1900–2000.* Armonk, NY: M. E. Sharpe.

Boyd, R., and P. Richerson. 1985. *Culture and the evolutionary process.* Chicago, IL: University of Chicago Press.

———. 2005. *Not by genes alone: How culture transformed human evolution.* Chicago, IL: University of Chicago Press.

De Weerdt, H. 2006. Changing minds through examinations: Examination critics in late imperial China. *Journal of the American Oriental Society* 126 (3): 367–77.

Gintis, H. 2000. *Game theory evolving.* Princeton, NJ: Princeton University Press.

Graham, A. 2001. *Chuang-Tzu: The inner chapters.* Indianapolis, IN: Hackett Publishing Company.

Hamilton, W. 1964. The genetical evolution of social behavior. *Journal of Theoretical Biology* 7: 1–52.

Hobbes, T. 1994. *Leviathan: With selected variants from the Latin edition of 1668*, ed. E. Curley, part 1, chaps. 13–16, part 2, chap. 17. 74–109. Indianapolis, IN: Hackett.

Keightley, D. 1990. Early civilization in China: Reflections on how it became Chinese. In *Heritage of China: Contemporary perspectives on Chinese civilization*, ed. P. Ropp. 15–54. Berkeley: University of California Press.

Knoblock, J. 1999. *Xunzi: A translation and study, vol. 2*. Chángshā, Húnán: Húnán People's Publishing House.

MacIntyre, A. 2007. *After virtue: A study in moral theory*, 3rd ed. Notre Dame, IN: University of Notre Dame Press.

Mackie, J. 1977. *Ethics: Inventing right and wrong*. London: Penguin.

Miyazaki, I. 1981. *China's examination hell*, trans. C. Schirokauer. New Haven, CT: Yale University Press.

Nietzsche, F. 1997. Homer's contest, trans. J. Dieterich and J. Lungstrum. In *Agonistics: Arenas of creative contest*, ed. J. Lungstrum and E. Sauer. 35–45. Albany: State University of New York Press.

———. 2004. The problem of Socrates. In *Twilight of the idols, or how one philosophizes with a hammer* (*Götzen-Dämmerung, oder Wie man mit dem Hammer philosophiert*). In *Twilight of the idols and the antichrist*, trans. T. Common. 9–13. New York: Dover.

Plato. 1953. *Plato: Collected dialogues, vol. 1*, trans. B. Jowett. Oxford: Clarendon Press.

Redfield, J. 1975. *Nature and culture in the Iliad: The tragedy of Hector*. Chicago, IL: University of Chicago Press.

Sax, B. 1997. Cultural agonistics: Nietzsche, the Greeks, eternal recurrence. In *Agonistics: Arenas of creative contest*, ed. J. Lungstrum and E. Sauer. 50–58. Albany: State University of New York Press.

Siemens, H. 2002. Agonal communities of taste: Law and community in Nietzsche's philosophy of transvaluation. *Journal of Nietzsche Studies* 24: 83–112.

Sober, E. and D. Wilson. 1998. *Unto others: The evolution and psychology of unselfish behavior*. Cambridge, MA: Harvard University Press.

Warnock, G. 1971. *The object of morality*. London: Methuen.

Wong, D. 1996. Xunzi on moral motivation. In *Chinese language, thought, and culture: Nivison and his critics*, ed. P. Ivanhoe. 202–23. Chicago, IL: Open Court. Reprinted in *Virtue, nature and moral agency in the Xunzi*, ed. J. Kline and P. Ivanhoe. Indianapolis, IN: Hackett Publishing Company, 2000.

———. 2000. Fragmentation in civil society and the good. In *Civility*, ed. L. Rouner. 200–21. Notre Dame, IN: University of Notre Dame Press.

———. 2006. *Natural moralities*. New York: Oxford University Press.

Xià, Y. 夏勇. 1992. 人權概念起源 (The origin of the concept of human rights: A Chinese interpretation). Běijīng: Zhōngguó Zhèngfǎ Dàxué.

Xúnzǐ 荀子. 1978. 王先謙, 荀子集解 (Wáng Xiānqiān, collected commentaries on *Xúnzǐ*). In 諸子集成 (*Collected works of various masters*), vol. 2. Hong Kong: Zhōnghuá.

Zhū Xī 朱熹. 1996. 學校貢舉私議 (Private opinion on schools and selection through examinations). In 朱熹集 (*Zhū Xī's collected works*) 69.3632–43. Chéngdū: Sìchuān Jiàoyù.

11

Confucianism and Moral Intuition

William A. Haines

Much modern moral philosophy has sought theories that explain and correct our "moral intuitions" — as though feelings without apparent grounds can amount to prima facie knowledge of what to do or what is moral. The better we understand the possible mechanisms of intuitive knowledge, in general and about morality, the better we can evaluate or pursue this project.

Looking mainly at the *Analects*, the *Lǐjì* 禮記, and the *Mencius*, I shall argue that early Confucianism has much to show us about such mechanisms. The early Confucians developed, engaged in, and promoted a set of practices meant to improve our sensibility about the world around us, centering on matters of moral importance and on what to do. Central among these practices was what the Confucians called "ritual" or *lǐ* 禮. The early Confucians were not, however, theorists. (It is said that Confucius even flirted with the idea of dispensing with language altogether, *Analects* 17:19.) Their focus was instead the practical work of developing and using ritual, a body of largely non-linguistic signs. Most of the Confucians' speech and writing aimed not at theory but at other supports and extensions of ritual, such as poetry, rules and records, terse but persuasive conversation, and pithy sayings designed to focus various people's practical attention.

The flexible term "intuition" means something like "mysterious sensibility." It suggests knowledge we have on no readily apparent grounds, especially by some process analogous to seeing. Intuitive knowledge is knowledge that (for deeper reasons than limited memory) we cannot readily trace to a premise, a piece of evidence, or an authoritative pronouncement. An experienced footballer sometimes knows *intuitively* to sprint rightward; that is, she has no specific grounds that she or we could notice or report if asked.[1] But when one unconsciously turns right on the road to work, knowing to turn is not intuitive, for the grounds are no mystery.

Insofar as the Confucians were making moral sensibility less mysterious, then, one might suppose they were shrinking the realm of intuition. However, as we shall see, certain features of moral sensibility tend to keep its detailed workings partly obscure, so that understanding and applying techniques that expand our sensibility may yield more intuitive knowledge, not less. The footballer understands that, by long hours of attending and responding to certain kinds of cue, she has learned to attend and respond to similar but subtler cues, beyond her own ability to trace.

Knowledge and Non-Linguistic Signs

It will be helpful to consider at the outset some of the diversity of "knowledge," attending both to English and to early Chinese. The English word "know" and the early Confucians' "*zhī* 知" can each take sentences as direct objects ("How do you know I can?", *Mencius* 1A:7). They also take simple nouns as direct or indirect objects, such as "sprouts," "Confucius," or "governing." In such cases "*zhī*" is perhaps always translatable as "know about." The context narrows down what may be meant, such as knowing that X exists, being able to recognize or navigate X, knowing what parts or significance X has, or knowing what to do regarding X. In a smallish subclass of the Chinese cases, X is an activity. Among these are the cases when "*zhī*" may be translated more narrowly either as "know to" or "know how to."

The familiar overlapping categories (a) *propositional knowledge* or *knowing that p*, (b) *knowing-how*, and (c) *knowing-to*, might cover all this territory; for *knowing horses* arguably amounts to some complex of all three categories.[2] Someone who knows horses knows facts about them, knows how to ride them, and knows not to leave them too long in the rain. More important for our purposes, however, is a different kind of rough category, largely cutting across these.

By *sentential* knowledge I mean knowledge mediated by sentences. That is, the knower can somewhat readily review and express its content in true sentences, and the same sentences are natural media for giving and receiving the knowledge. Much knowing-how and knowing-to is not sentential knowledge. Also, it would seem that not all propositional knowledge is sentential. The dog Fido has no sentential knowledge, but he does seem to know sometimes that he is about to go for a walk.

Interestingly, "know" and "*zhī*" also take a kind of object that we might call a nominalized open sentence, as in "the officers do not yet know where you are going" (1B:16). Knowing "where you are going" is not a familiarity with that place, nor knowledge that it exists, nor skill in dealing with it. Rather, the noun phrase picks out an open sentence, "You are going to X," which if completed would give the content of the knowledge. It does not follow that anyone who has such knowledge is prepared to complete the sentence with words that convey the knowledge. You can know how potato chips taste, the layout of your home, how paisley looks, and what the moves of the Macarena are, even if you cannot find even remotely adequate words. To complete a representation for such knowledge, you may have to see or show something: a picture, diagram, model, or representative sample. Paisley looks *thus*.

Each of the examples just listed has only one foot in the category of sentential knowledge. They suggest a companion rough concept: knowledge that is mediated by signs other than sentences.

For convenience I shall borrow a taxonomy of signs from Charles S. Peirce, who once wrote, "A sign is something by knowing which we know something more" (1958, 390; I would amend his account to allow that we might only *seem* to know something more). Peirce distinguished three kinds of relation that can help one thing be a sign of another: similarity, contact or correlation, and convention. Where a sign functions by similarity or resemblance, as one flake of gold promises more gold or a sketch helps us learn a face, it is an *icon*; where it functions by contact or correlation, as smoke indicates fire, it is an *index*; and where it functions by convention, as an "L" or a "Large" on a shirt signifies a size, it is a *symbol* (1958, 368). We can call knowledge by way of icons *iconic* knowledge, and so on.

Often one can translate a non-linguistic sign into a sentence, based on two aspects of the sign. For example, some signs are both icon and index. By knowing the taste of one spoonful, I know the taste of the house soup in general. The former is both icon and index of the latter. Similarly, when a bag of chips bears a picture of chips, almost as though the bag were transparent, the picture is an indexical icon of the contents. Its coloring shows *what* and its location shows *where*. The sign says *such* are *here*. Or vice versa: *here* is *thus*. One can thus translate the sign into a sentence, or the framework of a sentence filled out by some showing. But one need not. Analogously, the L is not only a symbol of largeness, but it is also an index of the shirt. Hence it says "This is large." The leash in your hand has two indexical aspects: it correlates with walks and it is now. It says "A walk is coming now." Fido understands.

The ways a sign can be significantly attached to or correlated with an aspect of the world shades smoothly into the way one sign is significantly attached to another sign (syntax, if you like). As an "L" is significantly on a certain part of a shirt, so "Orly" or a picture of an airplane is significantly near a dot or patch on a map.

Some Basic Confucian Icons

Early Confucian ritual is full of iconic signs. Some seem designed to support awareness of distant circumstances.

> In bad years, when the grain is not growing well, the ruler at his meals will not make the offering of the lungs, nor will his horses be fed on grain. His special road will not be kept clean and swept, nor at sacrifices will his musical instruments be hung on their stands. Great officers will not eat the large grained millet; and (other) officers will not have music at their drinking.[3]

Here the people's hardship is depicted for the rulers in the medium of the rulers' own hardship, by way of our natural tendency to project our own circumstances onto the wider world.

Other iconic signs display relationships. In Confucian practice, standing beneath someone displays subordination. Walking behind someone displays followership. Such nonverbal diagrams resemble their objects to the mind's eye, partly because we use spatial metaphors to conceive vertical relationships.

More specifically, my walking behind you is a sign of my intention to follow you, my actually following you now and in future, and the propriety of my doing so. It is a sign of each of these things to me and to others; though of course it may be used to deceive. Here is a more complex example from the *Lǐjì*:

> That the ruler's kindred appeared at the reception in the inner court honored the family relation. That they took places according to their age, even those of high rank, showed the right relation between father and son. That they took places at the reception in the outer court according to their offices meant they formed one body with the other families. (8.11/58/22)

These arrays simultaneously show how things are at this court and how things should be. They are signs-of and signs-to, mediating knowing-of and knowing-to.

Similarity adjusted for scale operates in a sign of high rank whose misapplication disturbs Confucius: "Eight rows of eight dancers in the courtyard! If this can be tolerated, what cannot be tolerated?"[4] The wider your sway, the more people dance to your tune, as we were reminded at the opening ceremonies of the 2010 Beijing Summer Olympics.

Herbert Fingarette has stressed that Confucian ritual is imagery. He uses a handshake as an image of the way Confucian ritual is an image of social harmony in the abstract (1972, 9–10, 63, 67). Here is an example of the sort of thing he has in mind. In the *Shījīng* 詩經, Ode 209 describes a sacrificial festival. The song would presumably have been the conclusion of the festival, shaping the participants' sense of the event. In the song, each kind of participant, from lowest to highest, plays a distinct part in the festivities, until "small and great bow heads" in a unison prayer that completes the song and the ceremony. In the words of another scholar, the festival described in this and other such songs amounts to "a beatific vision of sacramental social harmony."[5] Thus the festival displays hierarchical social co-operation as the life of the party of community. The festival also displays to each person everyone else's *image* of social harmony, and displays that everyone is happily co-operating. Such an image of society might help make itself accurate.[6]

The idea that ritual is to guide non-ritual action (cf. *Analects* 12:2) is consistent with the idea that what ritual does is to *display* something.

> The ceremonies at the seasonal court audiences are to show (*míng* 明) the right relations between ruler and subject; those of friendly messages and inquiries, to secure mutual honor and respect between the feudal lords; those of mourning and sacrifice, to show the goodwill of subordinates and sons; those of rural drinking, to show the [proper] order between young and old; and those of marriage, to show the [proper] separation of males and females. Those ceremonies prevent disorder, like embankments preventing the overflow of water. (*Lǐjì* 禮記 27.4/134/19–21)

These rituals show what to do, or how to act, so that people will know. They are concrete metaphors for forms of social order, and thereby for order itself. Like the festival, these models are attractive to each person partly because they are the models others hold up and are prepared to follow.

Icons and Intuition

As icons are typically also indices, I shall usually refer to indexical icons simply as icons. Now, icons are better suited than symbols to support intuition. Granted, there is no sharp line between icons and symbols. The main work of the photograph on the bag of chips could be done by a pictogram logo or by the word "chips." But there is an interesting difference. Consider again the house soup. In tasting the layer that lies closest to my tongue, I taste the whole spoonful, and thereby this bowl of soup, and thereby what yours tastes like or would have tasted like, not to mention the actual and potential house soup of strangers at other tables today and other days. We can distinguish as many or few signs as we like, or we can simply speak of tasting the house soup. When I see your face in a photocopy of a drawing on television through a reflecting telescope, I am (as I said) seeing your face. While signs without similarity tend to draw attention to themselves and to the cognitive processes by which we pass from knowing the sign to knowing the signified, iconic signs are comparatively transparent or invisible. They are more easily overlooked. In that respect they better support intuition.

Icons suit intuition better than sentences do, partly because they fit a model of the extension of knowledge as *projection* rather than inference. Where an inference model suggests deliberate verbal reasoning, a projection model suggests a more automatic or even involuntary nonverbal process (natural or trained), a process the knower may not notice. "[A cap] with strings hanging down five inches: the idle and listless officer. A dark cap with the roll round it of white silk: one excluded from the ranks of his compeers" (*Lǐjì* 13.11/81/11–12). The first cap depicts in a loose abstract way what one can expect from that officer. Because it is marginally less conventional than the second, it can be read with less training and less attention (if the two caps are equally vivid and commonplace). Even a dog can project: she can know how you will treat her by how you have been treating her. She need only form expectations in ways that track the truth. Hence while the inference-from-evidence model suggests coming to a final conclusion that we first formulate and then accept, the projection model suggests that our current knowledge extends indefinitely without our notice, gradually losing precision and warrant (not necessarily at the same rate) as it gains distance. In knowing how this spoonful tastes, you know how the soup would taste to me, and perhaps roughly how it would taste to bears, or bears next Tuesday, even without articulating or even noticing such topics.

Conversely, while the inference model suggests that I have a good grasp of my premises, the projection model is friendlier to the idea that I need not distinctly conceive very near signs, such as those bits of soup that actually touch my tongue, or a three-second time-slice of Mount Tài that I see for a second, or the moving patches of color on the television screen. Our knowledge of very near signs may often conceive them indistinctly, at least indistinctly from farther things they signify.

Iconic Feelings and Action-Guiding Signs

We often take as a mark of knowledge by intuition or sensibility that it is carried in the medium of feelings. There is nothing unusual about a feeling's being an iconic sign, most simply for *further feelings*. I know whether you and I would enjoy the soup by trying one spoonful (see *Mencius* 6A:7). I know how I am feeling this morning by how I feel right now. The pleasure in the anticipation of a kiss is an image of the pleasure of the kiss. If you kick me I may reciprocate, showing how it feels. Similarly, when the ruler's unswept road and unhung lutes represent a lean year for the people, feelings are the most clearly iconic element in the sign, as the ruler's discomfort represents the people's discomfort. And when a happy festival depicts happy social harmony, the participants' enjoyment would seem to be part of the picture.

Because feelings can be signs and parts of signs, iconic vehicles of awareness can be inherently action-guiding. The tingle draws me to the kiss. It can be a sign to kiss now, helping me know to kiss. Thus the idea that feelings can be signs and parts of signs helps *knowing-that* overlap with *knowing-to*. It can help explain how and when propositional knowledge about morality can be motivating.

By "feelings" one might mean *raw feels*: qualities of experience analogous to colors on a Cartesian view. We might thus conceive iconic feelings on the model of Cartesian iconic colors: in getting a red patch from a rose, I see what private color the geometric rose occasions for others and for me later. This conception of iconic feelings may suit a sort of knowledge that is mainly contemplative rather than practical: knowing-of and knowing-about rather than knowing-to.

If a Cartesian drops the inner theater but keeps a Cartesian view of what remains, she may think of feelings instead as wrinkles, jiggles, motion vectors, or machine programs. Chad Hansen sometimes seems to recommend interpreting early Chinese texts in a framework of post-Cartesian physicalism: "We shouldn't elaborate the Confucian view using the mythology of the inner individual. We have no evidence of the beliefs and desires of a child aside from her behavioral tendencies. Let us speak directly of those tendencies, of natural human inclinations and capacities" (1992, 77). He uses machine programming as a model of the early Chinese view of the function of language and characterizes Mencius's sympathetic bystander at the well as having only "motivational tugs" toward helping. Still, there is room even in post-Cartesianism for iconic feelings. In bad years, when the people are fidgeting, the rulers can be made to fidget too. And if I am properly sensitized or magnetized to others, I will go with the flow, or at least be tugged.

More likely the early thinkers would have had the *naïve* view, if that is the word I want, that the red is in the rose. The naïf might have no thought of inner red patches; for if such patches do exist, one's own may be hard to distinguish from the rose. Easier to notice are one's own and others' feelings. And just as the naïf locates the red in the rose, she might locate pain in an elbow, or other feelings in the face or elsewhere in the person, if she locates them at all (see, e.g., *Mencius* 6A:7). You and I can both see the color of my rose-colored glasses, at least when they are not in my pocket, out of our view; we can both feel how hot my hands are when we touch or almost touch; and we can both feel my feelings, at least when I wear them in my face and demeanor and do not bury them only in my heart, where you and I may apprehend them only indirectly (*Mencius* 1A:7).[7]

In feeling my feelings I can be feeling something further, such as your feelings. Your feelings too, then, can be icons for me: in feeling *your* feelings I can feel something further. Suppose you are distressed to see a child at a well, and begin to move. I see you and feel your distress, but I do not see the child or the well. In feeling your distress I am not feeling specifically the child's danger, but (especially if I know you) I *am* feeling that something very bad is imminent. My feeling is an icon for your feeling, which is an icon for further potential feeling. One person's sensibility piggybacks on another's. Hence to extend the vision of our affective sensibility on some topic, one effective procedure is to feel out our friends on the topic, by talking with them or at least thinking how they would feel, respecting their sensibility. We should find friends by whom we can see well, and respect their feelings. Perhaps that is why Confucius says, "Friends who are upright, honest, or well-informed are a gain. Friends who are biased, eager to please, or smooth-tongued, are a loss" (*Analects* 16:4).

Ritual that involves displays of feelings, like Confucian mourning ritual, helps display a person's feelings to herself and to others.

> When [one's father] has just died: quite overcome, as at wits' end. When the corpse has been put into the coffin: quick and sorrowful glances, as seeking and unable to find. When the interment has taken place: alarmed and restless, as looking for someone who does not arrive. At the end of the first year's mourning: sad and disappointed. At the end of the second year's: vague and uncertain. (*Lǐjì* 3.19/13/1–2)

Such a display is a sign of that mourner's own character, or general attitudes (*Mencius* 3A:2), and of the *proper* feelings in such cases. More directly, the sorrow displays the magnitude of the mourner's loss. This in turn, as a representative sample, displays to everyone the importance of everyone's family.[8] Naturally, the ritual display of feelings led to problems about sincerity, which drew attention to distinctions between gesture and feeling.

Feelings can be displayed in other ways than by facial expressions and gestures. Music, for example, can communicate feelings. Pieces of music are indeed not faces or persons, and so arguably cannot have feelings, nor be perfect icons for feelings. There must be limits to how far an aspect of music can be similar to a feeling, although a piece of music can certainly "feel sad" and thereby represent a film character's mood. People concerned about icons for feelings will be concerned about these issues, as the *Yuèjì* 樂記 book of the *Lǐjì* seems to be. It catalogues at length which specifically musical qualities cause and are caused by which feelings and temperaments, so that music can help bring people's hearts together (*tóng mín xīn* 同民心) as ritual and government do.

> When the mind [of the musician] is moved to sorrow, the sound is sharp and fading away; when it is moved to pleasure, the sound is slow and gentle; when it is moved to joy, the sound is exclamatory and soon disappears ... (19.1/98/14–15)

> When [the ruler] is generous, harmonious, and of a placid and easy temper, the notes are varied and elegant, with frequent changes, and the people are satisfied and pleased; when he is coarse, violent, and excitable, the notes, vehement at first and distinct in the end, are full and bold throughout the piece, and the people are resolute and daring ... (19.11/100/28–29)

Confucian Protocols for Perceptiveness

One reason to think about sensibility is to judge its authority and scope. A second is to extend our view, and aim it in the most important directions. Here I shall focus only on the second project, and only in connection with one kind of sensibility: knowing of feelings by way of similar feelings. I shall argue that much early Confucian self-cultivation is intelligible as the application of procedures to extend the range of our affective sensibility, especially in the direction of what is morally important.

I have already suggested that many elements of Confucian ritual extend affective insight, for the participants and other observers. Let us turn for a moment to procedures for the individual knower.

Confucius gives some advice that could be designed to extend our sensibility by removing interference: he recommends that we avoid pursuing or dwelling on glory, fine clothing, fine food, sex, or drink, so as to avoid feeling too strongly about them (*Analects* 1:1, 1:14, 4:9, 16:5).

We can classify other procedures by the positive lines of insight or directions of projection they promise to help with. (1) Some procedures help me feel my own past and potential future feelings regarding particular persons or projects. I can be more self-sensitive by being more constant and orderly, avoiding "confusion." To train myself against confusion I might follow Confucius's practice: "On a day when he had wept, the master did not sing" (*Analects* 7:10). And again: "[Confucius asked the messenger about Zǐlù's death.] 'They have made him into pickle,' said the messenger; and forthwith Confucius ordered the pickles [in the house] to be thrown away" (*Lǐjì* 3.7/11/21–2). I might also follow his advice: In any task, do the hard part first (*Analects* 6:22); put the work before the reward (12:21). Be blind to small gains and attend to the big picture (13:17). Avoid the cheap pleasure of announcing your good deeds in advance; and if you do give your word, keep it (4:22, 4:24).

(2) To make my feelings better reflect how *others* are feeling *now,* I might follow Confucius's practice: "When eating in the presence of a mourner, the Master never ate his fill" (*Analects* 7:9). And again: "When the Master saw people in mourning, in ceremonial garb, or blind, he would . . . rise to his feet, even if they were young" (9:10). I might also follow his advice: be attentive to the words and faces of others (12:20). Respect and care about others, and pursue fellowship (e.g., 1:6). Mencius tries to lead rulers to think about their people, to imagine what it is like to be in their shoes, to sympathize, and to "share enjoyment" with the people by sharing objects of enjoyment such as music and parks (1A:7, 1B1–5).[9] He says that if the ruler is happy at the people's happiness and sad at their sadness, they will reciprocate (1B:4).

(3) A more directly practical line of projection is from a person's feelings about her *current options* to the broad implications of her options, so that her feelings about her options better reflect the overall implications of those options, and she will favor an enterprise insofar as it is beneficent. To some extent we naturally project in that direction. When the infant is at the edge of the well, a bystander will find inaction distressing, feeling the distress it risks for others (*Mencius* 2A:6). To expand practical compassion, Mencius proposes procedures for deliberation and for longer-term self-training. In deliberation I can make my feelings better reflect what is at stake for others by paying imaginative attention to those others and to my heart (1A:7). In the longer term I can train myself to be more practically compassionate by regularly acting on whatever compassion I already have. Mencius believes my sympathy will then grow (1A:7, 2A:2, 6A:8). Confucius gives another piece of advice:

> As for the *rén* 仁 person, insofar as he wants to be established, he establishes others, and insofar as he wants to achieve, he helps others to achieve. The ability to understand by analogy with what is near may be called the method of *rén*. (*Analects* 6:30)

Here Confucius states a rule of action and then seems to recast it as a deliberation procedure in which I take the felt desirability to me of certain hypothetical outcomes as an iconic sign of the goodness, or overall desirability, of my promoting similar outcomes for others. The fact that he offers this procedure as second-best to "benefitting the people extensively and saving the multitude" suggests that he may be thinking of it as a way of feeling out what is at stake for others in what I might do, either those I might help or for those *they* aspire to help (Chan 2000).

Now, one might wonder how the three directions of projection I have distinguished could be sorted out in practice. It cannot be right to project every feeling in all three directions. And if the people to my north are happy and those to my south are sad, what am I to feel?

My schematic exposition prompts these questions because it neglects the indexical aspect of iconic feelings. In fact the meaning of a feeling depends on its precise placement or context, rather as the meaning of a bit of color depends on its location in a surface, picture, map, or traffic light. If a patch of red is on the nose in a portrait, we should project it to the look on other occasions of that person's nose and that portrait's nose. (For learning the real face from the portrait, what matters is not the absolute size and brightness of the patch, but its size and brightness relative to the rest of the portrait's face.) And my pleasure of the moment might show me that I would like a kiss or that you would like the soup, depending on whether the pleasure is correlated with my mental approach to a kiss or my tongue's encounter with soup.[10]

We can simultaneously apprehend many colors in many positions. For the placement of feelings, time plays a more prominent role.

> When he went past the station of his lord, his expression became serious, his step brisk, and his words halting. When he [began] to ascend the hall, he drew himself in, and seemed not to be breathing. When he came out and descended the first step, he released his expression, as though relaxed. Having descended the stairs, he moved quickly as though on wings. When he resumed his station his bearing was respectful. (*Analects* 10:4)

Here the official displays different feelings or attitudes in connection with different places, drawing (or reflecting) an emotional diagram for himself and others. The inner coherence of the diagram helps, as apprehension when ascending matches relaxation when descending. Viewers will understand the arrows of importance, and empathetic viewers may absorb attitudes that cohere with the values displayed. Further, one presumably understands that the official's display is not simply to the lord on the official's behalf, nor simply to the audience of subordinates on the lord's behalf. Rather it is public, in all directions at once; and so it has a kind of claim to present a balanced, objective view. And since one understands that the official's performance is ritual, carrying perhaps a notional antiquity and meant to be replayed indefinitely, his display is not specifically his. It inherently refers not only to his current lord or the state of their relationship that day. Rather, as a sign of other performances on other occasions, it refers more universally to the nature of the roles involved. Perhaps such objectivity and universality are part of what Confucius has in mind when he suggests that one should conduct oneself in public affairs as though playing a role in a major public ritual (*Analects* 12:2).

We have sentential knowledge even when we are not attending to sentences, if we have the right dispositions. Similarly, we can have knowledge mediated by iconic feelings even when we are not having the feelings, if we are disposed to have the right feelings in the right connections. (Indeed we are never having all the feelings integral to a temporally extended representation.) By my disposition to feel good when contemplating Smith and bad when contemplating Jones, I know what each person's company would be like for me, now or later.

Therefore, to have a strong sensibility, one must have enough character to have firm and complex affective dispositions. These are the opposite of the emotional fickleness that Confucius calls *huò* 惑, or confusion. "When you love someone, you want him to live, and when you hate someone you want him to die. If, having wanted him to live, you want him to die, that is confusion" (*Analects* 12:10). Constancy of feeling allows a person to have attitudes. Perhaps that is why Confucius, who associates the quality of *rén* 仁 with stability, says that "only the *rén* person can love people or hate people" (4:3), and that one who is not *rén* "cannot long endure pressure and cannot long endure pleasure" (4:2). Steady pressure or pleasure would erase weak dispositions.

Moral Sensibility

Confucius relied on his sensibility to such an extent that one might almost suspect that his concerns were aesthetic *rather than* moral (e.g., *Analects* 17:18). His general sketches of how to live have nothing like the clarity we want in a good theory. But his emphasis on the golden rule, respect, good faith, and concern for others leave little room for doubt about his moral focus.

Sensibility by way of iconic feelings seems to be a key part of how the early Confucians tried to give and gain knowledge of what to do, or moral knowledge. (Of course any sensibility we have operates in combination with all our other knowledge.) The Confucians do not therein seem to have been barking up entirely the wrong tree. A person's feelings are prima facie marks of her intentions and of her interest or welfare. If my feelings about my options somehow reflect and respond to a wide range of others' feelings at stake in what I might do, then my preferences are moral in the sense that they strike some sort of balance of respect or care for a wide range of other people's intentions and interests.

More specifically, the utilitarian conception of morality as spreading happiness and preventing suffering suggests an especially simple account of how iconic feelings can help give moral knowledge. The best-developed sensibility would be built by procedures that tend to make moving toward any current option feel good in proportion as the option would tend to bring about happiness (so far as can be known in deliberation).

One might suppose that utilitarianism's problems disqualify it from playing a part in even the sketchiest defense of the claim that the Confucian sensibility is a genuine moral sensibility. In reply I shall argue that the kind of sensibility I have been describing can go some distance toward resolving utilitarianism's main problems.

The most pressing objections to utilitarianism, I submit, depend on the assumption that the only way to be genuinely aiming at the general happiness is to deliberate by articulately instrumental calculation or "sentential" thought about the effects of one's options, because such calculation is the only or best way to pursue such knowledge as can be had about how one can best promote happiness. Once that assumption is granted, utilitarianism is in deep trouble. For such a mode of deliberation toward the general happiness seems counterproductive in terms of the general happiness, and seems to oppose elements of moral common sense (or intuitions). As a general practice it promises to alienate one from others, stunting one's perceptiveness and understanding of the human condition.

The example of Confucian sensibility suggests, however, that the assumption may be wrong. Surely between two people who are not prepared to articulate the arcane concept "aggregate happiness," one can do a better job than the other of aiming at aggregate happiness. Verbally articulate knowledge about "aggregate happiness" is surely not the only kind of knowledge we can have of the implications of our options for aggregate happiness, and perhaps it is not the farthest-seeing or best-warranted kind of knowledge on that topic available to us. The epistemic shortcomings of the calculative approach lend support to the idea that our best mode of knowing the utilitarian value of our options takes some other form. If the epistemically best way to pursue utilitarian knowledge relies in some large part on our affective sensibility, then the best utilitarian is largely not a "calculator" but rather someone who pursues practical knowledge by developing her integrity, seeking and respecting good friends, opening her specific deliberations to them, and respecting their feelings.

I have not seen that contrast between methods drawn in Confucian literature.[11] But Confucius does sometimes make a point that is related, given certain Confucian assumptions about social psychology. Confucians saw themselves as transmitters of patterns: ritual and virtue. They expected to be copied. Insofar as they were right, their ritually proper conduct was an image of some of its own consequences. Confucius's view that patterns of conduct will be imitated (especially the traditional virtues, and especially the conduct of rulers) implies that conduct images some of its own consequences, the conduct of others. Confucius often used this point to argue against more crudely instrumental ways of influencing others' conduct. To promote virtue, he said, it is unnecessary and self-defeating to kill the vicious, or to issue commands and threats, or even to enter the government. The way to promote the virtues is to exemplify them, trusting in their contagion (*Analects* 2:3, 2:21, 12:19, 13:6; cf. 13:4; *Mencius* 1A:1, 6B:4).

Now, the traditional virtues have readily apparent local benefits: improving personal relationships and making projects go better. Our good feelings about the virtues presumably reflect those benefits. Insofar as the main important expectable further consequence of conduct is usually by way of the *propagation* of the same kind of conduct, so that the main farther consequence of virtuous conduct is more virtuous conduct with its local benefits elsewhere, one would in general be correct to project the local quality and benefits of one's conduct as an image of the conduct's overall consequences. Sensing the overall value of a form of conduct would then be fairly easy. One might even do it by simply neglecting to notice that one's conduct has non-local consequences. Hence it may be possible to see Confucius's argument against reliance on the coercive tools of government as part of an argument that the best way to promote happiness is to attend mainly to the shape of one's own conduct and character, or the people with whom one associates directly — largely obviating the need for sentential knowledge that is distinctly about farther consequences.[12]

One can see how an interest in lines of projection for moral sensibility might lead someone to be interested in questions about which forms and patterns tend to be replicated where, interested in promoting the replication of forms and patterns, and perhaps excessively optimistic about the extent to which one thing will copy another. When one thing matches another, sensibility can see farther (cf. 2:23).

NOTES

1. Looking at a leaf, I temporarily know that it has *that shape*, knowledge that I cannot put all into words. I want to say the reason such knowledge is not "intuitive" is that it is articulated for me in the *look* of the leaf, or the leaf itself, while I attend.
2. Chad Hansen holds that *zhī* 知 often refers to a species of knowledge beyond all these, which he terms *knowing-of, knowing-about*, and *knowledge by acquaintance* (Hansen 1983, 66; 1992, 8, 44). His examples suggest that he means knowing of X's existence, but he does not say how that might differ from knowing that X exists.
3. Lau and Feng (1992, 2.10/8/9–10). All citations to the *Lǐjì* are from this edition. Translations are adapted from Legge (1885).
4. *Analects* 3:1. Translations from the *Analects* are adapted from Lau (1979).
5. Schwartz (1985, 49). For further discussion see Haines (2008).
6. Michael Chwe has argued that a main function of most ritual is to solve co-.ordination problems by creating common knowledge (2001).
7. If smiles include feelings as the rose includes its fragrance, or the flame its heat, then one might wonder: Can feelings waft?
8. P. J. Ivanhoe has described public funerals as "opportunities to reflect upon" such matters (2002, 225). Confucians might have valued grief partly because it is so transparently *not* part of an exchange; it is not self-interested. The modern Western emphasis on elective affinities puts more emphasis on reciprocity and the negotiation of relationships. One thinks of the communication involved in looking someone in the eye. Confucianism, by contrast, stresses unconditional duties in non-discretionary vertical relationships.
9. At least because they are common objects, ritual ceremonies tend to put their participants on the same emotional page. A powerful recent example is China's national three-minute silence in memory of those who died in the 2008 earthquake. Such occasions can remind us of Roger Ames's point that some Confucians identified accurate imaging with things themselves *getting through* (1991, 230). The ceremony might well feel like an open window or channel through which powerful feelings flow.
10. Downplaying the explanatory importance of raw feels, Hansen notes that the difference between guilt and shame is not in their raw feels, which might be the same, but rather in "what kinds of considerations lead to the feeling" (1992, 397 note 29); that is, in what connection we feel bad. Indeed, the rawer the conception of "feelings" we are working with, the more fully the meaning of a "feeling" depends on its context.
11. But see Haines (2008).
12. Thanks to Chad Hansen and Dan Robins for helpful comments.

References

Ames, R. 1991. Meaning as imaging. In *Culture and modernity*, ed. E. Deutsch. 227–44. Honolulu: University of Hawai'i Press.

Chan, S. 2000. Can *shù* be the one word that serves as the guiding principle of caring actions? *Philosophy East and West* 50 (4): 507–24.

Chwe, M. 2001. *Rational ritual: Culture, coordination, and common knowledge.* Princeton, NJ: Princeton University Press.

Fingarette, H. 1972. *Confucius: The secular as sacred.* New York: Harper & Row.

Haines, W. 2008. The purloined philosopher: Youzi on learning by virtue. *Philosophy East and West* 58 (4): 470–91.

Hansen, C. 1983. *Language and logic in ancient China.* Ann Arbor: University of Michigan Press.

———. 1992. *A Daoist theory of Chinese thought.* New York: Oxford.

Ivanhoe, P. 2002. Confucian self-cultivation. In *Essays on the moral philosophy of Mengzi,* ed. X. Liu and P. Ivanhoe. 221–41. Indianapolis, IN: Hackett.

Lau, D. 1979. *The Analects.* London: Penguin.

Lau, D., and F. Chen, eds. 1992. *A concordance to the Lǐjì.* Hong Kong: Commercial Press.

Legge, J. 1885. *The sacred books of China: The texts of Confucianism, vols. 3 and 4.* Oxford: Clarendon Press.

Peirce, C. 1958. *Selected writings (values in a universe of chance),* ed. P. Weiner. New York: Dover.

Schwartz, B. 1985. *The world of thought in ancient China.* Cambridge, MA: Harvard University Press.

12
Chapter 38 of the *Dàodéjīng* as an Imaginary Genealogy of Morals

Jiwei Ci*

1

I want to discuss two short passages from Chapter 38 of the *Dàodéjīng* 道德經. The first, given below, contains a laconic description of a process of decline, beginning with the loss of *dào* 道 and culminating in the breakdown of order:

> When *dào* is lost, then arises *dé* 德;
> When *dé* is lost, then arises *rén* 仁;
> When *rén* is lost, then arises *yì* 義;
> When *yì* is lost, then arises *lǐ* 禮.
> *Lǐ* bespeaks the shortage of loyalty and fidelity
> and heralds the breakdown of order.[1]

This passage (call it the "decline" passage) tends to be approached without any distinction between an ordinary historical narrative, a historically true genealogy, and an imaginary genealogy.[2] Given a cultural phenomenon, say a morality, a historical narrative as such merely describes how it came about, while a genealogical narrative makes sense of it by showing, as in a historically true genealogy, or imagining, as in an imaginary genealogy, what conditions of life made its emergence necessary and possible. Without the benefit of some

---

* I presented an earlier version of this chapter at "Dao, Mind, and Language: A Conference in Honor of Chad Hansen," held at the University of Hong Kong in May 2008. I am grateful to fellow participants in that conference for challenging comments and helpful suggestions. Special thanks go to the editors of this volume, Chris Fraser, Timothy O'Leary, and Dan Robins, for further suggestions that have proved very useful. Tang Yun has been a source of much appreciated help, both philosophical and practical.

such distinction, an interpreter could easily be distracted from the philosophical import of the passage. One way of preempting such distraction, for those who are primarily interested in a philosophical interpretation, is to treat the passage as an exercise in imaginary genealogy, that is, as a series of what Nietzsche (1954, 690) calls backward inferences that serve to illuminate, say, moral phenomena by imagining, in a way that makes best sense from where we are, how they could have come about. The upshot of such an exercise constitutes, as one might say, the "meaning" or "inner logic" of the phenomena in question.

In the light of my reading of the "decline" passage, I will go on to interpret the second passage. It goes like this:

> The man of superior *dé* 德 does not consciously possess *dé*,
> And thus he is in possession of *dé*.
> The man of inferior *dé* never tires of cultivating and displaying *dé*,
> And in so doing he falls short of *dé*.

This passage (call it the "consciousness" passage) is about what it is for one to have and not to have *dé* and what consciousness has to do with it. It thus invites a moral-psychological reading. Although only *dé* is treated in this passage, the rationale that informs the treatment seems to cover *rén* 仁, *yì* 義, and *lǐ* 禮 equally well, and in any case this is how I will try to make sense of this passage.

In discussing both passages, I will have much to say about *rén*, *yì*, and *lǐ*. The conjoining of these three concepts cannot but remind one of the four virtues (*sìdé* 四德, the fourth and last being *zhì* 智, which is beyond our concern) in Confucian thought, especially as developed by Mencius. Although all four virtues appear in the *Analects*, it was in the *Mencius* that they were first brought together in one scheme. What is particularly noteworthy about this scheme, for our purposes, is that while *rén* is in a sense the most important member of the scheme, *rén*, *yì*, and *lǐ* are not conceived as belonging to a scale of descending importance. Rather, *rén* and *yì* are viewed as complementary, and so are *yì* and *lǐ*. This is consistent with the way in which all three virtues, even *lǐ*, are treated as inner capacities as distinct from mere patterns of behavior. Thus — and this can serve as a gloss on *rén*, *yì*, and *lǐ* as understood in Confucian thought — according to Mencius, *rén* is the inner capacity for compassion (*cè yǐn zhī xīn* 惻隱之心), *yì* is the inner capacity for shame and resentment (*xiū wù zhī xīn* 羞惡之心), and *lǐ* is the inner capacity for respect and reverence (*gōng jìng zhī xīn* 恭敬之心) (*Mencius*, 6A:6).

Now, this is clearly not how *rén*, *yì*, and *lǐ* are understood in the *Dàodéjīng* chapter under discussion, if only because there *rén*, *yì*, and *lǐ* are rank-ordered without ambiguity. Whatever the historical relation between these texts, the *Dàodéjīng* and the *Mencius*, it does not seem at all far-fetched to see the

Dàodéjīng chapter as pitting itself against the kind of Confucian understanding that is represented by Mencius. How, then, are we to approach the terms *rén, yì,* and *lǐ* as used in the *Dàodéjīng*? To begin with, these terms must, obviously, be construed in such a way that it makes sense to say what the *Dàodéjīng* says about the relationship between them, especially: "When *rén* is lost, then arises *yì*; when *yì* is lost, then arises *lǐ*." Provided that this requirement is met, I prefer, as far as possible, to operate at a high enough level of abstraction to capture what I believe are insights of a quite general character to be found in the *Dàodéjīng*. In Chapter 38, there is no mistaking a process of decline. It is nearly as obvious that the decline follows two axes: from a state of natural, non-moral orderliness to a morally ordered form of life and, within the latter, from the more natural (*rén* being next only to *dé*) and sincere to the more artificial and superficial. In keeping with the general tendency of the latter trajectory, I propose to understand *rén, yì,* and *lǐ*, somewhat freely perhaps (but I certainly hope not gratuitously), as spontaneous goodness, cultivated goodness, and cultivated propriety, respectively. Thus understood, *rén, yì,* and *lǐ* are highly abstract moral concepts that can accommodate a great variety of instantiations. Such instantiations give specific substance to the general concepts but do not affect the relationships that hold between these abstract concepts. It is what the *Dàodéjīng* passages have to say about these relationships that I want to examine here.

As general concepts, *rén, yì,* and *lǐ* can each be taken to mean a virtue or, more broadly, a type of morality centered on that virtue. It does not substantially matter, for my purposes, which meaning is adopted, for the important thing is to grasp the nature of the relationships that hold between *rén, yì,* and *lǐ*, whether these are taken to mean different levels of virtue or, more broadly, of morality. For simplicity and greater openness of implication, however, I shall more often than not take *rén* to be a type of morality centered on the virtue of *rén*, and I shall do the same with *yì* and *lǐ*.

2

This is what I take to be the central insight of the "decline" passage: there is a sense in which what a morality lacks is something that is the defining feature of a higher morality. Thus, *lǐ* lacks the cultivated goodness that is characteristic of *yì*, and *yì* in turn lacks the spontaneous goodness that is characteristic of *rén*. *Rén*, in turn, lacks whatever (say, the state of *wúwéi* 無為 that is natural and beyond good and evil) is characteristic of *dé*, but since this lack is not a moral deficiency, I will leave it, as well as *dé*'s lack of *dào*, out of my discussion. According to this way of looking at the matter, each level of morality is to be understood not so much in terms of what it has, its constituent elements, as by what it lacks, that is, by that whose absence makes it necessary in the first place. In this sense, what each morality lacks is identifiable as a positive feature of a higher morality.

To speak of lack (of something higher) is also to speak of need (for something lower). In each case it is the lack of something possessed by (what would be) a higher morality that makes a lower morality necessary, that gives it its *raison d'être*. Thus it is only because, or to the extent that, the spontaneous goodness characteristic of *rén* is lacking, in a person or in a society, that *yì*, with its conscious and conscientious attempt at goodness, is necessary. Otherwise there would be no need for, and no point in promoting, the morality of *yì*. Something analogous is true of the relationship between *yì* and *lǐ*. An ethic of rule-following that requires proper behavior but not necessarily proper motive has to be established whenever *yì* — the effective desire to do the right thing because, and in the conscious knowledge that, it is the right thing — is in short supply. It is this *one-way* relationship of lack or need that allows us to rank-order moralities, to regard one morality as superior to another.

As this relation of lack or need is presented in Chapter 38 of the *Dàodéjīng*, it is open to both an imaginary-genealogical and a historical reading. The reason is that the abstract concept of lack can easily be translated into the empirical concept of loss. With the latter concept, it is natural to speak of moral decline, from *rén* to *yì* and then to *lǐ*. Now, if we speak *strictly* of moral decline, the relationship between the three levels of morality is understood no longer simply in terms of inferences in the spirit of imaginary genealogy but more ambitiously in terms of real causes in real historical time.

Such a causal-historical reading, superimposed upon what need be no more than a series of imaginary-genealogical inferences, would have us believe that a process of decline actually occurred. It says that each of the three levels of virtue or morality has existed at some point and that the disappearance of each higher level led to the emergence of the immediately lower level. For those who go to Chapter 38 of the *Dàodéjīng* for philosophical illumination, such a reading unnecessarily raises the historical question of how the decline actually occurred, how each higher morality made way for a lower one. And the question itself assumes without proof that the morality of *rén* actually prevailed and then disappeared, followed by the emergence of the morality of *yì*, and so on.

As a matter of fact, the essential philosophical insight of the "decline" passage is quite independent of the apparently historical narrative in which it is embedded. We can reject, or leave aside, the validity of the implicit claim to historical truths without giving up the philosophical insight. Once this insight is approached in the spirit of imaginary genealogy, the process of moral decline depicted in the passage need not be assumed to have actually taken place. What is left is just the claim, a highly thought-provoking one, that insofar as a certain morality, say, the morality of *lǐ*, exists, it is a sign that something is lacking, something we have reason to assign to a higher morality. This claim tells us nothing, however, about whether the higher morality is real or imaginary.

When the "decline" passage says, "When *rén* is lost, then arises *yì*," it seems more in keeping with what is known of human history to suggest that the relationship between the two levels of morality is one of imaginary rather than actual decline, because there seems never to have been sufficient *rén* to make *yì* unnecessary. The superiority of *rén* to *yì* is a matter, therefore, only of inferences that belong to an imaginary genealogy. Something similar can be applied to the next step in the decline: "When *yì* is lost, then arises *lǐ*." Just as *yì* is called for in the absence of *rén*, so *lǐ* is made necessary by the lack, rather than necessarily the loss, of *yì*. In both cases, a rank-ordering of moralities rests on the basis of inferential rather than causal relations that hold between them.

Such inferences neither deny nor affirm that the emergence of *lǐ* actually followed the loss of *yì* or that the emergence of *yì* actually followed the loss of *rén*. To determine that would require a historical inquiry. If such an inquiry were to establish the actual historical sequence, it would turn mere inferences into causes. I am concerned here only with the more modest, and more purely philosophical, task of spelling out the inferences.

Such an inferential reading can already tell us a good deal about a morality by revealing its *raison d'être*, the conditions that would make sense of its emergence. In the case of the "decline" passage, there is a striking conclusion to be drawn from the insight that different levels of virtue or morality are marked by a *one-way* relationship of lack or need. From such a one-way relationship, it follows that any attempt to promote a morality by appealing to a higher morality — say, an attempt to promote a morality of *yì* by appealing to a morality of *rén* — is a self-contradictory enterprise that is doomed to failure from the start. Any such attempt would amount to denying the very absence of a morality for which a substitute, and lower, morality is necessary in the first place. If the higher morality existed already, it would be unnecessary to promote a lower morality as a substitute for it. If it did not exist, it would be useless to appeal to it in cultivating the lower morality. Precisely this mistake — the mistake of appealing to a higher morality or a higher virtue to make up for the lack of a lower one — is all too often what happens under the rubric of moral education. Confucius made this fundamental mistake, one that has been endlessly repeated since.

3

To avoid this mistake, it is necessary to know what it means to be, say, a distinctively *rén* person. It means, among other things, that one does not suffer from any deficiency for which one can find, as it were, a second-best solution in being a *yì* person. The same applies to what it means to be a *yì* person, and so on. But is it possible to *become* a *rén* person if one is not a *rén* person to begin with? Common sense suggests an affirmative answer. The *Dàodéjīng* cautions us to think again, and this brings me to the "consciousness" passage, the second passage I want to discuss. Here it is again (and, as I said earlier, I take this passage to be saying something important about all conscious virtues):

> The man of superior *dé* does not consciously possess *dé*,
> And thus he is in possession of *dé*.
> The man of inferior *dé* never tires of cultivating and displaying *dé*,
> And in so doing he falls short of *dé*.

How so? The answer has a lot to do with the nature of moral consciousness. Such consciousness arises from trying to make up for a deficiency, say, the lack of *rén*. Where a moral deficiency exists, effort needs to be directed at it, and such effort cannot but be conscious. Only a naturally and spontaneously good person, one who has no moral deficiency and therefore requires no moral effort to make up for it, can be good and yet not self-consciously so. There is a clear sense, then, in which the function of moral consciousness is remedial.

Something of great consequence follows from the remedial function of a conscious virtue. It is this: that the process of acquiring such a virtue has to rely on motivational resources that are not only other than but also lower than the motive that supposedly informs the virtue in question. One cannot rely on *rén* to become *rén*, or on *yì* to become *yì*, and so on. Nietzsche says it well: "To become moral is not in itself moral" (1982, aphorism 97). In the same spirit, we might say that to become *rén* is not in itself *rén*; to become *yì* is not in itself *yì*; and so on.

It would be misleading to counter this observation by taking *rén* and *yì* as matters of degree and suggesting that one can use, say, what little *rén* one has to become more *rén* or even completely *rén*. After all, a *rén* person or a *yì* person does not have a moral deficiency describable in terms of any considerable lack of *rén* or *yì*. For such a person, the question of *becoming rén* or *yì* does not arise: he already is a *rén* person or a *yì* person, already someone who acts as *rén* requires or as *yì* requires even when it is most difficult to do so. Consider, then, someone who does have a moral deficiency describable in terms of a considerable lack of *rén* or *yì*, someone who tends to fall short of *rén* or *yì*, at least when the going is tough. How can such a person become *rén* or *yì*? Surely not by drawing on *rén* or *yì*, for, *ex hypothesi*, *rén* or *yì* is precisely what is in short supply in the first place.

This is not merely a matter of description. Given the nature of the virtues we are discussing, one either has enough of a virtue, say, *rén*, in which case one would not need to rely on other motives to do what the virtue requires, or one does not, in which case one would. Indeed, having no need to draw on other motives to do whatever the virtue in question requires is what it means to have enough of that virtue. It might be objected, with physical strength as an example, that one can improve the strength of a weak muscle by exercising it in gradually more challenging ways until it is strong. It is not clear what is meant to be the counterpart of a weak muscle in a virtue such as *rén*. On its face, the exercising of a weak muscle into a strong one, presumably without the aid of steroids, shows one's capacity for muscularity to be fully present and in need only of that which can straightforwardly turn it into actuality. Nothing of the sort can be said of someone who has only a little *rén* to begin with. And it does not help that the case of physical strength lacks the motivational dimension that is constitutive of *rén* and *yì*. A more suitably analogous example is thus called for, and, given the relative ease with which introspection can tell its presence and absence, love should serve as a particularly fitting analogue.

Suppose that you do not love someone enough (by a standard with which you yourself identify), and as a result you do not sufficiently display the outward signs of love, say, through acts of care and sacrifice. By love here we mean, in line with common usage, the spontaneous feeling of love — as distinct from the desire to have that feeling, as when you want to love someone but cannot. What can you do? You certainly can learn to better display those outward signs in which you are now deficient, but just as certainly you will not do so from the spontaneous feeling of love, for such feeling is precisely what you do not have enough of to begin with. You must therefore rely on other motives, such as gratitude or sense of duty or sheer convenience, among countless others. You must rely on those of such motives of which you happen to have plentiful supply. No matter how well you thus succeed in displaying the outward signs of love, it is no use pretending that you have learned to do so from the spontaneous feeling of love. To be sure, your very willingness to draw on extraneous motives in maintaining the relationship may (or may not) show a modicum of spontaneous love, but this does not change the fact that you have a considerable lack of spontaneous love for the person in question and that what you lack in spontaneous love you can only make up for through extraneous motives. It is even possible that, in the course of repairing the relationship in this way, you make new discoveries about yourself or your partner until you chance upon a wellspring of spontaneous love that is strong enough to dispense with all mixed motives. What this happenstance changes, however, is only the initial premise, namely, that you do not love someone enough, not the fact that *as long as* you do not love someone enough, you are in no position to draw on spontaneous love to make up for your lack of spontaneous love. Whatever it is you draw on to overcome, that lack must be something else.

The same applies to moral learning. One overcomes the manifestations of a moral weakness by drawing on motives one has in abundance, whatever these happen to be, not by drawing on motives that are weak or scarce, even though in theory they are the best. It is in this way that one improves one's ability to act as *rén* or *yì* requires, much as one can improve one's ability to act as love requires in the absence of a sufficiently strong feeling of spontaneous love. But it is one thing to say that what is improved is one's ability to act as *rén* or *yì* requires and something altogether different to suggest that what causes this improvement is *rén* or *yì* itself, the counterpart of the spontaneous feeling of love. When one is not already *rén* or *yì*, there is no choice but to descend below *rén* or *yì* in search of motives to make one do what *rén* or *yì* requires. But then these lower motives cannot be what we mean by *rén* or *yì* motives proper, motives by which we define the exemplary *rén* person or *yì* person.

4

This conclusion is, obviously, very close in spirit and substance to the one I have earlier drawn in my discussion of the "decline" passage. Thus my two lines of inquiry, based on two separate passages in Chapter 38 of the *Dàodéjīng*, have converged. The first concludes, from the one-way relationship between different levels of morality, that it does not make sense to promote a morality by relying on motivational resources that belong to a *higher* morality. The second, taking the nature of moral consciousness as its object, reaches a similar but even more radical conclusion, namely, that the cultivation of a morality has to draw on motivational resources both different from and *lower* than those that supposedly inform it.

These conclusions strike me as unavoidable; the more so given that they are reached via different routes and yet point in the same direction. I am inclined to see them as belonging to what may be called the logic of moral cultivation: they set the limits of moral cultivation, showing in what ways moral cultivation cannot possibly work. These conclusions do not deny the existence of morality, say, of *rén* or *yì* or *lǐ*. What they suggest instead is that morality — *becoming* moral, to be more precise — rests on a misunderstanding. The misunderstanding is that it is by drawing on motives that define a virtue, or even motives that define a higher virtue, that one acquires that virtue. It is commonly believed, for example, that one becomes *yì* by drawing on the *yì* motive or by drawing on the higher, *rén* motive. This, according to our logic of moral cultivation derived from the *Dàodéjīng*, is a mistake.

How does one become *yì*, then? (I again use *yì* as an example to illustrate a general point.) Strictly speaking, one cannot become *yì* if one is not already *yì*. Less strictly speaking, one becomes *yì* by coming to behave as *yì* requires and yet on the basis of motives lower than *yì*. To become *yì*, then, is to acquire the ability to act *as if* one were *yì*. Because the *yì* thus acquired has an "as if" character, one can, without contradiction, rely on lower motives than *yì*, and the availability of such motives in one's moral makeup is entirely compatible with one's lack of *yì* proper to begin with.

This does not mean that a person who has become *yì* in this way is aware of the "as if" character of his acquired *yì*. Quite the contrary: it is an integral part of becoming a *yì* person, a person who lives up to what *yì* requires and does so from what he *sincerely takes to be* the *yì* motive, that this "as if" character is hidden from his conscious awareness. Otherwise we would be forced into the highly implausible view that anyone who has become a *yì* person by cultivation is deceiving others, and that he knowingly acts from motives lower than the *yì* motive and yet tries to pass for a *yì* person. To give a plausible picture of the *yì* person by cultivation, a picture that keeps him or her free from the unnecessary taint of conscious deception, and at the same time not to run afoul of the logic of moral cultivation, we must allow for the possibility that the *yì* person by cultivation misunderstands how he or she has become *yì*.

This misunderstanding, we may further surmise, is a social rather than an individual deed. In promoting *yì*, or any other virtue for that matter, society encourages or compels a certain pattern of behavior in the name of *yì* (or some other virtue) while leaving people to draw on *whatever motives they happen to have* in learning this pattern of behavior. As long as such motives, in all their empirical diversity, conduce to the expected end result, society has no reason to expose them as false ones. Only individual agents need to know, and even they know only imperfectly, what motives they actually have when they succeed in behaving as *yì* requires. The important thing is just that each person develops a *stable* connection between a subset of his or her actual motives and what *yì* requires. Substantively, such effective subsets of motives will vary from person to person, and yet they are united by having a common, social rubric (in this case *yì*) according to which each moral agent can understand his motives and represent them to others. It is because this common, social rubric is available and because one can regulate and interpret one's conduct with reference to it, that it is possible to become a *yì* person by cultivation: to learn not only to behave as *yì* requires but also to understand one's motives for so behaving in terms of *yì*.

This understanding is essential to being a *yì* person by cultivation. And yet, given the logic of moral cultivation, it will always remain a misunderstanding, an act of interpretation that covers up the "as if" character of *yì* but cannot remove it. It is thus constitutive of being a *yì* person that, thanks to this misunderstanding, one both sincerely acts from what one takes to be the *yì* motive and fails to act from the *yì* motive. This is how it is possible to become *yì* by cultivation, and there is no other way.

As long as the "as if" character remains, however, the stability of any *yì* person's subset of motives necessary and sufficient for *yì* behavior is under threat. It is here that the insistence in Chapter 38 of the *Dàodéjīng* on seeing the "as if" motives as false ones has its point. As we have seen, those who act as if they were *yì* (or as if they were *rén* or *lǐ*, for that matter), no matter how sincerely, still actually do so from motives other and lower than *rén* or *yì* or *lǐ*. It is *Dàodéjīng*'s insight that this can make a world of difference: people who have become moral in this way will happily act in the *rén* or *yì* or *lǐ* manner only when their other and lower — in a word, ulterior — motives are satisfied, that is, only when those interests or desires of theirs that belong to the subset of effective motives get served in one way or another. Naturally, then, when their ulterior motives for acting in the *rén* or *yì* or *lǐ* manner are not satisfied by circumstances or by the behavior of others, they tend to stop acting *happily* in the *rén* or *yì* or *lǐ* manner or stop acting in the *rén* or *yì* or *lǐ* manner altogether. In this way, the synchronic composition of one's motives contains their diachronic evolution, such that the original, ulterior motives that seem to have been left behind are always ready to come to fore in the shape of resentment or even naked retaliation.[3]

This is most obvious in the case of a person of cultivated propriety, who acts in the *lǐ* manner conditionally and, failing to benefit in return from some expected *lǐ* behavior from others, flexes his muscles and forces them to reciprocate. When such resort to force ("rolling up one's sleeves and forcing them," as Chapter 38 puts it) takes a social form, we move from failure of *lǐ* to legal punishment. Thus "*fǎ* 法 arises when *lǐ* is lost," a suggestive later addition, is a logical extension of the series of inferences that in Chapter 38 of the *Dàodéjīng* ends with "*lǐ* arises when *yì* is lost." And where *fǎ* — explicit laws or standards — plays an essential role, where everyone acting properly is conditional on everyone else doing so or else being forced to do so, we are not very far from the breakdown of order. Whether such a breakdown will happen is a contingent (rather than inevitable, as the *Dàodéjīng* has it) matter, but that this is an ever-present possibility follows from the nature of the relationship that the *Dàodéjīng* discovers between higher and lower moralities and between the lowest morality and disorder.

5

The insights of the *Dàodéjīng* into the nature of morality — into the relationship between higher and lower moralities and between the lowest morality and disorder — do not figure prominently, if at all, in what has evolved into the mainstream of Chinese moral and political thought. They have been ignored or rejected in favor of the Confucian view of the matter, as in the Mencian version sketched earlier. The upshot, in the domain of morality, is a certain belief in moral perfectibility coupled with a tireless and tiresome reliance on exhortation and exemplification to call it forth. In politics, itself treated as seamlessly continuous with morality in the mainstream, Confucian tradition, these features translate into an unswerving subscription to the idea of rule by virtue (*dézhèng* 德政 or *dézhì* 德治), founded on the hope, all too often against hope, for the emergence of the sage (*shèngrén* 聖人) — or re-emergence of the reputed sages of the past. No matter how effectively or admirably Chinese civilization has conducted itself under the influence of Confucian thought, it is far from obvious that either morality by exhortation and exemplification or politics by sagely rule has done the trick. It is arguable, rather, that such morality tends to produce more hypocrites than real *jūnzǐ* 君子, or virtuous people, and that such politics can easily degenerate into an ideological defense of a system whose appeal in theory, the conjunction of "inner sageliness" and "outer kingliness" (*nèi shèng wài wáng* 內聖外王), almost never materializes. To the extent that this is true, Chapter 38 of the *Dàodéjīng* helps explain why. And insofar as both the morality and the politics have stood firmly in the way of better alternatives, we will continue to ignore such insights as those of the *Dàodéjīng* at our peril.

Notes

1. Translations from the *Dàodéjīng* throughout this chapter are my own.
2. For this distinction, see Williams (2002, ch. 2).
3. I develop such an account of moral motives at length in Ci (2006).

References

Ci, J. 2006. *The two faces of justice*. Cambridge, MA: Harvard University Press.
Nietzsche, F. 1954. *Nietzsche contra Wagner*. In *The portable Nietzsche*, ed. and trans. W. Kaufmann. New York: Viking Press.
———. 1982. *Daybreak*, trans. R. Hollingdale. Cambridge: Cambridge University Press.
Williams, B. 2002. *Truth and truthfulness*. Princeton, NJ: Princeton University Press.

13

Poetic Language: Zhuāngzǐ and Dù Fǔ's Confucian Ideals

Lee H. Yearley*

Zhuāngzǐ and Dù Fǔ

Zhuāngzǐ 莊子 not only lives within the later poetic tradition, but that tradition also grapples with, even is mesmerized by, both the "core" text and the early interpretive attempts that appear in the volume entitled the *Zhuāngzǐ*. Zhuāngzǐ's effect on specific poets is often clear, and illuminating examples include Táo Qián 陶潛, Lǐ Bái 李白, and Sū Shì 蘇軾, to note just poets who represent different perspectives, come from significantly different periods in history, and are acknowledged to be among the tradition's very greatest poets.[1]

I examine here, however, a different kind of example, the one presented by Dù Fǔ 杜甫 (712–770). This example features an explicit attempt to marry early Confucian ethical ideals with Zhuāngzǐ's ideals, and it thereby focuses our attention on features more often than not absent from Zhuāngzǐ. Most notable are tensions that, for Dù Fǔ, define the human situation, especially ones that have an ethical component, such as those between service to one's own genuine needs and service to the larger community, and thus also among the competing roles each endeavor produces. The Dù Fǔ of tradition might not seem prey to such possible strains because he is a solid, upright, and unbending Confucian. This picture may capture one part of Dù Fǔ, but it probably tells us more about how and even why a tradition like Confucianism operates than it does about Dù Fǔ. It is, in fact, a picture that both honors and truncates him, as is the dual wont of most traditions' acts of reverence.[2]

---

* Thanks are due to many, but let me highlight the editors of this volume, the referees for the press, and the following individuals: Kenneth Fields, Sally Gressens, Jason Protass, and Zhaohua Yang.

Most important to us, this picture drains the very complexity and depth that makes both the person and the poetry compelling. It fails to reflect the tensions, often creative tensions, that inform any vital, aware person or tradition, especially any operating in the milieu of the Táng's (618–907) social upheavals and religious syncretism. Examples from Dù Fǔ that illustrate this point are many, but let me briefly note one especially relevant to Zhuāngzǐ before moving on to our central subject.

In the poem, "Broken Boat" (c.764), Dù Fǔ returns home from a forced absence to find ruined the boat, moored on a stream by his house, that he had planned to use to wander over the water. Dù Fǔ knows he could easily replace or refit the boat, but he comes to understand that its presence represented a comforting yet false spiritual ideal, an ideal at variance with who he really is. Zhuāngzǐ's ideal of free and easy wandering, that is, functioned simply to mask Dù Fǔ's own capacities and even inclinations. Worse, it consoled him and distorted his own self-understanding. It obscured important questions about either the possible changes he should entertain or self-cultivation practices he might undertake. His image of a boat in which he can wander, he now recognizes, is an illusory spiritual ideal: all he really wants to do is putter around in the gentle streams near his home.

Other fascinating examples appear throughout Dù Fǔ's poetry, but I will focus here on just one lengthy poem, "A Song of My Thoughts on Traveling from the Capital to Fèngxiān." (The Chinese text and a translation are at the end of the chapter.) Although it may appear not to resonate with, even draw on, the *Zhuāngzǐ*, it directly treats one of the most significant issues Zhuāngzǐ addresses and, at times, tangles with — but never to my mind resolves. The question is how to square the *Zhuāngzǐ's* primary message with basic ethical ideals, especially in a time when the society appears unlikely to support ethical changes or even to provide hope to those trying to aid other people.

In pursuing this subject, the poem displays well the ways in which poetic language operates, including one of special importance to us: the treatment of conflicts that arise from emotions people usually reject because they challenge their ethical commitments. Those rejected emotions, if honestly faced, can separate people from conventional ethical mores and test ethical standards. Those consequences force us to consider the notion, as Owen puts it, that "the moralists who have always buzzed around poetry were quite correct; in their hearts they heard the Sirens singing them to shipwreck."[3]

Introduction to the Poem

Let us then turn to Dù Fǔ's poem probably written in December 755, when he was forty-four, having spent (or wasted) most of the last ten years in and around the capital looking for an appropriate government job. The current emperor, Xuánzōng 玄宗, was, as Lattimore puts it, "once a conqueror, reformer and patron of the arts [but he] was now an old man, controlled by his concubine and her vicious cousin, [the] chief minister" (1981, 54). Rule by such a regime produces situations in which people can encounter, as the poem says, wealth and ruin, grandeur and grimness, mere inches apart: "Within the palace gate, the reek of wine and meat / On the road, the bones of the frozen dead" (lines 67–69).

These failures will soon produce a massive uprising (the Ān Lùshān 安祿山 rebellion) that will not only destroy the present culture, at its zenith surely one of the greatest seen in China or any ancient civilization, but also bring years of chaos and prodigal suffering in its wake. A great culture, then, is about to die, but exceptionally perceptive people, like Dù Fǔ, neither foresaw nor forestalled that cultural death. (Those people, after the collapse, are haunted by questions about what they should have understood and done, if only to bear witness to the situation, one reason that those of us connected to the United States can find this poem so troubling.)

The poem, on my reading, breaks into three separable sections. The first 33 lines recount the conflicting thoughts, feelings, and attitudes of a character, Dù Fǔ. Lines 34–81 depict the journey of that character from the capital, Xī'ān, past the imperial pleasure palace, to a town, Fèngxiān, where he has sent his family. The final section, 82–100, portrays his reaching Fèngxiān, discovering his child has died of hunger, and reacting to that horrific fact and its implications. (My analysis distinguishes the poet Dù Fǔ and the journeyer in the poem, also referred to as Dù Fǔ; context usually makes clear which Dù Fǔ is being discussed, and therefore I rarely use formal nomenclature to distinguish the author from the journeyer.)[4]

The poem, thus described, appears to be a realistic narrative, perhaps even one that describes actual events. Closer attention, however, makes us realize that that the poem depicts events the protagonist either could not have witnessed or could not actually have seen as they are portrayed; e.g., he depicts masses of water that loom as high as the eye can see and make one fear a mountain has come loose (74–75).

Most important to us, features of the opening section, as well as its relationship to the rest of the poem, make us question any notion that the poem conveys a realistic narrative. That section's complexity, use of language, and allusions to the *Zhuāngzǐ* lead us to differentiate two separable sections, the first twelve lines and the remaining twenty-one lines. The differences between the sections are many, including the use of the *Zhuāngzǐ*. Most striking, however, is the way in which the latter part displays an agitation in which thoughts collide with each other, with one line being followed by another that qualifies, queries, or rejects the previous line's declaration.

The opening section of the poem presents, in fact, a dramatic portrait of a person caught by the competing ideals found in the early Confucian tradition and in that part of the early Daoist tradition exemplified by Zhuāngzǐ. The tensions presented in that section are, moreover, lived out in the remainder of the poem. The apparently realistic depictions of the poem's later sections are part of an emotional journey the implications of which go considerably beyond the mere portrayal of external movements and events, however wrenching some of them are.

Relationship to the *Zhuāngzǐ*

The relationship to the *Zhuāngzǐ* takes many forms. The poem, like the *Zhuāngzǐ*, aims to express a vast and often disconcerting reality that contains elements of the sacred, and to do so through literary devices of a very complex sort. These devices, in both works, include pungent if often very concise depictions, poetic formulations, apparent non-sequiturs, the employment and subversion of narrative processes, and alternating validations and undercuttings of the author's authority.

Another complex literary procedure characteristic of the *Zhuāngzǐ* is a switching, even fluctuation, among perspectives, and it is a procedure that also informs the basic structure of Dù Fǔ's poem. The poem is best understood, then, not as a linear narrative, as we have so far presented it, but as a presentation that switches among very different perspectives and therefore invites the reader continuously to rearrange different sections and parts. This kind of presentation is complicated, however, and we best begin with a simpler subject, if one that exfoliates in various directions: the presence in the poem of allusions to the *Zhuāngzǐ*.

The use of allusions is, of course, a central feature of the poetry of this period and Dù Fǔ is a master of the art, using it for purposes that range far beyond a display of learning or of respect for the tradition. Telling allusions to the *Zhuāngzǐ* pepper this poem, and some of them set out its larger purposes, including the crucial problematics with which it deals. Allusions range from the reference at line 13 to rivers and seas as a way to identify the desire to retreat from society, to the more distinctive and complex reference to ants and leviathans in lines 21–24.[5] Rather than pursuing each of these allusions, however, let me treat one thematic allusion and then turn to several connected ones that set out ethical issues in the poem and inform its use and defense of poetic language.

The thematic allusion, one that gives a distinctive texture to the whole poem, occurs with Dù Fǔ's impassioned, vocal reaction to his son's death. This recalls, I believe, various treatments of the death of friends or family members in the *Zhuāngzǐ*, most famously the story of Zhuāngzǐ's singing after the death of his wife (in Chapter 18) but also the stories in Chapter 6 of those friends who celebrate death's arrival in ways observers find unintelligible. An important feature of the allusion is the depiction of Dù Fǔ's outburst on first hearing of the death. His outburst, we are told, violates the social convention that enjoins him to restrain his mourning; it is a convention that serves to represent symbolically a social hierarchy (87–88).

His outburst, then, resembles those found in the *Zhuāngzǐ* that also violate convention and thereby reflect a different perspective. But the two perspectives, the ones that underlie Zhuāngzǐ's and Dù Fǔ's actions, could hardly be more different. His son's death highlights for Dù Fǔ the importance of general human suffering and people's responsibility for it. That understanding, in turn, informs two key features of the poem's concluding lines: his anguished reaction to other people's sufferings and his pained reflections on the self-pity he expressed in the poem's opening section.

Even more important are the specific, connected allusions in the poem's opening lines. These lines introduce matters from the first chapter of the *Zhuāngzǐ* that reverberate throughout both this poem and that book. Most important are the related questions of the character of helpfulness and helplessness, or put more generally, the ethical question of how to understand what benefits others and what does not. The poem's very beginning recalls, then, several related motifs in the *Zhuāngzǐ*, a recollection that establishes crucial parts of the poem's agenda and determines its pulse. Most important is the motif of querying the criteria people use to determine whether a person, a kind of language, action, or an object is either useful or useless. Two facets of that question, each prominent in Zhuāngzǐ, are explored in the poem.[6]

The most obvious one concerns Dù Fǔ's uselessness as a parent or official. The question troubles him throughout and, at times, causes him great anguish. Moreover, it underlies a subject to which we will return because it both constitutes the poem's central ethical problematic and divides Dù Fǔ and Zhuāngzǐ's perspectives. The subject is the apparently irresolvable conflicts among four different roles and thus expectations: being a family member; contributing to the community; pursuing spiritual goals; and participating in the arts. Conflicts among these roles and their accompanying expectations, the poem declares, define the journeys that Dù Fǔ and all of us must undertake.

The other, less obvious question concerns apparently useless language: Are odd kinds of language, kinds that most people would say can be disregarded as useless, vital in certain areas or for certain subjects? More specifically, is there a need for poetic language, for language that by definition both exceeds the boundaries normal language works within and aims to depict matters normal language either cannot or does only inadequately? This question may be the most important, if also the most elusive, of the questions about uselessness. If Zhuāngzǐ's or Dù Fǔ language is such that most people consider it useless, they will disregard it, and therefore they will miss the ethical insights it conveys.

That precise subject is, of course, highlighted at the end of the treatment of uselessness in the *Zhuāngzǐ*'s first chapter. (Examples of such language also appear in that chapter's opening, which takes readers on a poetic ride in which metamorphosis is central, as well as in the next chapter, which asks us to listen to reckless words with recklessness.) Zhuāngzǐ's reasons for employing this kind of language are many, and they include the dire situation he addresses and the grip of convention on nearly everyone. Most important, however, is the seemingly paradoxical notion that underlies discontinuous religious perspectives and becomes the poet's credo: the notion that people cannot get where they need to go by starting where they are, even though they must start where they are.[7]

Notions like these also underlie Dù Fǔ's poem, and we can best examine them and their implications by considering two topics. First are the ways in which Dù Fǔ's poem can be seen as a superb example of what Zhuāngzǐ identifies as the special kind of language he calls "goblet language." Second is the way in which Dù Fǔ's general vision is characterized by tensions that Zhuāngzǐ's usually is not, most notably the tension between service to a larger community and service to one's self. The two topics illuminate each other because poetic language, an instance of Zhuāngzǐ's goblet language, enables one to treat well the tensions that define, for Dù Fǔ if not always for Zhuāngzǐ, a well-lived life. Let us begin with a brief treatment of Zhuāngzǐ's account of such language and then turn to consider how it helps us understand the form of Dù Fǔ's poem.

Goblet Language

Goblet words or language is the third of the three kinds of language the *Zhuāngzǐ*'s twenty-seventh chapter describes, and examples appear in the work's most distinctive passages. *Goblet* or *spillover language* (卮言 zhī yán) behaves like a goblet that spills over when full but rights itself when the excess liquid flows out. It is a fluid language in which equilibrium is kept despite, or perhaps because of, the presence of changing genres, rhetorical forms, points of view, and figurative expressions. This language follows, then, neither the usual rules of argumentation nor ordinary rhetorical forms, but it does manifest a skill that both moves from and transforms those rules and forms.[8]

Goblet language utilizes features of ordinary kinds of language, as it must in order to be intelligible, but it serves to enable people to represent, and thus keep alive, features that ordinary language cannot. Such language, moreover, attracts and holds a reader's attention; it generates a distinctive fascination, an attentive perplexity, and a mysterious suggestion of beauty. For all these reasons, its significance can hardly be overestimated: as the plaintive cry in one passage puts it, a cry Dù Fǔ will echo, without such language "how could I survive for long?" or (to translate it as applicable to everyone) "who could ever keep going for long?" 孰得其久 *shú dé qí jiǔ*).

With goblet language, then, we have a response to the question of how to represent matters that differ dramatically not only from those matters ordinary language presents well but also from what any language can present adequately. It enables us to employ language that is odd, often very odd, and yet still have it render what needs rendering. To attain the needed representation we must, however, stretch language beyond its apparent limits and recognizable shapes while also acknowledging that such stretching seems to breach the conditions that allow language to convey meaning.

Goblet language involves, then, entering the provinces that contain Zhuāngzǐ's and Dù Fǔ's most distinctive poetic language. One way they use this language is to express elusive and mysterious higher states. Examples in Zhuāngzǐ — like depictions that reflect "heavenly equality" or trance-like perfections — are myriad, and some of Dù Fǔ's most famous poems also qualify, including "Viewing Tai Shan" (望岳 *Wàngyuè*) and "Thoughts Written While Traveling at Night" (旅夜書懷 *Lǚyè shūhuái*).

In this poem, however, Dù Fǔ usually uses goblet language to treat the conflicts that can characterize both people's internal life and some of the external events they encounter. (A muted version of this use appears in Zhuāngzǐ, say when he attempts to disrupt ordinary forms of understanding or to depict involvement in governmental affairs.) We will examine this use of poetic language when we consider the conflicts among roles that underlie Dù Fǔ's poem. First, however, let us focus on the way in which goblet language determines the very form of Dù Fǔ's poem, a form that makes possible, or even demands, a continuous switching of perspectives.

Linear Versus Non-Sequential Presentation

Dù Fǔ's presentation invites us, I think, to switch perspectives, and therefore it employs a procedure that Zhuāngzǐ's analysis and use of goblet language commend. The poem is best understood, then, not as a linear narrative, as on the surface it appears to be, but as a presentation that switches among very different perspectives and therefore asks the reader continuously to rearrange different sections and parts. (The lengthy, "experimental" genre the poem employs makes congenial such a presentation.) The poem can, of course, be read as a linear narrative: the opening section (1–32) portrays a conflicted person who in the second part (33–81) sets out on a journey and then concludes the journey in the last section, with his anguished reflections on what he finds and what has occurred. Three parts, then, and three activities and perspectives sequentially presented, with a conclusion that displays a fundamental change in point of view. Seen this way, the poem portrays a sequential unfolding that generates those new discoveries and narrative surprises that characterize complex narratives.

We can, nonetheless, approach the relationship between the three parts in a different fashion and say the poem's structure manifests the kind of switching among perspectives that often is near the heart of Zhuāngzǐ's message and deployment of language. The simplest use of this approach just switches the order of the poem's sections. (We can, for example, start with the middle section and end with the first section or start with the last and then go to either the first or the second section.) An even more powerful reading, as well as more consonant with Zhuāngzǐ, keeps in view the whole as one reads the separate parts of each section. In that way, the many singular parts of the poem reflect off and resonate with each other in a multitude of ways.

This latter approach not only allows or even forces us to read with the knowledge of what occurs at other places in the poem, but it also tempts us continually to consider other perspectives on the same events. Reading this way we cannot simply hold to one perspective, especially a linear one, but must move among different perspectives. Indeed, the poem educates us about how both to make such movements and to see their implications.

The self-pitying, distressed, and angry person we encounter at the poem's opening, for example, is read both as that person and through the lens provided by the events and understandings the other two sections provide. That approach changes the very character of the specific, portrayed emotions by placing them within the context provided by fluctuating perspectives. It also therefore undercuts immersion in, even attachment to, any specific emotion. It can, for instance, make the actual and symbolic shocks Dù Fǔ receives on the actual journey less important and make more critical what occurs when he encounters his child's death and realizes that his self-absorption helped cause it. That deeply emotional realization, in turn, transforms our understanding of the emotions portrayed in each of the first two sections. The goblet fills, and spills, and fills again and spills again . . .

This approach to the poem is much enhanced by the ways in which separable parts of the poem function as self-contained components. The ever-changing kaleidoscopic character of this kind of reading engenders a depth and texture to our understanding of each component, but it also preserves ordered relationships among them. It enables readers to reflect continually, in myriad ways, upon themselves and events in the poem at the same time as their experience is held together by both the specific poetic forms and the overall narrative structure.

The spiritual exercise involved in this switching among perspectives is both especially possible with and particularly relevant to the genre of poetry. (The exercise is, of course, made more effective if the poem is memorized or even just known well, attended to very closely, and considered repeatedly, possibilities poetry allows for and exploits.) One of poetry's most crucial features is the way in which it invites and rewards repetition, these multiple readings that draw on, augment, and change each other. A single poem's manageable form and apparently settled shape allow readers to return continuously to it — whether they do so in fact, in memory, or in their imagination. Those re-examinations permit, even encourage, the rearrangements of parts or the pursuit of the resonances of part to part. That process generates, in turn, a continuing ethical re-education of the self.[9]

Such a moving among different perspectives is also important because the central ethical problematic of the poem involves the ways in which, in Dù Fǔ's case, different modes of action and the perspectives they manifest can clash with each other. This conflict among perspectives is, then, at the heart of the poem, and we may now consider it more systematically.

Conflicts between Roles

Dù Fǔ's point of view is characterized by a concern with tensions, usually of an ethical sort, that Zhuāngzǐ's either does not treat or treats very differently.[10] Most notable and general is the apparently irresolvable tension between service to a larger community and service to one's self, especially in the less than auspicious situations that Zhuāngzǐ, Dù Fǔ, and, I would hazard, most of us live. This general tension exfoliates to create those distinct strains that define for Dù Fǔ the human condition.

Put another way, the great theme of the poem is the character of journeys, or more precisely, the nature of and relationship among the separable journeys that make up the voyage of any single life. The overarching question, therefore, is what Dù Fǔ is to do, feel, and be, given that he is defined by roles that fit uneasily, at best, with each other. Tensions are most prominent among four roles that, telegraphically put, are being a family member; contributing to the community; pursuing spiritual goals; and participating in the arts.

One role consists, then, in meeting the demands of being a parent, spouse, or member of an extended family. Another role consists in participating in the life of a community larger than the family, a role that manifests itself in various civic virtues. A third is the role of spiritual seeker, using "spiritual" to refer to those qualities that define people's appreciation of what surpasses the trivial and transient and allow them to deal admirably with common woe and bear uncommon woe well. The last is the role either of an artist or of anyone for whom imaginative representations of reality are crucial. (We will treat this last role separately, because it rests on a conception of artistic activity that is alien to many contemporary sensibilities.)

The notion of "roles" that operates in Dù Fǔ rests on Confucian ideas of ritual performance and selfhood, rather than on those often-vapid notions that inform current sociological thinking. In a Confucian understanding, roles are not the whole story, but they are a necessary part of any story because each role contains defining demands and responses. Apart from roles, humans often are indeterminate and plastic, a mere history of accidents and occasions, unknowable either to self or to others, and perhaps responsible to neither. Roles are, then, those patterned practices, those ways of participating in specific situations with explicit goals and expected activities, that allow humans to be other than just erratic, unknowable, and unresponsive.[11]

Two basically unmanageable features of life inform, for Dù Fǔ (and also I think for Zhuāngzǐ), the ways that relationships among roles work themselves out for any specific individual. One is the character of the times in which a person lives. The other is the character of a person's individual inclinations, whether those inclinations arise from nature, training, or some combination of each. (The sunflower bending toward light in line 19 displays the second, just as the ironic or acidic comments about the court in lines 16–18 and 48–64 manifest the first.)

A person in a harmonious era who was also blessed with a temperament, and thus inclinations, that fit the opportunities the era offers could live without conflicts, or at least such was the Confucian dream. Conflicts are inevitable, however, in most times and surely in the disarray (or incipient chaos) that marked both Dù Fǔ's and Zhuāngzǐ's times. In any time, moreover, a person will usually lack one or another of the inclinations needed to produce a harmonious reconciliation of roles.

The conflicts between the role of public servant and the roles of spiritual seeker and family member are clearest in the poem. With most spiritual pursuits, the simple need for seclusion constitutes one part of the conflict. Far more important, however, are the ways that the demands of public service crowd out spiritual aspirations or even crush them because of the time, energy, and often attitudes they demand. (This problem has, of course, been highlighted throughout Chinese history.)

Less obvious is the conflict between public service and familial obligations, a conflict this poem highlights in a shocking (and figurative) way with Dù Fǔ's return to his family and discovery of his son's death. Dù Fǔ sent his family from the capital in order to ensure their well-being, but he comes to realize his decision was far more than a simple miscalculation. He understands that his absence contributed directly to his son's death (89–90).

That event and Dù Fǔ's recognition of his responsibility is a metaphor for, even a metonym of, a much larger conflict among roles. The missing nourishment the poem presents is actual food, but the poem leads us to consider all those kinds of nourishment that a parent can withhold from, or only partially present to, a family member. Dù Fǔ's situation also highlights a failure with which we are all familiar: parents whose energy is taken up with helping the general community while the people for whom they have special responsibility and love wither or even perish.

These situations, as the poem makes clear, are less a matter of simple selfishness or indifference than of conflicts among the demands of constitutive roles. An especially perplexing instance of such conflict appears with the artistic role. Let us then turn to that subject, beginning with an account of the place of artistic activity, especially poetic activity, in Dù Fǔ's — and almost certainly Zhuāngzǐ's — perspective. (Poetry is not, of course, the only relevant kind of artistic activity, nor is it as clearly separable in China as it often is in the West from musical or graphic activities, but it is our focus here.)

Poetic Activity and Its Conflicts

Within Dù Fǔ's perspective, the tensions between this and other roles are both complex and difficult for moderns like us to grasp. The *complexity* of poetic activity, its variegated character and aims, is such that some features resemble the pursuit of spiritual goals. The *difficulty* (for us) arises from the ways in which this understanding of poetic activity differs from most of our contemporary understandings.

Poetic activity, from this perspective, involves participation in a demanding discipline, but one evident only when the subject and expression are neither conventional nor predictable. It involves participants, whether they create or read poetry, in a unique spiritual practice, even meditational discipline, that produces insights available in no other way. That discipline and those insights, furthermore, are crucial to a well-lived life for almost all people in almost all times.

Either the production or appreciation of poetic language is especially challenging because it aims to transform some of the most damaging and recalcitrant human features, features central to ethical failures because of the ways in which they affect our ability to attend to the salient characteristics of situations and to measure our actual intentions. One feature is the tendency to either truncated perception or full-fledged self-deception, maneuvers that seek to avoid danger and dissonance. Another is the tendency to inertia and thus to an acceptance of the familiar and trivial, maneuvers that aim to avoid those matters in memory or aspiration that challenge settled states.

This challenging discipline involves four distinct processes. One is a training of people's imagination that allows its capacious qualities to flower. A second is a nursing of people's mental flexibility that cultivates their native capacity to see internal and external events from different and ever-changing perspectives. Third is a sharpening of people's capacity to perceive disquieting external events, a honing of their ability to attend steadily and continuously to what they would rather flee from or block off. Fourth, and perhaps most difficult, is a nurturing of people's aptitude to attend to rejected emotions and thoughts, and therefore a shaping of their skill to reappropriate and probe things they have turned away from, even buried.

This discipline, in concert with the poetic language on which it works and from which it gains sustenance, produces understandings available in no other way. It informs and sustains the capacity to grasp well both our interior life and exterior occurrences. It helps us overcome the fact that most of us, most of the time, are strangers to ourselves and insensitive to much of what happens to us.

Proponents of this perspective reject, then, the common contemporary notion that artistic expression is an incidental, usually private, activity or pleasure that may even fit best within the category of the self-indulgent. They think, simply put, that poetic expression is extremely important because of two facets of human life. One is a universal human need to grasp accurately and to witness well to what occurs. The other is a combination of the difficulties, especially those concerning appropriate action, that accompany that need's satisfaction and the ethical problems for each of us that arise if it is not satisfied.

Poetry's ability to help us with these matters makes crucial a pursuit of its excellence. That excellence rests on various features, including technical matters in poetics in which Dù Fǔ's abilities are unexcelled. The most important feature to us, however, concerns a subject our poem displays in a most compelling fashion: the intentions that motivate poetic expression.

Forms of Poetic Expression in Dù Fǔ's Journey

The poem displays the more and less credible intentions that can inform poetic expression. Dù Fǔ the poet exhibits for us the array of motives that animate the poetic expressions of Dù Fǔ the journeyer in the poem. They range from personal bitterness, to the rage of the unjustly slighted, to the need to express for others and one's self something of the greatest ethical and spiritual significance.[12]

In displaying this range of motives, the poem uncovers another arena — artistic expression — in which one of the most crucial distinctions in Confucian (or most) virtue theories operates: the distinction between real virtues and semblances of virtues. Semblances occur when someone acts in an apparently virtuous manner but does so for motives, like a desire to curry favor, that a non-virtuous person would have. Confucians call someone who manifests only semblances of virtue the "village honest person" (鄉原 *xiāngyuàn*). They think such people are especially dangerous because they do not exemplify virtue — as most think — but rather are, as they put it, the thief of virtue. In poetry as in ordinary life, semblances of virtue provide dangerous models that distort rather than illuminate the most important human endeavors.[13]

The poem embraces the idea of the need for poetic expression, but it combines that embrace with a depiction of the range of motives that can animate such expression, a range that appears in the poem's different uses of the notion of "singing" or its surrogates. These locutions, which designate the desire to give poetic voice to a subject or a response, appear at various places. Nonetheless, they are most evident, revealingly, at the close of each subsection of the first thirty-two lines and at the poem's conclusion.

The first subsection (lines 1–12) presents a Dù Fǔ who is still strong, if battered, although he surely has failed to meet well the conventional expectations of his public role. (He has, in an image that will resonate with all who have encountered "truly successful" acquaintances, earned only sneers from the old men who were once fellow students.) Nevertheless, at the section's end he still sings loudly and passionately, aiming to express artistically a spirit that remains unbowed despite adversity. He depicts, moreover, the surrounding world in ways that lead us (and him) to entertain an ironic detachment from the conventional standards that gauge success in those roles and the people who use those standards with such ease. Dù Fǔ the poet can express both his strong if divided character and his understanding of the situation through poetic means that shape the attentive reader. (They may even influence some people who either sneer at people like Dù Fǔ or swim easily in the conventional world.)

At the very end of the second subsection (13–33), a section marked by bitterness and an agitation that takes away what is said as soon as it is said, Dù Fǔ conjoins with pained song the kind of drinking that aims not at illumination but at oblivion. (He dives into drink, he says, to banish these thoughts and then bursts into sorrowful song.) This poetic expression is driven by self-enclosed, even self-indulgent motives. It shows a release of primitive emotions, even ones that harbor notions of revenge, and a nursed sense of injury and aggrievement. It expresses, then, self-feeding frustration at one's self, other people, and the whole world.

Finally, in the poem's last line (line 100), we encounter the most complex use of the poetic voice, one that highlights crucial parts of the poem's overall objectives and strategies of presentation. The poet here aims to express the admittedly inexpressible, the "huge and formless" (澒洞 *hòngdòng*), and therefore to articulate something that exceeds people's abilities to treat it adequately. This huge, formless reality includes all he has seen, however imperfectly, as well as all that constitutes his attempts to negotiate the tensions among the roles that make him who he is. It generates for him worries as gigantic as a massive mountain, worries that contain all the subjects that the poem's final two sections present, as well as the tensions and anxieties that appear, however inchoately, in the first section.

Dù Fǔ expresses all this through goblet language, the only kind of language that can render it at all adequately. The whole poem, then, aims to witness through the uniquely expressive, if also oblique and admittedly inadequate, language that poetry provides. That witness enables Dù Fǔ the poet to express what he must for his own self-understanding, or more accurately self-preservation, and that of other people. (His intent resembles the intent that animates parts of the *Zhuāngzǐ*, such as the choice at the end of Chapter 2 to speak reckless words that need to be listened to recklessly.) Dù Fǔ's poetic writing, then, does not just manifest the literary features of goblet language but also functions to preserve his own and other people's ability to persist. As the plaintive cry, noted earlier, from the *Zhuāngzǐ* puts it: Without such language "how could I survive for long?" or "who could ever keep going for long?"

Dù Fǔ must express what occurs both to him and within him, to his encounter with events, feelings, and thoughts that exceed his ability to describe them with any adequacy. But he also writes to help other people, even while knowing that many will scorn and most will misunderstand what he writes. The poem conveys, then, something both about how the world actually is and about how it ought to be, suggesting the latter by presenting those absences that are also presences.

Underlying the poem is the attempt, expressed concisely at the end but evident throughout, to depict something characterized as being huge and formless, something that surely cannot be grasped by any ordinary conceptual means but can, if imperfectly, be expressed by goblet language. Those disciplined exercises as well as the disciplined exercises of those who read the poem operate well, however, only if they are unalloyed by the false consolations or self-serving illusions that turn true poetic expression into one of its semblances.

Conclusion: Dù Fǔ and Zhuāngzǐ's Confucius

It is central to Dù Fǔ's understanding that he must live with and witness tensions among the first three roles and between the last role and the first three. This poem, like almost all of Dù Fǔ's poems, expresses a far darker picture than does Zhuāngzǐ of the world's possibilities, or at least of the possibilities the world offers to people who share Dù Fǔ's ethical concerns.

Indeed, Dù Fǔ's situation resembles the portrait in the "core" *Zhuāngzǐ* of the figure of Confucius. It is a portrait that highlights Confucius's accomplishments as well as his limits, and the difficulties and anxieties the latter produces.[14] Dù Fǔ, tellingly, remains haunted by the differences between what age has brought him and what it should bring to a person like Zhuāngzǐ or the Confucius who appears in some of the *Analects*' portraits. (A muted allusion in line 2 to *Analects* 2:4 highlights Dù Fǔ's fear that he is older but only more foolish and therefore ill fits the exemplary picture in the *Analects*' passage of the sage's development.) These people develop through the stages that lead them not just to knowing larger, sacred purposes but also to being able to follow them easily and unerringly. The poem may also, of course, present a picture that squarely faces some of the continuing conflicts missing in that if not all of the *Analects*' portraits.

Most important here, the poem articulates persuasively the role of enduring tensions among roles. These are tensions that Zhuāngzǐ resolves in ways that may seem less than convincing, whether our concern is personal or political. Or at least those resolutions can appear inadequate for people who lack the qualities that allow some adepts (as is said in the *Zhuāngzǐ*'s sixth chapter) to wander outside, not within, the boundaries, as does Confucius. Whether, if we are to be fully human, we should see the people who wander outside the boundaries as really human, or rather as wondrous creatures of a non-human sort, or even just as wondrous creatures that ought only haunt us, is a question for another day. Our main task here has been a far simpler one: to see how Dù Fǔ employs and tests Zhuāngzǐ's ideals in a poem presenting tensions among roles as a feature of life that defines the human situation, a feature that only poetic language can present well.

The Poem

For notable translations, see S. Cherniack, A. R. Davis (almost complete), W. Hung (in prose), C. Kizer ("free"), D. Lattimore, S. Owen, and D. Young. My rendition is often, I fear "flat, prosaic, dumpy," to quote Robert Bly on one of his eight stages of translation (1983, 15). The Chinese text follows.

Dù Fǔ, "A Song of My Thoughts on Traveling from the Capital to Fèngxiān"

1. Dressed as a commoner, living at Dù-Líng
2. He grew older and got impractical ideas.
3. He devotes himself to mad dreams
4. Secretly he thought he was like the best men of old.
5. And so, he became at last too large to be useful.
6. His head white but still he relishes the privations endured.
7. Until the coffin lid slams and the matter ends
8. He ever hopes to fulfill his dreams.
9. Year in, year out, he worries about the people
10. And sighs for them, his guts in turmoil.
11. He earns sneers from old men, once fellow students
12. Yet he sings out loudly with fierce intensity.
13. Not that he doesn't cherish dreams of rivers and lakes
14. Free and aloof, sending the days and months on their way.
15. But he was born in reign of a brilliant ruler
16. And couldn't bear to withdraw forever.
17. Yet ample materials in the Halls of State
18. No gaps in that mansion's structure.
19. Still sunflower and clover lean to the sun
20. Truly, nothing can rob a creature of its nature.
21. He considers the tiny ants

22. Who can only seek their own little holes
23. Why should they admire great whales
24. And plan to sprawl, like them, in the ocean's deeps?
25. From this, he realizes how he must live
26. The only man ashamed to strive for favors.
27. Thus he has gone on stubbornly until now
28. And must suffer hereafter to vanish in dust.
29. Shamed to the end by ideal recluses
30. But unable to change his principles.
31. He dives into drink to console himself a while
32. And sings a loud song in the utmost grief.
33. In the year's twilight, when all grasses wither
34. And swift winds cleave the high ridges
35. As darkness looms in the Royal Avenue
36. The traveler sets out at midnight.
37. The frost is harsh. His coat belt snaps.
38. His fingers are too stiff to tie it.
39. At dawn, he passes Mount Lì
40. The imperial couch rests on its towering crest.
41. Ill-omened auroras fill the cold void
42. Trampling feet slicken the cliffs and valleys.
43. Over Jasper Pool, steam hangs, thickly clotted
44. Imperial guardsmen grind their halberds together.
45. Ruler and minister are detained by pleasure
46. Music is struck, and resounds in the distance.
47. All those granted permission to bathe wear long hamstrings
48. None invited to feast wear short coarse tunics.
49. But the brocade distributed in the crimson court
50. Came from the home of poor cold women.
51. Whose husbands were flogged with whips
52. By tax collectors, who delivered the exacted to the palace.
53. His Majesty bestows chests of treasure
54. Because he truly desires that the nation thrive.
55. But if a minister ignores his duties
56. Need a ruler throw away such objects on him?
57. When many such gentlemen fill the courts
58. Good men may well tremble with fear.
59. Even more so, hearing that the gold platters of the imperial family
60. Are all in the homes of the imperial hangers-on.
61. In the main hall, goddesses dance
62. Smoke-and-mist gossamer floats from their jade bodies.

63. They warm the guest with sable cloaks
64. As grave pipes play, after the pure-toned zither.
65. They urge the guest to camel-pad broth
66. And frosty oranges that lie, crushing fragrant tangerines.
67. Within the crimson gate, the reek of wine and meat
68. On the road, the bones of the frozen dead.
69. Grimness and grandeur a mere foot apart
70. Anguish overcomes me. I can't tell you any more.
71. My carriage headed north. We reached the Jīng and Wèi rivers.
72. Took the government ferry across. Again we changed course.
73. Chunks of ice were coming down from the west
74. Jutting up high, as far as the eye could see.
75. I wondered whether they came from Kōngtóng Mountain
76. Feared they would ram and snap pillars of sky.
77. Fortunately, the bridge across the river hadn't yet broken
78. Yet the sounds of its core beams creaked and groaned.
79. As we made our way across, clinging to one another
80. If the river grew broader, we could not cross.
81. I sent my old wife to a different district
82. The ten of them separated from me by wind-driven snow.
83. Who could leave them long uncared for?
84. So I went to share their hunger and thirst.
85. As I entered the gate, I heard wails
86. My little son had starved to death.
87. I could not suppress a wail of my own
88. When the whole lane is sobbing.
89. What shames me is that I was his father.
90. I didn't provide food. I caused his early death.
91. How could I have known that before the autumn harvest
92. Our poverty would be visited by a calamity.
93. All of my life I have been exempt from taxes
94. Nor has my name been registered for military service
95. Going over events, I still feel aching bitterness
96. The common people are surely tormented.
97. I think silently of those among them who have lost their livelihood
98. Then think of our troops on far campaigns.
99. The springs of worry rise level with the South Mountains
100. Huge and formless, they can't be grasped.

杜甫：自京赴奉先縣詠懷五百字：案：原注。天寶十四載十一月初作

杜陵有布衣，老大意轉拙。許身一何愚【過】，竊比稷與契。
居然成濩落，白首甘【苦】契闊。蓋棺事則已，此志常覬豁。
窮年憂黎元，歎息腸【腹】內熱。取笑同學翁，浩歌彌激烈。
非無江海志，蕭灑送【迭】日月。生逢堯舜君【堯為君】，不忍便永訣。
當今廊廟具，構廈豈云缺。葵藿傾太陽，物性固莫【難】奪。
顧惟螻蟻輩，但自求其穴。胡為慕大鯨，輒擬偃溟渤。
以茲悟生理，獨恥事干謁。兀兀遂至今，忍為塵埃沒。
終愧巢與由，未能易其節。沈飲聊自適【遣】，放歌頗愁絕。
歲暮百草零，疾風高岡裂。天衢陰崢嶸，客子中夜發。
霜嚴衣帶斷，指直不得【能】結。凌晨過驪山，御榻在嵽嵲。
蚩尤塞寒空，蹴踏崖谷滑。瑤池氣鬱律，羽林相摩戛。
君臣【聖君】留歡娛，樂動殷樛嶱【膠葛】【蠍蝎】【崛嶱】【湯嶱】。
賜浴皆長纓，與宴【謀】非短褐。
彤庭所分帛，本自寒女出。鞭撻【笞】其夫家，聚斂貢城闕。
聖人筐篚恩，實欲【願】邦國活。臣如忽至理，君豈棄此物。
多士盈朝廷，仁者宜戰慄。況聞內金盤，盡在衛霍室。
中堂舞【有】神仙，煙霧散【蒙】玉質。煖客貂鼠裘，悲管逐清瑟。
勸客駝蹄羹，霜橙壓香橘。朱門酒肉臭，路有凍死骨。
榮枯咫尺異，惆悵難再述。北轅就涇渭，官渡又改轍。
群冰【水】從西下，極目高崒兀。疑是崆峒來，恐觸天柱折。
河梁幸未坼，枝撐聲窸窣。行旅相攀援，川廣不【且】可越。
老妻寄異縣，十口隔風雪。誰能久不顧，庶往共飢渴。
入門聞號咷，幼子飢【餓】已卒。吾寧舍一哀，里巷亦【猶】嗚咽。
所愧為人父，無食致夭折。豈知秋未【禾】登，貧窶有倉卒。
生常免租稅，名不隸征伐。撫跡猶【獨】酸辛，平人固騷屑。
默思失業徒，因念遠戍卒。憂端齊【際】終南，澒洞不可掇。

Notes

1. Lǐ Bái is a particularly illuminating example, as certain of his poems evoke states that resonate with, and are even spiritual heirs of, states we see expressed in the *Zhuāngzǐ*. For example, his "Beneath the Moon Drinking Alone #1" contains a stunning presentation of three such matters: how people can imaginatively populate a world and then live in it; how they can both query and employ an idea of a self or "I" (我 *wǒ*) and do so sequentially; and last, how they can express, without sentimentality, the profoundly naïve kind of joy that parts of the *Zhuāngzǐ* exhibit. The volume the *Zhuāngzǐ* presents a multitude of textual issues that we need not consider here, but I follow, in general, the work of Graham (1979, 1981), Roth (1991), and Liu (1994);

their accounts draw on a general but not universal consensus. (When I refer to the "purported author" of the *Zhuāngzǐ*, the reference, more precisely put, is to that work's first seven chapters and the few other spiritual progeny of those chapters evident in the larger work.)
2. We know little about the person save through the poetry, although there is some very illuminating non-poetic evidence, such as exams he set when he was an official. Hung's biography (1952) occasionally tilts in the traditional direction, but overall it remains an extraordinary and quite balanced work. Chou (1995) addresses the larger implications of the traditional picture at considerable length; also see Davis (1971).
3. Owen (1989, 195). For a detailed treatment of this notion in a work that often focuses on the ethical dimensions of poetry and draws on both Adorno and Benjamin, see Williams (1998).
4. The distinction I draw here resembles closely the one between Dante the poet and Dante the pilgrim that informs most writing about the *Divine Comedy*; see Yearley (2004). For detailed and often contrasting interpretations of the poem, see Cherniack (1988, 99–158) and Yu et al. (2000, 146–72). Cherniack's work (a dissertation) provides a detailed account of controversies in the commentarial tradition about both interpretative and philological issues.
5. Some of these references to the *Zhuāngzǐ*, however apt, are part of any decent poet's repertoire; e.g., the reference at line 13 to rivers and seas as a way to identify the desire or even intention to seek a life outside ordinary society (from Chapter 15 of the *Zhuāngzǐ*). More complicated is the reference to the notion that a fish large enough to swallow a boat will, if cast ashore by waves, become food for ants and crickets (from Chapter 23).
6. The notion in line 2 of being foolish, inept, clumsy, or even stupid (拙 *zhuó*) recalls (the character is the same) the interchange between Zhuāngzǐ and Huì Shī 惠施 near the end of Chapter 1; the allusion acquires further resonances by the explicit reference to uselessness in line 5. Zhuāngzǐ's rejoinder to Huì Shī focuses on the gourd's "usefulness" in producing a wandering ride, and Huì Shī's failure shows not only his lack of imagination but also his inability to consider the realms that may lie beyond ordinary notions of usefulness. (The ride demands not that he become a natural object but rather that he be a person who reflects both nature's contours and a human being's characteristics.) Even more important in this context, however, is the turn on uselessness that occurs when, at chapter's end, Huì Shī declares that Zhuāngzǐ's words are too grand to be useful.
7. For the notions of continuous and discontinuous religions, and the importance of this typological distinction, see Yearley (1996, 2005).
8. See Yearley (2005) for a lengthy and, at times, labored examination of goblet language. The audience for this article, incidentally, helps explain the approach taken: it is aimed at ethicists.
9. Williams (1998) highlights the role both of arbitrary form and of repetition in poetry.
10. See Yearley (forthcoming, "Zhuāngzǐ") which treats, among other matters, the first three stories in Chapter 4; also see the conclusion and note 15. Those stories concern action in the human world and thus the perils involved in service to others, participation in government, and ethical aspirations in a usually inhospitable

environment. They all highlight, moreover, how those activities are likely to produce conflicts within a person.
11. See Yearley (forthcoming, "Xúnzǐ").
12. Each of these motives is more and less laudable, and they establish different relationships to the three other roles. For example, the least laudable, personal bitterness, never presents a real option to the other aims, and therefore it is never part of an irresolvable tension; it usually just distorts other intentions, say, those of the virtuous citizen. In contrast, the last aim, to express something of great significance, can conflict in virtually irresolvable ways with the intentions that inform family membership.
13. See Yearley (1990, 17–23) for a discussion of the distinctions between virtues and their semblances.
14. See Yearley (forthcoming, "Zhuāngzǐ") for an examination of Zhuāngzǐ's portrait of Confucius, especially as it appears in the fourth chapter. The chapter contains two statements, both in stories that prominently feature Confucius, that illuminate this subject and are instances of goblet language. The first states the most important thing of all is to fulfill what is ordained for one — an apparent bromide that transforms itself into something evocative with the addition of the notion that doing this is the most difficult challenge that humans face. The other is an image near the end of the first story that has all the resonance of those fine verbal images in poetry that have no corresponding physical image: keeping from walking is easy, it is said; what is hard is walking without touching the ground.

References

Bly, R. 1983. *Eight stages of translation*. Boston, MA: Rowan Tree Press.
Cherniack, S. 1988. Three great poems by Dù Fǔ: "Five hundred words, a song of my thoughts on traveling from the capital to Fèngxiān," "Journey north" and "One hundred rhymes, a song of my thoughts on an autumn." Ph.D. dissertation, Yale University, New Haven, CT.
Chou, E. 1995. *Reconsidering Tu Fu: Literary greatness and cultural context*. Cambridge [U.K.], New York: Cambridge University Press.
Davis, A. 1971. *Tu Fu*. New York: Twayne Publishers.
Graham, A. 1979. How much of Chuang-tzu did Chuang-tzu write? In B. Schwartz and H. Rosemont, eds., *Journal of the American Academy of Religion Thematic Issue* 47 (3): 459–502.
———. 1981. *Chuang-tzu: The seven inner chapters and other writings from the book. Chuang-tzu*. London & Boston: Allen & Unwin.
Hung, W. 1952. *Tu Fu, China's greatest poet*. Cambridge, MA: Harvard University Press.
Kizer, C. 1965. 100 lines from Tu Fu. *The Sewanee Review* 73 (3): 358–61.
Lattimore, D. 1981. From the capital to Feng-hsien: Five hundred words to chant my feelings. *Ironwood* 17 (Spring): 52–54.
Liu, X. 1994. *Classifying the Zhuangzi chapters*. Ann Arbor: Center for Chinese Studies, University of Michigan.

Owen, S. 1989. *Mi-Lou: Poetry and the labyrinth of desire.* Cambridge, MA: Harvard University Press.

Roth, H. 1991. Who compiled the Chuang Tzu? In *Chinese texts and philosophical contexts: Essays dedicated to Angus C. Graham,* ed. Henry Rosemont. 79–128. La Salle, IL: Open Court.

Williams, C. 1998. *Poetry and consciousness.* Ann Arbor: University of Michigan Press.

Yearley, L. 1990. *Mencius and Aquinas: Theories of virtue and conceptions of courage.* Albany: State University of New York Press.

———. 1996. Zhuangzi's understanding of the skillfulness and the ultimate spiritual state. In *Essays on skepticism, relativism, and ethics in the Zhuangzi,* ed. P. Kjellberg and P. Ivanhoe. 152–82. Albany: State University of New York Press.

———. 2004. Genre and the attempt to render pride: Dante and Aquinas. *Journal of the American Academy of Religion* 72 (2): 313–39.

———. 2005. Daoist presentation and persuasion: Wandering among Zhuangzi's kinds of language. *Journal of Religious Ethics* 33 (3): 503–35.

———. Forthcoming. Xunzi: Ritualization as humanization. In *Xunzi as religious philosopher,* ed. J. Kline. Albany: State University of New York Press.

———. Forthcoming. Zhuangzi's radical virtue ethics: A journey. In *The ethics of ease — The Zhuangzi on the norms of life,* ed. D. Schilling and R. King. Lun Wen — Studien zur Geistesgeschichte und Literatur Chinas. Wiesbaden: Harrasowitz.

Young, D. 2008. *Du Fu: A life in poetry.* New York: Random House.

Yu, P., et al. 2000. *Ways with words: Writing about reading texts from early China.* Berkeley: University of California Press.

14
Dào as a Naturalistic Focus

Chad Hansen

Modern ethical naturalism has the challenge of showing how normativity, broadly speaking, is a feature of the natural world — a description, roughly, acceptable in the language of modern natural science. I argued in 2005 that a concept like *dào* (ways) could be a key to doing this, but the conclusion was overstated. The concept can be used in expressing a positivist traditionalism, social or rational constructivism, or emotivism, among other positions, as well as naturalism. Its usefulness in expressing normative judgments needs to be buttressed by a claim that *dào*-expression helps make the case for naturalism better. I argue here that it helps dispel the queerness that John Mackie attributes to traditional attempts to naturalize ethics.

In this introductory section, I will refine my claims about the overall role and value of a concept in normative language that functions as *dào* does. I will use Shelly Kagan's distinctions between factors, foci, and foundations in normative theory. I will argue that *dào*-like concepts are foci and thus are alternatives to actions, laws, facts, virtues, properties, and so on. *Dào*s delineate a helpful generic category for clusters of important normative concepts, and analyzing *dào* as a focal concept shows that it need not rule out particular normative theories (factors), nor, by itself, entail particular foundational approaches (naturalism, constructivism, etc.).

In the next section, I will discuss Mackie's queerness objection to ethical naturalism and briefly illustrate how I envision *dào*-like concepts dispelling it. I will argue that normative claims explicated in natural *dào* terms would not seem as strange, particularly given other salient features of Chinese normative vocabulary. This, I will suggest, buttresses the naturalism of Chinese, and especially Daoist, thought. Besides changing the focus of such claims, *dào* versions of naturalized norm claims are claims of attractive possibility and are inherently normative — though they are normative qua invitation or recommendation, reversing the Pauline/Kantian focal priority on obligation or prohibition (law as command).

In the remaining sections, I will briefly sketch a picture of the larger gradations in plausible naturalistic stories illustrating continuity in the emergence of normative from natural *dào*s. In "Natural Scientific *Dào*," I will highlight some important features of normative "discourse" *dào*s that share structural parallels with naturalistic description (e.g., object emergence, relativity, and *dào* supervenience). In "The Emergence of Interest," I will argue that evolutionary *dào*s can underwrite talk of a *dào*'s serving interests (or failing to). In "Community *Dào* and Individual *Dào*," I will show how we can think of the *dào*s of clusters of natural living kinds, and in particular how we can think of communities of animals as creating *dào*s that guide members of those communities. Finally, in "Human *Dào* and Full Moral Normativity," I will explore some of the ways that human normative *dào*s are further developments and refinements of these emerging natural *dào*s. I will argue that a plausible *dào*-focused naturalism strongly suggests that moral *dào* will be relative, though neither subjective nor culturally relative.

I have argued that *dào* has a counterpart in English ("way") and probably in most other languages. "Way" is what Ian Hacking calls an "elevator word" (1999, 21–22). Attempts to fashion a species-difference definition fail because chains of definition tend to lead back to the original term.

A salient difference between *dào* and "way" is that, while *dào* was the explicit focus of most of Chinese philosophy, it is hard to find analytic treatments of the term "way" in our philosophical tradition, although all know of extensive analyses of "the," "some," "believe," and "know" and of our central elevator words, "truth," "law," "fact," and "reason." Analyses, however, are common for subtypes of ways, such as modes, practices, plans, causal processes, conventions, and institutions. Noticing that the dominant role for some *dào* subtype (plan, practice) is ethical analysis suggests that focusing on a more generic concept may be an interesting approach to metaethics. In that conceptual role, *dào* should make metaethical naturalism seem less "queer" and its detailed elaboration more intuitive.

Start with the normative category appropriate for *dào* (way). Shelly Kagan's (1992) analysis of normative ethical theories will help. Kagan distinguishes three components of a normative ethical theory: its factors, its foci, and its foundation. The proximate action-guiding item is some factor: qualities or attributes of right/good acts, persons, or things that count in their evaluation. Kagan puts it this way: "I mean to be making the ontological claim, that the interplay of the various morally relevant factors is what makes it *be* the case that the given act is right or wrong."[1] The factor property would typically be generalized in a fundamental principle or rule of the normative theory.

Kagan's "foundation," by contrast, is this: "Roughly, we propose and evaluate alternative 'devices' or 'mechanisms' that purport to generate and thus explain the favored list of normatively relevant factors" (1992, 225). His examples include contractualism, rule utilitarianism, and ideal observer theories. These would be background explanatory accounts of why certain factors count as considerations that favor some behavior. These foundation theories, as Scanlon suggests (1982, 108), can be used to explain different sets of normative factors; e.g., a contractarian could justify using maximizing benefit as a factor on the grounds that such is what we would implicitly agree on in the specified contract situation and procedure. A rule utilitarian, might, in practice (in terms of factors), be a retributivist, and an ideal observer might, like Adam Smith, treat egoistic prudence as a moral factor. Some passages in the *Mencius* suggest his foundation might be an ideal observer theory: the factors would be generated by the heart-mind judgments of the sages.

Confucius, were he to reflect on his implicit foundational attitudes, might rely on obedience to moral superiors. Kant's foundational account would be the free, self-willed legislation of a universal legislature of rational beings, and so forth.

Kagan's third aspect is foci:

> [It is] . . . helpful to distinguish as well a third activity, involving debate over what I will call *evaluative focal points*. . . . Rule consequentialists select *rules* as their primary evaluative focal point; they then evaluate acts in a secondary or derivative way, in terms of the directly evaluated rules. In contrast, act consequentialists select *acts* as their primary evaluative focal point, evaluating them directly . . . motive consequentialism, which asks which set of motives would lead to the best results overall. . . . We might similarly consider the merits of motive contractarianism, motive egoism, and so on for the various other foundational theories. (1992, 17)

Other possible primary evaluative focal points might include institutions, norms, character traits, and intentions (1992, 17).

With these distinctions in hand, Kagan suggests that virtue ethics is more like a shift in focus than some new normative factor or alternate foundational theories of moral norms. A virtue ethics could be consistent with normative factors that are consequences for human benefit. Hence, virtue ethics per se does not contrast with utilitarianism at either the foundational or the factoral level. Its departure is that most utilitarian theories focus on acts or rules. We may view Mencius's ethics as overlapping Mòzǐ's in their factors — benefiting humans — even more than it does Confucius's (conforming to a traditional formulation or practice such as 禮 *lǐ* ritual).

Accordingly, we can think of *dào* or "ways" as foci and of a *dào*-ethics as complementing or contrasting with a 德 *dé* (virtuosity) or virtue ethics, motive-ethics, act-focused ethics, or principle- or law-focused ethics. Introducing talk of *dào* or ways is not to offer a new normative factor or consideration but something analogous to the distinction between act and rule utilitarianism — a different normative focus. A *dào* utilitarianism, like Mòzǐ's, would take a broader focus than rule utilitarianism (cf. Rawls's practice utilitarianism). Rawls (1971) focuses on institutional structure; pragmatists on "practices"; Gibbard (2003) and Bratman (1987) on "plans." These would be subclasses of the focus on "ways." Picking a structural focus does not rule out relating or translating other normative structures into the favored structural form. So we should be able to translate *dào*-talk into act-talk, law-talk, or virtue-talk and vice versa. The role of the foci is as the primary form in which the foundational theory justifies its factors.

A normative focus on "ways" in ethical discourse, then, should mesh better with naturalistic foundational theories of normativity. The general structure is a variation on a classical Daoist theme — that normative *dào*, including social/moral *dào*, is grounded in natural *dào* — normatively valid plans, practices, and projects must mesh appropriately with natural processes. We would focus on concepts in the explanatory processes of science rather than on analyses of properties, truths, or laws.

John Mackie has argued that such analytic naturalism leaves a bizarre feel. Our complex and interacting heritage of dualisms (mind-body, divine-secular, value-fact, ought-is) bequeaths a kind of skepticism about what seem like reductive normative claims. Mackie expresses this reluctance via "the queerness objection." It seems queer to imagine that we have duties or obligations to reality or that reality can impose or command us to such duties and obligations. Metaethical naturalists typically seek some more permissive account of naturalistic, physical concepts, something more congenial to explaining and justifying norms. It is for this role that I nominate "*dào*" (ways).

Queerness and Dào

Mackie's metaethics poses a dilemma for metaethical stances that analyze moral propositions or moral facts: either we must accept error theory — ordinary normative talk is technically false — or we must make normative naturalism (moral realism or objectivism) seem plausible. Mackie suggests the latter is virtually impossible. Moral naturalism will seem queer, and the queerness of ethical naturalism weighs in favor of Mackie's error theory: that moral statements are strictly all false.

> [The queerness] has two parts, one metaphysical, the other epistemological. If there were objective values, then they would be entities or quantities or relations of a very strange sort, utterly different from anything else in the universe. Correspondingly, if we were aware of them, it would have to be by some special faculty of moral perception or intuition, utterly different from ordinary ways of knowing everything else. (1977, 38)

Mackie's queerness objection, here, has a greater prima facie plausibility because the conceptual candidates traditionally available to serve as foci for a foundational moral naturalism come from the metaphysics of sententials. The sentence-sized clumps of reality include facts, truths, propositions, events, and actions — all bits of reality that correspond to sentences. General sentences would similarly correspond to laws, duties, commands, and obligations. Other metaphysical realities that correspond to grammatical roles of sentences include objects, particulars, substances and their properties, and attributes or qualities. These are instances of traditional metaphysical categories that are motivated by the implicit focus on sentences and their subject-predicate structure. Conversely, naturalism seems intuitively plausible to ancient Chinese philosophers. I suggest the reason for this is that their dominant focal concept is *dào*. This invites them to reflect on the coincidence of social practices (cultural practices) and natural processes.

In recommending that naturalists adopt a *dào* focus in ethics, I can elaborate on the familiar claim that Chinese ethical theorizing seems not to face a Western "fact-value" or "is-ought" problem without suggesting that they have "solved" those problems. Rather, I would argue that Chinese thinkers simply never encountered these puzzles in the forms they confronted classical Western thinkers. How normative *dào*s emerge within natural *dào*s can be a complicated issue but need not involve a conceptual mistake. Ethical naturalism presents a starker puzzle when we use the available Western elevator foci that Mackie targets.

Natural normativity seems "queer" when we try to imagine *legitimate obligations* arising from descriptive properties, facts, truths, or laws. No particular queerness is posed by suggesting that normative 道 *dào* (guide) and 德 *dé* (virtuosity) are comprehended in natural processes and dispositions embodied in physical structures.

The hurdle for Western theorists is obvious, as Mackie announces, when we consider these *available* conceptual candidates: laws, truths, facts, properties, essences, relations, forces, objects. The centrality of "laws" in this nexus brings a corollary that paradigm normativity is the authoritative *command* or *obligation*. The Western emphasis has been on the forbidden/required aspect of doxastic logic, whereas the traditional Chinese emphasis was on the permissive among the possible courses of behavior. Classical science shared this emphasis on necessity (causation) and impossibility. In effect, classical Western practice was to view permission as the absence of prohibition, while the Chinese practice was to treat obligation as "not permissible not to."

The lingering effects of the popular conception of scientific knowledge of laws, facts, and reality have further shaped these concepts. That, combined with the traditional Western understanding of values, leave us with the consequence that value, moral, normative, or ethical truths, laws, and properties cannot be verified by scientific method. Thus we feel forced to divide each into two stark types: natural versus ethical properties, truths, relations, and forces, and events versus actions. The scientific types can be studied empirically, while the moral or ethical cannot. This dynamic was given particular impetus in positivist verificationism. Mackie uses this issue to cement his conclusion while acknowledging the repudiation of strict verificationism:

> This queerness does not consist simply in the fact that ethical statements are "unverifiable." Although logical positivism with its verifiability theory of descriptive meaning gave an impetus to non-cognitive accounts of ethics, it is not only logical positivists but also empiricists of a much more liberal sort who should find objective values hard to accommodate. Indeed, I would not only reject the verifiability principle, but also deny the conclusion commonly drawn from it, that moral judgments lack descriptive meaning. The assertion that there are objective values or intrinsically prescriptive entities or features of some kind, which ordinary moral judgments presuppose, is, I hold, not meaningless, but false. (1977, 39–40)

Given our modern criterion of naturalism — employing the language of and being broadly consistent with our best scientific account of the natural world — it is not surprising that most Western accounts stumble. Our longest historical tradition, natural law theory, relied on a supernaturalism — a lawgiver for both moral and scientific laws. Over a century ago, the march of science had already triggered a reaction — positive law — which still required a *legitimate* lawgiver. Traditional supernaturalism had postulated an explanans of nature that also functioned as the ultimate normative authority, whose absence, as Nietzsche emphasized, threatens our conception of morality.

Mackie's examples draw on the philosophical ancestor of that supernaturalism, Plato, and his twentieth-century heirs such as G. E. Moore. Plato postulated forms that simultaneously embody a word's definition and give teleological purpose to their natural emergence — items or objects that exemplify the good.

> Plato's forms give a dramatic picture of what objective values would have to be. The Form of the Good is such that knowledge of it provides the knower with both a direction and an overriding motive; some thing's being good both tells the person who knows this to pursue it and makes him pursue it. And objective good would be sought by anyone who is acquainted with it, not because of any contingent fact that this person, or every person, is so constituted that he desires this end, but just because the end has to-be-pursuedness somehow built into it. (Mackie 1977, 40)

Apart from being non-observable, Mackie notes, normative values would have to have Plato's teleological *force*, to-be-pursuedness, inherent in them. No scientifically natural object, property, relation, or law seems plausibly to satisfy this demand. Although Mackie does not argue this way, this implicit requirement seems even to undermine Plato's and Moore's *non-natural* objects or properties. Russell (and later emotivists) famously turned Moore's open-question argument against his own attempted solution — an unanalyzable simple, non-natural, but real property of good perceived by intuition. Isn't it still possible, they wondered, to perceive or apprehend this curious property and still not care to pursue it, not feel any appeal, invitation, or demand from it? Moore's open-question argument thus led us to *emotivism*, an essentially subjective analysis of morality and norms.

A similar line of reasoning that Plato had elaborated in the *Phaedo* led to related philosophical argument against supernatural obligation — God's laws, commands, rules, etc. Hearing God's command, we still can ask, "Why should we care?" Don't we rely on an additional reason to obey God? Moore's open-question argument works against supernaturalist definitions of normativity as it does against intuitive perceptions of non-natural properties. And Kant wrestled with how to spell out the good will's commitment to moral law. It is not the norm naturalism that is puzzling but that objects of a sentential or sentential-role metaphysical type — substances (subjects), properties (predicates), facts (true sentences), or laws (necessarily true universal sentences) — could have the required normative force.

Mackie also argues that non-naturalist accounts, like Moore's and Plato's, invariably give rise to intuitionism, because of a related epistemological queerness. Objective non-scientific foci end up, Mackie argues, committed to epistemological intuitionism. "Intuitionism merely makes unpalatably plain what other forms of objectivism wrap up" (Mackie 1977, 38).

Mackie's take on the interactions in this structure of Western concepts also explains why interpreters, noticing the widespread Chinese assumptions of ethical naturalism, characterize Chinese moral epistemology as intuitionism rather than either empiricism or rationalism.

So this chapter has several subtasks:
- To explicate the nature of *dào* in a way that ties it to contemporary scientific naturalism, in concepts grounded and broadly coherent with natural science;
- to explain how normativity (normative *dào*) can emerge from and be fundamentally coherent with natural *dào* — that is, to elaborate the quintessentially Daoist view that all the rival moral *dào*s (discourse *dào*s) are embedded in and presuppose natural *dào*;
- to explain how *dào* can also serve as a general normative concept intertranslatable with the familiar cluster of Western candidates for the focal role in normative theorizing;
- and to illuminate how *dào* can be accessible to "our ordinary ways of knowing everything else" in a way consistent with a broadly natural empiricism.

Natural Scientific Dào

The first of these tasks is the perennial central question of Chinese philosophy: What is *dào*? Ancient Chinese Daoists simply used and illustrated the term. Successive generations of interpreters have all addressed it in interpretation — particularly interpretations of classical Daoist philosophy texts. I have objected to a common feature of traditional answers to the question, namely, the claim that Daoists used the word to mean something different from what Confucians mean, i.e., to refer to a natural force of creation versus Confucian morality (and thus implicitly detaching natural from normative *dào*).

My approach implied an alternative distinction — between what I called *discourse dào* and *performance dào*. The model is the type-token relation, or that between a play and its performance, or a score and a concert. I treat a performance as of some discourse *dào* type, as an interpretation in practice, in real time, of a discourse score or play. A performance *dào*, a concrete course of performance, is subject to evaluation as being a performance of some discourse *dào* and a discourse *dào* subject to interpretation in a performance. Discourse *dào*s are changeable in the sense that we can interpret them in different performances. (Alternatively, one can think of a given *discourse dào* as a sum or collection of possible *performance dào*s.)

The notion of constant *dào* here would thus combine two ideas. A discourse *dào* could be the single correct one for everyone at all times to follow or execute, and it can have only one correct performance *dào* — only a particular concrete history would count as *correct*. I theorized that Shèn Dào 慎到 is an example of how an early Daoist thinker applied the discourse-performance model to natural cosmology — exploiting the tendency of Confucians, Mohists and other disputants to insist that their chosen discourse was 天道 *tiān-dào* (natural path). Great *dào* — the actual history of everything's movement — counts as the correct performance of whatever is the natural *dào*. (The tone of determinism arises from the implicit implication that actual history is also the only performance — that no *interpretation* is required.)

So *tiān-dào* would be constant in both senses: we have no choice but to follow or be subject to it, and we do not need to interpret it. It was constant in still another sense, in that, like the movement of heavenly bodies, the paths are constant. This third is the sense that makes it such that *tiān-dào* can function as a rough counterpart of natural physical laws.

I held that the central focus of classical Chinese theory, including Daoism, addressed discourse *dào*. The cosmological focus in Daoism has a role mainly in the context of metaethical reflection on human normative *dào*s. Clearly, both human and natural *dào*s have metaphysical status, though they are embodied in different structures (as human *dào*s may be embodied in speech, practice, writing, penal codes, etc.). Human *dào*s are broadly socially constructed objects, and linguistic *dào*s are tightly integrated with them.

Two modifiers characteristically mark a more cosmological use of *dào*: 天 *tiān* (nature:sky) *dào* and 大 *dà* great *dào*. Shèn Dào's "Great Dào" (*dà dào*) is minimally relevant to a portion of the *Lǎozǐ*'s theorizing and to vanishingly little of the *Zhuāngzǐ*'s. The writers of both texts, I suggest, concluded that Shèn Dào's Great *Dào* was nearly irrelevant to a normative project, since, trivially, everything that happens constitutes Great *Dào*. The *Zhuāngzǐ*, I theorize, reflects a similar conclusion about *tiān-dào*: any socially constructed human *dào*s are results of the operation of natural *dào*s. The *Lǎozǐ*, by contrast, seems to presuppose more of an opposition between socially constructed and "natural" *dào*s.

Here, I will follow the *Zhuāngzǐ* and illustrate some interesting continuities linking natural *dào* smoothly to distinctively normative *dào* — including social discourse *dào*s. My goal is not so much to repeat or endorse the *Zhuāngzǐ*'s theory, since the understanding of nature and naturalism prevalent among the text's contemporaries would have been very different from ours. Theirs probably assumed a broadly organic conception of nature, and ours is the still unresolved combination of general relativity and quantum mechanics — which singly and together challenge both common sense and our traditional materialist metaphysics. Part of understanding the concept of *dào* would thus lie in seeing how we can express our current best natural theory in *dào* terms.

Other commentators have noticed, probably with excessive ardor, some of the ways that classical Chinese concepts fit modern physics rather more neatly than they would have fit classical mechanics. It is, for example, interesting to note with Graham that the Chinese word we translate as "universe," *yǔ zhòu* 宇宙, is composed of terms that are, respectively, spatial and temporal (1978, 365). So like post-Einsteinian and unlike classical physics, the ancient Chinese would think of reality as a space-time history rather than as some huge composite object in space with a history.

Another example is the Chinese concept of the fundamental stuff, the fundamental constituent of everything that has a history: *qì*. Wing-tsit Chan and Frijof Capra excitedly note parallels with relativity's blend of mass and energy.[2] The Chinese conception involved its being the source of living vitality (breath) as well as a counterpart of Western matter — the basic stuff of all things, including spirits (if there are spirits). What we are noticing in the two cases is a relatively continuous way to express some of the features of a modern conception in the language of ancient Chinese cosmological concepts.

My version of a similar project for *dào* will also exhibit this kind of partial continuity with a pattern of Chinese use that still fits modern natural science — again perhaps better than the traditional sentence-linked foci that triggered Mackie's queerness reaction. I suspect that the implicit standard *meaning* theory of *dào* — signaled in the conventional dictionary translations — is substantially correct. A standard dictionary list includes "road," "path," "channel," "course," "way," "route," "method," "art," "means," and "line." Dictionaries frequently also include some of the things we think of as socially constructed discourse *dào*s, such as "doctrines," "teachings," and "morality." Finally, we may find the concepts with which Western theorists have tried either to link the two or to do approximately what Chinese theorists did with their talk of constant *dào*: "truth," "principle," "justice," and "reason." These, however, I find less plausible as meaning analyses than as attempts to reflect the central role of *dào* talk in Chinese thinking by linking it to central Western "elevator words," the West's similarly pivotal concepts.

My own preferred replacement definition of *dào* is that *dào*s answer "how" questions. Such answers tie a *dào*'s explanatory and guiding role together. Besides instrumental guidance, however, we take a *dào* to answer categorical "What to do?" questions, the "Where should we go?" that underlies "How do we get there?" I treat answering this "what to do" question as a further "how" question — how to choose a *dào*. We normally do this *in consideration of some end*, but we can choose paths for deontological reasons or for evidentially available qualities of the path other than where it leads, e.g., aesthetic qualities.

To make sense of choosing a path, we presuppose some range of naturally existing *dào*s among which we can choose. The categorical question is exchanged for a recursive procedural one — a constructivist approach. Additional meta-questions are how to search, identify, choose, and interpret *dào* structures. Again, the answers generate a recursive hierarchy of "how" questions, with answers also to be found, if at all, in naturally available processes for creatures like us to make and performatively interpret such choices of naturally available guidance structures.

So a *dào*-based naturalism does not entail normative absolutism; there need not be a single correct answer to the "what to do" question. It is still nomically realistic naturalism, that is, not in the one-right-answer sense but in the sense that available *dào*s are part of the natural structure of the world. Whether in the end the recursive application of ways of answering the prior question will terminate in a single outcome is unknown but seems improbable. Hence, the upshot of *dào* naturalism is skeptical relativism.

This picture of the link between normative *dào*s (natural processes or histories) draws on developments in philosophy of science stemming from Russell and recently elaborated by Wesley Salmon. They are motivated by the physics of relativity and quantum mechanics and Hume's challenge (resembling Mackie's) that we should not invoke "hidden causal springs." Salmon explains as follows:

> The general idea is quite simple. . . . A process is something that, in the context, has greater temporal duration than an event. From the standpoint of cosmology a supernova explosion — such as occurred in

our cosmic neighborhood in the last year of the fourth decade — could be considered an event; the travel of a photon or neutrino from the explosion to earth (requiring thousands of years) would be a process. In ordinary affairs a chance meeting with a friend in a supermarket would normally be considered an event; the entire shopping trip might qualify as a process. In microphysics a collision of a photon with an electron would constitute an event; an electron orbiting an atomic nucleus would qualify as a process. A process, whether causal or pseudo, will exhibit some sort of uniformity or continuity. Something that, in one context, would be considered a single process (such as running a mile) would often be considered a complex combination of many processes from another standpoint (e.g., that of a physiologist). (1989, 108)

A natural worry about this ontology of the proposed continuity between nature and normativity is my implicit further distinction between discourse and performance *dào*s (type-token) in normative discourse (cf. Salmon's *sets* of uniform/constant processes). Both seem to entail a one-many structure like Platonism, inviting a Mackie-style debunking of an abstraction. The abstract score or play stands still in contrast to the intuitively concrete actual performance history as well as to the physical printed copies. The easiest defense is to note the pervasive role of similar type-token relations in scientific discourse.

The most obvious of these is talk of the symmetry of a path of light in various directions, in regions of space and time, and to observers in different inertial frames. To all, the "path" of light in space-time will appear the same. This translational symmetry is the most familiar form of constant *dào*s or physical laws. That reality has symmetrical structures need not give rise to anti-Platonic scruples.

Other examples come from quantum mechanics, in which an electromagnetic energy packet's probability of striking a detector is calculated by thinking of it as travelling, wavelike, by all actually possible *dào*s to the detector and then summing the probability of arriving by each route.[3] Richard Feynman, who pioneered this "sum-of-histories" approach to quantum mechanics, admits that the resulting picture is strange, but the strangeness belongs to natural physics, not to transcendent abstraction. We use the method to compute the percentage of light that is reflected by its passing through a medium, but the classical experimental two-slit experiment shows that the wavelike interference pattern of probabilities is best explained as each photon moving through both slits simultaneously and thus setting up an interference pattern with itself that generates the probability of where it will strike the detector. In following each possible path, the light particle exhibits the symmetrical constancy mentioned above, the speed of light.

The one-many relation of supervenience also is implicit in scientific accounts of nature. Process A supervenes on underlying process B when changes in B need not entail changes in A, but changes in A always entail changes in B. If two underlying B processes are symmetrical, then their A processes will be. But A processes can be symmetrical when B processes are not. Such relations among paths account for how quantum processes, paths of energy packets, interact to form neutrons, protons, and electrons, from which atomic nuclei emerge with their supervenient *dào*s, and so on through atoms and molecules, up to stars, galaxies, clusters of galaxies, and super-clusters. These "objects" emerge from underlying realities and have their own individual *dào*s, features of which are constant/symmetrical under a wide range of transformations. They form populations (clouds) which can also have *dào*s. All such emergent objects have *dào*s that supervene on the *dào*s of their components.

The language of natural science, as much as that of morality, is characterized by supervenience relations and real modalities: possibility, probability, and necessity. Modern physics also contemplates explaining things in a world with extra dimensions. Probability waves are taken to "collapse" into determinate events when processes interact (a photon strikes an electron shell). Scientists speculate about holographic features of reality — ways all the "information" in a region can be on a "surface" of that region. Broader theories of physical processes, string theory or loop quantum gravity, offer more models of how reality-grounded analogues of type-token relationships constitute the architecture of reality. We need not resort to assertions that the *dào* of the actual universe contributes to some larger planning *dào* or exemplifies some *dào*-type transcending the actual processes occurring symmetrically in reality.

Natural processes also aggregate temporally: *dào*s have a network-like structure in which relatively constant sub-processes occur in a wider variety of temporal sequences. Both the snippets and the larger segments count as *dào*s. The points of interaction events are like nodes in the network of subroutines that may be assembled into larger temporal *dào* sequences. Emergent objects with their supervening *dào*s aggregate both spatially and temporally in the *dào*s of other objects whose structure they are parts of. The layered scheme of *dào*s is a conception of the interconnectedness of things. While we can speak of a *dào* of the universe, we should think of the universe as a collection (probably of 10,000-plus super-clusters) and of its *dào* as the limit of the probabilities of such temporal sequences, not a repeatable *dào* in some larger reality or scheme. The actual world is the one-time *dào* of the universe (setting aside speculations about alternate universes and big-bang/collapse scenarios).

Consequently, the *dào* of the universe is not another source of normativity. We find normativity within the plethora of actual *dào*s within which we routinely conceive of *dào* types as real, structural, symmetrical probabilities of histories actually arising in the world. Assimilating scientific and normative *laws* only seemed to confront us with a stark choice between mechanical necessity of transcendent purpose and guidance. Whatever spookiness we find in the counterparts of *dào*-types in modern physics, they do not require scientists to resort to supernatural, mental, moral or other radical dualisms of the sort Mackie objects to.

Once we see the processes from which normativity can be instituted, the natural structure of probable *dào*s will provide the material of choice, and it can become natural to see such *paths* as the range of options available to choice (and practical interpretation). Daoists used the analogy of the invitation of a channel, valley, or ravine to water. It is natural to think of paradigmatic *dào*s as *wú* 無 (lack, non-being or absence) since, as the *Lǎozǐ* argues, it is the emptiness that invites movement through it. Treating *dào*s as probable or possible places to go gives them the modality of permissibility rather than obligation. They portray water as following a course (so "channel" is among the definitions of *dào*). Equally relevant, water can, over time, carve a channel. This invitational focus of normativity, in place of the obligations implicit in a focus on law, also reminds us that a *dào* is neither a thing (an emergent object) nor a force. It is rather analogous to open structures created by the configuration and distribution of stuff or force.

Epistemically, such *dào*s are configurations we *can* access and use in guiding our behavior. One result of seeing guidance as originating in *dào*, the available open network of options for normative purposes, rather than as duties, is to see *dào* guidance as the two-phase sequence described above: a choice phase, when we pick some road to follow; and the practical interpretation phase. We read a physical structure as triggering a sequence of routines yielding our intended historical path as one of the probabilistically available histories embodied in that structure used as a *dào*-type — a discourse *dào*. The interpretation phase gets relatively more attention in China, and it is the basis for my describing even physical roads as "discourse *dào*s." There is a sense in which we "read" the road (though we may notice we are doing so only when it is somewhat harder than a superhighway with marked lanes). We are treating the structure as guiding our action. When we come to a fork or crossroad, we re-enter a choice phase that is also (from the point of view of the whole way to X) part of the interpretation.

We might take some comfort in the Chinese model of a mass-like notion of *dào* (the play consists of all of its physical copies, editions, productions, performances, and recitations, past and future). This allows us to aggregate *dào* in different ways. We can aggregate, as above, your way to Aberdeen and mine as our way of getting there, and we can also aggregate levels of *dào* where physical *dào* constitute artifactual *dào*. My physical execution of the physical *dào* of moving my right foot to the right, crossing my left behind, then replacing my weight on the right, constitutes my performance of the *dào* of a samba right whisk.

The elements of fully normative *dào* emerge gradually from this natural base. Suns forge heavier atoms whose trajectories and histories may bring them together in solar systems, and in some of these — maybe only in one — the courses and interactions of the atoms in molecules form some molecules with an important structure. The structural *dào* gives that molecular structure a probabilistic disposition, in appropriate environments, to shape and convert some of these more complex elements and molecules into protein molecules. The *dào* of one of these possible (seemingly rare) protein structures has a supervening probabilistic *dào*, e.g., of that molecule's splitting and replicating. That such a structure exists is not nature's judgment that such a molecule should form a population of replicants. The emergence of the processes of life does not, by itself, import normativity into nature.

Students puzzled by "intelligent design" alternatives sometimes ask when the "theory of evolution" will become a law. The question resembles a category mistake. Evolution is not even lawlike — it is a *dào*. Evolution can be explained by scientific laws — like Mendelian laws of hereditary inheritance, which together with random variation (which, being random, hardly counts as a *law*), interact with the probabilities in the interaction of their histories and of things around them to result in a distribution of similar structures in a population. Similarly, the big bang theory is a *dào* — it is a scientific reconstruction, based on lawlike retrodiction — of the early history of the universe. So if we seriously want to find a reference for the idea that *dào* is source of everything or the force behind creation, there is no such *dào*. However, there is a *dào* that consists of everything being created, i.e., the world's actual history.

The crucial discovery associated with Zhuāngzǐ (though it seems to have first been realized by the Later Mohists) is that most of natural *dào* is not normative. Normativity emerges gradually from and is grounded in a non-normative natural *dào*.

The Emergence of Interest

The present account, so far, can only be normative by reverse projection — typically by us attributing normativity to unguided natural processes. We may, like Mòzǐ, think that the formation of the solar system and the emergence of plant life is an example of nature behaving "correctly." Scientific explanatory *dào* does not directly lead to normativity. However, we can regard the progression of complex structures as gradually introducing the elements out of which normativity emerges.

The possibility of replication introduces a crucial element, a systematic way of talking about a structure's *interest*. Its process involves interaction with conditions under which the structure is replicated so the structure's proliferation — its forming a population — depends on which of the *dào*s of varying probability it traces. It does not seem as queer to talk of the interest of a bacterium or a plant or even of a gene pool, population, or ecosystem as it does to talk of the interest of a galaxy of helium molecules. We can talk about how a species of plant interacts with other plants in an ecosystem that enhances their population growth and the diversity and enlargement of the ecosystem. However, it is still *we* who use the concept of interest to make judgments about what this plant or that species is right or wrong to do, not the organism or population itself, far less nature or the quantum processes on which the whole story supervenes.

We may conceive of these interests or ends, as Aristotle does, as a species of causation. But, while the living emergent thing's *dào* is part of a description of how the universe works and the natural *dào,* nothing guides the structure via anything like a choice or an interpretation or consists in following (in the sense of performing) some available probabilistic *dào*. At this level, life processes are still descriptive *dào*s and the "guidance" consists simply in the fact that the *dào* supervenes on highly probable *dào*s of underlying and surrounding things. We may project that, besides the natural *dào* of the plant, the plant has some goal or end state. We still cannot plausibly attribute that goal to the plant, nor the choice, collective or individually, to co-operate with other plants in its ecosystem. Things happen.

Forms of life have clusters of physical structures embodying dispositional probabilities excited by interactions with external environmental processes. Broadly, these structures constitute what Chinese thinkers called *dé* 德 (virtuosity) and define as "*dào* within." The interactions of these internal processes and external processes trigger that life form's propensity to follow *dào*s. Such a cluster of structures is *dé* when (a) the *dào* it guides toward is normatively right and (b) it follows that *dào* reliably. A plant's *dé* consists in a persistent feature of its physical structure that embodies its dispositional propensity to follow path times conducive to some interest. A plant bends its stems to capture more light, extends its tendrils toward suitable anchor points or nourishment, gives protection or attracts co-operative species, and so forth. Neither the emergence of these structures nor their highly probable operation would count as normative, but we can meaningfully talk about how that *dé* guides the plant toward its (or its population's, or ecosystem's) interest. When full normativity emerges, we may attribute normativity to a *dé* if we already attribute normativity to the processes toward which it *guides* the plant's growth.

What we characterize as a normative structure may be a product of interactions of a population of creatures, each acting according to its own *dé*. These interactions may create physical marks or structures that may guide others toward performances conducive to some interest. This process may involve the magic of large numbers, threshold effects, and the emergence of order from the interaction of a seemingly chaotic plethora of paths.

So we can speak of guidance embodied in the historical *dào*s of populations, of emergent objects, and of encompassing ecosystems — *dé* of communal co-operation. However, we would not call the plants' movement along the *dào*s marked by past behavior a choice nor their execution of these movements morally right or wrong. As the *Zhuāngzǐ* argues, Mencius and his interpreters who try to extract morality from natural inclinations have jumped prematurely to this conclusion. Interests and ends are only a first step toward normativity. Socially generated guiding signals conducive to an interest are a second. Claiming normativity at the plant or insect stage relies heavily on imaginative projection — on something like the personification of nature.

Community Dào and Individual Dào

Vertebrates, however, give us more structure and more recognizable *dào*s. Their internal guidance is rooted in the probabilistic interactions of electromagnetic energy with chemical structures in the nerve endings. It involves a considerably more obvious way an animal's *dé* can respond to and trigger interactions with relevant external environmental processes — and thus guide the animal through some *dào*. Animals do process information and, in a still closer sense, can be said to "choose" their paths and to have phases of learning to read and follow both social markings and natural signs in ways that satisfy an interest.

A carnivore may calculate an interception route for its prey. It does so in response to photons hitting receptors in its eye and "preserving" information about the continuous temporal "collapse of probabilities" of the prey's path of escape. This information collection and calculation process launches the animal — say, a cheetah — on its interpretive performance *dào* of capture. Given the distribution of stuff in the situation, including the prey, the environment, and the cheetah, there either is or is not a path, both a direction and speed within the cheetah's range, such that, should the cheetah execute it, it will successfully intercept the antelope. We can meaningfully judge that the cheetah *should* turn at a specific angle. The cheetah has an internal *dào*, the chemical-electromagnetic physical processes of its central nervous system, for calculating its angle of pursuit. We can speak in an even more familiar way of the animal's *dé* (virtuosity) than we do of a plant's. Some animals may be more efficient than others, and their efficiency may result from the quality of their learning.

The animal level allows a richer way of bringing in the relevance of a community — although community is relevant to *dào*s of plants. But in animal communities, we find not only co-operative *dào*s, but the laying down, learning, and transmitting of *dào*s. Community conformity plays a role in animal behavior even outside of our more familiar vertebrates. Cockroaches normally choose the darker of two hiding spaces, but a herd of micro-robots programmed to choose a lighter space produces a change in cockroach behavior. More of them choose the lighter hiding space. Ants have notoriously orderly and efficient methods of path finding, marking, selecting, adapting, and following. The mechanism that explains the emergence of ant trails is ultimately a physical, chemical one, but it reveals how elements of complex *dào*-guiding behavior emerge in a community context and how such ant-*dé* can be a distributed property of the colony as much as that of individual ants. Individual ants do not lay the trail, but the chemistry of ant trails makes it so that when the numbers of ants in a region get large enough, a threshold is reached and the ants begin to march on trails marked by other ants.

The community's *dé* selects and marks or signals a path, and this facilitates that community behavior. The path becomes an "attraction" to the ants. This is an intuitively clear example of how a social *dào* can be naturally "inviting." Ants do not, of course, have normative autonomy, so we should not speak of their being under an obligation to follow the trail, whether hypothetical or categorical. Ant *dé* exhibits a vestige of "choosing" the *dào* they follow, but they do not, as it were, choose the whole but only to follow this scent here. They similarly exhibit a rudimentary kind of interpretation — at least in the sense that they can lose the trail, be forced off it by overcrowding, etc.

Here bees may seem to show us a richer insect version of this kind of *dào*. Where the ant gets only the equivalent of a *shì-fēi* 是非 (this-not this) for a contextual choice of a marked segment of the ant-trail, the bee dance seems to encode direction and distance to a nectar source. We similarly need not treat the observing bees as choosing whether or not to fly as indicated (it seems the dance, like human music, gets them worked up). But there is a more complete sense in which they internalize the message instructions and interpret the whole in their flight performances. A bee must have a *dé* that reads, stores, and executes the correct flight path from encoded instructions — some, no doubt, better than others. That day's flight has not been genetically programmed, but the dance, interpretation, and inclination to hive co-operation seemingly are. The dance is an act of altruism triggered by a chemical probably linked to a reward system in their brain. The *dé* of individual bees to read, store, and execute the *dào* conveyed in the dance can differ. A virtuoso dancer and virtuoso readers of its dance have a high probability of reliably contributing to finding the food source.

Besides the core programming to read and execute some form of language or signaling, more temporary but still traceable three-dimensional paths — patterns generated by past histories of animal behavior — guide many other animals through mimicry. Sometimes guidance takes place that is not co-operative, as when a predator follows a prey's trail, including its prints and scent. All these paths are emergent objects in their own rights and are physically present for other animals to choose and interpret. Other non-co-operative species and enemies may also use such a trail, as when many animals follow a shared path to water.

Learning can be observed among a more restricted range of animal species. Cultural differences have been noticed not only in primates' but in aquatic mammals' skill. Deliberate educational activities have recently been observed in meerkats (Thornton and McAuliffe 2006), even including progressive teaching of skills based on the student's readiness and/or their requests for more challenging exercises. Animals learn *dào*s of finding, reading, and following other natural *dào*s.

Human animals join other species in both following physically accessible paths and trails, in copying animal behavior of other species — mimicry — and education. Recent animal behavioral studies have begun to track a whole range of progressively more complex forms of pre-normative behavior — from varying degrees of education, to signaling vocalizations, dances, or songs, to accumulation and transmission of culture, to a sense of justice (Range et al. 2009). The mirror test and associated behaviors involve simulating the *dé* of others in ways that enable mimicry, co-operation, and deliberate interference.[4] Humans are different in their normative capacities, of course, but we are discovering with the Daoists that there is a progressively smooth blending of natural *dào* behind even capacities that show huge jumps in outcome capacities.

Humans, obviously, have significantly greater degrees of blending and sophistication in *dào*-use. Much of this pivots around the capacity for using more complex forms of signaling via conventionally malleable and grammatically compositional language. The familiar form of this difference lies in vocalization, but we see it in the variety of ways to create readable three-dimensional physical paths — from blazing trees to rock piles to broken branches to gingerbread crumbs. These form part of both co-operative and individual adaptive behavior.

The capacity to mirror or simulate the *dé* of another allows us to learn their *dào*s. The internal *dé* mechanism (the nervous system) that underlies and enables this gradually more complex capacity for co-operative community behavior also exhibits gradually greater plasticity culminating in *dào*s interwoven with a syntactically structured language. Many components of eventual full human normativity emerge gradually — while we retain, of course, elements of other animal mechanics, habit, routine, and blind mechanism.

Remarkably few animals come with all their behaviors genetically guided — as we saw, including even cockroaches, ants, and bees. We can join Daoists in reminding humanity-worshipping Confucians that most animals join us in having an evolutionary capacity to detect and follow *dào*s and to bolster the capacity by broadly educational means. These vary in degree within populations and play a role in the mechanism of further evolution. Warning and distress signals among animals are increasingly being discovered, so we can see widespread hints of less complex forms of "discourse *dào*" in nature. We are discovering greater degrees of "compositionality" in these ways of communicating, e.g., among birds who seem to compose their songs from a repertoire of fragments in response to training and for expressive effect.

Salient roles for this kind of signaling, besides co-operation and warnings of danger, are sexual attraction, mating, and bonding. Birds' mating calls and rituals introduce aspects of normativity we could characterize as aesthetic value. It is probably an exaggeration that nature does not waste any *dào*, but the economy of nature in preserving and reusing DNA structures as well as of animal communities using and exploiting each other's *dào*s and their tastes is remarkable in nature. Hummingbirds, bees, and humans all find flowers attractive. Both humans and peahens find peacock feathers and their display beautiful, though humans may respond less to the peacock's "dance."

In summary, layered on top of the emergence of interests in an organism, group, species, or ecosystem in following a *dào*, we find in animals a wide range of progressively more complex and interrelated patterns of *dào* creation, sharing, signaling, reading, and following. *Dào*-guidance seems very smoothly embedded in natural behavior. The autonomy we associate with morality should emerge as elaboration and completion of these elements of normativity.

Forms of life allow us to conceptually divide possible *dào*s into aggregates that serve some interests of species, ecosystems, populations, communities, or individuals and do not serve or interfere with those interests. Adaptive central nervous systems allow individuals to register some of these, select, and execute them; they have a capacity, *dé*, to register roughly the same distinction internally and to initiate interest-serving *dào*s with a certain reliability. Populations, communities, other species in the ecosystem may evolve co-operative ways to interact with these internal capacities to increase their accuracy. Primates that also have capacities to simulate the inner process of choosing and following *dào*s in others can internally create *dào*s of aiding, co-operating, or interfering. This ability may be further developed and enhanced by more complex forms of communication, from simple warning, attracting, etc., to complex expressions of a discourse *dào* that can be shared with others.

Human *Dào* and Full Moral Normativity

Full normativity, especially Kantian normativity, as Mackie would argue, is still not found in our story of nature so far. It says nothing about reason or autonomy or the kind of full-fledged choice that justifies talk of moral responsibility. However, we can see in the gradual build-up of full normativity the beginnings of a distinction between "a reason" and "a cause" that can underlie the full notion of a language — a scheme of giving and asking for reasons.

An animal that registers information, marks, or indications of a natural "discourse" *dào*, a structure that would reliably guide that animal's behavior — its performance of the *dào*-type — can be said to have perceiving the mark as a reason for its behavior. That reason, in conjunction with the animal's *dé*, is also a cause. The mark could count as a reason for the animal to pursue that *dào*. Had it executed some information-gathering routine within its repertoire (looking, smelling, listening, etc.) it would have registered and responded to the mark and chosen or followed the *dào*.

This use of *a* reason is broadly normative but not yet sentential. When registered as an input, it initiates a process that generates an output, but the process need not be inferential or mediated by concepts. When we add the capacity to simulate the process in conspecifics, we can appreciate their reasons in this underlying sense, where they may or may not be causes. Armed, then, with an appropriate method of communication, we could convey or share such a reason with another creature when we appreciate it has failed to register the mark. The method of communication would be guided by its own *dào*, which could involve inferences (e.g., concepts). Then the articulation of that communication would give it an inferential role among other communications guided by the *dào* of that language. The articulation would be a premise in some possible reasoning process leading to a choice of behaviors.

We think of reasoning, in the sense needed for Kantian autonomy, as an inferential process. It comes, as opponents of any talk of animal language insist, with a significant leap in complexity of the grammatical and inferential structure of a guidance signaling system. The use of a more powerful structural *dào* of co-operative signaling still clearly relies on the other features of natural normativity discussed above. The leap in complexity may be a magnified effect of small incremental changes in natural structure.

Anatomically modern humans with approximately our present brain size and raw intelligence did not become behaviorally modern until they began to exploit the power of language. Language and more advanced social ways of life certainly affected the distribution of capacities in subsequent populations but without requiring vastly greater brain size. What were our brains doing that could be so adapted to language use? One possibility is navigation, which similarly involves recursive elements and the storing of sequential performances (conditional dispositions) in structural physical form. Navigation would have been involved in group planning and rudimentary signaling (perhaps with gestures, pictures in the sand, etc.). We are distinguished from our ape cousins partly by an expanded period of adolescent dependency during which the training, enculturation, and learning necessary for language takes place. As the power of our signaling systems and the extent of the accumulated knowledge stored by means of them grow, the period of educational dependency expands.

We have treated *dào*s (ways) as a broad generic class that encompasses processes (causal and non-causal), histories, possible (probable) histories and their aggregations, and paths, whether marked or naturally generated from repetitive behavior. Ways can be marked or signaled by interactive and co-operative behavior, and internal repertoires of sequential *dào*s for choosing *dào*s and interpreting them in practice are stored in the nervous system. We have only hinted at the *dào*-like structure of the brain, the *dào* routines calling and executing subroutines, and so forth. In all this, we have meaningful senses in which we can identify correct or successful and flawed execution, tied, perhaps, to flaws in the learned *dào* or caused by random fluctuations in the *dào*s of underlying processes on which our guidance behavior supervenes.

In the human social realm, the counterparts of *dào* include rituals, practices, and games — and as Wittgenstein taught us, we understand language naturalistically when we see its functioning in the context of rituals, practices, procedures, and games — in the context of a "form" (way) of life. Language is one social practice embedded in a broad set of social practices. They are acquired as a package in the child's training and induction into the community. Language games involve such broad gamelike features as taking turns, having a range of choices (*dào*s) for each move, and adjusting one's move to those of other players.

Participation in games introduces normative notions of status and commitment that are autonomous in the sense that they are internal to the game's *dào*. They supervene on, but are not entailed by, underlying *dào*s. I am not committed by my desires but am by my participation in a co-operative *dào*. The predator in choosing a path of interception is "committed" to it mainly in the sense that, in the nature of movement, it takes time and effort to change direction. Commitment and status in the game change with the state of the game, the history of prior moves.

The big normative jump at a human stage is the degree of devotion and dedication to learning, practicing, and participating in such forms of social interaction. The change in *dé* consists more in the plasticity of using the physical mechanism via complex programming than in its storage of vastly more paths or routines. The efficiency of storage is based on a hierarchy of processes of finding, choosing, and interpreting segments of paths. This is a structure of inferential reasons that can be accessed and called from many points in choice and performance execution of naturally and socially marked *dào* types.

The child who says "gogo dooed it" has not *inferred* from our speech behavior that he or she should use a past tense form but has been inclined to do it from registering our speech behavior. The child had a reason for speaking that way but had not inferred that he or she should. The child is not a theoretician constructing a hypothesis or theorizing about the grammar but is learning a *dào*. The game or social practice the child is learning is the game of giving and asking for, sharing and communicating such reasons. The pieces in the game — words, concepts, and structures — have a range of patterned entitlements to each other, permitted, required, and forbidden inferences. Making an assertion — making a move in the game — commits us to those assertions required by it, while permitting and forbidding other assertions.

Social practices and interactive "taking turns" as in games can be observed in other natural species (songbirds' duets), but the complexity of human signaling systems allows us to speak of commitment to other speech acts (as well as behaviors) in ways that do not seem naturalistically plausible for less grammatically complex signaling systems.[5] Armed with this sort of game, we can extend it by attempts to give reasons for how we play the game: we theorize about the rules or laws enshrined in our linguistic and other practices. Here, finally, I suggest, we have full-fledged normative reasoning.

However, this account of how we arrive at normativity might not satisfy Mackie. The first problem is that social practices are not self-warranting. Morality is typically regarded as a standard by which we can evaluate, select, and reject social practices. And the language-assisted process of reconstructing principles enshrined in such practices — the norms that would justify the practice — can at best give us conventional mores, not full-fledged morality. The second problem is that Mackie was quite clear that hypothetical imperatives would not evade his criticism — his *error* theory of morality. We need unconditional and intrinsically obligatory natural structures and natural epistemic access to them.

Two more steps then lead to the Daoist result. The first is that developed by Blackburn (1984) and Gibbard.[6] Some social practices can emerge that, though they are *d*àos of existing communities with a history and a range of adherents, include an enshrined norm of an associated linguistic dào. This is a *dào* of inferentially justifying a practice (or justifying reform, adaptation, or rejection of it). One such practice that can emerge is a justifying practice that rules out appealing to the mere fact of social acceptance as the reason for the practice.

This meta-practice has evolutionary value because it facilitates reforming and adapting co-operative practices. The practice of giving reasons for our practices can become one in which we reject reasons relying on certain indexical information. "This is how *we* do it" is not a good enough reason.

Not all social practices are characterized by this quasi-objectivity, but there is no particular *queerness* associated with appreciating it as a characteristic of such a practice. If the practice permits this self-critical behavior, that is enough to block merely registering the fact of its being *ours* or the way we do it as a sufficient justification of doing it that way. Any *dào* that can be reflectively justified can also be reflectively criticized and reformed or changed.

The final step, according to Fernandez-Armesto (2003), is one of his "ideas that changed the world." A cultural innovation or invention he attributes to sometime in the ice age is an extrapolation from the autonomy of quasi-objective reason-giving practices. Having a social practice of making inferentially linked judgments with normative terms for commitments, obligations, and goodness, together with the emergence of quasi-objective justification, could have invited speculation about the good or recommendable *in itself*. The speculation could have been triggered by reflecting on a practice of ruling out appeal to the fact of the practice itself in considering reforms and objections. The idea, Fernandez-Armesto speculates, having occurred in human "Ice Age" pre-history, may have persisted and survived in all subsequent cultures.

The tempting feature of Fernandez-Armesto's historical story is the suggestion that universal human attitudes might stem not from genetics but from early innovation and persistence of practices. That story, however, seems to open the door to Mackie's "error theory." This early *superstition* may be a widespread human error that, like Fernandez-Armesto's other Ice Age "influential ideas," ritual cannibalism and tribal inheritance of leadership, is an innovation that a more realistic modern culture can abandon. If the story conflicts with Mencius (morality is not explained by innate or genetic inclination), it might still be made natural by Xúnzǐ's technique: the idea that something obligatory in itself persisted as a social practice because it promoted a human interest, namely, survival and flourishing in co-operative society. However, even that addendum cannot save morality from Mackie's critique. Mackie himself proposes such an account of the persistence of this massive error.

We seem to be faced with a dilemma. Either morality comes from the kinds of naturalistic structures we have outlined or from a cultural invention. If it is natural, then we should accept either a less ambitious, less Kantian, conception of morality, or accept that morality extends beyond humans to animals, or both. While the spirit of Daoism could accept either of these two results of basing human dàos on natural *dào*, there seems a Daoist way to escape the horns of the dilemma.

We could argue that morality expresses an ideal implicit in the *dào* in language itself — the extension of a *dào* of giving and asking for inferentially linked reasons. We can trace more widely the natural *dào*s of pre-linguistic reasons to choose a *dào*. The emergence of a rich, inferentially linked game allows us to see these reasons as sometimes inferentially justifying a natural choice or not. Language gives us a *dào* of choosing and interpreting *dào*. And as in other co-operative social practices, nature has equipped us with inclinations to use linguistic practice via pre-linguistic reasons. We naturally follow the *dào* enshrined in our community's practice. Then language gives us a *natural* reason to choose among existing social practices — yielding quasi-objectivity of social *dào*s. As we oscillate between the pre-linguistic and linguistic reasons for choosing and adapting a language and reasons expressed to each other using that language, we can recursively leverage the autonomy of morality out of existing social practice. We then have a language practice in which the fact that it is our shared social practice does not count as a sufficient reason for following it. At the same time, success or satisfaction in use of this structure of moral reasoning gives us a natural base for testing this reasoning via "reflective equilibrium."

In China, the *Zhuāngzǐ* version of this idea focuses more on interpretation of a *dào* in natural execution. Language gives us a way more reflectively to identify the *dào* enshrined in a social practice — in our actual past history. Consequently, it gives us ways to evaluate performance *dào*s as correct or incorrect expressions of the *dào* of the practice. We have two kinds of *dào* of *dào*: a *dào* of choosing and of interpreting in execution. We can use these *dào* of *dào* on both natural and social *dào*. We can appreciate morality both as uniquely human and as based on and grounded in our *dào* of using natural *dào*.

Conclusion

We started with a conception of ways or *dào* with varied dimensionality and the familiar metaphorical link of a path, road, or way in a three-dimensional space and a four-dimensional course of possible or permissible events or actions. We traced the variety of ways in nature by which a lower-dimension *dào* can *guide* higher-dimension execution of these processes. A three-dimensional "object" (a road) is a natural structure that contains information about a relatively favorable (i.e., convenient, fast, and reliable) possible future performance.

We are equipped to extract this guidance — an ability to read and execute a space-time course of walking-to some interest-related goal. The road-to-walking relation is an instance of the type-token relation between my "discourse" *dào* and "performance" *dào*. Similarly, a two-dimensional map is a discourse *dào* relative to selecting and following such a three-dimensional road — or to constructing one — a possible future history of creating a three-dimensional discourse *dào*. Similarly a one-dimensional pointing (orientation) guides us in reading/following the map or determining which way to follow a road represented on it.

The existence of *dào* is different from the existence of objects that emerge from *qì* (energy-stuff) but still fully naturalistic. The structure of reality, the distribution of such "stuff," either makes it the case that there is a way to . . . or not. However, *dào* is not, as religiously portrayed, a force, a transcendent origin, or a creator — physical or supernatural object counterpart of God. *Dào*s are possible or actual histories of objects, aggregations, populations, or eco-communities. They supervene on *dào*s of the structural parts of these emergent objects. What is mysterious and vague about *dào* is, I suggest, less the broad outlines of its metaphysics than the promiscuity with which we can individuate *dào*s — an effect of the promiscuity with which we can identify such aggregates, compositions, or emergent objects.

We traced the emergence of this kind of lower-dimension guide in natural life — routines stored in function and sub-routine format in nervous systems (vaguely corresponding to *dé* in Daoism — *dào*s "within"). The nervous system stores such routines (like a dance move) in a three-dimensional composition that we can "call" recursively in a real-time performance. The ant repeatedly executes the simple sub-routine of choosing the direction marked by the strongest pheromone odor and a community discourse dào in the form of a pheromone trail can emerge from a large enough population of ants simply executing the sub-routine when triggered. The three-dimensional *dào* is marked by the past history of the aggregate and is *read* and executed in real-time performance by the neural *dé* subroutines in each ant. Registering the stronger odor gives the ant a pre-linguistic "reason" (reality, which, if registered by the animal, *would* guide its sequential behavioral history) to walk toward some interest-related goal. Ways may or may not be marked, and a creature's *dé* may or may not reliably execute that *dào*. Hence, such "reasons" may or may not be causes. Ways can become complex networks composed of components, each of which is also a way — each sub-*dào* running to a linking node to which the next sub-*dào* (and alternatives) connect. The actual network structure of *dào*s can make it the case that multiple ways exist, that only one does, or that none do. The existence of *dào* is world-dependent. *Dào*s may be either effectively marked or not — though this relation is a natural one between structures in nature and the *dé* of the creature performing it.

I have argued that the classical Daoists were both naturalists (realists in my sense) and relativists. This does not mean they had access to anything resembling Einsteinian arguments. They were intuitively assuming a "constant" natural *dào* (perhaps from the semantics and associations of *tiān* (nature: sky) and noticing that, from different perspectives, different naturally available paths could be the normative paths of choice. The parallel is not purely accidental but also not to be taken as an indication of puzzling access to modern physical theory, even if, as formulated, their rough conception of *dào* seems like a modern insight to a Western tradition shedding its attachment to sentential metaphysical focal concepts. The point of this argument is to demonstrate the plausibility and natural access to the focal concept around which classical Chinese thinkers developed their more naturalistic ethics. We do have the counterpart "way" in Western languages but have not elevated it to a focal role in ethical naturalism where it can defuse the queerness some find in natural normativity.

Chinese naturalism about *dào* seems a reflection of how *dào* makes smooth the continuity between morality and nature. Many of the familiar features of morality can be traced to natural *dào*-like structures, but we can still join those who insist that full autonomy of normative morality is a peculiarly human development. We accommodated this conception by naturalizing reason as *dào*ing *dào*s. Languages with inferential semantics can give us ways of choosing, interpreting, and evaluating the execution of natural and social ways. They give us ways not only to signal *dào*s but to signal reasons for them — *dào*s of choosing and interpreting natural possible histories. Linguistic discourse *dào*s initiate the full natural emergence of morality.

NOTES

1. I take this analysis and the concept of normative foci from Kagan (1992, 224). The concept helps us keep our attention on issues of formulation rather than the familiar focus on factors that dominates normative debates. Settling how best to

formulate ethical claims should facilitate formulating the foundational (metaethical) issue without being distracted by issues of the factors or grounds for settling those disagreements.
2. See the gloss on *qì* in Chan (1969). Capra (1975) could barely be said, however, to be offering a translation or interpretative claim as much as guessing at a parallel in the conception.
3. For an accessible account of this "sum of histories" approach, I relied on Feynman (1985).
4. See especially Gallup (1994). Also see Bayne, Cleeremans, and Wilkin (2009, 446).
5. There is a phenomenon of assuefaction noticed in squirrels in which a persistent use of a distress call when not in distress leads the community to ignore later calls from the squirrel who cried "wolf."
6. See the discussion of quasi-objectivity in Gibbard (1990).

References

Bayne, T., A. Cleeremans, and P. Wilken, eds. 2009. *The Oxford companion to consciousness*. Oxford: Oxford University Press.

Blackburn, S. 1984. *Spreading the word*. Oxford: Oxford University Press.

Bratman, M. 1987. *Intentions, plans, and practical reason*. Cambridge, MA: Harvard University Press.

Capra, F. 1975. *The tao of physics*. Boulder, CO: Shambala.

Chan, W. 1969. A *sourcebook in Chinese philosophy*. Princeton, NJ: Princeton University Press.

Fernandez-Armesto, F., 2003. *Ideas that changed the world*. New York: DK Publishing.

Feynman, R. 1985. *QED: The strange theory of light and matter*. Princeton, NJ: Princeton University Press.

Gallup, G., Jr. 1994. Monkeys, mirrors and minds. *Behavioral and Brain Sciences* 17: 572–73.

Gibbard, A. 1990. *Wise choices, apt feelings*. Oxford: Oxford University Press.

———. 2003. *Thinking how to live*. Cambridge, MA: Harvard University Press.

Graham, A. 1978. Later *Mohist logic, ethics and science*. Hong Kong: Chinese University Press.

Hacking, I. 1999. The *social construction of what*? Cambridge, MA: Harvard University Press.

Kagan, S. 1992. A structure of normative ethics. *Philosophical Perspectives* 6: 223–42.

Mackie, J. 1977. *Ethics: Inventing right and wrong*. Middlesex: Penguin.

Pepperberg, I. 2008. *Alex and me*. New York: Harper Collins.

Range, F., et al. 2009. The absence of reward induces inequity aversion in dogs. *Proceedings of the National Academy of Sciences* 106 (1): 340–45.

Rawls, J. 1971. *A theory of justice*. Cambridge, MA: Harvard University Press.

Salmon, W. 1989. *Four decades of scientific explanation*. Minneapolis: University of Minnesota Press.

Scanlon, T. 1982. Contractualism and utilitarianism. In *Utilitarianism and beyond*, ed. A. Sen and B. Williams. 103–28. Cambridge: Cambridge University Press.

Thornton, A., and K. McAuliffe. 2006. Teaching in wild meerkats. *Science* (July 14): 340–45.

Afterword

Chad Hansen

I am humbled that so many of my academic friends and colleagues have honored me by writing about themes related to my work. Reading and thinking over their contributions have led me to reflect on the courses that brought me into my pleasant and productive relations with each of them. A conceptual theme in Zhuāngzǐ shapes my reflections: his concept of dependence. I have seen this concept as central to his thinking in the region where Western thinkers struggle to tease out the puzzling interplay of reasons and causes. Each of us is dependent broadly on our past *dào*s. Each of us interacted because of our respective trajectories and by that interaction changed each other's paths.

I share with many the trauma of adolescent deconversion. In my case it occurred in the context of my first disequilibrating contact with Hong Kong. The style of philosophy grounded in the concept of valid inference helped me in what I saw as a liberation of mind. Philosophy helped me detach from an "only true church" fundamentalism by undermining its central "God" premise. A recurring fundamentalist defense against criticism of that premise is to appeal to a compelling commitment to God's existence, arising from extended, conscientious practice of and immersion in a conception of religiosity, and perhaps understood as engendered by the divinity as a reward for fidelity. I sought to neutralize this defense in advance by following the rules of my faith meticulously. No compelling religious experience ensued.

Later, an advocate from a rival evangelical sect in Japan asked me why I would not devote equal treatment to her brand of fundamentalism. The question provoked an existential moment for me. Detaching from a lifelong way of thinking goes beyond simply intellectual conviction. I had already confronted the choice of being a "liberal" apologist for a familiar tradition, working from within to reform it and from without to give it an acceptable veneer. And I had dealt with my awareness that others, whom I still respected intellectually, had reflectively chosen to maintain their commitments. Clearly, my "liberation" was not to a clean slate. Since I had already processed a battery of arguments against rival religions (mainly, of course, those of "The Book"), my way out of my own faith effectively extinguished the appeal of similar supernaturalisms. The decision was pragmatic, though, because in principle I could have committed another decade each to many such experiential tests. However, as Zhuāngzǐ puts it: "my life is bounded and knowing is unbounded." Unable to follow all paths, I choose now from where I have arrived on the trajectory I have already completed.

Obviously, I did not similarly dismiss Chinese thought — its concepts and arguments were new and intriguingly different. So I had chosen two paths in the same process: one to philosophy and another to understand Chinese thought. Frustrated, however, with the obstacles to getting much insight into Chinese reasoning from traditional translations and other sources, I first simply returned to philosophy. When I went to study at Michigan with Professor Donald Munro, he reignited my aspiration to work on Chinese thought. Reading his generous comments, I am reminded how much our interaction conditioned my academic path — via both his *jūnzǐ*-like kindness and my appreciation of his way of understanding Chinese philosophy. I had arrived at graduate school with much momentum from my history in Hong Kong and my atypical introduction to Chinese (for me, Cantonese), which meant I had not been schooled in the ideology of the Western Chinese language classroom. These experiences intensified my fascination with that amazing language and spurred my life's quest to understand Chinese philosophy in its own terms. Don changed that quest from a private aspiration to a professional direction.

I cherish the many collegial friends I encountered pursuing similar goals along the way. I am impressed by how much I have gained from my interactions with the group of wonderful scholars who have contributed to this volume. I offer the above narrative more to explain than to argue about the areas where we differ. Our respective paths exerted a mutual pull but left each on independent trajectories — dependent on prior choices of direction. Clearly I have a more Panglossian perspective on professional philosophy than some and a less open attitude toward the more religious aspects of Chinese thought than others. My decision not to be an apologist persists in the context of my growing insights and understanding of Chinese thought. I need a positive reason to remake such entrenched decisions about my path in life.

My debts to Don are obvious and pervasive. They range from minor kindnesses, such as his willingness to provide Chinese characters along with Mandarin romanizations in his lectures, to major, pivotal events. Two of the latter were his encouraging me, when he understood my interest in language, to meet with Henry Rosemont and then to participate in the Society for Asian and Comparative Philosophy, where I first met Roger Ames and David Wong. My association with same-generation colleagues has been unwaveringly pleasant and constructive — and at times epic, as when we theatrically presented Chinese philosophy in drag in Sydney to an audience of, frankly, mostly each other. I share with Henry his appreciation of how formal theory of language can enrich our understanding of Chinese thought and with both him and Roger the awareness that studying and appreciating conceptual differences are crucial to understanding Chinese thought. On philosophical issues, I am closest to David Wong, who joins me most consistently in his appreciation of Zhuāngzǐ's relativist message, which he illustrates here with his impressive breadth of historical examples. Within this fellowship our differences are few, but, as they each pointedly remind me here, we have debated them endlessly, though always professionally and in good humor, over many wonderful years.

My Stanford associations came soon after and were psychologically crucial. Lee Yearley's encouragement was pivotal and his appreciation of my work generous, since our styles and directions were even more profoundly divergent. I might not have persisted in my academic life without the confidence he and David Nivison sustained in me. Our lively and friendly discussion circle included Sally Gressens (Lee's spouse) and P. J. Ivanhoe, who still had his own complex path to travel. Those cherished academic friendships are among my most treasured and enduring.

I had, by the time I went to Stanford, already honed my understanding of semantic theory at Pittsburgh, where fellow junior professors included Robert Brandom and John Haugeland. So my leanings toward pragmatic inferentialism became even more entrenched and central to my method. They were also leading me further from orthodoxy in my understanding of Chinese philosophy. My initiation into Chinese linguistic theory drew on Graham's reconstruction of the Later Mohists, which convinced me that, while profoundly distinct in conceptual structure, philosophy had thrived in Classical China before the emergence of a dominant Confucian orthodoxy. The gravitational pull of my Stanford colleagues was insufficient to sustain my interest in Mencius or the schisms and sects of Confucian orthodoxy. My aversion to apologetics could not be so easily dislodged. However, my delight at debating with these colleagues has never ceased.

Lisa Raphals crossed my path in some memorable conferences in New England while I was at the University of Vermont. Much of our work has been mutually reinforcing and productive. She shared my interest in theory of language and the centrality of knowing-how in Chinese thought. I always appreciated her interdisciplinary training in history, religion, and philosophy at Chicago. The value of such a background is well represented in her essay here, as in so much of her recent work on broad aspects of Chinese culture linked to thought. Jane Geaney approached me by email, also from Chicago and with similar training but with research interests and inclinations closely related to mine — the Later Mohist texts. She asked me to be a *really* long distance supervisor of her dissertation. (I had by then started teaching at the University of Hong Kong.) So she became my first graduate student by extension, and working with her was most satisfying. I was awed by her analytic critical instincts and quick grasp. Her critique of Graham's assumptions and her subsequent work on Chinese views of the role of oral-aural versus visual perception and guidance have provoked and challenged my own ideas. Her chapter here on rectifying names shows the excellence of this work.

My interest in Confucianism declined as I came to better understand its central concepts and their inferential roles. It was not the exemplar of sound Chinese reasoning but the beneficiary of the patronage of a political class. My gradual disaffection with Confucianism differentiates me even from some of my closest academic "siblings" — other students of Don Munro. We all derived diverse value from Don's open-minded breadth of learning, which allowed each of us wide berth in our approaches and interests. Steve Angle and Manyul Im, whose chapters appear here, are among these (along with several others, including, especially, Robert Eno and Sin Yee Chan). Steve shares my appreciation of Brandom's pragmatic inferentialism, and Manyul has illuminatingly retraced and revised my steps through the white horse paradox. We have honest and respectful disagreements about how sound Confucian arguments are. I have met and interacted with many others whose interests intersect with mine, and I am honored that Franklin Perkins has contributed here. He joins Manyul (and many others) in urging me to soften my criticism of Mencius. I tend to agree with Manyul that Mencius is a closet consequentialist, but, as my chapter here suggests, I think of virtue as an ethical focal point, not a factor, so I do not contrast virtue ethics with utilitarianism.

My personal narrative above is intended partially to explain my differences from Steve, P. J. and others on moral tradition respect. I was not motivated, as they suppose, by MacIntyre as much as by my own experiences. These made more real for me the insights I found in Bernard Williams (along with Gilbert Harman, Alan Gibbard, Simon Blackburn, and others) and in the ascendency of internalism in ethics and epistemology. I accept that we should discipline our reasoning about Chinese texts by Chinese norms, as embodied in the inferences implicit in their concepts (call this "reasoning"). But I find no sufficient reason to judge Confucianism viable in the face of contemporaneous rivals' criticisms — an evaluation rooted in the relation between early Confucianism and its homegrown critics, not in differences between Confucianism and modern Western thought. I was less critical of Mencius's normative utilitarianism than of his reasoning and his responses to objections from his peers.

My own students, Dan Robins and Chris Fraser, have not only organized this collection but done the bulk of the work of sending out invitations and editing these papers. Their own work shows one thing I cherish in my students: independence from me. I have learned a great deal from both of them, particularly when they work as a team. Dan's sensitivity and ability to express nuance and Chris's ability to marshal and elaborate detail are both splendidly demonstrated in their contributions.

Finally, my long-time colleague here at the University of Hong Kong, Jiwei Ci, and visiting colleague Bill Haines both honor me by participating. Jiwei's stunning originality of thought, together with his seemingly unerring ability to grasp the thrust of my interpretive arguments, enlivens his delightful piece on a long-time favorite passage of mine. Bill's work also engages a number of issues that have occupied me and shows his own deft handling. Finally, let me especially thank another HKU colleague, Timothy O'Leary, who planned and presided over the conference from which this volume grew, as well as organizing its publication, and to all my colleagues and the staff in the Department of Philosophy at HKU for their generous support.

Index

Acampora, C., 198
Achilles, 199, 203
act consequentialism, 57–9, 269
aestheticism
　in Confucianism, 22
　judgments, 162–3
After Virtue (MacIntyre), 169
agon, 211, 212
　in Chinese culture, 204–9
　in Greek culture, 198–204
all-things-considered judgments, 165, 172n
allusions, in poetry, 248–50
altruism, 86, 210
Ames, R., 117, 136n, 206
Ān Lùshān 安祿山, 247
Analects. *see* Confucius
Angle, S., 207–8
animals
　dé and *dào* of, 283–7
　group rights, 171n
　and physical exercises, 150, 151, 153n, 155n
　physiognomy of, 150
"appraisal respect," 163, 171n
appropriateness. *see yì* 義
Aquinas, 193n
archery, 145–6, 153, 204
aretaic judgments, 46–7
　aretê. *see* virtues

Aristotle
　comparative study of, 18
　concept of excellence, 19–20, 30–3
athletic performance
　defined, 143, 144
　and embodied self-cultivation, 144–50, 154n, 155n
　Greek *vs* Chinese views of, 151–3, 199, 200, 203, 204
　types of, 153n
authoritative conduct. *see rén* 仁

Bales, R.E., 48
beautiful, 22
Behr, W., 131, 133
Behuniak, J., 78n, 79n
belief-desire model, 88, 100n
benefit. *see lì* 利
benevolence. *see rén* 仁
Bentham, Jeremy, 28
biàn 辯 (discrimination/distinction-drawing), 88–9, 92
Blustein, Jeffrey, 29
breath cultivation, 149, 154n–5n
"Broken Boat" (Dù Fǔ), 246
Buddhism, 165
Burke, E., 74

carpenter, Mohist analogy, 92
Ceremonies and Rites. see *Yí lǐ* 儀禮
character consequentialism, 57–9
character development. see formation of character
civil service examination, 209
Classic of Family Reverence, 20–1, 25
Classicists. see Confucianism
A Cloud across the Pacific (Metzger), 179–80
command, 134
communities
  of animals, 284
  Aristotelian notion of, 31, 37n
  Confucian notion of. see *xiào* 孝
  Mohist notion of, 98
comparative ethics, 17–20, 161. *see also* moral tradition respect
  disaggregative approaches, 179, 186, 188–91, 193n
  holistic approaches, 175, 177–80, 186–8
competence/incompetence. see *zhī* 知
Confucianism. *see also* Confucius; Mencius; role ethics; Xúnzǐ
  archery and physical self-cultivation, 145–7, 153, 204
  defense of tradition, 65–6, 68–74
  four virtues, 234. *see also* individual virtues
  iconic signs of ritual, 220–1
  modern Confucianism, 175, 181–91, 193n
  moral intuitions, 217, 225–6
  Mòzǐ's criticisms of, 49–50, 66–7
  vs Western ethics, 1–3, 17–20, 26–35, 151–3
Confucius
  on archery, 145, 204
  on court order, 221
  on family reverence, 26
  on foundation of normative factors, 269
  on friendship, 224
  on harmony, 205
  on *jūnzǐ*, 204
  on laws, 23–4, 32
  moral practice, 226, 227–30
  on music of Zhèng, 127–8

on ruling/rulers, 206
on strength, 209
on study of The Odes, 132
on tradition, 65
use of paronomasia, 131
and Yán Huí, 205
in *Zhuāngzǐ*, 108, 112, 119, 259, 265n
on Zǐjiàn, 21
consequentialism
  characteristics of, 42–9
  Mohists vs Mencius, 41–2, 49–60
  normative focus, 269
conservatism, 74
consummate person/conduct. see *rén* 仁
contest. see *agon*
contractualism, 269
cosmos
  aural/visual balance, 126
  concept of, 276
  dào of the universe, 279–80, 281
  origin of, 105, 106, 115–16, 117, 119
criminal punishment, Mohist notion, 96
Critias, 201
cultural inventions, 290–1
cultural pluralism, 212–13

dà dào 大道, 275–6
dào 道
  of adaptiveness and skill, 108–12
  and the ancestor, 115–19
  beyond skill, 112–15
  constant, 106, 275–6, 277
  cultivating of, 181–3
  discourse, 275, 277, 280
  of *dào*, 291
  and ethical naturalism
    community and individual, 283–7
    emergence of interest, 282–3, 292–3
    generic concept of, 268
    human *dào* and full moral normativity, 87–91
    interpretations of, 274–6, 292
    natural and normative, 276–81
    as normative focus, 270
    normative pull of, 107–8

performance, 275, 281
two uses of, 105–6
Dàodéjīng 道德經
   on competition, 204, 205
   on *dào*, 106, 276, 280
   motivations, 238–42
   nature of *dào*, 115, 116, 117, 118
   relationship between individual virtues, 235–7
   translation of Chapter 38, 233–4
Daoists. see also *dào*; *Dàodéjīng*; *Zhuāngzǐ*
   on competition, 204–5
   material virtue, 148
   relativism vs pluralism, 172–3n
   self-cultivation, 147
   use of terminology, 106
dàotǒng 道統 (tradition or "interconnecting thread" of *dào*), 175, 190
   defined, 181–2
   and moral traditions, 184–5
   religious dimension, 182–3
dǎoyǐn 導引, 149
Darwall, S., 163
dé 德 (power, charisma, virtuosity)
   defined by Confucians, 1–2, 20–1
   defined by Daoists, 110, 148, 205, 282–3
   in organisms, 283–7
deontological ethics, 43, 28–30, 32
Descartes, 75–6, 80n
desires, 89
DeWoskin, K., 129, 132, 134, 138n
dietary, 149
dikaiosune, 200
discourses, defined, 179, 181
Discourses of the States, 206
discrimination. see *biàn* 辯
discrimination-and-response model, 89
Doctrine of the Mean, 145–6, 209
Dù Fǔ 杜甫, 245–6

è 惡 (crude, ugly), defined, 22
education
   civil service examination, 209
   and language, 288–9
   Mohist notion of, 94–6, 101n
   and music, 129, 132
   New Confucian view of, 182–3, 192n
   in organisms, 285
elenchus, 199–200
elevator words, 268
embodied virtues, 144–5, 146–50
embodied self-cultivation, 144–5, 144–5, 146–50, 154n, 155n
emotivism, 273
Eris, 198
esteem-based moral good, 45–8, 60
ethical egoism, 43
ethical naturalism. see also *dào*
   challenges to, 267, 270–4
   community and individual, 283–7
   dào and natural science, 274–81, 292–3
   emergence of interest, 282–3, 292–3
   human *dào* and full moral normativity, 287–91
ethics of virtue. see virtue ethics
eudaimonism, 43
evolution, 201, 210, 281
exemplary persons. see *jūnzǐ* 君子

fǎ 法, 95, 242
Fǎ Yán 法言, 128–9
family feeling, 18–19, 72, 87–88
   in Tang poems, 249
family reverence. see *xiào* 孝
Fāngjì 方技 ("Recipes and Methods"), 149–50
feelings, iconic signs, 223–5
fēng 風, 128
Féng Yǒulán, 184, 185
Fernandez-Armesto, F., 289–90
festivals, 221
Feynman, R., 278–9
filial piety. see *xiào* 孝
final moral synthesis, 167–9, 170, 186
Fingarette, H., 221
first-order moral judgments, 176
formation of character, 57–9
   and improper sound, 128
   Mohist notion of, 92–3, 94
Frankena, W., 43, 45–6, 61n
friendship, 29

functionalists, 201–2
funerary and mourning rituals
    Mencius view of, 73, 224–5, 231n
    Mòzǐ's criticisms of, 49–50, 66–7, 72
    in Zhuāngzǐ, 249

Gàozǐ 告子, 56
gentleman. see *jūnzǐ* 君子
GMWER, 180
goblet language, 249–51, 258
God, 75
goods, 203
Graham, A., 276
Great *Dào*, 275–6
Great Modern Western Epistemological Revolution (GMWER), 180
Greece
    athletic performance, 143, 151–3
    human nature and culture, 198–204
Greek, language, 26
group rights, 171n
group selection, 210
"grudging respect," 163–4
Guǎnzǐ 管子, 114, 154n
Guó Yǔ 國語, 206
Gūyè 姑射, 148

Hacking, I, 268
Hall, D., 117
Hansen, C., 105. see also ethical naturalism; moral tradition respect
    on *dé*, 7
    ethics in global context, 77–8
    language and reasoning, 6–7
    on *lǐ*, 10–11
    on Mencius, 65–6, 68, 69–70, 223–4
    metaphysics of *dào*, 107
    on modern Confucianism, 181
    on Mohist criticism of Confucianism, 67
    on *yì*, 138n
Hànshū Yìwénzhì 漢書.藝文誌, 149–50
happiness, 48
hé 和 (harmony)
    and *agon*, 197, 202–9, 211, 212
    image of, 221
    and music, 225

health, moralization of, 147
Heaven. see *tiān*
Hector, 199, 203
hedonism, 43
hegemon, 55
"Homer's Contest" (Nietzsche), 198
Hú Hóng 胡宏, 182
Huángdì Nèijīng 黃帝內經, 147, 149
Huì, King of Liáng 梁惠王, 53
Huìzǐ 惠子/Huì Shī 惠施, 107–8, 120n, 211–12, 264n
human beings
    Aristotle vs Confucius, 19–20, 27–8, 33–4, 198–213, 208
    Mencius's view of, 65–6, 68–71, 72–4, 75
    Mohist view of, 67–8, 71–2, 85
    Wáng Yángmíng 王陽明 on, 80n
human body
    in Greek traditions, 152–3
    and *qì*, 146–7, 148
human excellence. see also virtues
    moral/nonmoral value distinction, 44–8
    scope of, 44
human judgments. see also *shì-fēi* 是非 attitude
    aesthetic judgments, 162–3
    all-things-considered judgments, 165, 172n
    aretaic judgments, 46–7
    first-order moral judgments, 176
    Mencius vs Mohists, 66–7, 71, 74–5, 74–8
    in teleological theory, 44–5
human nature. see human beings
Hume, D., 47

Ice Age ideas, 290
iconic knowledge, 219–20, 222–3
ideal observer theories, 269
Ihde, D., 139n
Iliad, 151–3, 199
illumination. see *míng* 明
inclusive care/concern. see *jiān ài* 兼愛
inclusive fitness, 210
inclusivism, 172n

incompetence. see *zhī* 知
individualism, 27–8, 199
intrinsic moral value. see virtue ethics
intrinsic nonmoral value, 46
intuitionism, 274
intuitive knowledge, 217–18, 222–3
Ivanhoe, P., 57–9, 70, 231n

James, William, 37n
Jì Yàn 季彥, 126–7
jiàn 諫 (remonstrance), 25–6, 206, 208
jiān ài 兼愛 (inclusive care/concern), 50–1, 51–2, 85, 87–8, 98
jiào 教 (teaching), 182–3, 192n
Jiāo Xún 焦循, 74–5
jīng 精 (vital essence), 148
jīngfāng 經方 (recipes), 149
jūnzǐ 君子 (gentleman/exemplary person)
    actions judged by Mencius, 41
    and archery, 145, 204
    body and appearance, 146–7
    defined by Confucianism, 21, 25–6, 119, 128, 209, 243
    Mohist notion of, 67, 95
justice (*dikaiosune*), 200
Jūyán 居延, 150

Kagan, S., 268–70
Kant, I, 28, 162–3
Kern, M., 130
kin selection, 210
kinship relationships. see *xiào* 孝
know-how. see *zhī* 知
knowledge, categories of, 200–1, 217–20
knowledge of the forms, 200–1, 273
Kǒngcóngzǐ 孔叢子, 126–7
Korsgaard, Christine, 36n
Kuí 夔, music master, 130
Kupperman, J., 37n

language
    goblet language, 249–50
    and reasoning, 6–7, 288–9, 291, 293
    in Tang poems, 248, 250–3
    uselessness of, 250

Language and Logic in Ancient China (Hansen), 6–7
Láo Sīguāng, 189-190
Lǎozǐ 老子. see *Dàodéjīng*
Lattimore, D., 247
laws
    Aristotelian notion of, 32
    Confucian notion of, 23–4, 25, 32
    Daoists' notion of, 242
    levels of concept, 19
learning, 182, 183, 192n, 285
lǐ 禮 (ritual, ceremony, propriety)
    athletic performance, 144, 146–7, 204
    defined by Confucianism, 10–11, 21, 24–5, 31, 68, 73–4, 234
    defined by Daoists, 235–42
    and feelings, 224–8
    funerary and mourning rituals, 49–50, 66–7, 72, 73, 224–5, 231n, 249
    and human character, 128, 129
    iconic signs, 220–1
    and moral intuitions, 217
lì 利 (benefits/profits), 52, 53, 72, 97–8
Lǐ Bái 李白, 263n
Liberalism, 193n
Lǐjì 禮記 (Records of Ritual)
    on archery, 145–6, 204
    court order and human relations, 220
    on sounds and music, 127, 128, 137n, 225
Liú Zōngzhōu 劉宗周, 182
longevity, 148
Lǚshì Chūnqiū 呂氏春秋, 132–3, 148

MacIntyre, A., 37n, 167, 191n
    concept of traditions, 177–9, 185, 187, 188, 193n
    on contest and motivations, 203
    on modern Confucianism, 181, 191
    unified moral order, 168–9
Mackie, J., 270–4, 289–91
Makeham, J., 181
Maritain, J., 188
material virtues, 144–5, 146–50
material incentives, 96
Mǎwángduī 馬王堆, 149, 150, 154n

medical practice, 148–50, 154n
měi 美 (beautiful), 22
Mencius
   on archery, 145
   as consequentialist, 41–2, 57–60
   contestation of, 206–7
   on feelings and rituals, 223–5
   foundation of normative factors, 269
   four virtues, 234
   on human nature, 65–6, 68–71, 72–4, 75, 78n, 79n
   moral practice, 226, 230
   on moralities, 283
   on qì and physiognomy, 146–7
   on ruling/rulers, 55–6, 207, 226
   vs Mohists, 49–55, 56
metaethical naturalism, 270
mêtis, 151–2
Metzger, T., 181, 188–90, 179–80, 187
Militiades, 198
Mill, John S., 28
míng 明
   interpretations of, 113, 136n
   musical aspects of, 131–5
mìng 命 (command), 134
míng 名 (names/titles/fame), 125
Miyazaki, I, 209
model emulation, 95–6
models (fǎ 法), 95, 242
"Moderation in Funerals" (*Jié zàng xià* 節葬下), 49–50
Mohists
   concept of action, 88–93
   consequentialism, 2, 41–2
   criticisms of Confucianism, 49–50, 66–7, 71–2, 74, 207
   Jiāo Xún's criticism of, 74–5
   laws of nature, 76–7, 78
   Mencius' criticisms of, 50–5, 56
      practical project, 93–6, 98–9
      reform program, 83, 84, 85–8, 99–100
      sources of motivations, 96–9
Moore, 273, 274
moral goodness. see rén 仁
moral intuitions, 217–18, 228–30
moral naturalism. *see* ethical naturalism
moral rightness. see yì 義
moral tradition respect
   conditions for, 164–6
   interpretations of, 162–4
   role for comparative ethics, 161, 166–70, 176–7, 186–7
moralities
   cultivation of, 239–40
   cultural pluralism, 212–13
   defined, 197–8, 289, 291, 293
   functional view of, 201–2, 211, 213n–14n
   narrative approaches to, 233–4
   raison d'être, 237
   utilitarian conception of, 229–30
moral/nonmoral value distinction, 44–8
mothers, as role term, 19, 30
motivations
   defined, 84
   models of reasoning, 88–9, 92, 100n
   Mohists' concept of, 89–99
   and moralities, 201–2, 209–11, 238–42
   in poetic expression, 257–8
motive consequentialism, 269
Móu Zōngsān 牟宗三, 182, 183–5
Mòzǐ 墨子, 84, 114
MTR. *see* moral tradition respect
music. see also yuè 樂
   as analogy of consummate conduct, 21–2
   metaphors for rulership, 131
musical conversation, 130

names, 125
Nèiyè 內業, 148
Neo-Confucianism, 182
Nestor, 151–2
Nichomachean Ethics, 32
Nietzsche, F., 198–200, 234, 238
Nivison, D., 100n, 101n
nonmoral/moral value distinction, 44–8
"The Normative Impact of Comparative Ethics" (Hansen), 161, 176
normative naturalism. see ethical naturalism
"Numbers and Techniques," 149, 150
Nylan, M., 129

objective act-consequentialism, 58–9
objective consequentialism, 49
The Odes. see *Shījīng*
Okin, Susan M., 36n
Olympic Games, 143
orchestras, 72, 74
Owen, S., 246

pànjiào 判教, 182, 184
parents
    Aristotelian notion of, 29–30, 32
    Confucian notion of, 25–6
    Mohist notion of, 87
    in Tang poems, 249
paronomasia, 131–2, 133
peer approval, 98
Peirce, C., 219
perfectionism, 43, 44
persuasion, 93, 95
phenomenology, 34
philosophy, vs authority, 77–8
physical performance. *see* athletic performance
physiognomy, 146–7, 150
Picken, L., 132
Plato
    agon spirit, 199
    divine and traditions, 75–6, 79n, 273
    on Socrates, 200
poetic tradition, 245–6, 255–7
positivism, 272
power. see *dé* 德
practical reasoning, 2–3, 88–9, 92, 100n
propriety. see *lǐ* 禮; *yì* 義
psychological behaviorism, 92
public concert, 72, 74
puns, 131–2, 133

qì 氣 276
    Confucius's notion of, 112
    Daoist notions of, 147, 148
    Guǎnzǐ's notion of, 154n
    Mencius's notion of, 146

Railton, P., 49
Rawls, J., 43–5
reasoning. see also *shì-fēi* 是非 attitude
    and language, 6–7, 288–9, 291, 293
    models of, 2–3, 88–9, 92, 100n
    nature of, 6–7, 287–8
"Recipes and Methods," 149–50
"recognition respect," 162–3
Records of Ritual. see *Lǐjì* 禮記
Regan, T., 171n
remonstrance, 25–6, 206, 208
rén 仁 (moral goodness/benevolence/ consummate person/authoritative conduct)
    and archery, 145–6
    and compassion, 54, 68
    defined by Confucians, 1–2, 18–24, 31, 32, 33, 34, 145–6, 227, 234
    defined by Daoists, 235–42
    defined by Mohists, 86
    moral value of, 48
    in ruling, 55–6
Republic (Plato), 200
right, *vs* good, 44–5
right-derived moral good, 44–5
ritual propriety. see *lǐ*
Robins, D., 79n
role ethics, 208
    conflicts between roles, 253–5
    consummate conduct, 20–4
    exemplary persons, 25–6
    ritual propriety, 24–5
    and Western ethics, 17–20, 28–35
role models. see *jūnzǐ* 君子
Rosemont, Henry, 206
Ruists. see Confucianism
rule consequentialism, 269
rule utilitarianism, 269
ruling/rulers
    Mencius on, 55–6, 207, 226
    Mohists on, 98–9
    and music, 129, 131, 134–5, 225
    and people's hardship, 220
    relationship with ministers, 206
    Xúnzǐ on, 126
    and *zhèngmíng*, 135n–6n
Russell, B., 273

sages
  Confucian view of, 56, 71, 243
  Daoists view of, 148
  Guǎnzǐ on, 154n
Salmon, W., 277–8
Saussy, H., 130
Scanlon, T., 269
scholarship, 182, 183, 192n, 285
scholastic tradition, 181
Schwartz, B., 6
"Seesaw Effect," 180
self-cultivation. *see* embodied self-cultivation
self-interest, 97–8
sentential knowledge, 218–19, 228
sexual arts, 149, 150
shén 神 (spirit), 112, 148
Shèn Dào 慎到, 275–6, 277
shén rén 神人, 148
shēng 聲 (sound), 127, 128–35, 139n
shèngrén 聖人. *see* sages
shí 實, 125, 136n
shì-fēi 是非 attitude, 88–91, 92–4, 96–7, 100n
  Daoist notion of, 114
Shījīng 詩經, 129–31, 132, 138n
  sacrificial festival, 221
Shīzǐ 尸子, 134
shù 恕 (sympathetic consideration, moral imagination), 28
Shū Jīng 書經, 129–30
Shùn 舜, 207
Shun, K., 78n, 79n
Shuō Yuàn 説苑, 127
  on moral instruction, 129
  on music and ritual, 128
Shùshù 數術, 149, 150
Siemens, W., 199
signs, 219–20
Slater, M., 172n
Sober, E., 210
social encouragement, 96
social order. *see zhì* 治
social reform, 85–8
Socrates, 75–6, 199–200, 201
Sòng Kēng 宋鈃, 53

"A Song of My Thoughts on Traveling from the Capital to Fèngxiān" (Dù Fǔ), 250–1
  allusions to *Zhuāngzǐ*, 248–50
  background and depictions, 247–8
  ethical commitments, 246
  ethical tensions, 253–7, 259–60
  forms of poetic expression, 257–9
  linear and non-sequential presentation, 252–3
  texts of, 260–3
Sophocles, 153
sound, 127, 128–35, 139n
speech, 95, 130, 137n–8n
spirits, 148
sports. *see* athletic performance
state of nature, 89–90, 91–2
statements, 95, 130, 137n–8n
Sterckx, R., 127
sú 俗 (custom) vs *yì* 義 (right), 66–7
subjective consequentialism, 49, 58
supernaturalism, 273
Svensson Ekström, M., 138n
Symposium (Plato), 79n

Tang dynasty, 247
teaching, 182–3, 192n
teleological theory, 34, 43–6
"Ten postures," 155n
thin values, 188
Thrasymachus, 200
tiān 天 (nature, heaven)
  Mohists on, 76, 86–7
  potter's wheel of, 113, 114
tiān-dào 天道 (way of nature/heaven), 275, 276
Tiwald, J., 172n
tolerance, 168, 176, 177
tǒng 統 ("interconnecting thread"), 182
traditionalists, 66, 74
traditions. *see also lǐ* 禮; moral tradition
  respect concept of, 177–8, 181, 187
type-token relations, 275, 278–9

unified moral order, 167–9, 170, 186
unity, 207–8

Universal Declaration of Human Rights, 188
universal love, 50–1, 51–2, 85, 87–8, 98
universal moral synthesis, 167–9, 170, 186
universalism, 28–33
universe, 276
uselessness, 109–10, 120n, 249, 250
utilitarianism
    characteristics of, 43, 269
    conception of moralities, 229–30
    status of persons, 165
    vs Confucianism, 28–30, 32

Van Norden, B., 78n, 171n
Van Zoeren, S., 128, 129, 131
verificationism, 272
vice, 48
"village honest person," 257
virtue ethics
    Western vs Chinese, 1–3, 17–20, 26–35, 151–3, 271–2, 293. *see also* ethical naturalism; role ethics
    defined, 46–7, 60, 143, 268–70
virtues
    Aristotelian vs Confucian, 1–2, 18–24, 31, 32–4, 151–3
    Confucian notions of, 144–50, 234, 257
    Daoist notions of, 147, 148, 235–7
    Hume's notion of, 47, 60
    Mohist notion of, 86–8, 92, 93, 94, 97
voluntarism, 101n

Walzer, M., 188
Wàn Jùnrén 万俊人, 37n
Wáng Chōng 王充, 147
Wáng Yángmíng 王陽明, 69–70, 80n
way. see dào
wén 聞 (hearing/smelling), 126, 128
Whose Justice? Which Rationality? (MacIntyre), 187
Wilson, D., 210
wisdom, 21, 68–9
Wittgenstein, L., 288
Wong, D., 172n
worthlessness, 109–10, 120n, 249, 250
wù 物 (things), 117

Xià Yǒng 夏勇, 207
xiào 孝 (family reverence/filial piety), 28–33
    Confucian notion of, 20–6, 59–60, 220
    Mohist notion of, 87
xīn 心, 29
xìng 性. see human beings
Xióng Shílì 熊十力, 182, 183, 184
Xuān, King of Qí 齊宣王, 55
Xuánzōng 玄宗, Emperor of Tang, 247
xué 學 (learning/scholarship), 182, 183, 192n, 285
Xúnzǐ 荀子
    on human nature, 70
    on *jiàn* 諫 (remonstrance), 206
    and Mencius, 207
    on moral instruction, 129, 201
    on physiognomy, 147
    on *shēng yuè* 聲樂 (sound and music), 127, 132, 138n
    on *zhèngmíng* 正名 (right names), 125–6, 133–4

Yàn 晏, 206
yán 言 (speech/statements), 95, 130, 137n–8n
Yán Huí 顏回, 112, 119, 205
Yáng Zhū 楊朱, 56, 74–5
yǎngshēng 養生 (cultivating life). see embodied self-cultivation
yì 義 (moral rightness/appropriateness/propriety)
    defined by Confucianism, 21, 22, 24, 28, 53–4, 68, 234
    defined by Daoists, 235–42
    defined by Mohists, 86–7, 90, 96–7
    and *qì*, 146
    vs *sú* 俗 (custom), 66–7
Yì lǐ 儀禮, 204
Yí Zhī, 51
yín 淫, music, 127, 128, 132, 133, 138n
Yínquèshān 銀雀山, 150
yù 欲 (desires), 89
Yu, J., 18
Yu Yingshi, 182
yǔzhòu 宇宙 (universe), 276

yuè 樂, 72, 74, 127–31, 132–5, 137n
  and feelings, 225
"Yuèjì" 樂記, 127, 137n, 225
yuèyǔ 樂語, 130

Zhāng Zǎi 張載, 182
Zhāo Wén 昭文, 115
zhèng 正 (right/straight), 125
Zhèng Jiādòng 鄭家棟, 182, 183
Zhèng 鄭 and Wèi 衛, sounds of, 127, 128, 132
zhèngmíng 正名
  graphs or oral/aural, 126–7
  musical aspects of, 131–5
  and rulership, 135n–6n
  Xúnzǐ's notion of, 125–6
zhī 知 (know-how)
  Confucian concept of, 218, 219
  Daoist concept of, 205
  Mohist concept of, 91–2, 94
zhì 治 (social order)
  defined by Confucians, 135n–6n, 220–1
  defined by Mohists, 85, 87, 97
zhì 智 (wisdom), 21, 68–9
zhōng 忠, 28

"Zhōngyōng" 中庸, 145–6, 209
Zhōulǐ 周禮, 130
Zhū Xī 朱熹, 182, 209
Zhuāngzǐ 莊子
  altruism, 86
  the ancestor and dào, 115, 118, 119
  on competition and knowledge, 205
  Confucius and swimmer, 108–9
  on dào, 105, 106, 276, 281, 283, 291
  Huìzǐ, 107–8, 120n, 211–12, 264n
  Kitchen Dīng, 110–12
  mourning practice, 249
  philosophy of learning, 198
  and poetic tradition, 245–6, 248–53, 258
  portrait of Confucius, 259, 265n
  Artisan Qìng, Yán Huí, and monkey keeper, 12–14
  on shén rén (spirit-man) and qì, 148
  shì-fēi and three masters, 114–15
  use of paronomasia, 131–2
  uselessness, 109–10, 120n, 249, 250, 264n
Zǐdào 子道, 206
Zǐjiàn 子賤, 21
Zǐyú 子輿, 116
Zuǒzhuàn 左傳, 133